RACISM, SLAVERY, SALVATION AND THE BIBLE

What's Wrong With America
From A Christian Pastor's Perspective

―――――――――

―――――――――

Dr. Nathaniel T. Powell

Racism, Slavery, Salvation, and the Bible
What's Wrong With America From A Christian Pastor's Perspective
Nathaniel T. Powell

Published by Austin Brothers Publishing, Fort Worth, Texas
www.abpbooks.com

Copyright © 2021 by Nathaniel T. Powell

The copyright supports and encourages the right to free expression. The purpose is to encourage writers and artists to continue producing work that enrich our culture.

Scanning, uploading, and distribution of this book without permission by the publisher is theft of the author's intellectual property. To obtain permission to use material from the book (other than for review purposes) contact terry@abpbooks.com.

Paperback ISBN: 978-1-7359739-6-8
Hardcover ISBN: 978-1-7359739-7-5
LCCN: 2021909395

Printed in the United States of America
2021 -- First Edition

"There is not a Black America and White America and Latino America and Asian America—there is the United States of America"
— President Barack Obama

"No matter what, you give everybody a fair shake, and when somebody needs a hand, you offer yours"
— First Lady Michelle Obama

"Until justice is blind to color; until education is unaware of race; until opportunity is unconcerned with the color a man's skin, emancipation will be a proclamation, but not a fact
— President Lyndon B. Johnson

"None of us got to where we are solely by pulling ourselves up by our bootstraps, we got here because somebody bent down and helped us pick up our boots."
— Justice Thurgood Marshall

"There comes a time when silence is betrayal."
— Rev. Dr. Martin Luther King, Jr.

"We must learn to live together as brothers or we will perish together as fools."
— Rev. Dr. Martin Luther King, Jr.

"No one is born hating another person because of the color of his skin, or his background, or his religion. People must learn to hate, and if they can learn to hate, they can be taught to love, for love comes more naturally to the human heart than its opposite."
— Nelson Mandela

"I have learned that success is to be measured not so much by the position that one has reached in life as by the obstacles which he has had to overcome while trying to succeed.
— Booker T. Washington

"In this country, America means white. Everybody else has to hyphenate
— *Toni Morrison*

"Hate, it has caused a lot of problems in this world,
but has not solved one yet."
— *Maya Angelou*

"America is mad at black people for saying 'Black Lives Matter.' We mad for having to say it at all."
— *Unknown*

To
Lenore, my loving wife, and life-long partner,
without your sacrifice and help,
this book would not have been possible

My Agape Community Fellowship Church family
who inspired me to pursue this project

My Lord and Savior Jesus Christ—
My eternal gratitude
and thanksgiving

Contents

Introduction	1
Two Nations: Black America And White America	17
One Nation Under Who?	49
Created In The Image Of God	67
Am I My Brother's Keeper?	81
God's Command: Love Thy Brother	103
Who Is My Neighbor?	119
Knowing Who's Your Enemy	131
God's Answer To Racism	143
When Grace Overcomes Race	155
Christian Accountability	171
The Dangers Of Idol Worship	195
Religion And Politics	211
The Stain Of Slavery On America	243
God's Role For Government	255
It's All In A Name	275
When Your Skin Becomes The Problem	289
Physical Bondage Vs Spiritual Bondage	321
Where Do We Go From Here?	331
White Privilege On Steroids	377
Bibliography	391

INTRODUCTION

As a 57-year-old African American Christian pastor and a veteran who served for over 30 years in the U.S. Air Force, my heart has been deeply troubled for a long time because of America's sinful condition. We claim to be a great Christian nation, but I would argue that we have never remotely resembled what we declare. However, the position of many white evangelicals is that America was founded as a Christian nation.[1] In a book titled *The Search for Christian America*, the authors included the historical argument for a Christian America.[2] Hatch, Noll, and Marsden disagree with the premise of a Christian America, and throughout their book, they argue just the opposite.

> *We feel a careful study of the facts of history shows that early America does not deserve to be considered uniquely, distinctly, or*

---

1 John Fea, "Why White Evangelical Trump Supporters Believe America is a Christian Nation," 30 June 2018. [on-line]; accessed on 1 February 2021; accessed from ; Internet. Ever since the founding of the republic, a significant number of Americans have supposed that the United States is exceptional because it has a special place in God's unfolding plan for the world. Since the early 17th century founding of the Massachusetts Bay colony by Puritans, evangelicals have relished in their perceived status as God's new Israel—His chosen people. America, they argued, is in a covenant relationship with God. The defenders of this idea like to apply Chronicles 7:14 to the United States: "If my people, who are called by my name, will humble themselves and pray and seek my face and turn from their wicked ways, then I will hear from heaven, and I will forgive their sin and will heal their land."

2 Mark A. Noll, Nathan O. Hatch and George M. Marsden. *The Search for Christian America*. (Colorado Springs: Helmers & Howard Publishers), 1989, 129. For those who hold to the "Christian America" view, the situation may be summarized as follows: America was founded as a "Christian nation." But the nation turned from its Christian foundation and in recent decades has been taken over by secular humanism. The goal today is to become a Christian nation once again—by restoring America to its "biblical base," to the "biblical principles of our Founding Fathers.

even predominately Christian if we mean by the word "Christian" a state of society reflecting the ideals presented in Scripture. There is no lost golden age to which America Christians may return. Also, a careful study of history will show that evangelicals themselves were often party to blame for the spread of secularism. We feel also that careful examination of Christian teaching on government, the state, and the nature of culture shows that the idea of a "Christian nation" is a very ambiguous concept which is usually harmful to effective Christian action in society.[3]

As a retired Senior Air Force Chaplain, in the rank of Lieutenant Colonel, I am deeply proud of my African American heritage as well as my years of military service, including deploying twice to the Middle East in support of *Operation Desert Storm* and *Operation Enduring Freedom* for a combined total of 13 months. I was blessed to earn numerous military awards and accommodations for meritorious service. Also, I was blessed to have joined the Air Force as an enlisted member and earned the Staff Sergeant's rank before being commissioned as an officer. Furthermore, I am grateful to have a mother and father who encouraged me to strive for excellence, which led me to graduate from college and graduate school at Southwestern Baptist Theological Seminary. My background, experience, and training provided me a unique insight in writing this book. Therefore, at a bare minimum, I hope to start a public dialogue on the Bible, racism, American history, and the failure of the Christian church in America. Also, I hope we could be respectful, honest, and Christ-like toward one another, even if we do not look like one another or if we do not agree—but hopefully, we will at least agree with the Bible.

As a student of the Bible, I realize that people behave the way they do because we are all sinners and desperately in need of a savior—but the only true Savior is Jesus Christ, our Lord.

Clearly, Christ's death was a substitutionary death, a death in place of others. Christ did not die for His sins, but for the sins of the world. Through Christ's death, all believers are reconciled to God. And because we have received reconciliation from Him, the body

---

[3] Ibid.

of Christ should strive to be reconciled with one other. Division and segregation among God's people do not honor nor glorify Him. Therefore, when believers from various races and ethnicities gather together in the name of Christ and worship Him as Savior and Lord, this picture reflects the glory of God to a lost world in need of a Savior.[4]

Proverbs 14:12 says, "There is a way that seems right to a man, but its end is the way of death." Proverbs 21:2 says, "Every man's way seems right in his own eyes, but the Lord weighs the heart." John 14:6 Jesus says, "I am the way, the truth, and the life; no one comes to the Father unless they come by Me." In these Old and New Testament passages, the Hebrew word for way is *derek*, which is also translated as road or journey, or as a metaphor for "way of life" or "course of life." In the New Testament, Jesus used the Greek equivalent of *derek*, which is *hodos*. I believe our Lord's choice of hodos was deliberate as well as profound. Because Jesus is the *hodos* for lost humanity, He is the world's only answer and cure for humanity's sinfulness, especially in America. This reveals to us how much we are in desperate need of a Holy Spirit revival to break the grip of systemic racism that still plagues us today.

To address the racial tensions in America, we must follow the teachings of Scripture because they contain the answers we need to glorify God—our Creator and sustainer of life. Before there was ever division between Blacks and Whites, there was a division between Jews and Gentiles. To unite these two people groups into one family of faith that He could use, Jesus died on Calvary's cross—which established the Christian church.[5] In Ephesians Chapter 4, the apostle Paul addressed

---

4   Nathaniel T. Powell. "Implementing the USAF's Chaplaincy Model of Racial Diversity in Agape Community Fellowship Church" (D-Min diss, Southwestern Baptist Theological Seminary) 2013, 6.

5   The Greek word for church is *ekklesia*. The first time this word is used is in Matthew 16:18 by our Lord Himself as He addresses Peter and the disciples. "I also say to you that you are Peter, and upon this rock I will build My church; and the gates of Hades will not overpower it." In addition to church, the word is also translated as assembly or congregation. This word is used in the New Testament to describe true followers of Jesus or the body of Christ. This word is used repeatedly throughout this book, in order to remove any confusion because the word "church" is often used in a generic sense in America.

the subject of unity between Jews and Gentiles, as well as the role of the pastor. Paul's message is relevant for our society because we are divided in many ways, especially racial lines. Paul addressed the church because it is the one entity within society that God has empowered to deal with the division among the races. When the church comes together in unity—led by the Holy Spirit—society benefits greatly. The church is God's biblical model to set the tone for racial reconciliation in a fractured society. However, if the church resembles society and remains segregated, it loses a tremendous opportunity to make a difference for the kingdom of God.[6] This is why the role of a pastor is so vitally important today. According to Paul, a pastor's role is to help bring about unity by constantly proclaiming God's truth to a lost and dying world to lead them to faith in Christ and helping them to grow in Christ. Also, the pastor needs to train the people of God to reflect the glory of God, inside as well as outside the church house.

Throughout this book, you will notice that I will use the term evangelical repeatedly. A term that is confusing to many. In my many years of scholarly study, I have found that many authors use this term, but they assume their audience understands exactly what they mean. The name evangelical has its roots in the Greek word *evangelion*, meaning "the good news" or the "gospel." Evangelicalism is a movement within the Protestant church and can be recognized by its foundational tenants. Evangelicals are Christians that advocate four fundamental principles. The first is that salvation—or being born again—is only possible by placing one's faith in Jesus Christ as Savior and Lord. To include, Christ died for all, and that anyone that calls on the Lord can be saved, regardless of their past. Second, Jesus Christ's death on the cross is the only sacrifice that could remove the penalty of my sin. Therefore, God does not have another plan of salvation apart from His Son. Third, the Bible is the authoritative Word of God, it is absolute and without error, and it is God's clear direction for all manner of life. Fourth is the importance of spreading the word of God through evangelization. Evangelicals come from all ethnic and racial backgrounds, but nearly

---

6   N. Powell. "Implementing the USAF's Chaplaincy Model of Racial Diversity in Agape Community Fellowship Church," 97.

90 percent of Americans who call themselves evangelicals are white.[7] This book focuses primarily, but not exclusively, on white evangelicals.

Making The Bible Relevant

Based on Paul's teachings, my job as a pastor is to preach the Bible correctly and make sure the sermons are relevant and applicable to everyday life, especially in these times of Covid-19 and financial uncertainty in America. To educate and encourage our church, I believe it is important to teach and preach the whole counsel of God—Old and New Testament—from Genesis to Malachi, from Malachi to the Gospels, and from the Gospels to Revelation. With the focus on the sinful state of affairs in American society, I preached a 12-week series on the Old Testament Minor Prophets, containing the last twelve books of the Old Testament. During this series, I pointed out how Old Testament prophecy was still applicable to what is going on in America today. In these prophetic books, God constantly reminded Israel about their disobedience and the consequences of their actions. God told Israel that they were facing their multitude of troubles because of their crimes against Him.

Conversely, Israel rebelled against the God who had consistently blessed them, and they constantly failed to obey His Word—which is exactly what's wrong with America! For example, Amos Chapter 2 says, "For three transgressions of Judah, and for four, I will not revoke its punishment, because they rejected the law of the Lord and have not kept His statutes" (Amos 2:4). These are God's Words that Amos spoke to Judah. In verse 6, Amos repeats the same judgment statement but directs it toward Israel, not their enemies. By this time in the nation's history, Israel was divided into two nations: The Northern Kingdom the Southern Kingdom.[8] The way that Amos presented his arguments

---

7   Michael O. Emerson and Christian Smith. *Divided by Faith: Evangelical Religion and the Race Problem in America.* (Oxford: University Press, 2000), 3.

8   William Sanford Laser, David Allan Hubbard, and Frederic William Bush, Old Testament Survey: The Message, Form, and Background of the Old Testament, (Grand Rapids: William B. Eerdmans Publishing), 1996, 197-198. Because Solomon had tolerated idolatry, disastrous divine judgment inaugurated the reign of Rehoboam, Solomon's son and successor. The prophet

about God's prophesies of judgment was compelling. He began with God's pronounced judgment on Judah and Israel's enemies in Chapter 1 and at the beginning of Chapter 2. When Judah and Israel heard the severely harsh judgment of their enemies, it caused them to celebrate. However, they were astonished when the Lord pronounced the same judgment against them that He had pronounced against the other six Gentile nations listed.[9] The main idea Amos portrayed was that God's judgment awaits any nation that forgets the basic rule of human decency, but it is even more certain when God's people forget Him, His teachings, and all He has done for them.[10]

Amos' message is just as relevant today as it was when he preached it. He reminds me of America in many ways. First, many Americans view other nations as sinful or heathen (except for some strange reason they give Israel a pass) with evil leaders. Still, they somehow view America as predominately a Christian nation that is better than all other nations. Unfortunately, Amos has something to say about that.[11] Second, America has convinced itself that it is not so bad, even though some are willing to acknowledge that we have some significant problems. Third, America has confused the ability to live a comfortable life with God's approval. Somehow, we are convinced that God is pleased with us because He allows us to be blessed as a nation. Unfortunately, America's false belief about where we stand with God is very similar to that of Judah and Israel, which again didn't end well for them, just like it won't end well for us—unless we repent.

Ahijah prophesied that Jeroboam, an able young Ephramite whom Solomon had appointed to supervise northern work gangs in Jerusalem (11:28), would lead the northern tribes to independence.

9   Max Anders and Trent C. Butler, Holman Old Testament Commentary: Hosea, Joel, Amos, Obadiah, Jonah, Micah. (Nashville: Broadman & Holman Publishers, 2005), 177. Damascus, Gaza, Tyre, Edom,, Ammon, and Moab. Note: Nations were often referred to by their capital cities. Amos accused these nations of crimes against God, but surprising he accused Israel and Judah of committing the same offenses.

10   Ibid, 169.

11   Ibid.

Amos Today

The Book of Amos, expressing as it does God's outrage against a society that had become insensitive to justice—a society that materialistically exalted profit over people—has been identified as one of the most significant of prophetic books for us today. Certainly, we too experience unequaled prosperity. Surely, there are great class distinctions in our society. And surely too there is oppression—oppression that has not been touched by institutionalizing a financial dole to the poor. Perhaps, and most importantly, Amos helps us review our values. He asks the question: Do our lifestyles reflect the heart of God? Or do we share the selfish heart of the indifferent of Amos' day? [12]

As a pastor who loves God and loves his country, I view life through the lens of Scripture, and when something is going on that affects the church, I address it from Scripture using proper Biblical Hermeneutics.[13] While preaching a series on the Old Testament Minor Prophets earlier this year (and constantly being reminded of Amos' prophecy), Covid-19 began to explode, the bottom began to fall out of our economy, and the nation began to freak out. By God's grace and His infinite wisdom of what was headed our way, this sermon series helped our church prepare for what we were witnessing going on around us and the country and the world. Besides, it was confirmed that preaching about Old Testament prophecy was beneficial to our congregation. Conversely, another issue exploded during that time that got my attention in a different way: the constant shootings of

---

12   L. O. Richards. *The Teacher's Commentary* (Wheaton: Victor Books), 1987, 463.

13   Ronald C. Potter, "Was Slavery God's Will?" *Christianity Today*, 22 May 2000 [on-line]; accessed 5 September 2020; available from https://www.christianitytoday.com/ct/2000/may22/29.80.html; Internet. This article states that some Christian writers have said slavery in America was divinely sanctioned because it helped bring Africans to Christ. The problem with that argument is the fact that Christianity had long been on the continent of Africa before America became a nation. Also, those that make this argument that slavery was God's will, arrive at that bogus conclusion because of poor Biblical Hermeneutics and taking Scripture out of context.

unarmed African Americans throughout the country. While a virus crippled America and led to one of the worst economic downturns in our nation's history, what we all understand from personal experience is that the virus was not a respecter of persons. As of this date, over 500,000 Americans have died from the virus, and over 30,000,000 are infected. Covid-19 reeked-havoc throughout the country, which led to enormous job losses, school closings, canceling sporting events, closing of businesses, government facilities severely limited, logistical supply chains turned upside down, and the shortage of everyday household supplies affected everybody—Whites as well as Blacks. However, police brutality that targeted Blacks (mostly men) was different because it was not universal across racial lines. There has been a consistent flow of these tragic stories that have made national news. The outrage from Blacks was joined by many Whites, which led to protests around the country and the world. During the many protests, it was amazing to see Whites marching alongside Blacks with Black Lives Matter signs and voicing their racial justice concerns. What Americans must understand is that the racial unrest did not happen in a vacuum. The following events I describe in this book were the catalyst that brought us to this point and changed America going forward, but not necessarily for the better.

In my first year of seminary, my family joined Cornerstone Baptist Church in Arlington, Texas, where the Senior Pastor was William Dwight McKissic, Sr. I recall him talking from the pulpit about a book he had written titled, *Beyond Roots: In Search of Blacks in the Bible*. Being a student of the Bible, I was intrigued by his discussion. From that moment on, I knew Mckissic was a bit radical in his thinking—in a good way. However, my view was reaffirmed when McKissic released another book in 2018 titled, *Controversial Conversations: Kingdom Reflections On Biblical & Contemporary Issues*. In this book, he deals with many of the controversial issues that Christians in leadership shy away from, especially in Baptist circles, such as the Southern Baptist Convention and Race Relations, and the church, homosexuality, and contemporary society. I can respect that an African American pastor of a megachurch can take a stand, knowing he will ruffle feathers among his white evangelical brothers. In the introduction of this book, McKissic stated the following:

> *I've been called "the racial conscience of the Southern Baptist Convention" by some and a "race-baiter" by others. In some news reports, I've been called "outspoken," "controversial," "a lightning rod," "once a rising star in the Southern Baptist Convention," and a "theological street fighter." Indeed, some, both friends and foes, have viewed my writings and speech as controversial. Being "controversial" is not my intent. Neither is that the goal of this book. However, I recognize and concede that topics that I'm burdened by the Holy Spirit to address are often topics where "angels fear to tread." Therefore, I titled this book Controversial Conversations because I hope that it triggers a discussion(s) for those who might share my convictions and even those who may challenge my convictions.* [14]

Mckissic's burden that led him to write this book and others he has written has inspired me to write this book based on the same principle. Therefore, I wholeheartedly understand what it means to be so burdened by the Holy Spirit to address controversial topics, especially for a local church's senior pastor. The burden the Holy Spirit placed on my heart was to address the issue of systemic racism in America since 1619 and how the Christian church was complicit by not only supporting slavery but many of the other ills that have placed African Americans at a serious disadvantage to this day.

A Breakdown Of This Book

Chapter 1 explains the tale of two Americas: A Black America and a White America. Since 1619, when the first slaves arrived from Africa, we have been divided along racial lines. From the very beginning, a caste system was put in place and has never been dismantled. This system set in motion the environment for systemic racism to flourish.

---

14   Wm. Dwight McKissic, Sr. *Controversial Conversations: Kingdom Reflections On Biblical & Contemporary Issues*. (Dallas: Saint Paul Press, Dallas, Texas, 2018).

In the two Americas, there are two separate systems of justice and policing, education and upward mobility, economics and financing, housing and homeownership, employment and job placement, and healthcare and pharmacy, just to name a few.

Chapter 2 challenges the myth of America being a nation under God. Although the phrase "in God we trust" is on our money, it is essentially an oxymoron because we do not trust God with our financial resources or hearts. "No one can serve two masters; for either he will hate the one and love the other, or he will be devoted to one and despise the other. You cannot serve God and wealth" (Matt 6:24). In a true nation under God, all citizens in that nation should be treated equally. No one should be treated better than the other, but one of the main reasons that does not happen in America is for two primary reasons: the root cause for everything else that's wrong with race relations in America. First, White supremacy, which led to the idea of white privilege, which I will explain in detail and give examples in Chapter 1. Second, systemic racism, which is covered throughout this book.

Chapter 3 explains what it truly means to be created in the image of God and how all races are created in His image. Therefore, the belief that one race is superior to another is not validated with Scripture. Also, I explain the significance of mankind being the pinnacle of God's creation. Because all men are created in the image of God, I explain the fallacy of separate but equal that dominated American life for years.

Chapter 4 explains the consequences of the fall of man. After Adam and Eve sinned against God, they were banished from the garden. Sadly, for humanity, they passed their sinful nature onto their offspring (including you and me). Cain was the oldest; therefore, he had a responsibility to be Abel's keeper. Out of anger, and because his offering was rejected by God (while Abel's was accepted), Cain killed Abel, even though God warned him about the dangers of sin. This chapter examines how racism—that has existed throughout American history—is a direct result of White America (the dominant race) not being their brother's keeper for Black America (the minority race).

Chapter 5 explains the amazing benefit we have when Christ is our advocate. Since America claims to be a Christian nation, we are commanded by God to love our brother. In the Gospel of John and

John's epistles, he extensively uses the term brother—which means one who is related in Christ. Therefore, since all Christians are brothers and sisters in Christ, regardless of race or ethnicity, there should be a genuine love displayed in America for one another—that's if we are truly the Christian nation we claim to be. Unfortunately, this is not a command of God we obey because our politics are more important to us than our faith. In fact, for many Americans, their politics is their religion.

Chapter 6 explains how the biblical application of the Good Samaritan story should be applied in America. Unfortunately, due to the extremely poor race relations throughout America's history, we don't look after our neighbor, especially when our neighbor does not look like us. In President Donald Trump's age, the division between Whites and Blacks in America is perhaps as worst as it has ever been. Therefore, if there was ever a time, we need to apply the principles Jesus taught in the Good Samaritan story; that time is now.

Chapter 7 explains how the U.S. Armed Forces can be a significant role model for America to follow, especially when it comes to understanding who our enemy is and the importance of working together as one unified nation. In 1942, the Tuskegee-trained 99th Pursuit Squadron deployed to North Africa. Before that time, African American military pilots were not allowed to fly in combat because of segregation and racism. However, out of mission necessity, they were given the opportunity, and they excelled—dispelling the myth of Black inferiority. The enormous contributions of the Tuskegee Airmen help change the laws on racism and segregation in the military.

Chapter 8 reveals God's answer to the problem with systemic racism in America, which is Jesus Christ. For God to implement His plan through Christ, He created the church and equipped the church with everything we need to carry out His Kingdom agenda. However, unless the church in America stops neglecting its God-given responsibility and works toward racial reconciliation, our country will continue to be divided and only worsen until Christ returns.

Chapter 9 describes what happens when grace overcomes race. We examine the story of Jesus and the Samaritan woman at the well. Jews and Samaritans hated one another. Jews would go out of their way to avoid Gentiles, which makes this story even more remarkable. Jesus broke all cultural norms to reach a lost woman with a broken life. This is a story to show America how to address poor race relations and reach those in need. This chapter's main point is to explain how God extends His divine grace to fallen mankind—through faith in Jesus Christ. By the way, we are all fallen individuals, regardless if we are Jew, Samaritan, or Gentile—the three people groups in Scripture.

Chapter 10 explains why Christian accountability is necessary for America. We examine what happened when one early church giant (Paul) was opposed by another church giant (Peter) for his racist behavior. This was a major problem that could have devastated the early church. If Paul did not dare to stand up against Peter in front of the other church leaders, it would have resulted in two separate churches: a Jewish church and a Gentile church. All true believers everywhere need to have the convictions and courage of Paul. However, one of the biggest problems we have in America is, we just don't like being held accountable for our actions, whether personally, professionally, politically, or spiritually. Just remember, when we fail to hold people accountable for their actions, especially people in positions of power or authority, we simply become enablers.

Chapter 11 explains the dangers of idol worship in America. "You shall have no other gods before Me. You shall not make for yourself an idol or any likeness of what is in heaven above or on the earth beneath or in the water under the earth" (Ex. 20:3-4). In America, we have many different objects of worship (idols), from money, positions of power and authority, to personal possessions. If that was not bad enough, we have a bad habit of worshiping people: athletes, movie stars, music groups, solo artists, and even presidents. However, this chapter's primary focus is the multitude of Confederate statues and monuments built in America during the Jim Crow era—to ensure that segregation and racism remained part of the American fabric. The sad reality is that these statues and monuments are still treated as sacred objects of worship by many Americans to this day. Some speak out against having these symbols of racism removed because of heritage. The question is, who's heritage? Certainly not African Americans—because we do not need any reminders of such a horrific time in our history.

Chapter 12 examines what happens when religion and politics collide, especially when it is man-made religion and sinful politics—which is what Jesus faced when He was brought before Pilate—to have Him crucified. What the religious establishment accomplished by getting in cahoots with the Roman government was a transactional business arrangement. Pilate wanted to keep his governorship position over Jerusalem, and he feared a rebellion that would have gotten the Roman Emperor's (Caesar) attention. The religious establishment (the Pharisees and the Sadducees) wanted the thorn in their side removed, which was Jesus—who threatened their religious positions of authority, so they wanted Him crucified. The transactional agreement was to make each other's problems go away. However, little did they know by putting Jesus to death would turn the Roman world upside down. Unfortunately, we are witnessing many white evangelicals making a similar mistake in America by aligning themselves with immoral politicians to have the political power to push their agenda.

Chapter 13 explains how the stain of slavery on America has directly led to the systemic racism that still plagues our nation centuries later. In the book of Philemon, Paul gives a guide on how to deal with racial reconciliation. Paul led a slave owner (Philemon) and his slave (Onesimus) to faith in Christ. The goal was for them to no longer treat each other according to the societal norms of slavery in the Roman Empire and treat each other like true brothers in Christ. Paul taught these men an important principle: that at the foot of the cross, the ground is level because there are no levels of hierarchy other than Christ Himself. Until America truly gets its heart right with God—through a personal relationship with Jesus Christ as Savior and Lord—the problem that slavery has done to this nation's foundation can never be fixed.

Chapter 14 explains how important the role of government is to the order and discipline of society. In the Bible, God created three covenants (institutions) to provide structure, a moral compass, and law and order for the entire world. These divine covenants are the family, the government, and the church. Each of these covenants plays an important role in how God intended for society to function. However, the *fall of man* led to the chaos of human life that has played out since the beginning of time. In Paul's day, the Roman government was a massive bureaucracy that had conquered much of the known world. The Jews hated being controlled by the Roman government, even Jews that became Christians. When the kings of Israel obeyed Yahweh, they were the most protected nation on this earth, even though they were not the most dominant. Yahweh caused His fear to fall on Israel's enemies, which gave them peace on their borders. However, their continued pattern of sinful behavior brought an end to Israel's monarchy. A vast majority of the Jews believed that he would restore Israel's earthly kingdom and supplant the Roman government when the Messiah came. Most Jews rejected Jesus as the Messiah because He did not set up the type of kingdom they were looking for—instead, he revealed His heavenly kingdom, which was eternal, not temporary.

Chapter 15 explains the significance of a personal name and how it was extremely important in Jewish culture in the Bible and African culture throughout history. A personal name had great significance in the Bible because it was tied to your purpose or destiny. Therefore, I examine how significant it was for slave owners to change the name of African slaves. Today, in American culture, we hate when someone calls us out of our name, especially if it is derogatory. For a slave to be stripped of their African heritage, it was as derogatory as you could get. However, that was the purpose of slave owners stripping slaves of their identity and making them into what they wanted them to be—a pliable useful tool for the sole purpose of free labor and financial gain.

Chapter 16 explains how America has a history of judging black people solely based on their skin color. Even today, this still takes place. When Barack Obama was elected as the first black president of the U.S. in 2008, some Whites referred to him as the "Tragic Negro." He was harassed for years and even told he was not born in the U.S.; therefore, he was a fraud and not a legitimate president. Therefore, a sitting president was forced to produce his Hawaiian birth certificate. Astonishingly, President Donald Trump's rise in the political world was achieved by pushing this false conspiracy.

Chapter 17 explains how the skin color of Blacks became a problem early on in America's racist history. Whites in positions of authority and wealth cruelty was fully displayed. They tried to exterminate Indians

(Native Americans), even though they were here first. Also, they tried enslaving poor whites, but that did not work out too well because it did not fit into their worldview. However, for Africans, their dark skin set them apart because they stood out and could be easily recognized in society. Furthermore, this fit into their worldview because most Whites (at that time) believed Blacks were not human, only savages. So, enslaving someone and deeming them to be an animal or monkey allowed Whites to settle their conscience—no matter how sinful their actions—racism.

As you read this book, I hope you will keep an open mind, especially if you did not have the recorded experiences. My aim in this book would be to start a dialogue concerning the problems of race in America. Whereby African Americans and Caucasian Americans, and all other Americans, would be willing to face the truth. However, to do so, we must be willing to examine at least our sinful past of how Blacks were enslaved for the sole purpose of improving the quality of life for white Americans.

CHAPTER 1

TWO NATIONS: BLACK AMERICA AND WHITE AMERICA

The Hierarchy of America's Structure

It is not original, but it can be said that if you wanted to keep a people group down, the best way to accomplish that is to do so socially, economically, and politically; however, I would add educationally as well. In a book by Isabel Wilkerson titled, *Caste: The Origins of Our Discontents*, the author describes this "putting down" and "keeping down" as a caste system. Wilkerson describes caste as an artificial hierarchy that places certain groups above others to create some as inferior and some as dominant.

> *A caste system is an artificial construction, a fixed and embedded ranking of human value that sets the presumed supremacy of one group against the presumed inferiority of other groups based on ancestry and often immutable traits, traits that would be neutral in the abstract but are ascribed life-and-death meaning in a hierarchy favoring the dominated caste whose forbearers designed it. A caste system uses rigid, often arbitrary boundaries to keep the ranked groupings apart, distinct from one another and in their assigned places.*[15]

Wilkerson identifies three types of caste systems throughout human history: The tragically accelerated caste system of Nazi

---

15   Isabel Wilkerson, *Caste: The Origins of Our Discontents*, (New York: Random House, 2020), 17.

Germany, the lingering, millennia-long caste system of India, and the shape-shifting, unspoken, race-based caste pyramid in the United States. She adds, what allows a caste system to endure is that it is often justified as divine will, originating from sacred text or presumed laws of nature, reinforced throughout the culture and passed down through generations.[16]

The American caste system began in 1619 with the arrival of African slaves to American soil and continued to build through 1776 when the Thirteen Colonies declared their independence from Great Britain. Once they defeated the British in the Revolutionary War in 1783, enslaved Africans became the foundational institution for the survival of a new nation. Free African slave labor allowed America to build an economy and international trade system that benefitted Whites but abused Blacks. One would have to ask the question, what would have happened to America without enslaving Africans? Would Whites have been able to produce the hard labor that Blacks were forced to endure without compensation? The obvious answer is no!

I make this point for three reasons: 1. There was not a pool of white workers lining up for the job. 2. If somehow you could have convinced enough white Europeans to come to America, they would have demanded to be paid fair compensation. It would have taken at least 4 million of them because that's how many Africans it took to build America. However, due to the fact these white colonists were poor, this was a nonstarter. 3. White Europeans would not have wanted to give up everything to come to America to be treated as someone else's slave when they understood their white privilege. Although many Whites did come to America as indentured servants, there was nowhere enough of them to build this country on their backs. In a book by Michael Eric Dyson, titled *Long Time Coming: Reckoning with Race in America*, he eloquently sums up the point of how Blacks were taken advantage of by Whites.

> *When you think of it, so much of the nation has been built to establish and preserve white comfort. Slavery existed to provide white folk enormous comfort—providing all the energy needed to*

---

16   Ibid.

maintain farms and plantations. Black folk did all this to support the nation's bottom line as white folk collectively reaped untold financial benefits and the American economy grew to monstrous proportions. Jim Crow, and in many ways white life ever since was constructed for white comfort: to keep Blacks and others from drinking from the same water fountains, eating at the same restaurant riding on the same buses, sitting in the classrooms, playing on the same diamonds, gridirons, or courts, worshipping in the same sanctuaries, and, God forbid, being buried in the same cemeteries, all because white folk believed they were superior and that they should be spared the discomfort of having to be near what and whom they were better than. And, just in case their heightened view themselves proved to be false, they spared themselves the discomfort of the ugly truth.[17]

Therefore, these white European men's goal was to set up a "white America," whereby everyone else would serve their majority, and they would be allowed to do as they pleased. Speaking as an African American professional, I seriously believe this is what "Make America Great Again" means.

The Myth of Black Inferiority

In, *Oneness Embraced: A Fresh Look at Reconciliation, The Kingdom, and Justice*, Dr. Tony Evans explained how the myth of Black inferiority has been one of the primary issues that have plagued Americans since its inception.

Hundreds of years since the first arrival of slaves to these shores, the myth of Black inferiority is still very much with us. It is visibly seen in the rejection and continued disenfranchisement of Blacks by many Whites and the inability to get beyond the issue of color. Unfortunately, the problem is often as replete in the church as it is in the secular community. Why is this? I would like to posit that it is primarily because of the failure of Christians to approach

---

17 Michael Eric Dyson, *Long Time Coming: Reckoning with Race in America*. (New York: St Martin's Press, 2020), 185.

the issue of race from a theological rather than anthropological perspective.[18]

Evans went on to explain the power of a myth. He defined a myth as a story or tradition passed down to justify an event lacking evidence or a historical basis.[19] One reason why myths are so powerful is that people are gullible enough to believe them without checking the source. If a myth already fits into a person's way of thinking, they are more likely to believe it no matter how ridiculous or farfetched it may be. For instance, Donald Trump (before he was President) rose to prominence in the right-wing of the Republican party by falsely claiming that President Barack Obama was not born in the U.S. but was born in Kenya. Although he might not have been the source of the myth, he used his platform to repeat it often enough that it resonated with many Whites, who still believe it to this day. Unfortunately, this myth was not just a lie that was told for amusement; it was blatant racism. In an attempt to dispel a myth—which was pushed to say Obama was an illegitimate President—a sitting President was forced to publicly display his birth certificate from Hawaii to dispel the rumors. Unfortunately, some Whites in America believed the lie because they refused to accept the fact that a Black man was now leading their nation, which I believe stemmed from the myth of black inferiority.

In a book by President Barack Obama titled, *A Promised Land*, he delivered an excellent summation of what happens when racism and politics collide. Obama stated he believes the reaction to his Presidency played a role in someone like Donald Trump, a reality TV host, being allowed to ascend in politics and cause the dark transformation of the Republican party.

> *"It was as if my very presence in the White House had triggered a deep-seated panic, a sense that the natural order had been disrupted, which is exactly what Donald Trump understood when he started peddling assertions that I had not been born in the United States and was thus an illegitimate president. For millions*

---

18   Tony Evans. *Oneness Embraced: A Fresh Look at Reconciliation, the Kingdom, and Justice.* (Chicago: Moody Publishers, 2011), 87.

19   Ibid, 88.

of Americans spooked by a Black man in the White House, he promised an elixir for their racial anxiety."[20]

Obama remained relatively quiet during his eight years in the White House, but in this book, he revealed how much he had a grasp on what was going on: before, during, and after his Presidency. Ironically, in 2008 John McCain chose the worst person to ever be on a Presidential ticket, arguably in U.S. history, when he selected the Governor of Alaska, Sara Palin, as his running mate—until Donald J. Trump completed a hostile take-over of the Republican party. Obama explained what happened to the Republicans and what led to the party's current dismal climate, which he blamed on John McCain, and rightfully so.

"The ideological shift in the Republican party can be traced back to when John McCain chose Sarah Palin as his running mate during the 2008 campaign. Through Palin, it seemed as if the dark spirits that had long been lurking on the edges of the modern Republican party — xenophobia, anti-intellectualism, paranoid conspiracy theories, an antipathy toward Black and brown folks — were finding their way to center stage."[21]

I don't think the Republicans realized the seismic shift in their party when they were willing to launch Saran Palin into the national spotlight as a Vice Presidential candidate in 2008 without properly vetting her. If they knew Palin would end up being the laughing stock of the political world, they probably would not have chosen her. She proved she was not ready for political prime time shortly after she was introduced. Palin provided constant laughing material for weekly late-night comedians from the major networks and increased Saturday Night Live ratings as long as she remained in the spotlight. You would think that a Republican like McCain, with his political smarts, would have rethought this move, especially knowing that Palin would have

---

20   President Barack Obama, *A Promised Land*, (New York: Crown Publishing, 2020), 672.

21   Ibid.

been a heartbeat from the Oval Office.[22] However, in hindsight, McCain knew he was losing and willing to do just about anything to win. He needed someone to take President Obama's shiny varnish, so he hired an attack dog. Palin's over-the-top racist rhetoric exited the base because they felt the same way.

As a result of that awful McCain-Palin presidential ticket, which failed miserably, it severely angered the conservative far right, who hate losing elections and did not even want McCain as their candidate in the first place.[23] Of course, after Obama won the presidency, that stoked racist anger had not subsided. The racist reaction to President Obama's election opened the door for Trump to fan the flames of hatred, division, and racism among many Whites in America, which launched him into the national spotlight. Furthermore, Trump took all that resentment and anger among those same Whites, who felt their white heritage and white privilege (or white supremacy) were slipping away and filling the void. So, Trump played them like a fiddle—even though he did not care about anyone but himself—and rode it to the White House. He needed someone to take "off" President Obama's shiny varnish.

---

22   Isabel Wilkerson, *Caste: The Origins of Our Discontents*, 312. John McCain, a beloved war hero from Arizona, a wise and measured moderate Republican, was at the top of the ticket of a party that had grown far more conservative. He ran a less-than-energetic campaign and made several misjudgments, the most significant of which was choosing an unpredictable former governor of Alaska, woman prone to gaffes and to quirky, word-salad misstatements, as his running mate.

23   President Barack Obama, *A Promised Land*, 170. Palin's nomination was troubling on a deeper level. I noticed the start of her incoherence didn't matter to the vast majority of Republicans; in fact, anytime she crumbled under questioning by a journalist they seemed to view it as proof of a liberal conspiracy. I was even more surprised when prominent conservatives—including those who'd spent a year dismissing me as inexperienced, and who'd spent decades decrying affirmative action, the erosion of intellectual standards and the debasement of Western culture at the hands of multiculturalists—suddenly shilling Palin, tying themselves into knots as they sought to convince the public that in a vice presidential candidate, the need for basic knowledge of foreign policy or functions of government was actually overrated. It was, of course, a sign of things to come, a larger, darker reality in which partisan affiliation and political expedience would threaten to blot out everything–your previous positions; your stated principles, even what your own senses, your eyes and ears, told you to be true.

I do believe that President Donald Trump believes in white supremacy as well as black inferiority. His racist actions against Blacks for many years have led me and many other African Americans to that conclusion.[24] The whole birther movement conspiracy theory he leveled against President Obama was a classic example of clear-cut racism. Trump has been very effective in getting his base to believe that President Obama was not born in America and believe anything else he says. People fail to realize that it would not have mattered if Obama was born in Africa. As long as his mother, Ann Dunham was a U.S. citizen; it did not matter; according to our U.S. Constitution, he would still be an American citizen—full stop. [25]

A book by Tom Burrell, *Brainwashed: Challenging the Myth of Black Inferiority*, provides an interesting perspective on this issue concerning the myth of Black inferiority.

> *The marketing of black inferiority and white superiority, as building blocks for the founding of America, is a chicken that has finally come home to roost. Now we must ask ourselves: Did the world's greatest brainwashing campaign work? Fast-forward 233 years. "Yes, it worked brilliantly." That response, however, is incomplete. To discover the real answer, we must strip away multiple layers of complex conditioning. Part of the black inferiority marketing campaign is to convince us that we can't handle the truth... that we're better off not knowing. It's an extremely patronizing message.*

---

24 Errol Louis, "Why Americans think Trump is a racist," CNN, 2 March 2018 [on-line]; accessed on 20 November 2020; accessed from Why Americans think Trump is a racist (Opinion) - CNN; Internet. As the nation approaches the 50th anniversary of the Rev. Martin Luther King Jr.'s assassination, we are more divided than we should be—thanks in no small part to a President who chose to build his power on the quicksand of racial resentment rather than a firm foundation of tolerance.

25 Although Obama would still be a U.S. citizen, he would have been ineligible to run for president. The U.S. Constitution states any person running for that office must be born on American soil or a U.S. territory. If you recall, John McCain was eligible to run for president even though he was not born on U.S. soil. He was born in Canal Zone, Panama when his father was serving in the military. This tactic was used to denigrate Obama as well as claim he was illegitimate, even though he was born in Hawaii. To claim he was born in Africa was racism because it attacked his name and heritage.

We are capable enough and strong enough to handle the truth. More importantly, if we are to reverse the mindless perpetuation of the "black inferiority" or BI campaign we must go to that painful place so that we may claim our peace.[26]

Burrell's perspective comes from his 45-year background in the advertising industry. As a result, he presents his arguments from this view. He uses his background as a salesman to explain how he believes White America has sold the rest of the nation a false premise on the condition of the Black man. He even talked about when he was growing up on the Southside of Chicago and how his community was indoctrinated with the idea that they needed help from Mr. Charlie in the form of government programs, including public assistance, food stamps, and any other "gifts" the government bestowed. He explains this from what psychologists call "learned helplessness."[27] This is a strong point because we can see this in some families in America, especially in how they raise their kids.

When I was in Air Force Basic Training in 1985, I recall serving with some grown men in my squadron who did not know how to do simple tasks such as making a bed, folding clothes, sweeping or mopping a floor, or cleaning latrines. When we were not in the presence of the drill sergeant, I would hear them whine and complain because they had to help clean the dormitory and clean their areas. These men would say they never had to clean up back home because their mothers would do it for them. Needless to say, they struggled throughout Basic Training. By no means am I comparing slavery to military basic training; I am only making the point of similarities in learned helplessness. Although many Blacks have overcome learned helplessness—and have made major contributions to this country in many career fields—some have not. There is a reason for this phenomenon. Some of the problems reside with the individual. Still, I would submit that the bigger problem or issue is derived from systemic racism that remains in many, if not all, American social structures. This includes education (K-12 and college),

---

26 Tom Burrell, *Brainwashed: Challenging the Myth of Black Inferiority* (New York: Smiley Books, 2010), 25.

27 Ibid, 1.

housing and homeownership, economics and finances, policing and criminal justice, corporate America, employment, and how we receive goods and services.

What is interesting about the resiliency of Blacks in America is the amount of us who have great achievements in the areas of science, humanities, literature, education, college professors, senior military leaders (in the enlisted and officer ranks), law enforcement, accountants, doctors, lawyers, architects, corporate America, judicial judges, mayors, governors, Congress, Secretary of State, U.S. Attorney General, and even the President of the United States. Furthermore, Blacks have made these huge contributions in American society, despite the many structures in place to hold us back. My military and educational achievements, as well as the countless other successful Blacks in the United States and around the world, are living proof that the myth of "Black inferiority" is just that, a myth.

A Myth Sets the Groundwork for Systemic Racism

The problem with systemic racism in America is not just a 2020 problem. It is a problem that this country has faced from the very beginning. In 1776, when the Thirteen Colonies proclaimed their independence from England, systemic racism was already ingrained in the New Nation's fabric.[28] Between 1761 and 1860, the slave population in America was approximately 350,000.[29] According to the U.S. Census of 1800, there were a total of 5,628,506 people in America, of which

---

28   Nina Strochlic. "How Slavery Flourished in the United States, *National Geographic*, 23 August 2019 [on-line]; accessed 1 September 2020; available online from https://www.nationalgeographic.com/culture/2019/08/how-slavery-flourished-united-states-chart-maps/#close; Internet. By 1776 when the United States severed ties with Great Britain and declared independence, the 13 former colonies had already participated in the Atlantic slave trade for 157 years. A ban on the slave trade would go into effect in 1808, but was often disregarded. By then some 300,000 Africans had already been uprooted and pressed into slavery. Nearly half of them—150,000 people—had been brought in through the country's largest slave port, Charleston, S.C.

29   Khushbu Shah and Juweek Adolpe. "400 Years Since Slavery: A Timeline of American History, 16 August 2019 [on-line]; accessed 27 August 2020; available from https://www.theguardian.com/news/2019/aug/15/400-years-since-slavery-timeline; Internet.

996,917 were Black slaves.[30] According to a news article in *The Atlantic*, slavery helped produce many wealthy people in the South, which is why the Confederate States fought so hard to keep their way of life—even if it meant going to war with their countrymen.[31] Sometimes war is an unavoidable necessity, such as when Japan bombed Pearl Harbor on December 7, 1941, which led to the U.S. entering WWII. However, the Civil War was based on greed, systemic racism, and maintaining white supremacy.

> *By 1860, there were more millionaires (slaveholders all) living in the Lower Mississippi Valley than anywhere else in the United States. In the same year, the nearly 4 million American slaves were worth some $3.5 billion, making them the largest single financial asset in the entire U.S. economy, worth more than all manufacturing and railroads combined. So, of course, the war was rooted in these two expanding and competing economies—but competing over what? What eventually torn asunder America's political culture was slavery's expansion into the Western territories.*[32]

So, there is no denying that slavery was the engine that drove economic success for the country. As the nation grew beyond the original Thirteen Colonies, slave labor was utilized to benefit Whites while disenfranchising Blacks. Even in the states that outlawed slavery, they still benefitted from products produced by free slave labor from the South. While the quality of life for many Whites improved, the quality of life for most, if not all, Blacks suffered.

The first slaves arrived in Jamestown, Virginia in 1609, and since that time, life for Blacks has been drastically different from any other

---

30 U.S. Census Bureau. "An Act Providing for the Second Census or Enumeration of the Inhabitants of the United States [on-line]; accessed 27 August 2020; available from https://www.census.gov/content/census/en/library/publications/1801/dec/return.html; Internet.

31 Ta-Nehisi Coasts, "Slavery Made America: The Case for Reparations," *The Atlantic* [on-line]; accessed 27 August 2020; available from https://www.theatlantic.com/business/archive/2014/06/slavery-made-america/373288; Internet.

32 Ibid.

people group that arrived in America.[33] Blacks are the only people group that primarily came to America, not on their initiative (at least not in large numbers), but came involuntarily for the benefit of being subservient to Whites. Although many Whites had nothing to do with Blacks being enslaved, they still benefited from their labor and suffering. Furthermore, enslaving Blacks was not done just for economic gain; it also demoralized and denigrated them. Sadly enough, many Whites did not even view Blacks as human. As a result, black families have been damaged in so many ways that still affect us negatively to this very day.

Finally, one other major point needs to be addressed (because it is often overlooked). That is the economic, psychological, and emotional impact slavery had on the African nations that lost millions of their citizens. Countless families were destroyed for generations. There were children left behind for someone else to raise; there were wives left without their husbands (and vice-versa); there were children snatched from their parents; there were men and women taken that were vital to the function of the tribal community. In many ways, tribes were left defenseless because of the number of African men kidnapped and taken hostage. Likewise, the role of women changed as well. Slavery destroyed their tribal structure of a community and stripped them of power and dignity. There is no way you can remove approximately 12.5 million people from a continent,[34] mostly males, but females and children as well, over many years (16th to the 19th century) without doing irreparable harm for generations.

Many of the African countries and tribes still struggle in modern times because of what Whites broke, from several different continents and nations but have not lifted a finger to try and fix. What is sad, African nations are still put down to this day by many White nations around the world—that played a role in their demise and benefited

---

33   Jemer Tisby, *The Color of Compromise: The trust about the American church's complicity in Racism.* (Grand Rapids: Zondervan, 2019), 32-33.

34   Henry Louis Gates Jr. "Slavery By The Numbers," *The Root*, 10 February 2014 [on-line]; accessed 1 September 2020; available from https://www.theroot.com/slavery-by-the-numbers-1790874492; Internet.

from it due to the Trans-Atlantic Slave Trade—many of them continue to struggle to this day.[35]

Government Sanctioned Segregation

In a book by Richard Rothstein, *The Color of Law*, he explains how the U.S. government played a major role in America's segregation. Rothstein points out how laws in America, passed by whites, have created the structure of all citizens. However, this system or structure was not designed to advance the lives of black people, only white people. He deals with such topics as public housing: black ghettos, racial zoning, state-sanctioned violence, and suppressed incomes, to name a few. Rothstein describes a concerted effort to use public housing by federal and local governments to herd African Americans into urban ghettos.

At the same time, from WWII to 1955, the housing authority built attractive low-rise (six-story) unsubsidized housing in New York City. However, the authority maintained a list of twenty-one disqualifying factors for prospective tenants. This was designed to ensure that undesirable tenants were not accepted, which included African Americans, Hispanic Americans, and even low-income Caucasian

---

35   Nathan Nunn, "Understanding the long-run effects of Africa's slave trades." Vox EU, 27 February 2017 [on-line]; accessed 1 September 2020; available from https://voxeu.org/article/understanding-long-run-effects-africa-s-slave-trades; Internet. Between 1400 and 1900, the African continent experienced four sizeable slave trades. The largest and best-known was the Trans-Atlantic Slave Trade where, beginning in the 15th century, slaves were shipped from West Africa, West Central Africa, and Eastern Africa to the European colonies in the New World. The three other slave trades – The Trans-Saharan, Red Sea, and Indian Ocean slave trades – were smaller in scale and predated the Trans-Atlantic Slave Trade. During the Trans-Saharan Slave Trade, slaves were taken from south of the Saharan desert and shipped to Northern Africa. In the Red Sea Slave Trade, slaves were taken from inland of the Red Sea and shipped to the Middle East and India. In the Indian Ocean Slave Trade, slaves were taken from Eastern Africa and shipped either to the Middle East, India, or the plantation islands in the Indian Ocean. In total, close to 20 million slaves were taken from the continent (Nunn 2008). According to the best estimates, by 1800 Africa's population was half of what it would have been, had the slave trades not occurred (Manning 1990).

Americans.[36] Another example involved the New Deal[37] construction in many states such as Tennessee and New Jersey. State agencies were created to bring jobs and economic growth to regions whose suffering during the Great Depression had been usually severe. However, those same agencies housed African American workers in shoddy barracks, some distance away from job sites, while Caucasian workers were housed near job sites in nice facilities. As it related to the towns they were building, state officials stated, "Negroes do not fit into the program." [38]

> *After the Civil War, liberated slaves dispersed throughout the United States, seeking work to escape the violence of the post-war South. For several decades many lived relatively peacefully in the East, Midwest, and the West. But in 1877 the disputed presidential election of the previous autumn was resolved in a compromise that gave the Republican candidate, Rutherford B. Hayes, the White House. In return for southern Democratic support of their presidential candidate, Republicans agreed to withdraw federal troops who had been protecting African Americans in the defeated Confederacy. The period of black liberation known as Reconstruction then came to an end. In the South, the former slaveholding aristocracy renewed African American subjugation. Supported by a campaign of violence against the newly emancipated slave, southern states adopted segregation statutes—Jim Crow laws. Denied the right to vote, segregated in public transportation, schools, private accommodations, and victimized by lynching and other forms of brutality. African Americans in the South were*

---

36   Richard Rothstein, *The Color of Law: A Forgotten History of How Our Government Segregated America* (New York: Liveright Publication Company, 2017), 17-18.

37   "New Deal: United States History," *Britannica*, 10 September 2020 [online]; accessed on 1 September 2020; available from https://www.britannica.com/event/New-Deal; Internet. New Deal, domestic program of the administration of U.S. Pres. Franklin D. Roosevelt between 1933 and 1939, which took action to bring about immediate economic relief as well as reforms in industry, agriculture, finance, waterpower, labor, and housing, vastly increasing the scope of the federal government's activities.

38   Ibid, 19.

reduced again to a lower caste-status status. Plantation owners redefined their formers slaves as sharecroppers to maintain harsh and exploitative conditions.[39]

These actions led to racial zoning, which left Blacks at a serious disadvantage in society. It allowed local and state governments to create really nice and predominately White neighborhoods, while at the same time, relegating Blacks to lower-income ghetto areas. Racial zoning affected Blacks in the area of housing and education, and employment as well. It also led to Blacks having to settle for housing in less desirable neighborhoods, state-sanctioned violence used to keep blacks in their place, and make sure they never got out of the caste system Whites placed them in. As a result, their incomes were severely suppressed.

An Unequal Justice System

The story of Darryl Burton is all too familiar to Blacks in America. Burton was charged and convicted on March 27, 1985, of capital murder and armed criminal action. He was 26 years old at the time. His sentence was life imprisonment without the possibility of parole, plus a consecutive sentence of 25 years for armed criminal action. After serving 24 years, he was freed on August 29, 2008.[40] A separate article titled "The man who was falsely imprisoned for life due to alleged police fabrications" was about Burton's case.[41] The subtitle to the article was, "Sometimes the cops don't get the bad guy, so they create one." The article revealed that Burton was exonerated in 2008 when a judge released him after agreeing he was framed by the St. Louis Police Department. Burton sued the city of St. Louis, the board of police commissioners, and several police officers involved. It was alleged

---

39   Ibid, 39-40.

40   Darryl Burton, Other Missouri Exonerations with Jailhouse Informants, *The National Registry of Exonerations*, 12 June 2012 [on-line]; accessed 5 September 2020; available from http://www.law.umich.edu/special/exoneration/Pages/casedetail.aspx?caseid=3076; Internet.

41   10 of the Worst Wrongful Imprisonment Cases," *Oddee*, 9 November 2013 [on-line]; accessed 5 September 2020; available from https://www.oddee.com/item_98768.aspx; Internet.

that witnesses were coerced into accusing Burton of crimes he didn't commit. Also, the police fashioned false statements and concealed eyewitness accounts of the actual murderer.[42] Ironically, Burton's lawsuit was dismissed. In 1985, shortly after Burton's tragic dilemma first began, I was in an Air Force recruiter's office inquiring about joining the military. After taking and passing the ASVAB,[43] passing a criminal background check, and a military physical, I was placed on delayed enlistment for six months. I entered the Air Force in November 1985. I was sent to Lackland Air Force Base, San Antonio, Texas, where I attended Basic Training. I was living in the St. Louis area at the time of Burton's arrest. By the way, I was 20-years-old at the time, and Burton was only two years older—He was 22. If what happened to Burton had been my story, I would not have been able to join the Air Force because I would not have been able to pass the criminal background check. Even if I had been found innocent, the fact that I would have had an arrest on my record would have changed the trajectory of my life—for the rest of my life. The old saying, "There but for the grace of God, go I," was all I can think of when I learned about Burton's case. This injustice hit close to home for me since we both grew up not too far from one other and because we are both black men from a city known for racial inequality, especially in the policing of African Americans.

A CBS article titled, *Unequal justice under the law*, asked the question, does our criminal justice system truly guarantee justice for all? The answer was no if you don't have the money to hire your top-notched attorney.[44] The argument the article focused on was that not only does our criminal justice system favor the rich over the poor, but also White over Black. It told the story of a Black woman name Shanna

---

42   Ibid.

43   The Armed Services Vocational Aptitude Battery, "ASVAB Enlistment Testing Program," https://www.officialasvab.com/: Internet. The Armed Services Vocational Aptitude Battery (ASVAB) is a multiple-aptitude battery that measures developed abilities and helps predict future academic and occupational success in the military. It is administered annually to more than one million military applicants, high school, and post-secondary students.

44   Bright Stephen, "Unequal Justice Under the Law," *CBS News*, 13 August 2017 [on-line]; accessed 5 September 2020; available from https://www.cbsnews.com/news/unequal-justice-under-the-law/; Internet.

Shackelford. Her life was turned upside down when her home outside Atlanta, GA caught fire in 2009. She was not at home at the time of the fire. However, investigators became suspicious because she had taken out a small insurance policy on the home.

Based on only minimal circumstantial evidence, Shackelford was arrested and charged with arson. She was given a public defender to represent her, who recommended she accept a 25-year prison term. As the article pointed out, the U.S. Constitution may promise everyone legal counsel under the law; it says nothing about that legal counsel's quality. This is something Shackelford learned the hard way. Not only was it hard for her to get in touch with her public defender, but he also didn't seem to care about what she had to say. He automatically assumed because she was Black and because the police said so, that she was guilty. He asked her if she didn't do it, well, who did? Even after she emphatically denied his accusations, he still didn't believe her. She knew she was in trouble because of the racist lawyer assigned to her and that she could not afford a lawyer on her own.

She had never been in trouble with the law before this incident but feared the outcome. There was one strange fact about this case. Shackelford's insurance company was instrumental in her being charged because they did not want to pay out her claim. Shackelford took the initiative to research her case, which took years. She says her public defender was swamped with other cases, so he devoted very little time to her case, especially since he believed she was guilty.

During the process, she lost two jobs and her home. Also, she had a hard time finding a place to live because renters look very unfavorably at someone accused of arson, even if they were innocent. If it had not been for a Good Samaritan named Stephen Bright, Shackelford would more than likely still be in jail. Bright's investigation—which he did for free—proved faulty wiring, not arson. The article painted a grim picture for Blacks and the Criminal Justice system in America because Shackelford's case is common among people of color. The article stated that approximately 90% of African American cases often end in a plea deal, even if they are innocent. This is primarily because most poor defendants cannot afford bail and must wait in jail until trial, months, or even years. This further exacerbates the situation because Blacks often end up losing their jobs, cars, and homes in the process, just like Shackelford.

Depending on a person's political affiliation, whether a Democrat or Republican, often determines whether a person believes we have two criminal justice systems. To drive home the point about this important issue, I came across a *Washington Post* opinion article that dealt with this issue.

> *Of particular concern to some on the right is the term "systemic racism," often wrongly interpreted as an accusation that everyone in the system is racist. Systemic racism means almost the opposite. It means that we have systems and institutions that produce racially disparate outcomes, regardless of the intentions of the people who work within them. When you consider that much of the criminal justice system was built, honed, and firmly established during the Jim Crow era — an era almost everyone, conservatives included, will concede was rife with racism — this is pretty intuitive. The modern criminal justice system helped preserve racial order — it kept black people in their place. For much of the early 20th century, in some parts of the country, that was its primary function. That it might retain some of those proclivities today shouldn't be all that surprising.*[45]

This paragraph was about a conversation that took place at the beginning of this article that followed Senator Tim Scott's speech on the floor of the U.S. Senate. Scott talked about how police officers had repeatedly pulled him over for simply being Black when there was no other legal justification for the police officer's actions. Scott is the only black man serving in the Senate. When Scott made his remarks, not one white Senator stood up and said he was lying, not even one Republican. Why is it that these same Senators refuse to believe that this is a common experience for many black men in America, who don't happen to be U.S. Senators?

---

45 Radley Balko. "There's overwhelming evidence that the criminal justice system is racist: Here's the proof, *The Washington Post*, 10 June 2020 [online];. accessed 5 September 2020; available from https://www.washingtonpost.com/graphics/2020/opinions/systemic-racism-police-evidence-criminal-justice-system/; Internet.

The point being, if it can happen to someone as distinguished as a sitting Senator, why couldn't this happen to other ordinary black citizens that are not in such high-profile positions? Regrettably, many Whites have on blinders when it comes to understanding the Black experience in America. Awkwardly, some Whites try to relate their personal experiences with that of African Americans, which is a false equivalency. In a very unsympathetic way, with the underpinnings of racism, they say things like, "I made it as a white person, and so could black people if they get off food stamps and stop waiting on the U.S. Government to take care of them." While in reality, there are far more Whites on some type of government assistance than Blacks. This goes to show that ignorance and false stereotypes are also serious problems.[46]

In a book by Michael Eric Dyson, *Tears We Cannot Stop: A Sermon to White America*, he makes a really strong point about the two separate Americas: White and Black, when he said, "Black and white people don't merely have a different experience; we seem to occupy different universes, with worldviews that are fatally opposed to one another. The merchants of racial despair easily peddle their wares in a marketplace riddle by white panic and fear." [47]

Fortunately, for Whites in America, they never had to endure the heinous institution of slavery, nor their ancestors. Furthermore, they never had to face Jim Crow laws designed to keep them in the role of second-class citizens, being lynched by their neighbors, a criminal justice system that disproportionally incarcerates them, simply based on race, or being denied housing in certain parts of a city, simply based on race, or being shot for driving or walking while "white." Until all Americans, White and Black, can at least agree on the obvious—that racism remains a systemic problem that permeates throughout our

---

46   Barbara Ehrenreich, "Welfare: A White Secret." *Time Magazine*, 24 June 2001[on-line]; accessed 5 September 2020; available from http://content.time.com/time/magazine/article/0,9171,156084,00.html; Internet. The numbers go like this: 61% of the population receiving welfare, listed as "means-tested cash assistance" by the Census Bureau, is identified as white, while only 33% is identified as black. These numbers notwithstanding, the Republican version of "political correctness" has given us "welfare cheat" as a new term for African American since the early days of Ronald Reagan.

47   Michael Eric Dyson. *Tears We Cannot Stop: A Sermon to White America*. (New York: St. Martin's Press), 2017.

society—we will never have a solution for a problem that many White people don't believe exists.

Incidents That Inflamed Racial Unrest

George Floyd

On May 25, 2020, a black man named George Floyd died while lying on the ground with three police officers kneeling on him, one with his knee on Floyd's neck for eight minutes and forty-six seconds. Brazenly, while being videotaped by a teenager named Darnella Frazier on her cell phone, the officers continued their police brutality. Without the video of the incident, many Americans would not know that this sort of thing was still possible in this day and time—although African Americans are keenly aware of these everyday experiences. What began as a routine police call for a run-of-the-mill minor crime—someone allegedly passing a counterfeit $20 bill at a grocery store in the Powderhorn Park neighborhood of Minneapolis—ended in tragedy.[48]

The video went viral on local and national cable news channels. The outpouring of rage and anger led to unprecedented protest, not just in the U.S. but around the world. If this were a one-off, it would be one thing, but the fact that this has been the norm throughout our nation's history reveals the problem of systemic racism. What ignited the outpouring of frustration, activism, and support for Black Lives Matter was not just the Floyd shooting—even though it ignited a pent-up response—but the repeated deaths of Blacks at the hands of police officers in America for years.

Breonna Taylor

In March 2020, at 12:43 A.M., the Louisville Metro Police Department, with a no-knock warrant in-hand, burst through the front door of the apartment of 26-year-old Breonna Taylor, in which

---

48   Jorge Fitz-Gibbon, "Here's everything we know about the death of George Floyd" *New York Post*, 28 May 2020 [on-line]; accessed 28 August 2020; available from https://nypost.com/2020/05/28/everything-we-know-about-the-death-of-george-floyd; Internet.

she was there in bed with her boyfriend, Kenneth Walker. Ironically, the warrant was part of a narcotics investigation involving a previous boyfriend, not on the premises. The officers were in plainclothes and unmarked vehicles. According to Walker's statement, he and Breonna were in bed and heard someone burst through the door. He reached for his gun—which he had a license to carry—and fired because he and Taylor thought it was burglars. Also, he stated that the police never announced they were police, so he fired his weapon.

The police blindly sprayed gunfire into the residence with total disregard for human life, which at least 22 rounds were fired. Taylor was struck six times with bullets and died in the hallway of her apartment. Neither Taylor nor Walker had a criminal record or were drug dealers. Much of the nation was outraged because of this incident, and to this date, the police officers involved have not been charged.[49] Unfortunately, to justify the shooting, the Louisville police are trying their best to paint Taylor as a drug dealer, with no evidence that justifies that characterization. After more than six months had passed, the Attorney General of Kentucky, Daniel Cameron, held a press conference on September 24, 2020, to announce charges would not be brought against any of the officers responsible for Taylor's death. He announced that the grand jury failed to indict the two officers who fired the shots into Taylor's body, leading to her death. However, one officer was indicted on a lesser charge for firing three bullets into an adjacent apartment.[50] In an update to this case, the family was outraged because the Attorney General of Kentucky never asked the grand jury to consider charges against the two officers who killed Taylor.[51]

---

49   Minyvonne Burke. "Breonna Taylor police shooting: What we know about the Kentucky woman's death." *NBC News*, 15 May 2020 [on-line]; accessed 28 August 2020; available from https://www.nbcnews.com/news/us-news/breonna-taylor-police-shooting-what-we-know-about-kentucky-woman-n1207841; Internet.

50   Christina Carrega and Delano Massey, "Weeping resounded from the room where Breonna Taylor's mother learned the grand jury's decision" *CNN*, 24 September 2020 [on-line]; accessed 28 August 2020 available from https://www.cnn.com/2020/09/24/us/breonna-taylor-grand-jury-decision-reaction-tamika-palmer/index.html; Internet.

51   Timothy D. Easley, "Grand jury was never asked to mull homicide charged in Breonna Taylor case," *Politico*, 9 September 2020 [on-line]; accessed

Jacob Blake

In August 2020, America watched as 29-year-old Jacob Blake was shot seven times in the back by a Kenosha police officer as he leaned into an SUV while his three young sons were in the backseat of the vehicle. The cell phone video of the shooting was replayed over and over on local and national TV. Many details of what led up to the shooting remain uncertain. However, what can be pieced together, from two separate videos made public, showed Blake on the ground with police officers around him trying to apprehend him. He was tased by one of the officers, which is why he was on the ground. Somehow, Blake made it to his feet and walked around the SUV to the driver's side. At least three police officers followed him with their guns drawn.

Blake appeared to open the driver's door of the vehicle and lean inside. One of the officers, Rusten Sheskey, fired seven shots into Blake's back while holding on to the back of his t-shirt. Amazingly, Blake survived the ordeal but was paralyzed from the waist down due to his spine being ruptured from the gunfire.[52] Because of the continued outrage for police shootings of unarmed black men, there was a Black Lives Matter march in the city of Kenosha the following day. Later that evening, during a confrontation between protestors and a group of armed agitators, a 17-year-old white teenager named Kyle Rittenhouse fired an AR-15 long rifle— killing two people and wounding one other.[53]

---

5 October 2020; available from https://www.politico.com/news/2020/09/29/kentucky-grand-jury-tapes-breonna-taylor-422864; Internet. Kentucky's attorney general, Daniel Cameron said the only charge he recommended to the grand jury was wanton endangerment. The family felt misled because they thought that Cameron had tried to indict, but the grand jury declined, but he didn't attempt to indict.

52   Jordan Freeman and Justin Carissimo. "Police in Wisconsin shoot Black man in back multiple times, sparks protest," *CBS News*, 25 August 2020 [on-line]; accessed 27 August 2020 from https://www.cbsnews.com/news/jacob-blake-kenosha-shooting-wisconsin-police-black-man-protesters-gather; Internet.

53   Charles Davis, "Prosecutor announce homicide charges against Kyle Rittenhouse, the 17-year-old accused of shooting and killing 2 people at a Kenosha protest" *Business Insider*, 8 August 2020 [on-line]; accessed 28 August 2020 from https://www.msn.com/en-us/news/crime/prosecutors-announce-homicide-charges-against-kyle-rittenhouse-the-17-year-old-vigilante-who-shot-and-killed-2-people-at-a-kenosha-protest/ar-BB18rmSj; Internet.

What was interesting, Rittenhouse tripped and fell to the ground but still fired his fatal shots from a seated position while leaning back. He then got up, with his rifle in hand, strapped it across his shoulder, and walked toward the police with his hands raised. Onlookers shouted to the police in the background, which was nearby, that Rittenhouse had just shot and killed somebody. From the young man's actions, it appeared that he wanted to surrender to the police because he realized what he had just done, and he did not want to get shot by the police. However, the police just drove right past him in tactical vehicles, even though it was visible that he was carrying an assault rifle. What was also apparent from the video, even though it was night, was that he was White—but a White guy walking the streets of America with an AR-15 rifle is normal. This was a picture of White Privilege on full display. [54]

Somehow, Rittenhouse was able to make the twenty-minute drive back to his home in Antioch, Illinois. He was not arrested until the following day at his home and charged with two counts of homicide and other criminal charges for his deadly actions. According to news sources, Rittenhouse claimed self-defense for his brutal actions—although the only thing that the people he shot were armed with was a skateboard.[55] This reminds me of another case that involved another young man with a gun. However, there was a stark difference in the outcome of these cases.

---

54   Nicki Lisa Cole, PhD. "Understanding and Defining White Privilege: The U.S. Hierarchy in the 21st Century" 22 June 2020 [on-line]; accessed 29 August 2020 from https://www.thoughtco.com/white-privilege-definition-3026087; Internet. White privilege refers to the collection of benefits that white people receive in societies where they top the racial hierarchy. Made famous by scholar and activist Peggy McIntosh in 1988, the concept includes everything from whiteness being equated with being "normal" to whites having more representation in the media. White privilege leads to white people being viewed as more honest and trustworthy than other groups, whether or not they have earned that trust. This form of privilege also means that white people can easily find products suitable for them—cosmetics, band-aids, hosiery for their skin tones, etc. While some of these privileges might seem trivial, it's important to recognize that no form of privilege comes without its counterpart: oppression.

55   Robert Verbruggen, "Does Kyle Rittenhouse Have a Self-defense Claim?" *National Review*, 28 August 2020 [on-line]; accessed 28 August 2020 from https://www.nationalreview.com/2020/08/does-kyle-rittenhouse-have-a-self-defense-claim; Internet.

Tamir Rice

Tamir Rice was only twelve-years-old at the time. He was a Black child, minding his own business. He was not part of a gang, nor did he have a criminal record. He had a small build and did not have an intimidating appearance. Rice was on a playground by himself with a gun. By the way, the handgun he was playing with was a toy. As the story goes, a local 911 dispatcher was called concerning a Black person on a playground playing with a gun. Somehow, the dispatcher failed to convey to the police what the 911 caller said. What was left out was some very crucial details. The police were not told it was a child, that he was not harming anyone, and that the gun was a toy. In seconds upon the police arriving on the scene, Tamir Rice was shot and killed by Timothy Loehmann, a Cleveland police officer. The shooting was ruled to be justified by the Cleveland Police Department, and no charges were filed against Loehmann—although he was fired.

From the perspective of a trained former military police officer,[56] everything about how the Tamir Rice shooting was handled was wrong on so many levels. As a military police officer, when we could use deadly force was drilled into us daily. We were constantly required to undergo vigorous police training. We were required to pass annual and semi-annual firearms training and annual job performance quality control evaluation training. We even carried Military Police cards that detailed rules of engagement and use of deadly force. It was drilled into us that deadly force was only lawful as a last resort. We could not just roll up on a scene and begin firing as though it was the Wild-Wild West. Even if you gave the police officers the benefit of the doubt because they did not receive a full description of the incident, this should have been clear once they arrived on-scene. If they had taken the time to properly evaluate the situation, the outcome would have differed. As trained

---

56 The author served on active duty for 10 years in the Air Force as a Security Specialist. He graduated from the Security Police Academy, the Air Base Ground Defense School, and the M-60 Course, Lackland AFB, Texas as well as the Air Base Ground Defense Supervisors Course, Fort. Dix, and served in Operation Desert Storm as a police supervisor. He was also awarded marksmanship ribbons for M-9 handgun and M-16 Rifle.

police officers, we were also taught to assess the situation before taking action, especially action that could cost someone their life.

Furthermore, there was no way officer Loehmann was able to make the correct assessment from the time he drove up, got out his patrol car, and fired his 9mm Glock at a 12-year-old child, killing him instantly. Although Timothy Loehmann was fired in Cleveland, he was hired by the Bellaire Police Department, which patrols a community of about 4,000 residents just opposite the Ohio River from West Virginia.[57] How is it that a 17-year-old white teenager got the benefit of the doubt when he was a criminal, and someone five years younger was not, because he happened to be Black, even though he was innocent?

Kenosha, Wisconsin

The people involved in the two Kenosha, Wisconsin incidents in August 2020 (as well as the many other incidents like George Floyd, Breonna Taylor, and Tamir Rice) reveal why many Blacks believe there are two justice systems in America: one for Whites and another for Blacks. Here you have two individuals, Jacob Blake and Kyle Rittenhouse. Police in America treat people of color differently from the majority white race when they encounter each of them in the course of their normal duties. This was on full display in these two incidents and was evident to anyone rational and willing to open their eyes to the truth. Blake, who is black, was challenged by three to four police

---

57   Matthew Haag. "Cleveland Officer Who Killed Tamir Rice Is Hired by an Ohio Police Department," *New York Times*, 8 October 2018 [on-line]; accessed 28 August 2020; available from https://www.nytimes.com/2018/10/08/us/timothy-loehmann-tamir-rice-shooting.html; Internet. The department's chief said he had no concerns about hiring Officer Loehmann, who was not charged in Tamir's death but who was fired last year after a Cleveland Police Department investigation into the shooting uncovered that he had lied on his job application. "He was cleared of any and all wrongdoing," the Bellaire police chief, Richard Flanagan, told The Times Leader of Martins Ferry, Ohio, adding that it was unfair to "crucify" the officer. "It's over and done with." Just because Officer Loehmann was never charged for Tamir Rice's death, does not mean that he should be allowed to hold a job that he is obviously not qualified to serve in because he lacks judgment, temperate, and a respect for African Americans necessary for the position. This is the problem with the systemic culture of policing in America, which continues to uphold systemic racism.

officers unable to apprehend him. Blake ignored the orders of the police officers and ended up being shot multiple times.

On the other hand, Rittenhouse essentially shot three people, killing two of them, and was not even approached by the police. He was able to survive and be arrested at his home in a non-violent way, even though he proved he was extremely violent. Thinking of this situation, I am reminded of another situation that portrays America's two justice systems. For instance, a young white man named Dylann Roof went into an African American church in Charleston, South Carolina. He killed nine people, injuring many others during an evening Bible study. Dylann was not only treated with kid gloves; the officers even stopped and purchased fast food for him on their way to the police station because he was hungry.[58] It was stated that Roof told the police that the black people of the church were so nice to him that he started not to shoot them. I recall watching the news coverage of the surviving members and other members, who spoke on camera, with tears in their eyes; they said they forgave this young white man that shot up their church and killed their pastor.

If white America was paying attention, this African American church displayed genuine Christian love to a predominately white country with a history of doing vile things to them. By the way, there was a stark contrast to how law enforcement dealt with someone who was White, opposed to their normal interaction when they encounter someone Black. Dylann was not tackled, tased, thrown to the ground, harassed, humiliated, punched, kicked, shot in the back, nor was a knee placed on his neck. Not saying he deserved to be treated that way, even after what he did (because he did not), but neither do black people when they encounter the police, whether innocent or allegedly guilty of some infraction or crime.

White Privilege

---

[58] "Charleston shooting suspect's Burger King meal gets national attention," *The Charlotte Observer*, 24 June 2015 [on-line]; accessed 28 August 2020; available from https://www.charlotteobserver.com/news/local/article25394389.html; Internet.

One other issue I must discuss in more detail to make the point of this book clearer is the subject of White Privilege. Since I have already defined the term, I want to give a few clear examples. On May 27, 2020, a white woman named Amy Cooper crossed paths with a black man named Christian Cooper (no relation) in Central Park, New York. Christian was there bird watching, which was his hobby and his right to be in a public park. Amy was there walking her dog, her hobby, and her right to be in the same public park. What started the incident that went viral was when Christian asked Amy to follow the law and place her dog on a leash, which she had in her hand. From the video recorded on Christian's cell phone, you could see and hear their confrontation.

Amy was on her cell phone calling 911 to report a black man bothering her (which was false because he was minding his own business). She raised her voice to imply to the 911 operator that she was in fear for her life—as though she was about to be attacked by the black man. She told the operator that the man (Christian) was recording her and threatening her and her dog (which he does not do at any time). She also emphasized the fact that Christian was a black man. That's racism! The fact that Christian was black had nothing to do with the incident. Amy injected race into the situation because she understood her white privilege (and she knew Christian understood her white privilege as well), which is why he recorded her to protect himself from her false accusations. They both knew the police were more likely to believe her version because she had the upper hand due to her dominant race.

As Amy continued to talk with the operator, she again went into panic mode and raised her voice to sound as though she feared for her life. Ironically, her dog freaked out because of her actions and not the actions of the so-called threatening black man. Because Christian was smart enough to record the incident, and the fact that it went viral nationwide, the video saved a black man from being falsely accused by a white woman, which is not always the case.[59] This incident, once again, proves that systemic racism is alive and well in America.

---

59   Alicia Lee and Sara Sider, "99 years ago today, America was shaken by one of its deadliest acts of racial violence" *CNN*, 1 June 2020 [on-line]; accessed 29 August 2020; available from https://www.cnn.com/2020/06/01/us/tulsa-race-massacre-1921-99th-anniversary-trnd/index.html; Internet. What led to the Tulsa Race Massacre was an encounter between a Black man and

Brock Turner, a young white man, was charged for violently raping a female student while she was unconscious. To the surprise of many, he received a six-month sentence due to his "previous good character." Turner served only three of his exceptionally short six month sentence.[60] In contrast, there is the well-known story involving the Central Park Five, which was made into a Netflix mini-series.

> *In the first episode of the Netflix series When They See Us, members of the New York City Police Department lie to five teenagers as they were interrogated about the brutal rape of a jogger in Central Park. The scenes are painful to watch as the young actors portray the pain and desperation of hour after hour of deceptive interrogation tactics. Their parents, determined to get their children out of the police station and back home, plea with them to say whatever the cops want to hear. The teenagers, who became known in the press as the Central Park Five, didn't know each other before they got to the police station, and the cops played them off one another. They told 14-year-old Raymond Santana they had evidence against 15-year-old Kevin Richardson, and if he just helped them build a case against Richardson by placing himself into the crime scene, he'd get to go home. They made the boys believe they were acting merely as witnesses to a crime. In the end, four of the five boys falsely confessed. And even though no DNA linked them to the scene of the crime, and their descriptions of the victim's clothing*

---

a White woman that ended very differently than Christian Cooper and Amy Cooper.

60   Lynn Neary, "Victim Of Brock Turner Sexual Assault Reveals Her Identity," *NPR*, 4 September 2019 [on-line]; accessed 6 October 2020; available from https://www.npr.org/2019/09/04/757626939/victim-of-brock-turner-sexual-assault-reveals-her-identity. Internet. Chanel Miller was the young college student Turner victimized. Turner, who could have gotten 14 years in federal prison, was sentenced to six months in county jail. He served three months. That decision, by Judge Aaron Persky, was met with outrage. Critics assailed Persky for being too lenient. Turner was a first-time offender, promising student and swimming champion. The judge said a tougher sentence "would have had a severe impact on him" — and he did not think Turner was a danger to others. Critics of the decision started gathering signatures for a recall campaign. In June 2018, the campaign succeeded. Persky was the first California judge to be recalled in more than 80 years.

and injuries didn't match the crime scene, they were convicted. In 2002, after prison sentences that ranged from six to 13 years, they were all released when a murderer and serial rapist confessed to the assault—and his DNA matched with that found on the jogger. [61]

Donald Trump (not the President at the time), took out a full-page ad in a New York newspaper condemning the black boys, which placed their lives in danger. One of the boy's lawyers claimed that Trump's hateful unfounded article is what convicted the clients. The black boys were innocent of raping a white woman. However, they served between six to thirteen years for a crime none of them had committed.[62] Even when they were declared not guilty of the crime, the damage to their reputations was already done. To add insult to injury, Trump has never apologized to these black men. He still believes they are guilty, despite the lack of evidence. When a wealthy white man accuses a black man of a crime, even when he is innocent, many white Americans will still believe he is guilty because it is already baked into the psyche of American culture, which proves that systemic racism is alive and well in America.

Shanesha Taylor was arrested when she left her children in a car for 45 minutes to attend a job interview. Although she was homeless and desperately in need of a job at the time, and her children suffered no harm, Taylor pled guilty to felony child abuse. She received ten years' probation, was required to undergo parenting classes, and her children were able to remain in her custody.[63] What would have happened if

---

61   Kate Storey, "'When They See us 'Shows The Disturbing Truth About How False Confessions Happen," *Esquire*, 1 June 2019 [on-line]; accessed 6 October 2020; available from https://www.esquire.com/entertainment/a27574472/when-they-see-us-central-park-5-false-confessions/; Internet. The Netflix show depicts the Central Park Five case, one of the most important in the field of false confessions research.

62   Niloufar Haidari, "50 Examples of White Privilege to show family members who still don't get it," Vice, June 9, 2020 [on-line]; Accessed 29 August 2020; available from Https://www.vice.com/en_Uk/Article/4ayw8j/White-Privilege-Examples; Internet.

63   Shanesha Taylor, "Phoenix Mom Who Left Kids in Hot Car, Pleads Guilty to Child Abuse." *NBC News*, 16 March 2015 [On-line]; accessed 29 August 2020; available from https://www.nbcnews.com/news/us-news/shanesha-taylor-mom-who-left-kids-car-pleads-guilty-child-n324476; Internet.

Taylor did not accept the government's plea agreement? She probably would have received jail time and treated as though her children had died in the vehicle.

In contrast, a white woman, an assistant principal at an Ohio middle school, Brenda Nesselroad-Slaby's daughter died after she left her locked in her car for eight hours while she went to work. She was not arrested, nor was she indicted. The Clement County Prosecutor, Don White, said, "A mistake is not a crime." Furthermore, it was stated that Nesselroad-Slaby behavior did not meet the definition of "reckless conduct," and that she had already suffered enough.[64] Nesselroad-Slaby did not receive a felony on her record. She was not placed on probation, and she was not required to attend parenting classes. She was allowed to go home and grieve because of her loss. Why didn't Shanesha Taylor receive the same benefit of the doubt? Why wasn't it said that she had suffered enough? Why didn't the government consider her plight? Why were these two women treated so differently simply based on their race and financial position in life? The answer is white privilege that has led to a broken justice system, which proves that systemic racism is alive and well in America.

Lori Loughlin is a very successful white actress who was caught up in a college cheating scandal. She became a household name for her role in the acclaimed sitcom *Full House*. Her husband, Mossimo Giannulli, a fashion designer, was also her partner in crime in the scandal. In October 2019, Loughlin and her husband were charged in the college admissions scandal that spanned nationwide, which included dozens of other people such as Felicity Huffman from the show *Desperate Housewives*. Due to the seriousness of the charges, they faced up to 50 years in prison.[65] Loughlin and her husband pled guilty for paying a

---

64   "Mother not charged in hot car death," ABC News, 8 January 2020 [On-line]; accessed 29 August 2020; available from https://abcnews.go.com/gma/story?id=3570651&page=1; Internet.

65   Zach Friedman, "Lori Loughlin charged with Bribery, faces 50 years in Prison," *Forbes*, 22 October 2019 [on-line]; accessed 19 August 2020; available from https:// www.forbes.com /sites/ zackfriedman/ 2019/10/22/ lori-loughlin-bribery-college-prison/#784ea7c8679e; Internet. A grand jury in the District of Massachusetts has returned additional charges against 11 of the 15 parents, including Loughlin and her husband, fashion designer Mossimo Giannulli, in the largest college admissions case in U.S. history.

$500,000 bribe to falsify their daughters Olivia Jade and Isabella Rose's records, as recruits to the University of Southern California, USC.[66] What does not make sense to average Americans, like myself, is that Loughlin and her husband had the wealth and means to send their daughters to a multitude of colleges and universities in the country, as well as overseas. If their daughters could not get into the college of their choice, they could have done like the rest of us, who desired to go to college, and apply elsewhere. The tragedy is not just that they cheated to get their daughters into USC, but it denied someone else's child that deserved to get in, left out. Loughlin and her husband spent months lying about their involvement and initially claiming that the $500,000 they gave was simply a donation. They used their high price attorneys to get them every advantage they were afforded—due to their fame, enormous resources, and privilege.

Another tragedy was the lenient sentences they both received: Loughlin, two months, and her husband five months. However, the biggest tragedy is that Loughlin got to choose her country club prison.[67] Although the daughters were not indicted in the scheme, they were certainly involved. They both turned in phony documentation that stated they were star athletes in a sport they didn't even play.[68] The daughters dropped out of USC and were never charged.

66   Doha Madani and David K. Li "Lori Loughlin sentenced to 2 months, husband to 5 months, in college scam," *NBC News*, 21 August 2020 [on-line]; accessed 19 August 2020; available from https://www.nbcnews.com/news/us-news/lori-loughlin-s-husband-mossimo-giannulli-sentenced-5-months-college-n1237556; Internet.

67   Melissa Roberto, "Lori Loughlin's request to serve prison sentence at California's Victorville signed off by judge: court docs," *Fox News*, 18 August 2020 [on-line]; accessed 19 August 2020; available from https://www.foxnews.com/entertainment/lori-loughlin-prison-sentence-california-victorville-signed-judge-court-docs; Internet.

68   Carter Evans, "Alleged college resume of Lori Loughlin's daughters lists fake rowing achievements," *CBS News*, 10 February 2020 [on-line]; accessed 19 August 2020; available from https://www.cbsnews.com/news/college-admissions-scandal-lori-loughlin-daughter-olivia-phony-rowing-achievements-resume/. Internet. A phony resume is heavily redacted, but the graduation date of 2018 matches that of YouTube star Olivia Jade. The bogus document details an elaborate list of rowing accomplishments, including gold medals and top 15 finishes in the Head of the Charles Regatta in Boston, one of rowing's most prestigious events. All the achievements could have been easily

The final tragedy that played a major role in this college admission scandal was the school itself, USC. With a Division 1 school's tremendous resources, they could have easily checked and found that the Loughlin daughters were frauds. However, when the school is complicit in the crime, that tells you everything you need to know about how many college admission programs work. I included this story because it shows the other side of our broken criminal justice system, which is also white privilege. Let's face it, White people and Black people are not treated the same in our criminal justice system. Furthermore, Blacks get blamed for not going to college, often because they cannot afford it. At the same time, many Whites can simply buy their way in because the system is rigged in their favor, which is another major problem in America.

As I reflected on all these horrific issues this 2020 year, I am even more troubled with the Christian church's response in America, namely white evangelicals.[69] Although some white pastors and seminary professors have spoken out against the racial unrest in America, that is still not enough. More pastors and Christian professors, especially those with the biggest platforms, need to do much more. They need to speak out because their silence is not only deafening but also complicit. What is the church's responsibility to the nation and their communities during the time of this enormous racial unrest? How can the church remain silent while our nation continues down the road of self-destruction? How can white Christian pastors preach the Bible, while at the same time so many of them remain silent—when it comes to systemic racism in America? Why do so many Whites get so angry when Blacks say, Black Lives Matter? Why don't more white Christians

---

checked out. But USC's associate athletic director at the time, Donna Heinel, is accused of being in on the scam.

69   Mark Galli, "So, What's an Evangelical?" 18 September 2020. [on-line]; accessed on 20 September 2020; available from; Internet. Evangelical means "the religion of the born-again." The most obvious way that Evangelicals have stood out historically from the rest of the Christian movement is putting a great deal of emphasis the experience of conversion, and Christ's teachings in John 3 in particular about being born again. Evangelicals have put a distinctive and unique emphasis on the need for all people to experience the transformation of the new birth. That was what was new in The Great Awakening of the 1740s when the modern Evangelical movement is born.

join with black Christians and say, Black Lives Matter? Why don't white Christians ask a black Christian they trust the meaning of Black Lives Matter instead of responding with the insensitive statement All Lives Matter? Why don't more white Christians believe they have a definite privilege because of their race when it permeates our society?

CHAPTER 2

ONE NATION UNDER WHO?

The Sons Of Israel Did Evil

When Joshua had dismissed the people, the sons of Israel went each to his inheritance to possess the land. The people served the Lord all the days of Joshua, and all the days of the elders who survived Joshua, who had seen all the great work of the Lord which He had done for Israel. Then Joshua the son of Nun, the servant of the Lord, died at the age of one hundred and ten. And they buried him in the territory of his inheritance in Timnath-heres, in the hill country of Ephraim, north of Mount Gaash. All that generation also were gathered to their fathers; and there arose another generation after them who did not know the Lord, nor yet the work which He had done for Israel. Then the sons of Israel did evil in the sight of the Lord and served the Baals, and they forsook the Lord, the God of their fathers, who had brought them out of the land of Egypt, and followed other gods from among the gods of the peoples who were around them, and bowed themselves down to them; thus they provoked the Lord to anger. So they forsook the Lord and served Baal and the Ashtaroth. The anger of the Lord burned against Israel, and He gave them into the hands of plunderers who plundered them; and He sold them into the hands of their enemies around them so that they could no longer stand before their enemies. Wherever they went, the hand of the Lord was against them for evil, as the Lord had spoken and as the Lord had sworn to them, so that they were severely distressed. (Judges 2:6-15)

If there was ever a passage in the Bible that describes the state of affairs in the United States throughout its history, it is the second chapter of the book of Judges (although the entire book applies in many ways). If the claim is accepted that America is a Christian nation—or at least founded as a Christian nation or on Christian principles—then what happened to the Israelites mirrors in many ways what happened (and continues to happen) in America. For instance, if one buys the argument that most, if not all, of America's Founding Fathers were Christians who sought to establish a Christian nation, then a strong argument could be made that they failed miserably. When the Declaration of Independence was signed on August 2, 1776, at the Pennsylvania State House in Philadelphia, they declared that the former Thirteen Colonies were a sovereign nation—although they were still at war with England.[70] Included in the declaration was the Preamble written by Thomas Jefferson, "We hold these truths to be self-evident, that all men are created equal, that they are endowed by their Creator with certain unalienable Rights, that among these are Life, Liberty and the pursuit of Happiness." Throughout this book, I will examine the application of this preamble in American history.

A Generation That Knows Not The Lord

To understand the book of Judges, one must first understand the book of Joshua as well as the very important foundational Old Testament books (the Torah) that proceed them. The first five books of the Bible are often overlooked in their importance and not treated as one continuous message of the entire Bible. Immediately after the story of creation, we learn about the fall of man. After the fall, we learn about the downward spiral of humanity. However, in the same chapter in the Bible that records the fall of man (Genesis 3), we learn about the redemption of man. "And I will put enmity Between you and the woman, and between your seed and her seed; He shall bruise you on

---

70   Benjamin Elisha Sawe, "Who Signed The Declaration Of Independence?" *World Atlas*, 16 February 2020 [on-line]; Accessed 9 September 2020; available from https://www.worldatlas.com/articles/who-signed-the-declaration-of-independence.html; Internet.

the head, and you shall bruise Him on the heel" (Genesis 3:15).[71] This is the first prophetic statement in Scripture that reveals a Messiah to redeem lost man.[72] Genesis 12 reveals God was putting His redemptive plan in motion by choosing Abraham and making a covenant with him and his descendants. Joshua and Judges complement one another because they tell the story about God keeping His promise to Abraham. The book of Joshua records the transition from Moses leading God's people to Joshua assuming the mantle. God encourages Joshua by telling him, "…just as I have been with Moses, I will be with you; I will not fail you or forsake you" (Joshua 1:5). This had to be very encouraging for a young man who God handpicked to succeed such a faithful servant like Moses. Joshua knew the job was an enormous task and that he could not do it alone because he witnessed firsthand Moses, his mentor, struggle for years trying to shepherd over 2 million grumbling ungrateful people. This caused Joshua to choose godly men from among the people and appoint them to help lead the people. Consequently, Joshua was instrumental in leading the Israelites into the Promised Land, where he gave Israel God's final instructions before he died.

---

71 W.W. Wiersbe, *Wiersbe's Expository Outlines on the Old Testament: Genesis*, (Wheaton: Victor Books, 1993), 7-19. This is the first Gospel declared in the Bible: the good news that the woman's seed (Christ) would ultimately defeat Satan and his seed (Gal. 4:4–5). It is from this point on that the stream divides: Satan and his family (seed) oppose God and His family. God Himself put the enmity (hostility) between them, and God will climax the war when Satan is cast into hell (Rev. 20:10).

72 J.F. MacArthur Jr, *Genesis: The MacArthur study Bible: New American Standard Bible*,(Ge 3:15–16). (Nashville: Thomas Nelson Publishers, 2006). After cursing the physical serpent, God turned to the spiritual serpent, the lying seducer, Satan, and cursed him. *bruise you on the head … bruise him on the heel*. This "first gospel" is prophetic of the struggle and its outcome between "your seed" (Satan and unbelievers, who are called the Devil's children in Jn 8:44) and her seed (Christ, a descendant of Eve, and those in Him), which began in the garden. In the midst of the curse passage, a message of hope shone forth—the woman's offspring called "He" is Christ, who will one day defeat the Serpent. Satan could only "bruise" Christ's heel (cause Him to suffer), while Christ will bruise Satan's head (destroy him with a fatal blow). Paul, in a passage strongly reminiscent of Gen 3, encouraged the believers in Rome, "And the God of peace will soon crush Satan under your feet" (Ro 16:20).

The book of Judges recorded the transition from Joshua's leadership to the judges of Israel. Also, this book chronicled the "cycle of sin" of God's chosen people, as they rebelled against Him, dishonored the land, and worshiped the Canaanite gods. As a result, they were repeatedly humiliated by their enemies, faced numerous defeats, and cried out to God to rescue them.

Chapter 2 began with God's strong admonishment of Israel due to their blatant disobedience and ended with the Lord allowing some of the Canaanites to remain in the land because Israel failed to drive them out.[73] Because of Israel's unfaithfulness, the Canaanites became a thorn in their side for many years and was one of the primary reasons that the nation of Israel still struggles with maintaining their land to this day. After God chastised His people, Joshua dismissed them, and the sons of Israel went and possessed the land, each tribe to their inheritance (v. 6). Afterward, the next verses shed light on what happened to Israel and why they failed so miserably. Also, these verses explain why Israel struggled and never fulfilled its God-given purpose of being His divine people, under the Old Covenant, for reaching the Gentiles.

We read that the people served God all the days of Joshua, but he died at the age of 110 (vs.7-8). Furthermore, the elders who served under Joshua also died, which left a vacuum for consistent and strong godly leadership. The key verse that sets the tone for Israel's history throughout the remainder of the Old Testament and even into the New Testament is verse 10. It says there arose another generation (a sinful generation after Joshua's generation) who did not know the Lord, nor the work which He had done for Israel. The people did evil in the sight of the Lord and served the Baals, which revealed the degree to which they turned their back on the Lord (vs. 11-13).

This is one of the saddest turning points in the entire Bible. From this point on, it set the stage for how God dealt with His rebellious

---

[73] A. C. Bowling, *Judges: Evangelical Commentary on the Bible*, Vol. 3, (Grand Rapids: Baker Book House, 1996), 161. The angel begins by reminding the Israelites of the exodus, the gift of the land, and God's faithfulness to his covenant (v. 1). He then strikes directly at the heart of Israel's disobedience—the illicit covenants which legitimized the existence of pagan religion and peoples within Israel's territory. Such covenants led to the preservation of pagan shrines and even to the adoption of Canaanite religion by the Israelites.

people. Due to the void made available by the people rejecting the Lord, even after all that He had done, the people did evil in His sight and served the Baals—the Canaanites' false gods. They angered God by their actions. So, the Lord gave them into the hands of plunders who plundered them; and sold them into the hands of their enemies around them (v. 14). What was even worse, it says that wherever they went, the hand of the Lord was against them for evil (v. 15). [74] Instead of fighting for them, God would now fight against them. Wow! What a turn of events!

Another Generation That Knows Not The Lord

Now that we understand the context of the passage let's examine how it applies to America. Just like Israel, American turned its back on God. Although not all of the people who came to America to escape England's trouble and persecution for a better life were Christians, evangelicals today consider many of them to have been believers. However, the way that they conducted themselves was not Christian behavior. The way these wealthy white men (that ran the country and held all the power and resources) treated other people groups was sinful, such as how they treated Blacks and Natives. These same white men wrote a constitution designed to guarantee their way of life and create a society that would allow them to enjoy their white privilege.[75]

---

74   M. I. Duguid, E. A. Blum & T. Wax (Eds.), *Judges: CSB Study Bible: Notes* (Nashville: Holman Bible Publishers, 2017), 366. The consequence of Israel's covenant unfaithfulness was the covenant curse (Dt 28:48). Instead of the Lord fighting for Israel and handing their enemies over into their power, the Lord gave them over into the hand of their enemies, and they suffered greatly.

75   "The Founding Fathers," *National Geographic*, 24 January 2020 [on-line]; accessed on 9 September 2020; available from https://www.nationalgeographic.org/article/founding-fathers/; Internet. Historians have varied opinions about exactly who should be included on the list of Founding Fathers, or how large this list should be. Some names—George Washington, James Madison, and John Adams—are obvious, but others may be more debatable. Fifty-five delegates attended the Constitutional Convention, each of whom had an important part to play. There were also men—Thomas Jefferson, most notably—who were not at the Constitutional Convention but who nonetheless played a critical role in the foundation of the country. Jefferson not only wrote the original draft of the Declaration of Independence, but also provided counsel to the Constitutional Convention from Paris, France, where he was serving as the

George Washington set the tone for how America would deal with slavery because he had a personal stake in this sinful enterprise. His actions told the country that the enslavement of Blacks would be an acceptable practice in the new nation, which helped set the nation on the course for generation after generation of systemic racism.

A sad reality is that twenty-four of the forty-five Presidents of the United States have owned slaves, some were Founding Fathers. If the first president was allowed to own slaves, what message did that send to the rest of the nation? It screamed loud and clear that racism was an acceptable practice to benefit Whites! However, what would America have been like if slavery had been outlawed in 1776 during the Revolution, especially if the country had put God first and obeyed the Scriptures? Then, America could have been a Christian nation, and perhaps, avoided the Civil War.

Racism In The Church

In a book by Jemar Tisby titled, *The Color of Compromise*, the author made the following statement about the Civil War. He stated, there are two facts about the Civil War that are especially pertinent to our examination of race and Christianity in America: the Civil War was fought over slavery, and that countless devout Christians fought and died to preserve it as an institution.[76] Tisby says that many Christians supported slavery to the extent that they were willing to risk their lives to protect it. Also, he stated, the church, which prioritizes the love of God and love of neighbor, capitulated to the status quo—by permitting the lifetime bondage of human persons based on skin color. He added, the antebellum way of life had to fall, and the Civil War was the sledgehammer that knocked it down.[77]

Tisby made a strong argument for just how complicit the church was in prolonging the institution of slavery in America. He talked about how Methodists split over bishops that owned slaves, such as James Osgood Andrew, the Methodist Episcopal Church's bishop minister to France.

---

76   Jemer Tisby, *The Color of Compromise*, 71.

77   Ibid, 72.

(MEC). This was allowed even though the denomination had opposed slavery since it was founded in 1784. Even John Wesley, the founder of the Methodist movement, found slavery appalling.[78] Despite the Methodists' original opposition to slavery, as the denomination grew more socially conservative (at the time), views shifted in the South. In southern states, Methodist ministers became more comfortable with slavery and accommodated their preaching and practices to its presence. During the 1844 General Conference, there was a split in the denomination. Refusing to give up his church duties, Andrew and his allies split from the MEC. They formed the Methodist Episcopal Church, South (MECS), allowing their clergy to practice slavery.[79]

Tisby not only talked about Methodists, but he also discussed how Baptists split over slaveholding missionaries. A year after the Methodist schism, Baptists followed a similar course. In 1844, the Georgia Baptist Convention nominated James E. Reeve as a missionary to the Home Mission Society. Like James Osgood Andrew of the Methodist church, Reeve enslaved black people as well. In 1845, in Augusta, Georgia, the Southern Baptist Convention (a national convention) was born, which authorized their missionaries to own slaves.[80]

Tisby added that a third prominent protestant church in America struggled with slavery, which was the Presbyterians. Gardiner Spring, a Presbyterian pastor in New York, wrote a resolution that called all Presbyterians to pledge their allegiance to the federal government, which meant he supported the Union army at the Civil War outbreak and rejected slavery. However, the Presbyterian churches in the South supported the Confederate army, which meant they supported slavery. Many elders in the Presbyterian church rejected the ultimatum that derived from Pastor Spring's resolution because it was viewed as a "Christ vs. Caesar" argument. Those that viewed the ultimatum as forcing them to align with the government (Caesar), even though it meant rejecting slavery, sided with the Confederates. So, the Presbyterian church in the South formed the Presbyterian Church in the Confederate States of America (PCCS), which later changed its name

---

78   Ibid, 76.

79   Ibid. 77.

80   Ibid. 77-78.

to the Presbyterian Church of the United States of America (PCUSA). These churches were all in southern states that advocated for each state to have the right to determine the legality of slavery. To harden their stance toward slavery, southern Christians devised increasingly complex theological arguments to contend for the existence of slavery. In the process, southern Christians moved from viewing slavery as something permitted to something positive.[81]

In his book, Tisby does not detail the role of the Catholic church in slavery. However, he does comment on how some American Roman Catholics outside the South demonstrated their complicity in racism.[82] Tisby talked about how Catholic schools generally excluded black people or only included them on a segregated basis.[83] Not only did the Catholic church struggle with racism in their schools, but they also did so in the priesthood. Tisby told the story about Augustus Tolton. He was born a slave in Missouri in 1854 and fled to Illinois's free state during the Civil War. He was baptized as a Catholic and sought to become a priest. However, no Catholic seminary in the country would accept a black student. For Tolton to attend a Catholic seminary, he had to move to Rome—where he was accepted and allowed to pursue the priesthood.[84]

In an on-line article by Stacy Brown titled, "The Major Role The Catholic Church Played in Slavery," the author explained how the Catholic church performed a vital role in the Trans-Atlantic Slave Trade, according to historians. According to the article, the five major countries that dominated slavery and the slave trade in the New World were either Catholic or retained strong Catholic influences, including Spain, Portugal, France, and England, and The Netherlands.[85] It also

---

81   Ibid, 80.

82   Ibid, 112. Although Catholics had maintained a presence in North America since the sixteenth century, waves of immigration in the early 1800s—mostly German and Irish at first, but others from southern and eastern Europe—resulted in large populations of Roman Catholics in the urban North and the East Coast.

83   Ibid, 113.

84   Ibid.

85   Stacey M. Brown, "The Major Role The Catholic Church played in

stated that the Catholic church and Catholic missionaries could have also helped prevent the colonization and brutality of colonialism in Africa but did not. However, according to a 2015 Global Black History report, the Catholic church did not oppose the institution of slavery until the practice had already become infamous in most parts of the world. In most cases, Catholic churches and church leaders did not condemn slavery until the 17th century.[86]

When White Preachers Endorse Racism

When I was in seminary, one of my favorite subjects to study was church history. For my degree plan, I was required to take three semesters (or a year and a half) of church history, including Baptist history—because it was a Baptist seminary. However, during the entire time I was in seminary, I noticed that the accomplishments of black preachers in the advancement of Christianity were down-played severely. We learned about every prominent white pastor or minister from John Smyth (Baptist), to John Knox (Presbyterian), John Wesley (Methodism), Martin Luther (Lutheran), and many others. We even learned about those that were considered heretics and not true Christian ministers at all, such as Joseph Smith (Latter-day Saints), Charles Taze Russell (Jehovah's Witness), and Ellen White (Seventh-day Adventist). Sadly, the only mention of a prominent Black preacher was Richard Allen, the founder of the African Methodist Episcopal Church (AME). He was part of the white Methodist church but left because of racism.

Conversely, two white preachers were placed on a pedestal: George Whitfield and Jonathon Edwards. You would have thought that these men not only talked the talk, but they also walked the walk. However, when you study these two prominent white preachers, you discover a very disturbing truth.

Whitefield was an Anglin minister from England. He was heavily influenced by John Wesley, the founder of Methodism, and came to

---

Slavery," *Amsterdam News*, 18 September 2018 [on-line]; accessed on 7 October 2020; available from http://amsterdamnews.com/news/2018/sep/18/major-role-catholic-church-played-slavery/; Internet.

86   Ibid.

America to conduct revivals and spread Christianity. Whitefield was trained in theater and used his experience in his preaching.[87] While most preachers at that time read their sermons from a manuscript, Whitfield used a theatrical narration to provoke an emotional response from his crowds. He was one of the most prominent revivalist preachers during the Great Awakening. His emotional style appealed to the lower economic class of Whites and enslaved Blacks.[88] So, where did Whitefield stand on the issue of slavery? Well, it depends! When he had no stake in the game, he was moderately against slavery, but that changed when he needed free labor to support his ministry. What a hypocrite!

> Whitfield was more moderate on race than many of his white contemporaries. He excoriated enslavers for their physical abuse of slaves, calling them "monsters of barbarity." He expressed ambivalence about the practice of slavery itself, but he had no doubts about how masters should treat their laborers. "Unsure of 'whether it would be lawful for Christians to buy slaves,' Whitfield was positive that "it is sinful when bought to use them...as though they were Brutes.'" The worst abuse, in Whitefield's view, was some enslavers refusal to allow the enslaved to be evangelized. He and others like his wealthy, slaveholding Christian allies Hugh and Jonathan Bryan advocated for the rights of enslaved people to learn Christianity and to worship. Over time, Whitefield's moderation on slavery morphed into outright support.[89]

Whitefield purchased some land near Savannah, Georgia, to open a new orphanage, which he called "House of Mercy." However, due to mismanagement and the inability to raise money, Whitefield's orphanage struggled to stay open. As a result, Whitfield looked to slavery for the answer, instead of looking to God. Whitefield was virtually guaranteed a profit from his plantation activities if he did not have to pay laborers. Therefore, he began petitioning Georgia's political

---

87 Jemer Tisby, *The Color of Compromise*, 46.

88 Ibid, 47.

89 Ibid, 48.

leaders, which had been founded as a free territory, to allow slavery for his benefit. Whitefield advocated that allowing slavery would improve the land's financial fortunes and claimed that economic ruin was the only alternative. He said, "Georgia can never be a flourishing province unless Negroes are employed [as slaves].[90] Unfortunately, Whitfield's "house of mercy" became a "house of misery" for Blacks caught in his financial scheme. Whitefield's involvement in supporting slavery was never mentioned in any of my classes. He was portrayed as a "white knight" of the Christian movement in America among white, educated Christians at my seminary.

Jonathan Edwards was not British, like his contemporary, George Whitefield, he was an American. As such, many white Christians herald Jonathan Edwards as "America's Greatest Theologian." He is known for his famous sermon "Sinners in the hands of an angry God." A sermon that has been placed on the pantheon of biblical proclamations. Edwards became the pastor of First Church of Christ, Northampton, Massachusetts, after his renowned grandfather, Solomon Stoddard, died. Due to his preaching style that focused on emotionalism, a revival broke out in 1733.[91] However, Edwards compromised his Christian principles by owning enslaved Blacks. Although Edwards opposed the African slave trade, he did not oppose slavery in America. Ironically, Edwards, the theologian, accepted slavery as long as enslavers treated Blacks with dignity, an oxymoron. So, the question that should be asked asked, why would a Bible learned preacher like Edwards accept the evil, ungodly institution of slavery? The answer was his elite social status. Edwards represented an educated and elite class in New England society.[92] Also, wealthy and influential people populated his

---

90   Ibid. Historian Stephen J. Stein insists that financial concerns only partially explain Whitefield's advocacy for slavery. "The focus upon contrast and change in his ideas which has dominated discussion to date obscures a more significant feature of his thought, namely, his deep-seated fear of the blacks."

91   Ibid, 49. The revivals became the subject of ongoing controversy as more conservative preachers and theologians reviled the emotionalism of the events, and others defended the conversions and style of worship as authentic expressions of religion.

92   Ibid, 50. Evangelicalism focused on individual conversion and piety. Within this evangelical framework, one could adopt an evangelical expression

congregation, and slave-owning signified status—sort of like being the owner of a professional sports team in one of the three major sports today: NFL, NBA, or MLB.

Edwards and Whitefield represent a supposedly moderate and widespread view of slavery. Both accepted the spiritual equality of black and white people. Both preached the message of salvation to all. Yet their concern for African slaves did not extend to advocating for physical emancipation. Like these two preachers, many other Christians did not see anything in the Bible that forbade slavery. The Scriptures seemed to accept slavery as an established reality. Instead, white Christians believed that the Bible merely regulated slavery in order to mitigate its most brutal abuses.[93]

The problem with white Christian thinking, like Whitefield and his wealthy allies, is that it was okay to evangelize Blacks to lead them to faith in Christ, but it was also okay to never respect them; and treat them equally as brothers in Christ. The purpose of wanting a lost person to turn their life over to Christ is not just so they can go to heaven, but also to enjoy the journey on this earth and to make a difference for God's Kingdom. What was twisted about their thinking was that it sent a loud and clear message to Blacks. It's sad that it was okay for Whites to prosper in America, but not for Blacks, and that Blacks should have just been grateful that Whites shared their Jesus with them.

When white preachers say racism is okay, by their action or failure to act, it says to every black person that they are not equal according to their white interpretation of the Bible. What makes matters worse is when Christian seminaries and Bible colleges fail to set the record straight. Racial reconciliation will never be achieved in our local churches in America if our Christian schools of higher learning perpetuate the problem by ignoring the problem or masking the problem. There are certainly enough bad preachers and teachers in America that do not know the Bible, but that still does not stop them from drawing a crowd. However, what good does it do for a seminary-trained pastor or minister to learn the Bible correctly but have the wrong application? Does that not put the biblically illiterate and the

---

of Christianity yet remain uncompelled to confront institutional injustice.

93   Ibid, 51.

biblically knowledgeable in the same boat? Both are wrong in the eyes of God! Proverbs 4:7 says, "Wisdom is the principal thing; therefore, get wisdom: and with all thy getting get understanding." (KJV)

Scripture Is The Answer To Racism In The Church

All Scripture is inspired by God and profitable (or beneficial) for teaching (what is right), for reproof (what is not right), for correction (how to get it right), for training in righteousness (How to keep it right); so that the man of God may be adequate, equipped for every good work. (2 Timothy 3:16-17)

The apostle Paul wrote the Epistles of 1st and 2nd Timothy to encourage—the young pastor of the church in Ephesus—Timothy, to stay the course and preach the gospel during very difficult times for Christians. The answer to the problems we face today can also be found in Scripture, including racism in America.

"All Scripture," Old as well as New Testament, is inspired by God. "Inspired by God" or "God-breathed," as some Bible translations state, literally means filled with the breath of God. The Spirit of God enabled men of God to write the Word of God (2 Peter 1:20-21). [94] In layman's terms, God-breathed means that the Bible is God's own words. Profitable is translated from the Greek word opheleia primarily denotes "assistance"; then, "advantage, benefit,"; profit," in Rom. 3:1.[95] Therefore, Paul provides us with four primary benefits of the Word of God in this passage. 1. It is profitable or beneficial for teaching (what is right). 2. It is profitable or beneficial for reproof (what is not right). 3. It is profitable or beneficial for correction (how to get it right). 4. It is profitable or beneficial for training in righteousness (how to keep it right).

---

94 Wiersbe, W. W. *Wiersbe's expository outlines on the New Testament*. (Wheaton, IL: Victor Books, 1992), 650.

95 W. E. Vine, Unger, M. F., & White, W., Jr. *Vine's Complete Expository Dictionary of Old and New Testament Words* (Nashville: Thomas Nelson Publishers, 1996), 490.

Let's face it, we have never gotten it right when it comes to race relations in America, and the church has been a big part of the problem. Instead of the church setting the right example, it has been complicit instead. Early in this chapter, we looked at four early Christian denominations on American soil: Methodist, Baptist, Presbyterian, and Catholics. These denominations eventually became the most dominant for centuries in American culture. Unfortunately, they each share the responsibility of why the Christian church in America has failed African Americans.

The Bible is profitable for teaching (what is right). What is right is for us to love one another, "A new commandment I give to you, that you love one another, even as I have loved you, that you also love one another. By this, all men will know that you are My disciples if you have love for one another" (John 13:34-35). If only the church would turn to God's Word, it would know that slavery and racism are both sins. The Bible is profitable or beneficial for reproof (what is not right). "Direct my footsteps according to your word; let no sin rule over me" (Psalm 119:133, NIV). Although racism has ruled over America since 1619, it should have never ruled over the church.

The Bible is profitable or beneficial for correction (how to get it right). "For those whom the Lord loves He disciplines, And He scourges every son whom He receives" (Hebrews 12:6). If the church wants to act like a sinful world, then the church must accept the same discipline from God as the world. The Bible is profitable for training in righteousness (how to keep it right). "And He gave some as apostles, some as prophets, some as evangelists, some as pastors and teachers, for the equipping of the saints for the work of ministry, for the building up of the body of Christ; until we all attain to the unity of the faith, and of the knowledge of the Son of God, to a mature man, to the measure of the stature which belongs to the fullness of Christ" (Ephesians 4: 11-13). These verses teach us that God gave spiritual leaders to the church to aid us in our spiritual growth—meaning training in righteousness. Also, we learn that the congregation has a role in their spiritual growth and development as well. The pastors and teachers are to equip believers, but the members are to do the work of ministry. God's goal for His church is unity, not division, whether doctrinally or racially. Only if the church in America had applied these simple principles that Paul taught Timothy to deliver to the church in Ephesus it could have been part of the solution, instead of being part of the problem.

As I have already stated, racism has plagued America for centuries. However, if we apply the Scriptures to our problem with racism and the church takes the lead, we can send a powerful message to a sinful secular society on how to properly relate to one another.

When faced with anything that troubles us as Christians, our goal should always be to turn to Scripture for answers and guidance. The good news is, there is no subject or issue that we face that the Bible does not cover—and the Bible has plenty to say about racism, its origins, its devastating effects, and even reveals the only cure or remedy for the spiritual disease of racism, which is Jesus. These issues were covered in a series of sermons on racism and the Bible at our church last year. We opened the Scriptures, Old and New Testament, and searched for answers to the difficult subject of racism. I challenge you who are reading this book to open the Bible and search for the answers to the problems you face as well, not just racism.

Application of Judges 2:6-13

How does the book of Judges describe the failures of a nation that is supposed to be God's nation?

Israel Rebuked

1. **The failure to appreciate the land. (vs. 1-5)**

The Israelites waited a long time for God to bless them with their land, but they did not show God they appreciated it once He blessed them with it. They soiled the land with their constant sins and rebellion against God. The lesson we need to learn is to never to take God's blessings for granted.

2. **The failure to obey God's Word. (vs. 6-10)**

The Israelites were given God's Word in the Book of Exodus and again in the Book of Deuteronomy. Also, God sent His prophets repeatedly to remind them of what He said and what He required of His people. However, the Israelites constantly rejected God's Word as well as God's messengers. As a result, God not only allowed them to struggle in life, he also allowed them to be defeated by their enemies. The lesson we need to learn is God takes disobedience very seriously, even if we don't.

3. **The failure to remain with God. (vs. 11-15)**

To turn away from God (apostasy) is one thing, and a dangerous thing, but to deliberately abandon God altogether, to serve other gods, or put something or someone first before Him, is something that will always get God's attention—in a bad way. The lesson we need to learn is you cannot turn your back on God without severe consequences coming your way.

How does the book of Judges describe the failures of America that, according to some, is supposed to be a Christian nation?

1. **The failure to appreciate the land.**

Just like Israel defiled the land, America has defiled its land: Homosexuality, Adultery, Abortion, Violence, Murder, Strife, Division, Politics, Racism, the Broken Family, Abused Women and Children, Broken Justice System, and Broken Society.

Corrupt leadership in the church, corrupt leadership in the family, corrupt leadership in corporate America, Corrupt leadership in government.

The wealthy taking advantage of the poor. The poor turning to sin instead of turning to God.

Politicians willing to say and do anything to get elected, and citizens blindly willing to follow.

The failure to obey God's Word.

Just like Israel refused to obey God's Word, so does America.

Just like Israel did not want to listen to God's messengers, neither does America.

Just like Israel turned to false prophets, so does America.

The failure to remain with God.

Just like Israel, turned away from God, and turn to false gods and idols, so has America.

America today, in many ways, is like the Roman Empire—a polytheistic nation that is led by a corrupt government and a church that does not reflect the glory of God.

Just like all other great nations before us, America will face God's wrath if we do not repent from our sinful ways. Therefore, it is time for the Christian church to get its act together. To stop fighting amongst itself, especially along racial lines, and seek to work together for the glory of God.

Israel failed to be the beacon of light to a lost world, which is why God disciplined them repeatedly, even still, to this day. However, if America is ever going to live up to what it claims it was founded to be, a beacon of light to a lost world, it can longer fail to deal with systemic racism that has been an altostratus around our neck since 1619.

CHAPTER 3

CREATED IN THE IMAGE OF GOD

Mankind, The Pinnacle Of God's Creation

Then God said, "Let Us make man in Our image, according to Our likeness; and let them rule over the fish of the sea and over the birds of the sky and over the cattle and over all the earth, and over every creeping thing that creeps on the earth." God created man in His own image, in the image of God He created him; male and female He created them. God blessed them; and God said to them, "Be fruitful and multiply, and fill the earth, and subdue it; and rule over the fish of the sea and over the birds of the sky and over every living thing that moves on the earth." [Genesis 1:26-28]

The very first chapter in the Bible describes the origin of humanity. Regardless of race, ethnicity, nationality, or gender, all of humanity was created by God for a divine purpose. "Let Us make man in Our image, according to our likeness." Interestingly, the transition from the previous parts of creation is that it says, "Let there be." Now it says, "Let us make." The "Us" is the godhead or Trinity: Father, Son, and Holy Spirit. Image and likeness are the keywords in this verse. 'Image' comes from the Hebrew word tselem. This word signifies an "image or copy" of something in the sense of a replica.[96] "Likeness" comes from

---

96 W. E. Vine, Unger, M. F., & White, W., Jr., *Vine's Complete Expository Dictionary of Old and New Testament Words*, Vol. 1. (Nashville: Thomas. Nelson Publishing, 1996), 244. In Ps. 39:6 *tselem* means "shadow" of a thing which represents the original very imprecisely, or it means merely a phantom

the Hebrew word demut. First, it means "pattern," in the sense of the specifications from which an actual item is made.[97] Second, it means "shape" or "form," or the thing(s) made after a given pattern.[98] Image and likeness are used in tandem to have a special meaning. The idea is that man was created to be (the) replica or pattern designed to reflect God's glory. This defined man's distinct relationship with God, which is unlike anything else in creation. In the first twenty-five verses, we learn about everything else in God's creation. However, verse 26 is transitional because it describes the pinnacle of God's creation, which is mankind. The final day of the creation week is the most significant of the six. More space and detail are given to the creative events in verse six than to the previous five.[99]

Another keyword in understanding this passage (especially as it relates to sin and racism) is the words "rule over," which is from the Hebrew word radah. It means to rule, have dominion, or dominate.[100] God gave humanity dominion over the earth and the animal kingdom, not dominion over other people or races. However, since the fall of man, humanity still has the propensity to dominate. Unfortunately, this dominion is not for the purpose God originally intended; it is now influenced by man's sinful nature, which causes men to dominate other men. The fall of man has severely affected race relations among the various people groups and is why so many Whites have treated Blacks in America so poorly from the beginning of our nation's founding.

(ghost?), a thing which represents the original more closely but lacks its essential characteristic (reality).

97   Ibid, 136.

98   Ibid, 136.

99   K.A. Mathews, *Genesis 1-11:26*, Vol. 1A, (Nashville: Broadman & Holman Publishers, 1996), 159. The crown of God's handiwork is human life. The narrative marks the prominence of this creative act in several ways: (1) the creation account shows an ascending order of significance with human life as the final, thus pinnacle, creative act; (2) of the creative acts, this is the only one preceded by divine deliberation.

100   J. Strong, *Enhanced Strong's Lexicon*. Woodside Bible Fellowship, (1995).

The U. S. Constitution says what?

The Preamble to the Declaration of Independence, which was the foundation of the U.S. Constitution, reads, "We hold these truths to be self-evident, that all men are created equal, all men are endowed by their Creator with certain unalienable Rights, that among these are Life, Liberty and the pursuit of Happiness." Thomas Jefferson penned these words in 1776 during the beginning of the American Revolution. If you didn't know any better, you would think that these words came from a devout Christian, not from someone who believed Whites were intellectually superior to Blacks, not from someone who was having sexual relationships with his female slaves and even fathering children out of wedlock.

The Founding Fathers' role in Slavery

Surely, our Founding Fathers that are believed to have been Christians would have at least read the first chapter of the Bible, even if they didn't read the rest. They would have come across this all-important passage in Genesis that clearly states all human beings were created in the image and likeness of God.[101] Being created in the image of God distinguishes people from all other earthly creations. God's image is not described as being possessed in part or given gradually; rather, it is an immediate and inherent part of being human.[102] Therefore, God did not give His image to some races within His creation while withholding His image from others—Whites and Blacks were created in His image and likeness. Understanding this verse alone would teach naysayers that no race has, or ever had, supremacy over another.

Furthermore, if our Founding Fathers had ventured into the New Testament, perhaps they would have come across Galatians 3:27-28. "There is neither Jew nor Greek, there is neither slave nor free man,

---

101   J.F. Walvoord, & R. B. Zuck (Eds.), *Genesis: The Bible Knowledge Commentary: An Exposition of the Scriptures,* Vol. 1. (Wheaton: Victor Books, 1985), 29.

102   J.D. Barry, D. Mangum, D.R. Brown, M.S. Heiser, M. Custis, E. Ritzema, D. Bomar, *Faithlife Study Bible: Genesis 1:27.* (Bellingham, WA: Lexham Press, 2012).

there is neither male nor female; for you are all one in Christ Jesus. And if you belong to Christ, then you are Abraham's descendants, heirs according to promise."

Therefore, now that we understand the proper meaning of the phrase Thomas Jefferson included in our Constitution, the way he used the words "we" as well as "all men are created equal" did not mean all men, just white men. The reason we know that to be true is that Jefferson owned approximately 700 slaves during his lifetime. He even owned many, if not all, of these slaves while serving for eight years as the 3rd President of the U.S. In his Notes on the State of Virginia (in which he recorded his racist ideas), Jefferson believed in mass schooling (for Whites only), emancipation for Blacks, and the colonization of Africans back to Africa.[103] Although he never took any action on those issues, at least not as related to Blacks, even when he was President.

> *Aside from his Hemings children (and Sally Hemings), Jefferson did not free any of the other enslaved people at Monticello. One historian estimated that Jefferson had owned more than six hundred slaves over the course of his life. In 1826, he held two hundred people as property, and he was about $100,000 in debt (about $2 million in 2014), an amount so staggering that he knew that once he died, everything—and everyone—would be sold. He rested in the comfort of slavery.[104]*

Jefferson was a hypocritical leader on at least two fronts. First, even though he thought Blacks should be emancipated, he still believed they were inferior to Whites. Also, he stated that slave revolts against enslavers were even more evil and tragic than the millions of African people who died on plantations.[105] The problem with white, wealthy men, like Jefferson, at that time, was that they believed they were doing Blacks a favor by rescuing them from their savage lifestyle in Africa, and bringing them to America, and allowing them to at least hear

---

103   Ibram X. Kendo. *Stamped From the Beginning: The Definitive History of Racist Ideas in America.* (New York: Bold Type Books, 2016), 109.

104   Ibid, 110.

105   Ibid, 123.

the gospel message.[106] Second, Jefferson publicly assailed interracial relationships between white women and Black men or biracial men. He even wanted the White women banished (instead of merely fined) for bearing the child of a Black or biracial man.[107] Jefferson's hypocrisy was rich because he held this belief while secretly fathering children with Sally Hemings, who was biracial.[108]

The Constitutional Convention's role in slavery

As history has revealed, it was not only Thomas Jefferson who agreed that enslaving Black people was okay; in 1787, delegates to the Constitutional Convention hotly debated the issue of slavery, and the vast majority of them believed it was acceptable as well. However, George Mason of Virginia argued eloquently against slavery, warning his fellow white delegates: "Every master of slaves is born a petty tyrant. They bring the judgment of heaven on this nation for their actions."[109] Southern delegates were not fazed by Mason's appeal to human decency

---

106   Nana Ekua Brew-Hammond. "Blacks Were Christians Before Slavery and Before White-Jesus Pieces," *The Root*, 29 March 2013 [on-line]; accessed on 5 September 2020; available from https://www.theroot.com/blacks-were-christians-before-slavery-and-before-white-1790895789; Internet. Long before colonialism and slavery, Africans were practicing Christianity. "We know that Christianity has had a long history in Africa itself, pre-dating any kind of European influence," says. Dr. Lawrence H. Mamiya, Professor of Religion and Africana Studies at Vassar College and co-author of The Black Church in the African American Experience.

107   Ibid, 117. Ironically, Jefferson was outed by one of his rivals for his hypocritical actions, but even as president, it didn't affect his pollical career because it was common place in those days that White male plantation owners frequently slept with their Black female slaves.

108   Ibid, 117. Sally Hemings came to Monticello as an infant in 1773 as part of Martha Jefferson's inheritance from her father. John Wayles had fathered six children with his biracial captive Elizabeth Hemings. Sally was the youngest. As his peers penned the Constitution, Jefferson began a sexual relationship with Sally. Jefferson had a problem with white women having sex with black men, but it was acceptable for white men to have sex with black women, especially slave women.

109   James D. Beset. "George Mason, the Framer Who Refused to Sign the Constitution." 20 April 2011. [on-line]; Accessed on 5 September 2020; available from http://www.whatwouldthefoundersthink.com/george-mason-the-framer-who-refused-to-sign-the-constitution. Internet.

because they argued emphatically that the new government should not be allowed to interfere with the institution of slavery. Delegate John Rutledge of South Carolina, for example, told delegates that "religion and humanity have nothing to do with the questions of whether the Constitution should protect slavery." According to Rutledge, the issue was simply a matter of property rights, and because black slaves were property, they had no rights. The Constitution the delegates proposed included several provisions that openly recognized and protected the institution of slavery. Without these provisions, southern delegates would not have agreed to support the new Constitution.

If the southern states were not on board, the Constitution had no chance of being ratified. Therefore, the northern states gave in. Provisions allowed southern states to count slaves as 3/5 (three-fifths) persons for allotment in Congress (even though the slaves could not vote). These provisions expressly denied Congress the power to prohibit importing new slaves (until 1808) and prevented free states from enacting laws protecting fugitive slaves.[110] Slavery, as all students of history know, continued to be a divisive issue throughout the Civil War. Southern states worried that the balance in Congress might turn against slavery, and so, they were anxious to extend slavery to the new territories and states.

Congress enacted the Missouri Compromise of 1820 to address the issue. The law permitted slavery in Missouri but prohibited slavery in other portions of the Louisiana Purchase. As the U.S. continued to expand into the new territories, Dred Scott v. Sandford (1857) was the turning point. This was a landmark decision of the U.S. Supreme Court in which the court held that the U.S. Constitution was not meant to include American citizenship for black people, regardless of whether they were enslaved or free. Therefore, the Constitution's rights and

---

110 "Three-Fifths Compromise: United States History," [on-line]; accessed on 5 September 2020; available from http://www.whatwouldthefoundersthink.com/george-mason-the-framer-who-refused-to-sign-the-constitution; Internet. Many of the Founding Fathers acknowledged that slavery violated the ideal of liberty that was so central to the American Revolution, but, because they were committed to the sanctity of private property rights, the principles of limited government, and the pursuit of intersectional harmony, they were unable to take bold action against slavery. Moreover, the Southern Founders' thoroughgoing embrace of slave-based agriculture and their deeply ingrained racial prejudice solidified the barriers against emancipation.

privileges conferred upon white American citizens did not apply to Blacks.

Dred Scott was born into slavery, and he was eventually sold and purchased by a U.S. Army doctor named John Emerson. Scott would eventually move with Emerson into U.S. territories in the North that outlawed slavery. When Emerson died, his wife wanted to rent Scott out to make some money, but Scott filed a civil suit for his freedom because he had lived in a free territory for a while. However, Emerson's widow transferred the rights to own Scott and his wife to her brother, John Sandford. Thus the case was called Scott v Sandford. The Supreme Court decision in Scott v Stanford is believed, by many, to be the worst ruling in the High Court's history. Five of the nine justices that ruled in the case owned slaves at the time, which should have been a conflict of interest. However, with their racist bias, they had no problem ruling against Dred Scott and upholding slavery. The Supreme Court ruled that because Dred Scott was Black and from a slave state (even though he had lived in free territories), he was not a citizen, and because he was not a U.S. citizen, he had no standing to bring his case. Scott lost his appeal for freedom and remained a slave. [111]

Chief Justice of the Supreme Court, Roger B. Taney, issued the stingingly controversial majority opinion. When he finished his five-page report, Taney hoped that Blacks, Free Soldiers, and abolitionists would have no constitutional life to fortify their freedom fights against slaveholders. Since Blacks had been excluded from the American political community when the nation was founded, the United States could not extend the rights, according to Taney as the Chief Justice.[112] As a white supremacist with power and authority, Taney's goal was to crush any future efforts that would ever allow Blacks from under the foot of Whites.

Writing for the majority opinion in the case, Taney went much further than the original court's ruling, which stated Blacks who were slaves were essentially the property of Whites. Thus they did not

---

111   "Dred Scott Case," *A&E Television Network*, 27 October 2009 [on-line]; accessed on 5 September 2020; available from https://www.history.com/topics/black-history/dred-scott-case; Internet.

112   Ibram X. Kendo. *Stamped From the Beginning*, 204.

possess rights under the Constitution. Additionally, Taney stated that people of African ancestry (whether free or slave, including Dred Scott) could never become "citizens" within the meaning of the Constitution and could not hence bring suit in federal court. Finally, Taney stated that the Law approved by Congress, "the Missouri Compromise of 1820," was unconstitutional; therefore, Congress had no authority to limit slavery in the New Territories.[113] The decision invited slave owners to pour into the territories and pass laws and regulations that upheld slavery. Unfortunately, this horrible decision made the Civil War inevitable and set Blacks back in so many ways for centuries.

This brief synopsis of this period in U.S. History proves that White Supremacy was ingrained in our nation from the beginning and continues to affect our nation today. It is often said that the original sin of America was slavery; however, I would submit to you that the sin of white supremacy was our original sin.[114] Why? Because this is the foundational sin that has opened the door to structural racism in many ways, if not all, areas of society. The reason why we argue this point is that without white supremacy in America, there would not have been racism in America, and without racism in America, there would never have been slavery. I believe that one is simply a negative sinful domino effect of the other. Another example of the racist's madness is what happened in Charlottesville back in May 2017.

> *What happened in Charlottesville this past weekend is devastating, but not surprising. Over the past three years, white supremacists have been invited back to the streets, to the airwaves, into the White House. White supremacy is our country's original sin. The legacy of slavery, the genocide of Native Americans, and the exploitation of immigrants remain unresolved and largely unacknowledged. But in my lifetime, over the past 40 years, while racism festered in the back rooms, behind bars in the prison industrial complex, in discriminatory hiring practices, in segregated schools and*

---

113   Ibid.

114   "White Supremacy Is Our Country's Original Sin," *Jewish Journal*, 16 August 2017 [on-line]; Accessed on 5 September 2020; available from https://jewishjournal.com/commentary/opinion/223136/white-supremacy-is-our-countrys-original-sin/; Internet.

neighborhoods, and among internet trolls, it was generally sanitized in public discourse.¹¹⁵

Today, the U.S. is more racially divided than at any other time in our nation's history. The current Trump administration did its best to make matters worse with their divisive rhetoric, as well as those they sent out on television to defend that rhetoric. What makes this situation sad is the multitude of white evangelicals who supported a president primarily due to a transactional arrangement—no matter what he does or says, which the Bible does not agree with. What makes our current situation on racial unrest worst is that it has left the average citizen, who is tired of the chaos, to feel powerless because we all know a small number of white men, most of them extremely wealthy and influential, still rule America and set the policies for everyone else.¹¹⁶

The Fallacy of Separate but Equal

The phrase separate but equal is an oxymoron because it was placed into the Constitution, and upheld by the Supreme Court, to support a policy that disproportionally discriminated against Blacks.

---

115   Ibid. A presidential candidate (Donald Trump) launched his campaign with an unconscionable attack on Mexican Americans, a verbal assault that should have marked the end of his public career. Instead, it was only the beginning. Attacks against Muslims, Blacks and immigrants followed, along with a refusal to disavow endorsements from known anti-Semites and white nationalists ("I don't know anything about David Duke. I don't know what you're even talking about with white supremacy or white supremacist. I don't know. I don't know..."). Good people whispered their discomfort and went along for the ride. Cast votes ignoring what was clear as day, willfully ignored, justified and excused. Clergy were scolded when they entered the fray: let's not get too political! Journalists faced full frontal attack for pointing out what was clear to anyone willing to pay attention. This was a dangerous and deliberate fueling of white supremacist ideology, which-once uncovered, promised to wreak havoc on our already deeply fractured nation.

116   Allan J. Lightman, "Who Rules America," *The Hill*, 8 December 2014 [on-line]; accessed on 5 September 2020; available from https://thehill.com/blogs/pundits-blog/civil-rights/214857-who-rules-america; Internet. A shattering new study by two political science professors has found that ordinary Americans have virtually no impact whatsoever on the making of national policy in our country. The analysts found that rich individuals and business-controlled interest groups largely shape policy outcomes in the United States.

At its core, separate but equal, was simply lawful segregation as well as systemic racism. The way Whites sold this hogwash to the nation was that Blacks and Whites were supposed to receive an equal amount of public resources—so Blacks couldn't complain about segregation.[117] By the way, this was essentially the Supreme Court's position in the outcome of the Plessy v. Ferguson case.

Let's be honest; when people are separated solely based on race (which is racism), it is impossible to achieve equality for all citizens involved. In such a system, the people in power, which are White, will always be placed ahead of other citizens that lack power, which are Black, which has been the American way from the beginning. Segregation has never achieved equality in America because it was never designed to do so. Segregation was the same vehicle that was put in place to sustain inequality and reinforce racism.

So how did we get here as a nation? How did a nation that claimed to be a Christian nation treat its citizens in such a non-Christian manner? How could a nation that advanced such practices and codified them into law ever convince themselves that what they were doing was pleasing to God? How could Whites sit in their segregated churches, read the Bible, supposedly preach from it, and sing Christian hymns while praying to God, in good conscience believe they were going to heaven, while everybody else was going to hell, especially Blacks.

Once again, the separate but equal clause resulted from a landmark U.S. Supreme Court case, Plessy v. Ferguson. The outcome of the case reinforced racism in America by affirming that separate but equal was constitutional. At the time this case was filed, a Jim Crow law allowed passenger trains in Louisiana to have separate cars for Blacks and Whites. The law applied to passenger trains and many other areas of society, such as public restrooms and water fountains. However, a black man named Homer Plessey sat in the white section on the train.

---

117   Ibram X. Kendo. *Stamped From the Beginning*, 273-274. In the 1890s a series of separate but (un)equal laws were instituted segregating nearly every aspect of southern life, from water fountains, to businesses, to transportation—all to ensure White solidarity and Blacks submission and to ensure cheap Black labor. These separate and inferior Black facilities fed Whites and Blacks alike the segregationist's idea of Blacks being a fundamentally separate and inferior people.

He refused to sit in the "Black section" because it was inferior to that of Whites. In Plessey's lawsuit, he claimed that his constitutional rights were violated.

Still, the Supreme Court disagreed because it ruled, "a law that implies merely a legal distinction" between Whites and Blacks was not unconstitutional. The result of this terrible ruling spoke volumes. It told white America one thing, while at the same time, it told black America another. For white America, it upheld and validated white privilege, and for black America, it upheld and validated that nothing had changed because the nation was still racist. This ruling set the stage for Jim Crow legislation and separate public accommodations (based on race) to become the norm across the country.[118] Since America claimed to be a Christian nation, the nation should have turned to Scripture for guidance on how to deal with Blacks that were strangers in their land. "When a stranger resides with you in your land, you shall not do him wrong. The stranger who resides with you shall be to you as the native among you, and you shall love him as yourself, for you were aliens in the land of Egypt; I am the Lord your God." (Leviticus 19:33-34).

The book of Leviticus provided Israel with guidance from God on how to deal with strangers once they entered the Promised Land. The stranger or foreigner who resided among them was to be treated

---

118 "U.S. Supreme Court 163 U.S. 537 (1896) Plessy Vs Ferguson," *Justia* [on-line]; accessed On 5 September 2020; available from; https://Supreme.Justia.Com/Cases/Federal/Us/163/537/; Internet. The statue of Louisiana, acts of 1890, c. 111, requiring railway companies carrying passengers in their coaches in that state, to provide equal, but separate, accommodations for the white and colored races, by providing two or more passenger coaches for each passenger train, or by dividing the passenger coaches by a partition so as to secure separate accommodations; and providing that no person shall be permitted to occupy seats in coaches other than the ones assigned to them, on account of the race they belong to; and requiring the officer of the passenger train to assign each passenger to the coach or compartment assigned for the race to which he or she belong; and imposing fines or imprisonment upon passengers insisting on going into a coach or compartment other than the one set aside for the race to which he or she belongs; and conferring upon officers of the train power to refuse to carry on the train passengers refusing to occupy the coach or compartment assigned to them, and exempting the railway company from liability for such refusal, are not in conflict with the provisions either of the thirteenth amendment or of the fourteenth amendment to the constitution of the United States.

with dignity and respect, equal to an Israelite's treatment. They were not allowed to mistreat others just because they were different. The key part of the verse says, "you shall love him as yourself." In the New Testament, Jesus quoted from two separate passages Lev.18:33-34 and Deut. 6:5, and paired them together in Luke 10:27, "You shall love the Lord your God with all your heart, and with all your soul, and with all your strength, and with all your mind; and your neighbor as yourself." Jesus revealed what God expected from His people, which was to keep Him first, and second, to love the stranger, or neighbor, among us. Jesus quoted an important principle that applied to God's people in the Old Testament as well as the New Testament. Therefore, God reminded Israel how they felt when they were severely mistreated while in bondage for over 400 years in Egypt. By reminding Israel of its past, the goal was they would not repeat it in the present or future. What made this binding was that it ends by saying, "I am the Lord your God." Now, apply this principle to American history. How things would have been different for Blacks if they had been shown godly love and respected, not just as Americans, but as human beings, instead of being treated as outcasts, animals, or savages.

Application of Genesis 1:26-28

What are four unique attributes (qualities) that All men inherited from God to glorify God?

1. **DIGNITY (v. 26)**

    - Self-Respect
    - Self-Esteem
    - Self-Worth/Value

2. **Distinction (v. 27)**

    - Difference
    - Characteristic's
    - Excellence
    - Note: But no man was created better than another.

3. **Dominion (v. 28)**

    - Rule
    - Have authority over
    - Power
    - Dominion over the earth, but one another.

4. **Duty (vs. 29- 31)**

    - Responsibility/obligation
    - Job
    - Function
    - To love God and keep in first, and love our neighbor as we love ourselves. (Matt 22:36-40)

What are three valuable lessons found in Genesis 2:1-26-27?

1. **God broke the mold.**

All people have value and worth in the eyes of God. So much so, when God created you and me, He broke the mold because He got it right the first time. However, because of the fall of man, sin has marred that image, which is why we all need Jesus.

2. **No race is superior to another race.**

All men, women, boys, and girls, regardless of race, ethnicity, nationality, or social-economic status, are created equal in the image and likeness of God.

3. **Judgment day is coming.**

All of humanity will one day answer to God for how we treat others, especially those that look different from us.

CHAPTER 4

AM I MY BROTHER'S KEEPER?

The Consequences Of The Fall

Then the Lord said to Cain, "Why are you angry? And why has your countenance fallen? If you do well, will not your countenance be lifted up? And if you do not do well, sin is crouching at the door; and its desire is for you, but you must master it." Cain told Abel his brother. And it came about when they were in the field, that Cain rose up against Abel his brother and killed him. Then the Lord said to Cain, "Where is Abel your brother?" And he said, "I do not know. Am I my brother's keeper?" He said, "What have you done? The voice of your brother's blood is crying to Me from the ground. Now you are cursed from the ground, which has opened its mouth to receive your brother's blood from your hand. When you cultivate the ground, it will no longer yield its strength to you; you will be a vagrant and a wanderer on the earth." Cain said to the Lord, "My punishment is too great to bear! (Genesis 4:6-13)

The subject of racism is not a subject that many people like talking about, not even some Christians, whether Blacks, Whites, Hispanics, and Asians. However, racism is an issue that the church of Jesus Christ has either ignored or glossed over for far too long. No one who is paying attention, as well as those that know the true sinful history of our nation—as it relates to racism—can disagree that we have a serious problem—if they are honest. Let's face it; we have a systemic problem with racism in America. Video recordings have brought to light what many Blacks have known for years was a widespread problem all along.

Can we all just get along?

It is hard to believe that it has been almost 30 years since Rodney King became a household name. On March 3, 1991, multiple police officers were filmed beating a taxi driver named Rodney King—after a police pursuit through the streets of Los Angeles. The video shocked the city as well as the country. An innocent bystander named George Holliday captured the video on a *Sony Handicam* from the balcony of his apartment, just across the street from the incident. It was one of the first police brutality incidents of its kind that was caught on video, and it forever changed the conversation about police and race in America.[119] On May 1, 1992, Rodney King appealed for calm after things erupted in Los Angeles (and around the country) after the acquittal of the four police officers caught on tape beating him was announced. The verdict sparked the explosive riots.[120] At a public appearance, King uttered his famous statement, "Can we all just get along?" The obvious answer is no because police brutality in America has gone in the wrong direction:

---

119   Cydney Adams, "Rodney King beating caught on tape." *CBS News*, 3 March 2016 [on-line]; accessed on 5 September 2020; available from https://www.cbsnews.com/news/march-3rd-1991-rodney-king-lapd-beating-caught-on-video/; Internet. The footage taken by Holliday showed four officers tasing, kicking, and hitting King with their batons more than 53 times. King claimed he never resisted, which several witnesses supported. King was 25-years-old at the time. His injuries included multiple bruises, a broken leg, and a scar from a stun gun which jolted him with 50,000 bolt shocks. The officers involved, Laurence Powell, Timothy Wind, Theodore Briseno and Stacey Koon, were put on trial and acquitted by a majority white jury in April of 1992. The following three days were marred by riots, looting, arson, and extreme violence across the city of Los Angeles.

120   Anjuli Sastry and Karen Grigsby Bates, "When LA Erupted in Anger: A Look Back at the Rodney King Riots," 26 April 2017 [on-line]; accessed on 8 October 2020; available from https://www.npr.org/2017/04/26/524744989/when-la-erupted-in-anger-a-look-back-at-the-rodney-king-riots. Internet. The four officers were Sgt. Stacey C. Koon, Officer Theodore J. Briseno, Officer Timothy E. Wind and Officer Laurence Powell. Two served time in prison and all four lost their careers.

from racial profiling,[121] which has led to a multitude of unauthorized stops, to beatings and unarmed shootings of black men.

George Holliday ushered in a new era of civilian journalism. Since that horrible display of police brutality against Rodney King, this has become a common occurrence. The advancement of digital cameras, especially in cell phone technology, has brought more of these types of videos to light. Citizens are quick to whip out their cell phones and record police officers behaving badly. What is interesting is that police officers have been filmed for years taking down citizens behaving badly. The Fox network made millions of dollars off their famous reality TV show "Cops." The show ran for 30 years and was a huge cash cow for the network. However, the show was canceled this year over the issue of racism.[122]

For years the show intentionally depicted Blacks and Hispanics in a very negative racial light for entertainment. In a racist way, Blacks and Hispanics were shown as menaces to society. However, they refused to display Whites the same way, at least, nowhere near as frequent.[123] The

---

121   Michelle Alexander, *The New Jim Crow: Mass Incarceration in the Age of Colorblindness* (New York: The New Press), 2020, 156. The hyper segregation of the black poor in the ghetto communities has made it easy for police target them. Confined to ghetto areas and lacking political power, the black poor are convenient targets. Douglas Massey and Nancy Denton's book, *American Apartheid*, documents how racially segregated ghettos were deliberately created by federal policy, not impersonal market forces or private housing choices. The enduring racial isolation of the ghetto poor has made them uniquely vulnerable in the War on Drugs. What happens to them does not directly affect—and is scarcely noticed by—the privileged beyond the ghetto's invisible walls. Thus, it is here, in the poverty-stricken, racially segregated ghetto's, where the War on Poverty has been abandoned and factories have disappeared, that the drug war has been waged with the greatest ferocity. SWAT teams are deployed here: buy-and-bust operations are concentrated here; drug raids of apartment buildings occur here; stop-and-frisk operations occur here. Black and brown youth are the targets. It is not uncommon for a young black teenager living in a ghetto community to be racially profiled, stopped, interrogated, and frisked numerous times in the course of a month, or even a week.

122   Tracy Brown, "'Cops' cancelled amid nationwide protest against police brutality," *Los Angeles Times*, 8 June 2020 [on line]: accessed on 5 September 2020; available from https://www.latimes.com/entertainment-arts/tv/story/2020-06-09/cops-canceled-paramount-protests-police-violence; Internet.

123   Emma Polan. "*'Cops' Cancelled: TV Show Has Been Accused of Racism Ever Since It First Aired 31 Years Ago.*" *Newsweek*, 10 June 2020 [on-line]; accessed on 3 October 2020; available from https://www.newsweek.com/cops-cancelled-

picture the program left on America's psyche was that all dangerous criminals are either Black or Hispanic. The catchy theme song of the show, "Bad boys, bad boys, what you going to do when they come for you," became so popular that many citizens hummed the tune, often in a joking manner. Unfortunately, what America has been made painfully aware of for years now, by watching videotapes of some cops in action, is that some "bad boys" actually wear a blue uniform.

We fought for this?

It's no secret that America fought a Civil War over the issue of racism. Although that war ended (and some would argue that it hasn't), the racial divisions between Whites and Blacks have never ended.[124] Many would argue that the racial unrest in 2020 mirrors 1968,[125] triggered by the multitude of issues caught on videotape involving police brutality against Blacks. Although the vast majority of police officers are good officers and deserve our support, respect, as well as prayers (for the extremely dangerous job they do daily), the few officers that are caught on video abusing their authority must be held accountable for shooting or abusing unarmed black men, or anyone else for that matter.

---

racism-criticism-paramount-1509985; Internet. Long-running unscripted police series *Cops* has been canceled after 31 years amid widespread protests against racism and police brutality—but the show has been accused of racism ever since it first aired in 1989. Following the death of George Floyd, who died on May 25 when Minneapolis police officer Derek Chauvin knelt on his neck for eight minutes, Paramount Network announced it was pulling the plug on Cop with "no plans to return."

124   Joseph Wheelan, "How the Civil War Changed America Forever," *Dailey Beast*, 14 April 2017 [on- line]; accessed on 3 October 2020; available from https://www.thedailybeast.com/how-the-civil-war-changed-america-forever?ref=scroll; Internet. When the North emerged victorious on April 9, 1865, the U.S. entered a new era. However, the war's legacy of destruction would leave deep scars.

125   Dylan Matthews, "How today's protests compare to 1968, explained by a historian," *Vox*, 2 June 2020 [on Line]; accessed on 5 September 2020; available from https://www.vox.com/identities/2020/6/2/21277253/george-floyd-protest-1960s-civil-rights; Internet. Heather Ann Thompson is a professor of history and Afro-American and African Studies at the University of Michigan in Ann Arbor and a scholar of 1960s and 1970s protest movements, particularly against white supremacy and mass incarceration. She explains what's changed and what has stayed the same. She states she sees a lot of similarities in the protest then and now.

However, the police often close ranks and protect their own, even when they are guilty, which is referred to as "The Blue Wall." Those in law enforcement must realize that the bad behavior of these cops makes all police look bad, which is why you would think they would want to purge the wrongdoers, that are not fit to wear the uniform from their midst. Some would argue that police brutality only happens because there are a few bad apples. However, many argue that the problem plaguing policing in America is a cultural problem, making it a racial problem.[126] Policing in America does not happen in a vacuum. It is a problem that is only a subset of a much bigger problem: systemic racism. Some would argue that the current state of policing in America can be traced back to Jim Crow.

Michelle Alexander, a highly acclaimed civil rights lawyer, advocate, and legal scholar, made a strong argument about the current policing in America being a direct result of Jim Crow in her book The New Jim Crow.

> *By the turn of the twentieth century, every state in the South had laws on the books that disenfranchised Blacks and discriminated against them in virtually every sphere of life, lending sanctions to racial ostracism that extended to schools, churches, housing, jobs, restrooms, hotels, restaurants, hospitals, orphanages, prisons, funeral homes, morgues, and cemeteries. Politicians competed with each other by proposing and passing ever more stringent, oppressive, and downright ridiculous legislation (such as laws specifically prohibiting Blacks and Whites from playing chess together). The public symbols and constant reminders of Black subjugation were supported by Whites across the political spectrum.*[127]

---

126   David Brooks, "The Culture of Policing in Broken," *The Atlantic*, 15 September 2020 [on-line]; accessed on 5 September 2020; available from https://www.msn.com/en-ph/news/opinion/the-culture-of-policing-is-broken/ar-BB15ADY7; Internet.

127   Michelle Alexander. *The New Jim Crow: Mass Incarceration in the Age of Colorblindness*. (New York: The New Press), 2020, 43-44.

Say it ain't so!

Alexander's biggest argument in her book, which she does so eloquently, is that mass incarceration of African America can be compared to the racist Jim Crow laws that followed the end of the Civil War. As a trained lawyer, she puts America's whole criminal justice system on trial. Vividly, Alexander captures the results of our racist criminal justice system in the real-life story of Erma May Stewart, a thirty-year-old African American, single mother of two. As part of a drug sweep in Hearne, Texas, Stewart was arrested along with about three others, although she was innocent. After spending a week in jail, her court-appointed lawyer encouraged her to plead guilty. She declined because, again, she was innocent.

After a month had passed, Stewart remained in jail on the bogus charges. Her court-appointed lawyer again encouraged her to plead guilty. Eager to go home to her children, she accepted the plea deal. She feared going to trial and losing, which would have resulted in years in prison. By the way, this is the decision many people of color make when they cross paths with our criminal justice system. Stewart received ten years' probation, was ordered to pay a $1,000 fine and probation cost.

Look at the cost of a false arrest on an African American woman. Stewart had to live with the stigma of being a drug dealer; she was no longer eligible for food stamps to help feed her kids; she was almost evicted from public housing (ironically, she took the plea deal to try to avoid it). Also, without her plea, she would have been homeless and her children placed in foster care. After Stewart's downward spiral, she received even more devastating news.

During the trial, the judge dismissed all the charges against the other defendants arrested with her. The judge ruled that the entire drug sweep was illegal because the testimony from a single witness was invalid because he had lied. However, since Steward pled guilty to a false charge, her confession upheld her conviction because she confessed. Even though she was duped by our criminal justice system, Stewart moved on and tried to put her life back together. Although she was done with the criminal justice system, it was not done with her, even though she still had not committed any crimes. Her story continued by detailing what the police came after her for next.

Stewart returned home to Bryan, Texas, to attend the funeral of her 18-month-old daughter that had passed. Unannounced, the police showed up and cuffed her in front of her family and friends while still grieving for her child. She was alarmed and confused because she knew she hadn't broken any laws or violated her probation. When Stewart was finally told why she was being arrested, she was even more astonished. One of the individuals arrested with her during the original drug bust in her neighborhood, which led to all her troubles, was arrested for a new crime. The police told her they needed a witness against him. Although she told the police she was not present and did not know about any crime by someone she had not seen or talked to, she was still arrested. She was jailed for refusing to cooperate. After she was released and her charges were finally dropped, she lost her job, apartment, car, and the opportunity to say goodbye to her daughter.[128]

I agree with Michelle Alexander; this is the problem with America's racist policy on the war on drugs because the criminal justice system disproportionally targets people of color—and it does not care if they are innocent—as long as they fit the profile. What most Americans fail to realize unless they are people of color is that the criminal justice system owns you once you are swallowed up in it, even if you had been innocent before you crossed its path. Unfortunately, many Erma May Stewarts from the African American community have experienced the American criminal justice system ruining their lives.

This is nothing new

A model (or caste system) was set in place from the beginning to deal harshly with Blacks, which has never subsided to this day. As a result, the systemic racism that began with white supremacy during slavery and continued during, and after, the Civil War, which gave rise to Jim Crow, and the policing culture of Blacks during that time, is the foundation for the policing culture that singles out Blacks to this today.

---

128   Ibid, 121-22.

In an article by Joseph Wheelan, he described the anger of former white slave owners about ending slavery. More specifically, he talked about a white slave owner that lost two sons who fought in the Civil War for the Confederates. After the war ended, because slavery ended, he lost his livelihood—what irony!

Besides the staggering human cost, the war profoundly transformed the United States in other ways. If there were two distinct Americas before the war — the slower-paced, chivalric South; the ambitious, forward-looking North — the differences were even starker afterward. Emancipation had destroyed the South's slave-based agrarian economy. Its modest industrial capacity lay buried in blackened rubble, while its harbors teemed with Northern warships and commercial vessels. Where the armies had fought, foragers had denuded or burned towns and cities, forcing the destitute to subsist on Yankee handouts. Decades would go by before prosperity returned to the South. [129]

After the Civil War, Confederates blamed the people they had once owned for the loss of the war.[130] The South was bitter because their way of life was turned upside down. They were angry with the North; they were even angrier with the slaves they were forced to let go free and could no longer own as property. Since they could not take their anger out on Whites in the North, whom they despised, they took that anger and hate out on their former slaves with a vengeance. When Reconstruction in the South ended and federal troops were withdrawn, it opened the door for Black Codes and Jim Crow laws that became the norm. It revealed that even though the Civil War ended, the division between Blacks and Whites got even worse.

Unless you are blind to what's going on now, as well as unfamiliar with our nation's sinful past, there have always been two Americas divided along racial lines. Our current environment of racial unrest, and a president that stoked the flames every chance he got, as well forty percent of the country that agreed with him, no matter what, should

---

[129] Joseph Wheelan. "How the Civil War Changed America Forever" [On Line]

[130] Isabel Wilkerson, *Caste: The Origins of Our Discontents*, 192.

tell you everything you need to know about our beloved country—we are racist and proud of it. How can I make such a statement? Because many people in America are either racist or do not have a problem with racism.

In Chapter 1, I talked about George Floyd and the terrible circumstances surrounding his death in the streets of Minnesota, which has caused marches and protest all over the nation. The nation witnessed a black man die after laying on the ground and handcuffed with his hands behind his back—with his head pressed against the pavement. Floyd warned the police officers by telling them he could not breathe, and after 8 minutes and 46 seconds, with the white police officer's knee on his neck, he died as a result of a bad encounter with the police gone horribly wrong. This has sparked all the backlash, outrage, and protest we are still witnessing today. So, the question is, how did we get here? Why is there so much division between Whites and Blacks, in the U.S., and even around the world? Why do we keep witnessing blacks killed at the hands of white police officers? I would submit to you that it is not a skin problem, it is a sin problem, and all sin problems should be addressed with Scripture.

That's Not How You Are Supposed To Treat Your Brother

Genesis chapter four provides us an answer to America's problem with systemic racism. After the fall of man, Adam and Eve had two sons, Cain and Abel, which both inherited the sinful nature of their parents. As adults, Cain and Abel's actions set the stage for everything else that happened afterward—especially with Adam's family and their descendants. Despite the continued mistakes made by this family, God's grace was on full display.[131] Adam, Eve, Cain, and Abel were the

---

131   John Piper, Future Grace: The Purifying Power of the Promises of God. (Colorado Springs: Multnomah Books, 2012), 245. The experiencing of future grace often hangs on whether we will take refuge in God or whether we doubt His care and run for cover to other shelters. For those who take refuge in God, the promises of future grace are many and rich. Cain rejected God's grace, which impacted his life for access to God's future grace. Although God warned him, "If you do well, will not *your countenance* be lifted up? And if you do not do well, sin is crouching at the door; and its desire is for you, but you

first family of creation. By that fact alone, God gave them a prominent role in his creative order. As a result, their behavior mattered to God because they were His building block for humanity. The sinful nature of Adam and Eve played out in the life of their son Cain.

When both sons became of age and were serving in their profession, they wisely brought an offering to the Lord, which they would have learned from their father. God accepted Abel's offering but rejected Cain's offering. Some have argued that the type of offering caused God to accept one while rejecting the other. The reason why is because Cain's offering came from the produce of the ground, and Abel's offering was an animal sacrifice. However, this would be bad hermeneutics (biblical interpretation). Therefore, God's response toward Cain and Abel was not due to the nature of the gift per se, whether it was grain or animal, but the integrity of the giver. The narrative ties together the worshiper and his offering as God considers the merit of their worship:[132] "The Lord looked with favor on Abel and his offering, but on Cain and his offering He did not look with favor" (vs. 4–5). Both giver and gift were under the scrutiny of God.

Cain's offering did not measure up because he retained the best of his produce for himself, and what he was willing to part with was not his best.[133] After Cain rejected God's wise counsel, he allowed sin to rule in his heart, which revealed itself, by his actions, when he killed his brother Abel—a brother he should have loved and protected, especially since he was the elder of the two. The Lord approached Cain and asked, "Where is your brother?" Cain responded by giving one of the most disrespectful answers a human being could ever say to their Creator. "I do not know. Am I my brother's keeper?"[134]

---

must master it" (4:7). However, he rejected God's wise counsel. Let's learn from Cain's bad example so that our sin does not impact our lives, for the rest of our lives.

132 K.A. Mathews, *Genesis 1-11:26*, Vol. 1A. (Nashville: Broadman & Holman Publishers), 1996, 268.

133 Ibid.

134 Reyburn, William. D. and Euan M. Fry. *A Handbook on Genesis* (New York: United Bible Societies, 1998), 113. "Where is Abel your brother?" is a question similar to the question God asked Adam in the garden in 3:9. With this question God again assumes the role of judge, as he did in the crime and

What Cain got wrong is what America continues to get wrong regularly—as it relates to having love and respect for one another. First, Cain lied; he knew exactly where his brother's bloodied body was located—it was right where he left it—out in the field. Second, for Cain to question his responsibility, as being his brother's keeper, was absurd because the role of family was to look out for each other, not to harm one another.[135] Also, by the fact that Cain used a pun by playing on Abel's name, which means "keeper," he showed his contempt for God for even inquiring about Abel. God responded by asking Cain, "What have you done?" God did not ask for His benefit because He is omniscient, but for Cain's benefit, so he would know that God was aware of his sinful actions, especially since he thought he was alone and showed no remorse for his actions. God also told Cain, "The voice of your brother's blood is crying to Me from the ground." This is a very profound statement because it reveals something about human blood. Life is in the blood, and when that blood was spilled on the ground, that blood cried out to God, as the Lord told Cain. Notice that if you remove blood from a human body, and that body dies, the blood still lives and can be used to give another human being a blood transfusion, often to extend that person's life. WOW! How can people still believe there is no God.

Just like Cain, some Whites do not understand what they have done by taking the lives of their brothers (as well as sisters), which are the millions of Africans they enslaved in America, as well as their descendants that still live in America. The blood of Black men

---

punishment episode in 3:9–19. Cain replies falsely, I do not know, and then adds a rhetorical question, Am I my brother's keeper? The purpose of this question is not to get information but rather to make a negative statement: "I am not my brother's keeper." Keeper translates a noun related to the verb meaning "to watch over, care for." Some translations express it as a verb; for example, FRCL has "Is it up to me to look after my brother?" TEV and GECL "Am I supposed to be taking care of my brother?" and SPCL "Is it my responsibility to watch over him?"

135   Ellen Van Wolde, "The Story of Cain and Abel: A Narrative Study," *JSOT* 52 (1991): 38. The relationship between Cain and brother Abel impacts the relationship Cain has with God: "Gen 4:1–16 makes it clear to sever the tie with one's sibling is to sever one's tie with *yhwh* and the earth."

and women, at the hands of Whites, has been crying out to the Lord from the ground in America since 1619. The following are examples of extreme racism and inhumane treatment of Blacks by Whites for years on American soil. What made these events so deplorable was not just the acts themselves, but how the government (at local, county, state, and federal levels), as well as the church, were complicit.

The Trans-Atlantic Slave Trade.

Involved the capture of Africans from their homeland, chained to one another on the bottom of large cargo ships, and transferred on a 3-4-month voyage to the Americas. 12.5 million Africans taken. It lasted for 300 years and had more than 20,500 voyages. The fact that this lasted as long as it did, and involved as many nations as it did, revealed the total depravity of the human race, with Whites being the main instigator.

The institution of slavery.

Relegated Blacks to subservient roles to Whites for approximately 245 years. This included devaluing Black men; the raping of Black women and their teenage daughters.[136] The fact that this lasted as long as it did, and involved as many nations as it did, also revealed the total depravity of the human race, with Whites being the main instigator.

The Civil War.

War on American soil where Whites in the South fought Whites in the North to maintain the status quo of slavery. The fact that this war took place also revealed the total depravity of the human race, with southern whites being the main instigator.

Black Codes.

Strict local and state laws that detailed when, where, and how formerly enslaved people could work and for how much compensation.

---

136   Isabel Wilkerson, Caste: The Origins of Our Discontents, 40-48.

Throughout the South, the codes appeared as a legal way to put Black citizens into indentured servitude, take voting rights away, control where they lived and how they traveled, and seize children for labor purposes.[137] The fact that this even happened at all also revealed the total depravity of the human race, with southern whites being the main instigator.[138] The fact that these codes were allowed to take place also revealed the total depravity of the human race, with southern whites being the main instigator.

Jim Crow laws.

A collection of state and local statutes that legalized racial segregation. Named after a Black minstrel show character, the laws—which existed for about 100 years, from the post-Civil War era until 1968—were meant to marginalize African Americans by denying them the right to vote, hold jobs, get an education, or other opportunities. Those who attempted to defy Jim Crow laws often faced arrest, fines, jail sentences, violence, and death.[139]

Lynchings.

The violent act of killing Blacks without the benefit of a legal trial. Whites used this method to terrorize Blacks and reassert their dominance, especially after slavery ended. This was mainly carried out by mob rule, and often hanging from a tree was the preferred method. The racism and hate of Blacks were so strong it was often done for the sport.[140] The Ku Klux Klan was the main contributor to the lynching of Blacks in America. Unfortunately, this organized group of white terrorists would go so far as to lynch black servicemen returning from

---

137   Michelle Alexander, *The New Jim Crow*, 35-36.

138   "Black Code," *Britanica* [on-line]; accessed on 23 October 2020; accessed from https://www.britannica.com/topic/black-code; Internet.

139   Ibid, 38-44.

140   Ibid, 229-230. The Klu Klux Klan was the main contributor of the lynching of Blacks in America. These acts of murder as well as the plan to carry them out are the definition of domestic terrorism.

World War I, while still in uniform.¹⁴¹ These acts of murder, as well as the plan to carry them out, are the definition of domestic terrorism.

Rosewood Massacre (1923).

In 1997 John Singleton directed the movie Rosewood, which is based on the massacre in Florida. In A small, overwhelmingly black town in Florida, Rosewood was essentially destroyed in January of 1923. In the nearby town of Sumner, a 22-year-old white woman named Fannie Taylor was heard screaming and, when her neighbor came to check on her, she was covered in bruises. Claiming to have been assaulted by a black man, which was false, she reported that she had not been raped. However, the other white citizens in her town believed otherwise. Her husband gathered a mob of White men from the town and searched for Black men to abuse, even those with nothing to do with the incident. They were joined by 500 members of the KKK. When they arrived at Rosewood, Blacks were terrorized because they were blamed for aiding in the escape of the alleged black man in question. After some Whites were killed by Blacks, who were defending themselves, the white terrorist group burned the town of Rosewood to the ground. Somewhere between 6-27 black people were killed, and many lost their homes and possessions.¹⁴² These acts of murder and arson are the definition of domestic terrorism.

Atlanta Race Riot (1906).

Fearful of the growing power of the black citizens of Atlanta, the white elites in the city began using the local newspapers to push their racially motivated opinions. The governor's race of 1906 was especially repugnant, as various newspapermen utilized their positions to help their campaigns by spreading false information about the state of race

---

141   Michael Emerson and Christian Smith, *Divided by Faith*, 42.

142   Michael Van Dunsen, "10 Worst Massacres of African Americans," 23 October 2019 [on-line]; accessed on 8 October 2020; available from https://listverse.com/2019/10/23/10-of-the-worst-massacres-of-african-americans-disturbing-images/; Internet. In all, anywhere from 6 to 27 black people were killed, with the rest escaping with their lives but none of their possessions, as many of them refused to return to the area, fearful of more violence. 500 members of the KKK.

relations in Atlanta. A favorite of theirs: any lurid tale of a "pure" white woman being assaulted by a black man. White mobs terrorized majority-black neighborhoods, setting fire to black businesses while beating and shooting Blacks at random that crossed their path. 40 African Americans died.[143] These acts of murder and arson are the definition of domestic terrorism.

Wilmington Insurrection (1898).

This event was the only site of a coup d'é tat on American soil, which took place in Wilmington, North Carolina. Just like in many other cases, racial tensions played a major role. Having lost control of the state in 1894, the state's Democrats changed their tactics, relying on an explicitly racist campaign platform centered on the scourge of black men preying on innocent white women. However, the city council of Wilmington ended up being interracial, perhaps as a rebuff to the white supremacists. Unwilling to face the changing face of their city, nearly 2,000 white men launched an attack. First, they burned a local newspaper, The Daily Record, to the ground. Next, they marched through the city, exiling black citizens and killing those unwilling to leave, murdering as many as 60 people. Finally, they forced the duly elected local government to resign at gunpoint, installing their leadership who, only days prior, had promised to "choke the current of the Cape Fear River" with black bodies.[144] These acts of murder, arson, and coup d'tat are the definition of domestic terrorism.

Thibodaux Massacre (1887).

Approximately two decades after slavery was outlawed in the United States, African-Americans began to utilize their freedom in the South. Also, Blacks began to realize the power their labor represented. As a result, they began several strikes, especially among sugar workers in Thibodaux, Louisiana. To further strengthen their position, some sugar workers reached out to the Knights of Labor, the biggest union

---

143 Michael O. Emerson and Christian Smith. *Divided by Faith*, 42.

144 Miachael Van Dunsen, "10 Worst Massacres of African Americans."

of them all, at the time. With the help of organized labor, black workers soon began to demand appropriate wages to Whites. However, instead of negotiating, the plant owners began firing union members. When strikes began, they also hired strike-breakers and created militias, armed to the teeth and out for blood. On November 23rd, black workers were taken from their homes by force, by an armed white mob, and taken to the railroads. Once they arrived, the white mob told the black workers to run for their lives, before shooting them in the back. By the time the violence ended, at least 60 Blacks had died. Defeated and cowed, the workers all went back to the plantations, and not one person faced justice; in fact, one of the murderers even won a seat in Congress the following year.[145] This was the bloodiest labor dispute in U.S. history against black people, another example of domestic terrorism perpetrated by Whites.

Opelousas Massacre (1868).

Opelousas was near Ocoee, Florida, which was known as a "sundown town," a phrase used to illustrate to the black visitors to the city they were not welcome once night fell. The murderous actions against Blacks and the constant threats of violence were a constant reality if they dared step out of line. To improve their plight in life, Blacks looked to take advantage of their rights under the Thirteenth Amendment. Voting rights activists encouraged black citizens to exercise their right to vote. However, understanding the power of voting, many of the white citizens began to see it as an attack on their supremacy[146] (Isn't that the same thing going on today in America with Republicans trying to suppress the vote in this 2020 election to maintain the white status quo that has dominated since slavery.)[147] On November 2, 1920, an African-American man named Moses Norman tried to vote in Florida. Although he was wealthy, Norman was still

---

145 Ibid.

146 Ibid.

147 Andy Kroll, "The Plot Against America: The GOP Plan to Suppress the Vote and Sabotage the Election," *Rolling Stone*, 16 July 2020 [on-line]; accessed on 31 October 2020 https://www.rollingstone.com/politics/politics-features/trump-campaign-2020-voter-suppression-consent-decree-1028988/; Internet.

denied the right to vote. To protect himself, Norman took a gun with him. Members of the KKK took the gun away from him and ordered him to go home. Later that day, a mob of whites, many of them KKK members, navigated the black neighborhoods looking for Norman to lynch him. Unable to find his home, they were able to locate the home of another prominent black man: July Perry. Eventually, they captured him, lynched him, and burned down his neighborhood. The terror wrought by the mob was so great that Ocoee turned into an all-white town for decades. The Blacks were either killed or run out of town for decades.[148] These acts of murder, arson, and vandalism are the definition of domestic terrorism.

New Orleans Massacre (1866).

Today, we honor the men and women of our Armed Forces as true American heroes. However, that has not always been the case, especially during or after the Civil War. Remarkably, about 180,000 black men served in the Union Army during the Civil War; about 90,000 were former slaves from the Confederate states. 40,000 black soldiers died in the war: 10,000 in battle and 30,000 from illnesses or infections. It is amazing how Blacks were willing to give their life for a country that did not even treat them with the dignity and respect they deserved.[149] Ironically, only one year after the Civil War ended, Republicans in Louisiana were looking to give newly freed black men the right to vote. They went so far as to call a convention, trying to get it enshrined in the state constitution. On July 30, 1866, the convention began, Confederate veterans (white men) in the hundreds volunteered to serve as "emergency police officers." On that same day, dozens of black men, many of them Union veterans, marched through the streets to support their right to vote. Armed to the teeth and better prepared for violence than their counterparts, the white mob began attacking the black marchers. Lucien Jean Pierre Capla, a witness to the violence, later recalled: "I saw the people fall like flies." (Capla and his son were

---

148 Michael Van Dunsen, "10 Worst Massacres of African Americans."

149 "Black Civil War Soldiers," *History Channel*, 7 June 2020 [on-line]; accessed on 31 October 2020 https://www.history.com/topics/american-civil-war/black-civil-war-soldiers. Internet.

both brutally attacked, suffering incredible wounds.) When federal troops finally showed up, more than forty black men were dead, with over a hundred wounded from the fighting.[150] These acts of murder and disrespect against black veterans are the definition of domestic terrorism.

New York City Draft Riots (1863).

What started this riot was White opposition to a new federal recruitment law which greatly increased the number of men who faced being called into the war. Two other factors also angered much of the citizenry: it was possible to pay for a substitute, though it was only available to the very wealthy, and African-Americans were exempt, as they were not considered citizens. Like much of the racially motivated violence of the times, the anger of the working-class whites was inflamed by newspapers, publications that ran stories warning of freed men flooding the North with workers willing to undercut the pay of the whites of the area. As this continued, on July 13, 1863, the white mobs, initially only attacking federal buildings, would eventually turn their ire to the black working-class citizens of Manhattan. For four days, hundreds of black residents were forced from their homes, and over 100 were killed, many of them lynched in the sort of violence usually reserved for the South.[151] These acts of murder and racism against blacks that were minding their own business are the definition of domestic terrorism.

Ocoee Massacre (1920).

Thanks to the votes of recently freed black men, Republicans won a vast majority of the elections that year. Faced with the prospect of losing their stranglehold on local and state politics, many racists (who were Democrats), especially those in the Knights of the White Camellia (a pre-cursor to the KKK formed to stop Republican successes at the polls through intimidation) began violently oppressing all the black

---

150   Ibid.

151   Ibid.

people they could get their hands on. Similar to the KKK, the Knights of the White Camelia was a white supremacist terrorist organization, and they were extremely popular in the St. Landry Parish. (One Democratic newspaper estimated nearly one in four white people were members of the group.) On September 28, 1868, as the U.S. Presidential election was beginning to inch closer, a local newspaper editor was beaten. Around a dozen black men came to his aid, and they were subsequently arrested; however, they were later dragged out of jail and lynched. This was just the start of the violence that night: armed white mobs began scouring the countryside for every black person they could find and murdering them as soon as they did. By the time the violence subsided a few weeks later, somewhere between 200 and 300 African-Americans were killed. Republican Ulysses Grant won the presidency against the anti-black Democratic contenders Horatio Seymour and Francis Blair.[152] These horrific acts of premeditated murder and against blacks are the definition of domestic terrorism.

The Red Summer (1919).

Less of an isolated incident and more a collection of similarly-themed violence, the Red Summer took place in 1919, as numerous African-Americans adjusted to civilian life after returning home from WWI alongside their fellow white veterans. Faced with men who were no longer willing to live under Jim Crow laws, many whites began to assault random black men throughout the country, especially those who had fought in the war. Though much of the violence occurred in the North, as the Great Migration dramatically changed the demographics of several major cities, the largest instance of violence occurred in the small town of Elaine, Arkansas. For three days, unspeakable violence was meted out to black sharecroppers who were trying to improve their working conditions; over 200 men, women, and children were murdered because of it. [153] These horrific acts of premeditated murder and against blacks are the definition of domestic terrorism.

---

152   Ibid.

153   Ibid.

The Tulsa Massacre (1921).

Greenwood, also known as Black Wall Street, was the greatest picture of Blacks' achievement if given the opportunity. However, the jealously of many Whites and the racist hatred led to the burning down of their homes (often with them still inside) business and community in the Tulsa Massacre.[154] This is covered in more detail in Chapter 1. These acts of murder, hatred, jealously, and racism against black veterans define domestic terrorism.

Application of Genesis 4:6-16

What events did Cain's actions set in motion because he lost sight of being his brother's keeper?

1. The Confrontation (4:6-7)

God confronted Cain about his anger resulting from his offering being rejected, while Abel's was accepted. This was the time for Cain to make an about-face, but he kept going in the same wrong behavior. It allowed jealously and anger to become murder. The lesson for us is how dangerous our sinful nation can be when we don't listen to God or walk with Him.

2. The crime (4:8)

Because Cain refused to accept God's wise counsel, his sinful desires took over and opened the floodgates for sinful humanity: men, as well as women, have been killing those they should love ever since. The lesson for us is when you disobey God, and you allow jealously and hate to be your motives, it always leads to disastrous consequences.

3. The complaint (4:9-12)

Although Cain committed the first murder in the Bible when he killed his brother Abel, he dared to complain about God's consequences

---

154   Ibid.

for his actions. The lesson for us is that one day we will have to answer to God for our sins. However, if your heart does not belong to Jesus, and you die spiritually separated from Him, you will have no room to complain when you realize hell is real, and you are a resident forever.

4. The consequences (4:13-16)

For the rest of Cain's life, he was banished from God's presence. God told Cain he would be a wanderer and a drifter on the earth for the remainder of his life. This was bad for him because God caused him to live a long life on this earth in that state while being banished from His presence. The lesson for us is we must take sin seriously because God does.

What lessons should we learn from the relationship between Cain and Abel?

The sinfulness of parents is often passed on to their offspring. So, be careful what you teach your children, whether by your words or deeds. Remember, our kids do not always do what we say, but they will mimic what we do, whether good or bad. And if you teach them your bad, sinful habits, you cannot complain when you begin to see yourself in them instead of Christ.

Worship is not a competition. So, be careful you don't make it a competition. Remember, God is not going to judge us by the standards of our family, friends, neighbors, or church members. He is going to judge each of us by His Son, which He sent to die for our sins on Calvary's cross.

A refusal to accept God's correction has disastrous results. So, when you fail to heed God's warnings, when he is trying to get you to turn from your sinful ways, then don't blame Him when your life crashes and burns, or if you crash and burn in hell because you waited too late to repent and accept Jesus as your Savior and Lord before you died.

CHAPTER 5

GOD'S COMMAND: LOVE THY BROTHER

Christ Is Our Advocate

By this we know that we have come to know Him, if we keep His commandments. The one who says, "I have come to know Him," and does not keep His commandments, is a liar, and the truth is not in him; but whoever keeps His word, in him the love of God has truly been perfected. By this we know that we are in Him: the one who says he abides in Him ought himself to walk in the same manner as He walked. Beloved, I am not writing a new commandment to you, but an old commandment which you have had from the beginning; the old commandment is the word which you have heard. On the other hand, I am writing a new commandment to you, which is true in Him and in you, because the darkness is passing away and the true Light is already shining. The one who says he is in the Light and yet hates his brother is in the darkness until now. The one who loves his brother abides in the Light and there is no cause for stumbling in him. But the one who hates his brother is in the darkness and walks in the darkness, and does not know where he is going because the darkness has blinded his eyes. (1 John 2:3-11)

The United States of America began as a British colony in Jamestown, Virginia in 1607, but on July 4, 1776, white Europeans living on this soil decided they no longer wanted to be ruled by a nation on the other side of the Atlantic Ocean, so they rebelled and declared their independence. After winning their freedom in 1776, and a nation was born, a system was put in place that disproportionally benefited Whites over other races. At the time, the U.S. was by far predominately White. If you were not of white European descent, you were not given the same privileges or rights under the new independence. At that time, what became known as two Americas, a White America that sought to help Whites advance, and a Black America, where Blacks were kept from advancing and remained in a subservient role to Whites.

In 1790, the U.S. population was 3,532,379. The number of Blacks was 740,054. 33.94% of the population, which meant 681,777 Blacks were slaves or 92%. In 1860, the U.S. population was 14,800,072. The number of Blacks was 2,136,762, or 32.27% of the population. 3,953,731 Blacks were slaves or 89%.[155] Because of America's painful history with racism and the fact that we have never properly dealt with it is why after almost 250 years of our existence as a sovereign nation, racism is alive and well and remains a major cause of division.

Tracing the problem

The sin of racism can be traced back to the founding of America and has plagued this nation since then. During the Civil War, President Abraham Lincoln issued the Emancipation Proclamation on September 22, 1862, with an effective date of January 1, 1863. It only declared that slaves were to be freed in the Confederate States of America, not the entire country. This was because Whites had rebelled against the federal government. Furthermore, the Emancipation Proclamation did not end slavery in all of America; that did not happen until December 6, 1865, when the Thirteenth Amendment was ratified to the Constitution, abolishing slavery.

Interestingly, even after military hostilities ended, as a part of the former Confederacy, Texas did not comply with the Emancipation Proclamation. Texas was the only Confederate state not to comply, as it was the state that held the most slaves. However, on June 18, 1865, Union General Gordon Granger and 2,000 federal troops arrived on the island of Galveston, Texas, to take possession of the state and enforce

---

155 "Statistics of Slavery," [on-line] accessed on 5 September 2020; accessed from https://faculty.weber.edu/kmackay/statistics_on_slavery.htm; Internet.

the emancipation of its slaves. Therefore, Blacks in Texas experienced an additional two and a half years of slavery.[156] If Satan can keep you from knowing the truth, he can keep you acting like a slave, talking like a slave, walking like a slave, living like a slave, and using the laws he created to keep you there.

> *After the Civil War, liberated slaves dispersed throughout the United States, seeking work and to escape the violence of the post-South. For several decades many lived relatively peacefully in the East, the Midwest, and the West. But in 1877 the disputed presidential election of the previous autumn was resolved in a compromise that gave the Republican candidate, Rutherford B. Hayes, the White House. In return for southern Democratic support of their presidential candidate, Republicans agreed to withdraw federal troops who had been protecting African Americans in the defeated Confederacy. The period is known as Reconstruction then came to an end. In the South, the former slaveholding aristocracy renewed African American's subjugation. Supported by a campaign of violence against the newly emancipated slaves, southern states adopted segregation statutes—Jim Crow Laws.* [157]

When word came on June 19, 1865, that Texas slaves were free, parties broke out on plantations, Black people were excited, folks went to pack their stuff to make their way North because finally, they were free. For White Americans, Independence Day is July 4th, but for Black Americans, Independence Day is June 19th or Juneteenth.[158] Our nation's racist past provides insight into why we do not love one another as God commands.

---

156   Jemar Tisby. *The Color of Compromise*, 207.

157   Richard Rothstein, *The Color of Law*, 39-40.

158   Bonnie Kristian, "Juneteenth: A Truer Independence Day," *Christianity Today*, 18 June 2020. [on-line]; accessed on 5 September 2020; available from https://www.christianitytoday.com/ct/2020/june-web-only/juneteenth-truer-independence-day.html; Internet. The official end of slavery in America more fully embraces the self-evident truth of all people as created equal.

What does the Bible say about this?

The Epistles of 1 John clearly explains why America struggles with systemic racism. First John is built around the repetition of the three main themes: light vs. darkness, love vs. hatred, and truth vs. error. These days when many Christians think they have fellowship with God but do not, and when many religious people think they are true sons of God but are not, it is important that we apply these passages and examine our own lives carefully.[159] When we apply these principles to America, as a so-called Christian nation, we fail miserably. America has a history of walking in darkness and not in the light. Slavery was one of the darkest times we faced, and we have yet to recover from it because it helped lay the foundation for systematic racism.[160] Sadly, we, as a country, have a history of loving some people, while hating others, especially those that do not look like us. The division between Black and White has played a major role in the division between other races in America. We have a history of downplaying the truth while deliberately accepting errors or lies. This has never been more evident than it is today. Everything seems to be fake news, which has become the catchphrase when we do not want to accept the obvious truth or accept another point of view that does not agree with our own. The problem is not only that our politics and media are called fake news by a segment of our society, but many in America view our Christianity as fake news or irrelevant as well. This epistle of first John reveals why we do not love one another as God commands.

Faith in our nation, not in our Savior and Lord

The prophet Jeremiah says, "Let no wise man boast of his wisdom, nor let the mighty man boast of his might, nor a rich man boast of his riches; but let the one who boasts boast of this, that he understands and knows Me, that I am the Lord who exercises mercy, justice, and

---

159 Wiersbe, W. W. *Wiersbe's expository outlines on the New Testament.* (Wheaton, IL: Victor Books), 1992. 767.

160 White supremacy was the original foundation for which America's sinful foundation was built that created the atmosphere for everything else that followed.

righteousness on the earth; for I delight in these things, declares the Lord." (Jeremiah 9:23-24) This verse exposes America's arrogance. We boast in our wisdom (numerous scholars, schools of higher learning, intelligence agencies, and a multitude of highly trained intellectuals); we boast in our military might (our vast Armed Forces and industrial complex that supplies our weaponry and machinery); and we boast in our riches (world's largest economy and the most millionaires by far), but we do not boast in the Lord—because we put our faith in these three things, instead of Jesus Christ.

Furthermore, mercy, justice, and righteousness are extremely important to God, but not to America. We do not show mercy to those in need, which are the poor and less fortunate among us, nor do we show mercy to the people of color. We do not have a fair and equitable justice system because of how we treat the poor and less fortunate among us, as well as the people of color. And we do not practice righteousness because our nation's righteousness is as filthy rags (Isaiah 64:6), which means that even our best efforts, apart from a personal relationship with Christ, are no better than polluted garments. In Hebrew, "filthy garments" has a profound meaning because it is a figure of speech that has the idea of a menstrual rage. Isaiah employed the imagery of menstrual cloths used during a woman's period to picture uncleanness (cf. Lev 15:19–24). This is true of the best behavior of unbelievers (cf. Phil 3:5–8).[161] Jeremiah reveals why we do not love one another as God commands.

America from a Nigerian Christian's Perspective

The Aremu, Adegoke, and Adebiyi families are a very important part of our church leadership. Their view of America is different now than it was before they moved to Fort Worth, Texas, from Nigeria to attend Southwestern Baptist Theological Seminary, which is my alma mater. It was very interesting and refreshing to hear their perspective of how America is viewed in Africa.

In 2008, when Barack Obama was elected as our 44th President, Africa rejoiced because to them, he was a native son because Barack

---

161   J. F. MacArthur, Jr. *The MacArthur Study Bible* (Is 64:6).

Obama Sr. was from Kenya. In Obama, they saw themselves, and if someone that looked like them could become the leader of the free world, then the sky was the limit for black people everywhere. Therefore, our Nigerian brothers and sisters admitted they held a very high view of America in many areas, before their arrival, because they remember Obama and what his presence in the White House meant worldwide. However, after living in America under the Trump Administration, they are amazed because America now reminds them of Nigeria in many ways. The high view they once held has been seriously diminished. First, they do not understand how a former reality TV star became president of what is supposed to be the greatest nation in existence today. Furthermore, they do not understand why so many Americans continue to support President Trump after his years of abysmal behavior, poor leadership, and outrageous propensity to lead by tweet. Also, they wanted to know why these same Americans were not turned off from a man who only cares about himself and has corrupted all levels of the Executive Branch for personal gain.

According to our Nigerian brothers and sisters, the church (as a whole) in America is not the Christian example they thought it would be. This has been for two reasons: how well prosperity doctrine is so widely preached and accepted in America, just like in Nigeria, and how much the church is influenced by the government or entangled in its affairs, also, just like in Nigeria. Also, having come from an authoritarian-run government, they see our current president as something you expect to see in Africa, not in America. Perhaps, the biggest thing they are confused about is why so many white evangelicals support Donald Trump, no matter what he does or says, since his lifestyle contradicts Christianity in every way possible. However, I explained that the Christian church in America is more political than most people realize or willing to admit. For many white evangelicals, their support for our president is transactional, even if they have to sell their souls to the devil, figuratively speaking. Having conservative judges appointed to the courts is more important to these evangelicals than having a president that acts like a decent human being. They don't seem to care that Trump is not a person who truly respects the office of the President, nor respects the people that voted for him as well as those that did not.

If Trump cared for his supporters, he would not have had them show up for numerous large rallies, mostly not wearing a mask, during a pandemic, with a virus that has infected over 10 million Americans and killed over 250,000, just so he could stir up his base, to stay in office possibly. It is obvious that Trump only cares about himself and only uses people to get what he wants out of them until they are no longer useful, then he kicks them to the curb—by a tweet. He does not care about the country he was elected to govern, only the power that the office affords the occupant, not what's good for the country. He has used all levels of government for his purposes. Long ago, Trump revealed who he really was to America, but somehow, at least to forty percent of the country, he is still their hero, regardless of his autocratic behavior—even though he breaks every presidential norm daily—as long as he supports their agenda. White evangelicals don't seem to learn from biblical history and what happened to God's people when their focus became governmental affairs instead of God's kingdom affairs. An example would be a prophet named Balaam.

When appeasing government becomes our priority

Balak was the king of Moab. He was afraid of the Israelites as they traveled to the plain of Moab and camped along with the Jordan, near Jericho (Numbers 22:1). So, Balak summoned Balaam to get him to curse the Israelites. Balaam's relationship with the wicked king of Moab was transactional. Balak offered to pay Balaam handsomely for his services. Balaam was foolish enough to approach God and ask for His permission to curse His people, which He had already blessed (v. 19). As Balaam was on his way to meet with Balak, the angel of the Lord stood in a narrow path blocking the road (v. 22).

However, the only one that saw the angel of the Lord standing in the road, with a drawn sword, was Balaam's donkey, not Balaam (v. 23). In an attempt to avoid the angel of the Lord, the donkey pressed close to the wall, crushing Balaam's foot in the process, which caused him to beat his donkey (v. 24). What was remarkable was that God gave the donkey the ability to speak, and he asked Balaam why he was beating him, especially when he had been good to him (v. 28). Balaam responded by telling his donkey it was because he made a fool of him and that if he had a sword in his hand, he would have killed him (v. 29). You could imagine, at that moment, the donkey desperately wanting to tell Balaam that he had made a fool of himself without his help, but of course, God did give him those words to speak. After going back and forth arguing with his donkey, God opened Balaam's eyes (spiritually), which allowed him to finally see the angel of the Lord standing in the road with the sword in his hand. It was at that point, Balaam realized that his donkey saved his life. For his actions, Balaam is called a false prophet in the New Testament (2 Peter 2:15).

Many white evangelicals in America make the same mistake that Balaam made; they align themselves with a sinful leader for transactional reasons. However, unlike Balaam, white evangelicals behave the way they do for personal reasons, maintaining their political power. Moreover, the reason why Balaam was willing to entertain the thought of cursing his fellow Jews, even as a prophet that should have known better, is for the same reason many white evangelicals went along with slavery in America; they did not love their black brothers and sisters. Balaam did not love the Jews, and many white evangelicals still do not love all their black brothers and sisters—unless they are Republicans and agree with their political agenda. To many of us African American Christians, these evangelicals act like Pharisees, not disciples of Christ. Numbers chapter 22 reveals why we do not love one another as God commands.

To love others is a command, not a suggestion

As we turn our attention back to 1 John 2:3-11, the apostle John was not only one of the original 12 disciples, he was part of a trio (Peter, James, and John) that were closer to Jesus than the other nine. Two of the three (Peter and John) were vessels God used to write down His Words, which became part of Scripture. James had been martyred by this time. John was the youngest of the group but was given the unique privilege of not only writing epistles but also the gospel of John and the book of Revelation. In all of John's writings, the central figure is Jesus Christ, the Messiah.

To understand John's writings, certain words or phrases must be properly defined. This is because words in Greek (as well as Hebrew) often have a much richer meaning than they do in English. The words walk, fellowship, abide, light, and darkness are prominent in John's writings. The phrases walk in obedience, walk in love, and walk-in truth are prominent as well.[162] When the Bible uses the word walk, as it relates to faith, it is often used as a metaphor for lifestyle—the Greek word is peripateo.[163] The word fellowship means intimacy or participation—the Greek word is koinonia. The word abide means to remain, stay in place, or hang out—the Greek word is meno. Therefore, to walk in love means to live a lifestyle of reflecting the love of Christ to God and others. To walk in obedience means to live your life in a way that does not stray from God's commands. To walk in truth means your life lines up with the truth of God's word, and you do not live in error.[164] If you put all of this together, John tells us we can know if we have fellowship (meaning an actual relationship) with Jesus Christ, our Savior. According to 1st John 2, there are two ways you can know whether you are truly a believer.

1. If we keep His commandments

> *By this we know that we have come to know Him, if we keep His commandments. The one who says, "I have come to know Him," and does not keep His commandments, is a liar, and the truth is not in him; but whoever keeps His word, in him the love of God has truly been perfected. By this we know that we are in Him: the one who says he abides in Him ought himself to walk in the same manner as He walked. (vs. 3-6)*

---

162   W. E. Vine, Unger, M. F., & White, W., Jr., *Vine's Complete Expository Dictionary of Old and New Testament Words*, Vol. 1. (Nashville: Thomas. Nelson Publishing, 1996), 664. In John's epistle, we are provided three basic "tests" that all Christians should followed: obedience (walking in the light), love (walking in love), and truth (walking in the truth).

163   Ibid.

164   W.W. Wiersbe, *Wiersbe's expository outlines on the New Testament*, (Wheaton: Victor Books, 1992), 767.

2. If we love our brother

> *The one who says he is in the Light and yet hates his brother is in the darkness until now. The one who loves his brother abides in the Light and there is no cause for stumbling in him. But the one who hates his brother is in the darkness and walks in the darkness, and does not know where he is going because the darkness has blinded his eyes. (9-11)*

Based on these two important principles, John provides us with a litmus test of whether a person is a true believer. First, they must know Jesus as their personal Savior and Lord. This is what John means when he tells us that we must keep His commandments. An unsaved person cannot keep God's commandments because they do not have God's Spirit (Holy Spirit) within them to guide them. "As a man thinketh in his heart, so is he" (Proverbs 23:7 KJV). "The good man out of the good treasure of his heart brings forth what is good, and the evil man out of the evil treasure brings forth what is evil; for his mouth speaks from that which fills his heart" (Luke 6:45). "The human heart is the most deceitful of all things, and desperately wicked. Who knows how bad it is?" (Jeremiah 17:9 NLT). What all three of these verses make clear is the sinful condition of the human heart and lets us know how bad we need Jesus.

Second, we must love our brother. Brother means our brother or sister-in-Christ. Also, without a personal relationship with Jesus, human beings do not have the capacity to love God or others. The Greek word for love is *agape*. So, the type of love John is talking about is godly love or unconditional love. Godly love can only be accomplished if the Holy Spirit's presence is present in a person's life, allowing love to flow through their life. Human love toward other human beings that is not based on a relationship with Christ is conditional, but God's love is unconditional.

John goes further to drive home his argument when he says the one who does not keep God's commandments is a liar. However, this has more to do with that person's lifestyle than it does with their speech. Why? Because if your heart is wrong, then your speech will automatically be wrong as well because speech flows from what's in a person's heart—as we have already established.

How does what John reveals to us in this passage relate to the failings of America, and explain why systemic racism has dominated this country from the beginning, as well as continues to do so. Once again, America is supposed to be a Christian nation. Based on what John teaches us in this passage, the way many white Americans have treated African Americans, as well as Hispanic Americans, violates what we are commanded to do in this passage. A command from God is not a suggestion, nor is it optional; it is a command, which means it must be obeyed or followed. Jesus showed us how to love one another by putting our main need (the need for salvation) above His needs (He died on the cross). Greater love has no one than this: to lay down one's life for one's friends (John 15:13). It is one thing for the unsaved world not to love one another, but it is a whole other matter when Christians fail to love one another. This is why the white Christian church founded in the original Thirteen Colonies has to take a lot of the blame for their role in slavery. However, they bought into slavery for two reasons: 1. They wanted free labor, and even if they did not own any slaves, they didn't mind benefitting from slave labor because economic necessity trumped morality.[165] 2. They truly didn't love Blacks, mainly because they viewed them as savages or less than human.[166] The apostle John reveals why we do not love one another as God commands.

In a book by John Piper titled, *Bloodlines: Race, Cross, and the Christian*, he added some very important comments that explain America's history on systemic racism. He said, "What may be the clearest indicator of the disappearance of a moral texture to society is

---

165   Greg Timmons, "How Slavery Became the Economic Engine of the South," *History Channel*, 6 March 2018 [on-line]; accessed on 15 September 2020; available from https://www.history.com/news/slavery-profitable-southern-economy; Internet. Slavery was so profitable, it sprouted more millionaires per capita in the Mississippi River Valley than anywhere in the nation.

166   Thomas Bradford, "Why were African people taken as slaves and thought of as savages in early American?" 2 February 2020 [on-line]; accessed on 15 September 2020; available from https://www.quora.com/Why-were-African-people-taken-as-slaves-and-thought-of-as-savages-in-early-America; Internet.

the loss of guilt and embarrassment over moral lapses."[167] Piper didn't stop there; he talked about the sins of Whites (as they consistently blame Blacks) for the harm they have caused them since slavery. Whites do not blame slavery because they say that they have nothing to do with what their ancestors did but fail to realize they benefit from what they did. Furthermore, many Whites are just as dysfunctional as the Blacks they consistently put down, which is a profound point that Piper makes.

> *Together with every race, whites are killing their babies (abortions), and wallowing in their porn and taking illegal drugs, and leaving their wives and having babies without marriage. The difference is that when you develop patterns of sin in the majority race, they have no racial connotation. Since the majority of people don't think of themselves in terms of race, none of their dysfunctions is viewed as a racial dysfunction. When you are of the majority ethnicity, nothing you do is ethnic. It's just the way it's done. When you are a majority, everything you do has color.*[168]

What is interesting about Piper's comments is that he is a white pastor from Minnesota. He even admits his sinful past as a racist[169] and

---

167   John Piper. *Bloodlines: Race, Cross, And the Christian*. (Wheaton: Crossway Publishers), 2011, 67.

168   Ibid, 67.

169   Ibid, 33-34. Piper's words continued: I was a Racist. I was, in those years, manifestly racist. As a child and teenager my attitudes and actions assumed the superiority of my race in almost every way without knowing or wanting to know anybody who was black, except Lucy. Lucy came to our house on Saturday's to help my mother clean. I liked Lucy, but the whole structure of the relationship was demeaning. Those who defend the noble spirit of Southern slaveholders by pointing to how nice they were to their slaves, and how deep the affections were, and how they even attended each other's personal celebrations, seem to be naïve about what makes a relationship degrading. No, she was not a slave. But the point still stands. Of course, we were nice. Of course, we loved Lucy. Of course, she was invited to my sister's wedding. As long as she and her family "knew their place." Being nice to, and having strong affections for, and including in our lives is what we do for our dogs too. It doesn't say much about honor and respect and equality before God. My affections for Lucy did not provide the slightest restraint on my racist mouth when I was with my friends.

talks about how God changed his heart before becoming a pastor.[170] Piper told the story about his conversion experience to Christ when he was a senior at Wheaton College. During an Urban Missions Conference in December 1967, and during a question-and-answer time, before thousands of students, Warren Webster was asked the following question: What if your daughter falls in love with a Pakistani while you're in the mission field and wants to marry him? Webster was the general director of the Conservative Baptist Foreign Mission Society and former missionary to Pakistan. His answer shocked young Piper, as well as the other students. Webster said something like: "Better a Christian Pakistani than a godless White American!" This was truly a remarkable statement because interracial marriage was still frowned on in 1967 by a majority of Whites. Ironically, this was the same year the Supreme Court deemed interracial marriage between Blacks and Whites constitutional.[171] Webster's powerful testimony was the catalyst that caused Piper to turn his heart to God and delivered him from the sin of racism. If God can deliver John Piper, he can deliver every other white person in America that still has racism in their heart, even Donald J. Trump if he is willing. John Pipers' reflection of America reveals why we do not love one another as God commands.

---

170   Ibid, 35.

171   Loving v. Virginia (1967). United States Supreme Court. [on-line]: Accessed on 9 October 2020; available from https://caselaw.findlaw.com/us-supreme-court/388/1.html. Internet. In June 1958, two residents of Virginia, Mildred Jeter, a Negro woman, and Richard Loving, a white man, were married in the District of Columbia pursuant to its laws. Shortly after their marriage, the Loving returned to Virginia and established their marital abode in Caroline County. At the October Term, 1958, of the Circuit Court [388 U.S. 1, 3] of Caroline County, a grand jury issued an indictment charging the Loving with violating Virginia's ban on interracial marriages. On January 6, 1959, the Loving pleaded guilty to the charge and were sentenced to one year in jail; however, the trial judge suspended the sentence for a period of 25 years on the condition that the Loving leave the State and not return to Virginia together for 25 years. After their convictions, the Loving took up residence in the District of Columbia. On November 6, 1963, they filed a motion in the state trial court to vacate the judgment and set aside the sentence on the ground that the statutes which they had violated were repugnant to the Fourteenth Amendment. It was this case that finally made it to the Supreme Court. Their win opened the door for interracial marriage to be legal in America.

Application of 1 John 2:3-11

What mistakes does the unsaved world make that the church unfortunately follows?

1. **They do not keep God's Commandment. (vs. 3-4)**

    It is understandable why the unsaved do not obey God's commands because they do not have the Holy Spirit, which empowers us to obey Him. However, it is an oxymoron when those claim they are Christians but do not. If you fall into this category, you are either lying about your faith in Christ, or you are a really bad example, at best.

2. **They do not walk as Jesus walked. (vs. 4-6)**

    It is understandable why the unsaved do not walk with Jesus, because you can't walk with someone you do not know. For a Christian not to walk with God means they do not truly love God.

3. **They hinder God's light from shining on this earth. (vs. 7-8)**

    It is understandable why unsaved people hinder God's light because they live in darkness. Therefore, it is biblically impossible for God's light to shine through them. However, for a Christian to hinder God's light from shining through them, then it means they are living in sin, whether they attend church or not, read the Bible or not, or pray or not.

4. **They hate their brothers. (vs. 9-11)**

    It is understandable why unsaved people hate their brothers because you cannot genuinely love God's way unless Jesus lives in you. However, for a Christian to hate his brother-in-Christ, he is not a Christian, or he is just a really bad example (John 4:24).

What valuable lessons should we learn from John's Epistle?

1. Love should be the unifying force and identifying mark of the Body of Christ.

2. If you do not genuinely love your Christian brother, you do not genuinely love God.

3. To love your Christian brother is a commandment, not a suggestion.

4. Love is the key to walking in the light of Christ because we cannot grow spiritually if we hate our brother.

5. The Holy Spirit's dwelling in us gives us the ability to love others as Christ loves us.

6. Racism is the result of man not genuinely loving God, and without genuinely loving God, he cannot genuinely love his brother.

CHAPTER 6

WHO IS MY NEIGHBOR?

The Good Samaritan

And a lawyer stood up and put Him to the test, saying, "Teacher, what shall I do to inherit eternal life?" And He said to him, "What is written in the Law? How does it read to you?" And he answered, "You shall love the Lord your God with all your heart, and with all your soul, and with all your strength, and with all your mind; and your neighbor as yourself." And He said to him, "You have answered correctly; do this and you will live." But wishing to justify himself, he said to Jesus, "And who is my neighbor?" Jesus replied and said, "A man was going down from Jerusalem to Jericho and fell among robbers, and they stripped him and beat him, and went away leaving him half dead. And by chance a priest was going down on that road, and when he saw him, he passed by on the other side. Likewise a Levite also, when he came to the place and saw him, passed by on the other side. But a Samaritan, who was on a journey, came upon him; and when he saw him, he felt compassion, and came to him and bandaged up his wounds, pouring oil and wine on them; and he put him on his beast, and brought him to an inn and took care of him. On the next day he took out two denarii and gave them to the innkeeper and said, 'Take care of him; and whatever more you spend, when I return, I will repay you.' Which of these three do you think proved to be a neighbor to the man who fell into the robbers' hands?" And he said, "The one who showed mercy toward him." Then Jesus said to him, "Go and do the same." [Luke 10:25-37]

In a book by Carol Swain titled, *The New White Nationalism in America*, in Chapter 5, she describes how Whites used crime and the fear of violence to control Blacks, which was very effective in holding the majority of them in poverty. However, despite the continued oppressive behavior from Whites, many Blacks found a way to excel far beyond what many Whites ever thought they were capable of achieving on their own. As a result, another popular tactic that Whites incorporated against Blacks was riots. During the riots of the nineteenth and early twentieth centuries, accusations of black crimes against white women were the pretext for the destruction of prosperous black communities, such as Rosewood, Florida, and an affluent black community in Tulsa, Oklahoma; nicknamed "Black Wall Street."[172] For the white nationalist, their goal is not to be a neighbor but to rule over their neighbors, which is why they continue their tactics of fear, intimidation, and violence against African Americans, just as they have done in the past.

The Tulsa Race Massacre of 1921

June 1, 2020, marked the 99th Anniversary of the Tulsa Race Massacre when one of the worst racist events occurred that no race of people should ever have to endure. On that sad day, thousands of Tulsa's white residents mobbed and attacked a black community in Oklahoma. In the summer of 1921, the city of Tulsa, Oklahoma, was the location of the vilest outbreak of racist violence in American history. Astonishingly, over 1,400 homes and businesses were destroyed, mainly by fire, and nearly 10,000 Blacks were left homeless.[173]

The massacre began on a Tuesday and ended on Thursday (May 31 - June 2, 1921). By that Friday, sheer horror and destruction were left in the aftermath. Many American cities in the 1920s were

---

172   Carol M. Swain. *The New White Nationalism in America: Its Challenge to Integration*. (Cambridge: University Press), 2002, 114.

173   Jeff Wallenfeldt, "Tulsa Race Massacre of 1921," *Britannica*, 5 February 2019 [on-line]; accessed on 16 September 2020; available from https://www.britannica.com/event/Tulsa-race-riot-of-1921; Internet.

largely segregated, and Tulsa was no exception. Consequently, the neighborhood where most of the city's 10,000 black residents lived was called Greenwood, which was the most prosperous black community in the nation.[174] Dubbed "Black Wall Street" by Booker T. Washington due to its affluent black residents, the Greenwood neighborhood of Oklahoma was a picture of African American success. It featured black-owned homes and establishments, which included: banks, restaurants, hotels, churches, luxury shops, restaurants, grocery stores, jewelry and clothing stores, movie theaters, barbershops and salons, a library, pool halls, nightclubs, and offices for doctors, lawyers, and dentists. Also, Greenwood had its school system, post office, savings and loan bank, a hospital, and bus and taxi services.[175] Greenwood was everything that Whites claimed Blacks could ever achieve on their own. However, this affluent black community far exceeded many white communities, not only in Oklahoma but also throughout the country.

Racism was the norm in Tulsa at that time in the city's history, as well as throughout Oklahoma and the country. The nearby white communities constantly harassed the black residents of Greenwood—mostly out of sheer jealously—fueled by hatred and blatant racism. Also, Whites were emboldened by the fact the law allowed them to get away with terrorizing Blacks without any repercussions—which has been an ill-fated stain on American culture.

Unfortunately, tensions boiled over on May 31, 1921, when a 19-year-old black young man named Dick Rowland entered an office building on South Main Street to use the restroom. Who knew that an ordinary harmless stop by a teenager would become the catalysts for a racial explosion? As he entered an elevator operated by a 17-year-old white young woman named Sarah Page, it was alleged that Rowland accidentally tripped over Page's foot—causing her to scream. Rowland understood the climate of the times, so he naturally feared for his life when a white woman screamed in public in the vicinity of

---

174 Isabel Wilkerson, *Caste: The Origins of Our Discontents*, 229.

175 Alexis Clark, "Tulsa's Black Wall Street Flourished as a Self-contained Hub in Early 1900s," *History*, 2 Jan 2020 [on-line]; accessed on 16 September 2020; accessed from https://www.history.com/news/black-wall-street-tulsa-race-massacre; Internet.

a black man. Therefore, Rowland ran from the building in an attempt to flee. He was apprehended by the Tulsa police not too far from the location for alllegedly assaulting Page. By the way, Page never alleged that Rowland assaulted her, it was only assumed by an eager white community that already had a lot of pent-up venom against Blacks, which they did not appreciate as their neighbors. Therefore, they did not care that the alleged attack was built on a false assertion. They only cared about having an opportunity to pounce on a people group they utterly despised.

Consequently, it did not take long for the rumors to spread like wildfire throughout the city's white community. This incident happened in the morning, but by noon, the Tulsa Tribune newspaper (without any evidence) had printed a front-page story pushing the false narrative. It was reported that the police had arrested Rowland for sexually assaulting Page.[176] After Rowland's false arrest, he was held in the city jail. The encounter sparked widespread outrage among white people as well as the black community of Greenwood. While Rowland sat in Jail like a dead duck, an armed white mob of about 2,000 in number arrived at the jail to take him by force to hang him. They would have succeeded, but approximately 200 armed black men from Greenwood showed up to stop them, which they succeeded, even though they were outnumbered.

The mob turned their attention in a standoff against the black men. Because they were overmatched, they retreated to their homes in Greenwood. However, that same evening, the white mob went to take out their vengeance on the black neighborhood that they loathed: Greenwood. The white mob spent the next 24 hours looting and burning homes, schools, libraries, movie theaters, and other Greenwood businesses. Not even the famous historical Black Mount Zion Baptist Church, the pillar of the community, was spared. However, it was one of only a few rebuilt structures and now stands as a historic landmark. The angry white mob of Tulsans—some of whom were deputized and given weapons by city officials—committed numerous acts of violence against black people, including shooting an unarmed black man in a movie theater.

---

176   Ibid.

Eyewitnesses reported seeing planes hovering overhead as buildings burned from the top down on the streets below. Historians believe as many as 300 people were murdered, but there will probably never be an accurate death toll. According to *The Ringer News Paper*, eyewitnesses said they witnessed black bodies piled onto trucks and dumped into unmarked graves. According to other eyewitness accounts, the scope of the attack was equal to warfare: homeowners shot dead in their front yards, planes dropped turpentine bombs onto buildings, and a machine gun fired bullets on a neighborhood church. It was a living nightmare.

In the aftermath of the heart-rending massacre, 35 city blocks were left in charred ruins, and 10,000 black people that survived the ordeal were left homeless, and their lives severely changed forever.[177] In 2020 financial numbers, it is believed that an excess of more than 33 million dollars worth of property damage was sustained. After the rampage, many black Tulsans left the city in fear for their safety. And many black and white residents, who remained in Tulsa, remained silent about the tragedy for decades.

As time passed, vivid details about the massacre faded. No one was convicted for the incident, including Rowland, the black young man falsely accused. To this day, questions about the scope of the attack, including how many white people carried out the violence, and the degree of government involvement, remain unanswered.[178] Unfortunately, the Greenwood community—the staple of black success—never fully recovered from the incident.[179] The best way to sum up the Tulsa Massacre is a quote from Randy Woodley's book on racial diversity.

Call it dehumanization, ethnocentrism, racial homogenization, or cultural cannibalism—when one culture begins to lift itself as better than another and it has the power to do so, any inhuman act

---

177 Ibid.

178 Ibid.

179 Isabel Wilkerson, *Caste: The Origins of Our Discontents*, 145

or deprivation can be, and has been "justified." And when such atrocities take place, Satan has a field day.[180]

What is truly heartbreaking about this story involving the Tulsa Race Massacre is that the Whites and Blacks in Tulsa were all neighbors, but they still could not coexist because of the sins of white supremacy, hatred, and racism. In the parable of the Good Samaritan, Jesus addressed this issue of what it means to be a neighbor. If all races and ethnicities throughout the world would not only read and study the Bible but also obeyed what it says—the world would be a better place.

Jesus Explains Who Is Our Neighbor?

In Luke 10:25-37, Jesus was approached by a lawyer (a Jewish student of Old Testament Law) who wanted to test Him. The man wanted to know what he could do to inherit eternal life. Although the question was faulty—because there is nothing we can do to inherit eternal life— except trust our life to Jesus—the Lord appealed to the man's profession. He asked the lawyer a legal question, which he should have answered correctly. The Lord also asked the man his interpretation of the law—meaning his understanding of the Scriptures. The problem with Jewish rabbi's methods concerning the law was they enjoyed debating the law without understanding it or applying it, just like many church leaders and Christians today.

This lawyer wanted to hear what Jesus had to say to trap Him. We get the impression that the man was not seeking the truth but was only trying to involve Jesus in a debate that he hoped he would win. The lawyer proved to be evasive when it came to facing the truth and obeying it.[181] When the man answered, "You shall love the Lord your God with all your heart, and with all your soul, and with all your strength, and with all your mind; and your neighbor as yourself," he quoted Deuteronomy 6:5 and Leviticus 19:18. Jesus essentially told the

---

180   Randy Woodley. *Living in Color: Embracing God's Passion for Christ Diversity*. (Downers Grove: InterVarsity Press), 2004, 24.

181   W.W. Wiersbe, *Wiersbe's Expository Outlines on the New Testament*. (Wheaton: Victor Books, 1992), 173.

man to go and apply both Scriptures he cited. Proving the man did not understand the Bible, nor the passage he quoted, he asked Jesus who his neighbor was—to justify himself.

For a teaching illustration, Jesus told the famous parable of the Good Samaritan. Jesus replied by saying a Jewish man was robbed, beaten, and left for dead while traveling from Jerusalem to Jericho. Afterward, a priest came upon the scene and recognized that the Jewish man was in serious need of aid, but he walked to the other side of the road to avoid any contact. Next, a Levite (temple worker) came upon the same scene and did the same thing as the Priest. Afterward, a Samaritan came upon the same scene, but his actions were drastically different from the priest and Levite. He stopped and dressed the wounds of the Jewish man who was left on the side of the road bleeding. However, the Samaritan man didn't stop there; he went over, and beyond what anyone like him was expected to do, he placed the man on his animal, took him the distance to a nearby town, and paid his lodging bill.

Yet, the Good Samaritan went even further with his generosity. He told the innkeeper that if the injured man incurred additional debt (due to more time needed for recovery), he would pay the balance when he returned from out of town. However, for you to fully comprehend this story's magnitude, you must understand the context of the story. First, Jews despised the Samaritans as well as Gentiles. Samaritans were considered half-breeds because they were half-Jew and half-Gentile. Second, Jews were ethnocentric because they were God's chosen, which they took out of context. Therefore, Jews did not eat with or fellowship with Samaritans or Gentiles because they were both considered unclean.

When Jews traveled, they would go out of their way to avoid Samaritan towns, to avoid contact—even if it meant adding miles onto their journey. Due to the attitude of supremacy the Jews held, to take their precious time, stop, and render aid to a wounded man beside the road, was unthinkable. Now, let us go back to the actions of the priest and the Levite who avoided the man along the road. Both men, who were supposed to be servants of God, avoided the man, even though, he too, was a Jew. This was because they viewed their responsibility the wrong way. This would be like a pastor or deacon today walking along the road and refusing to render aid to an injured man near their church because they were possibly afraid to get their suit stained.

Every Jew who heard about this story would have been surprised because Jesus made the despised Samaritan the hero of the story, thus painting him in a positive light—which no self-respecting Jew would have done. Once Jesus had completed the story, he asked a very practical question to the lawyer, "Which of these three do you think was a neighbor to the man who fell into the hands of robbers?" The lawyer had no choice but to state the obvious. He answered, "The one who had mercy on him." Jesus drove home His final point as He told the man to go and do likewise—meaning go and be a neighbor to those that God places in your path, regardless of their race, ethnicity, or status in life.

Unfortunately, this is something that America has struggled with in the past and continues to struggle with in the present. Unless there are some fundamental changes in America, we will continue to struggle with racism in the future. As long as we can live in the same communities, needing the same resources to survive, and refuse to work together as neighbors, then we will never be the Christian nation we claim to be, nor will be the type of Christian neighbors God created us to be. When neighbors do not care about neighbors, it creates a caste system that allows systemic racism to become the foundation of American society.

Application of Luke 10:25-37

What three mistakes did the Jewish lawyer make in his misunderstanding of who was his neighbor?

1. **His first and greatest mistake was he assumed he had fulfilled the first commandment.**

   "You shall love the Lord your God with all your heart and with all your soul and with all your might." (Deuteronomy 6:5)

   It is only by having a genuine love relationship with Jesus Christ that we will ever have the capacity to love others God's way, as well as forgive those who have wronged us. Why? Because it is only by the indwelling power of the Holy Spirit residing in us, as faithful believers in Christ, that God can display His love through us, even to those that do not reciprocate God's love to us.

2. **He failed to realize unless he fulfilled the first commandment, he could not fulfill the second commandment.**

> *You shall not take vengeance, nor bear any grudge against the sons of your people, but you shall love your neighbor as yourself; I am the Lord. (Leviticus 19:18)*

If our vertical relationship with God is broken, then our horizontal relationship with others will be broken. We must follow all of God's Word and not pick and choose what we want to follow while ignoring what we don't.

3. **He failed to understand what it truly meant to be a neighbor.**

> *"Keep on loving one another as brothers and sisters. Do not forget to show hospitality to strangers, for by so doing some people have shown hospitality to angels without knowing it." (Hebrews 13:1-2)*

Being a neighbor is a command, not an option. Human decency requires that we are respectful and neighborly to one another, whether we agree, whether or not we look alike, or whether or not we are from the same socioeconomic status in life. Remember, the ground at the foot of the cross is level, so in God's kingdom, there is no racial, economic, or gender hierarchy as it relates to salvation.

What three mistakes do we still make today in misunderstanding who is our neighbor?

1. **We fail to realize our neighbor is whoever God places in our path, just like the Jewish lawyer.**

2. We fail to understand our neighbors will not always look like us or come from the same social, economic, or religious background, just like the Jewish lawyer.

3. We fail to realize God calls each of us—regardless of race or ethnicity—to be the type of neighbor that is willing to impact their surroundings for the glory of God, just like the Good Samaritan.

A Story That Matters

I recently read a story where Leon McCray, a black pastor in Virginia, looked out his window and saw some white men dumping an old appliance on his property. He went outside to tell them to stop while armed with his handgun for protection. Instead of heeding the pastor's warnings and stopping what they were doing, they argued with him and then physically assaulted him. They even told him, "Your black life doesn't matter!"

Ironically, when the sheriff deputy arrived, the black pastor was arrested and charged with brandishing a weapon on his property. He was handcuffed and humiliated in front of the white family. To add insult to injury, the black pastor was not allowed to tell his side of the story before being taken into custody by the sheriff deputy who had known him for 20 years. By the way, the pastor was the one who called 911.

The Shenandoah County Sheriff, Timothy Carter, dropped the charges against the black pastor because he said the arrest was not appropriate. However, the humiliation and abuse of racism had already taken its toll once again on another black man in America. After a real investigation, at least five members of the white family were arrested. Donny Salyers, 43, Dennis Salyers, 26, Farrah Salyers, 42, Christopher Sharp, 57, and Amanda Salyers, 26, faced hate crimes and assault charges. Also, they were charged with more serious crimes unrelated to the incident, due to outstanding warrants.

This incident did not change the fact that the black pastor was beaten, humiliated, and arrested on his property— when all he was doing was exercising his right to protect his property. This shows that America is more comfortable with Whites with guns than they are with Blacks with guns. Therefore, even how we apply the Second Amendment to the Constitution is also based on race. After the fact, the sheriff learned that the pastor had confronted the family members when he found two of them dumping a refrigerator on his property in Edinburg, Virginia, on June 1, 2020. Other white family members who were not part of the initial altercation showed up and helped escalate the situation.[182] This incident reveals that systemic racism is still prevalent in our society today and that law enforcement officials still tend to side against Blacks when they have confrontations with Whites. It also reveals that we still do not understand who our neighbor is, no matter what the Bible says.

---

182 Ralph R. Ortega. "Police apologize to black pastor who was arrested after he called cops because he was being beaten and abused by white family," *Mail Online*, 15 June 2020 [on-line]; accessed on 12 October 2020; available from https://www.dailymail.co.uk/news/article-8420801/Black-pastor-called-cops-beaten-white-family-arrested-pulling-gun.html; Internet. The police apologized to the black pastor from Woodstock, Virginia, who was arrested after he called police when a white family beat and cursed at him. Leon McCray, the pastor of Lighthouse Church & Marketplace Ministries International recalled the incident as 'a day that changed my life,' during his sermon that Sunday, he spoke about his encounter as well as the George Floyd protests and Black Lives Matter movement.

CHAPTER 7

KNOWING WHO'S YOUR ENEMY

The Armor of God

> *Finally, be strong in the Lord and the strength of His might. Put on the full armor of God so that you will be able to stand firm against the schemes of the devil. For our struggle is not against flesh and blood, but against the rulers, against the powers, against the world forces of this darkness, against the spiritual forces of wickedness in the heavenly places. Therefore, take up the full armor of God, so that you will be able to resist in the evil day, and having done everything, to stand firm. Stand firm, therefore, having girded your loins with truth, and having put on the breastplate of righteousness, and having shod your feet with the preparation of the gospel of peace; in addition to all, taking up the shield of faith with which you will be able to extinguish all the flaming arrows of the evil one. And take the helmet of salvation, and the sword of the Spirit, which is the word of God. (Ephesians 6:10-17)*

The United States Armed Forces, which includes the Air Force, Army, Navy, Marines, and Coast Guard, provide protection and security for our country against other hostile nations and evil entities that wish to do us harm and kill our citizens. To effectively provide our national defense, the primary strategy that makes our military successful, is not fighting amongst itself, but working together in unity, as one military force, not five separate branches of services with their agendas. Also, to be effective, our military must recognize who our allies are and who are our enemies. However, this has not always been the case because our U.S. Armed Forces once allowed segregation and racism to thrive among its ranks for many years, mainly because those issues thrived in everyday civilian life in America. An excellent example of this problem would be the Tuskegee Airmen.

The Tuskegee Airmen

In a book by Robert Edgerton titled, *Hidden Heroism: Black Soldiers in American Wars*, the author does an excellent job describing the heroism of African Americans throughout the history of the American Armed Forces. The book also documents how Caucasian Americans refused to recognize the multitude of achievements of black servicemen and women. The refusal by white Americans, in and outside the military, was based on racial hatred and bigotry that permeated the country. Many white Americans insisted for years that African Americans were "natural cowards" unsuited for military combat.[183] Also, Edgerton wrote that black men and women who served in America's military forces faced enormous racial discrimination and hatred, even in uniform. Unfortunately, even though black men and women wore our country's Armed Forces uniform, racism and hatred trumped patriotism. Like other minorities in society, our military had to struggle against Jim Crow laws in the South that affected almost every aspect of public and private life, including on military bases. (This why it is an absolute disgrace that we still have military bases named after racist traitors from the Confederate Army) Regrettably, America's Armed Forces were dominated by southern beliefs and values that degraded blacks, despite their military achievements.[184] Edgerton's book provides the backdrop of what the Tuskegee Airmen had to endure.

Until I joined the Air Force in 1985, I had never heard of the Tuskegee Airmen.[185] All airmen, regardless of rank or race, are taught the

---

183   Robert Edgerton. *Hidden Heroism: Black Soldiers in American Wars*. (Boulder: Westview Press), 2001,1.

184   Ibid.

185   The problem with American History is that it is told primarily through the eyes of white America, who control the narrative, including that for black history. Because our history has been suppressed, is why many Caucasian Americans do not know our story because many of us, as African Americans,

history of aviation in the military. One of the greatest stories of military achievement we learned about was the powerful story of the Tuskegee Airmen. However, I would argue that the Tuskegee Airmen were far more than a story of African American military accomplishments. It was also an amazing story that showed the resiliency, determination, and professionalism of Blacks, especially when we are oppressed by Whites. Unfortunately, not only did Whites in civilian society oppress and denigrate Blacks, but there were plans sanctioned by the federal government that sought to justify it.

> *Following World War I, several studies were made regarding the role of African Americans in the military. The studies were exercises to prove that blacks were inferior to whites and were suited only for menial positions. The War Department held the position that "The colored man had not been attracted to flying in the same manner or to the extent of the white man." African-Americans felt a strong and patriotic need to serve in their countries military service, however, and they fought to do so.*[186]

The Tuskegee Airmen were the first African American military aviators in the U. S. Armed Forces. When you look at their accomplishments, despite the racial climate of that day, they excelled, which was nothing short of amazing. Overall, 992 pilots graduated from the Tuskegee Air Field courses, and they flew 1,578 missions and 15,533 sorties, destroyed 261 enemy aircraft, and impressively won more than 850 medals.[187] During their years of operation, from

---

don't know our story either. Those of us that do know, need to take the time to educate others, which is another reason why I wrote this book. An additional problem is the truth of Black History is not taught in many American public schools, colleges, or universities, even those that I attended. Many Whites do not like talking about slavery, and only wish Blacks would stop bringing it up. The only problem is we cannot because we are still living under the lingering effects of it. As long as Whites write the textbooks for Blacks, especially without our input, many Blacks will never know our story, from 1619 until today.

186   Lynn M. Homan and Thomas Reilly. *The Tuskegee Airmen: Images of America.* (Chicago: Arcadia Publishing), 1998, 7.

187   Michael Ray, *"Tuskegee Airmen: United States Military Unit,"* Britannica, [on-line]; accessed on 13 October 2020; available from https://www.britannica.com/topic/Tuskegee-Airmen; Internet.

1940 to 1946, 996 pilots were trained at Tuskegee Army Air Field. Black fighter pilots from the 332nd were awarded close 1,000 medals, including 150 Distinguished Flying Cross medals. Seventy-six African American flyers were killed in action; others died in training accidents. Also, thirty-two were captured and held as Prisoners of War (POWs).[188] What made the Tuskegee Airmen such an inspirational story in our nation's sinful history are the conditions in which these black aviators had to operate and yet, still succeeded. These faithful airmen loved their country too, even though that country did not love them back—mainly because of the color of their skin. Unfortunately, the perception by many white military personnel, as well as Whites in civilian society at the time, was that Blacks were monkeys and lacked the intelligence and skillful ability to operate such a sophisticated piece of machinery, like a military fighter jet. Although well-trained for flying in combat, initially, the black pilots were not allowed to fly in combat because of racism.

> *While everyone in the United States was arguing whether a black man could fly an aircraft, in 1941, the First Lady, Eleanor Roosevelt, climbed into the cockpit with a black pilot, C. Alfred 'Chief' Anderson, for an aerial look at Alabama. Even after this vote of confidence, it still took another year and a lawsuit before the War Department finally announced the formation of an all-black flying unit. An unwelcome sight to many, these flying personnel broke yet another race barrier and dispelled the myth that 'blacks can't fly.' The story of the so-called Tuskegee Airmen from Alabama—highly successful black pilots in the Second World War—is a historic case about diversity in the Armed Forces. It testifies to the controversies that surround diversity, the difficulties it entails, and the successful ways in which it may be managed in the long run.[189]*

What sets military members apart for outstanding service and recognition to our country are the awards and decorations they earn

---

188   Robert Edgerton. *Hidden Heroism*, 145.

189   Joseph Soeters and Jan Van Der Meulen. *Cultural Diversity in the Armed Forces.* (New York: Routledge Press, 2007), 2.

in combat, which occur during the most hostile times our military personnel face in uniform. It is the highest honor to be recognized among your leadership and peers for performing in an outstanding manner under extreme pressure, especially in the military in a combat or deployment situation. Many Whites in the military, at that time, did not want to have to share their prestigious awards and medals with Blacks. If they did, they would have had to admit that Blacks were not monkeys but their equals. However, the same white supremacist attitude that poisoned civilian society adversely affected morale in the military.

Despite Racism, Blacks Excelled Anyway

What makes the story of the Tuskegee Airmen so interesting was that when black military aviators were finally allowed to participate in combat missions in Europe, it was not because many Whites' racist attitudes had changed, but due to necessity. White pilots were dying in combat while WWII continued to rage on. Therefore, trained pilots were needed desperately, even if they were black. This opened the door and allowed the well-trained black pilots from Tuskegee, Alabama, to show what they could do. They not only met the challenge, but they excelled far beyond what was expected of them. Their valiant efforts helped turn the tide of the war in favor of the allied forces.

Many valuable lessons were learned from the involvement of the Tuskegee Airmen in combat, especially since they had been previously denied because of racism. One major lesson, as well as an important reminder, was understanding how our U.S. Armed Forces essentially operate—it is mission-driven. That means it requires choosing the right personnel to execute a well-orchestrated plan to achieve a predetermined outcome. However, when plans don't go well—or if they are not thought through before being implemented—there will always be collateral damage or unintended consequences. In other words, military personnel, as well as civilians, die or are severely injured. Additionally, valuable resources are wasted. Therefore, if something hinders the U.S. Armed Forces from completing its plan or mission, it must make the necessary changes or suffer defeat. Well, segregation and racism were hindering the military from putting forth its best effort in WWII. Why? Because the military was not utilizing all its trained personal, so something had to change. As a result, senior military leaders, with the help of President Franklin Roosevelt, worked to change the culture in the military, by ending segregation and discharging Whites that refused to change their racist attitudes and actions toward Blacks.[190] Finally, white military personnel had to understand who was their enemy: The Axis alliance, which included Adolf Hitler and his German military, as well as the militaries of Italy, Japan, Hungary, Romania, and Bulgaria, and not the black soldiers in their ranks. This same principle can be applied today within society, but more importantly, in the Christian Church, especially in America. We need to understand who our enemy is, not our brothers and sisters in Christ, who do not look like us, but Satan and all his demonic followers, that work overtime to keep us divided.

What Americans Should Learn From The Tuskegee Airmen?

The U.S. Armed Forces made the necessary adjustments to rid itself of systemic racism—so that it could work together as one unified force to combat all our real enemies. However, America's civilian society has never made that adjustment. When Harry Truman ended racial segregation, as the President of the U.S., as well as the Commander and Chief of our Armed Forces, first he had to admit there was a problem that was adversely affecting our military personnel. Since Truman was

---

190   Andrew Glass, "Truman ends racial segregation in armed forces," *Politico*, 26 July 1948 [on-line]; Accessed on 16 September 2020; available from https://www.politico.com/story/2018/07/26/this-day-in-politics-july-26-1948-735081; Internet. On July 26, 1948, President Harry S. Truman signed an executive order aimed at ending racial segregation in the U.S. armed forces. Truman's 400-word directive, which bypassed Congress, stated: "It is hereby declared to be the policy of the president that there shall be equality of treatment and opportunity for all persons in the armed services without regard to race, color, religion or national origin. This policy shall be put into effect as rapidly as possible, having due regard to the time required to effectuate any necessary changes without impairing efficiency or morale."

in a position of power, he had the authority to do something about the problem, so he took action.

Just like our Armed Forces had to understand who their enemy was and make the necessary adjustment to change, there is still a valuable lesson to be learned. The Christian church in America desperately needs to learn that lesson. The church needs to understand who our enemy is, not each other, whether Black, White, Asian, Hispanic, or any other race or ethnicity. The apostle Paul addressed this issue with the church in Ephesus.

In the sixth chapter of Ephesians, Paul explained the true enemy of the church, as well as for every individual Christian, which is Satan. However, Paul used the illustration of the armor of a Roman soldier to explain the spiritual armor Jesus provides His true followers. Ephesians was one of Paul's prison epistles—meaning he wrote it while incarcerated under Roman authority. Therefore, Paul had an up-close, personal view of the Roman soldier's uniform and equipment. Not only was Paul keenly aware of Roman Soldiers, so was the early Christian church making this was a brilliant illustration.

In this final section of Chapter 6, Paul used several imperatives to challenge and strongly encourage Christians on how to be prepared and withstand Satan's constant attacks by completely obeying God's Word. Imperatives in the Greek language are very important to the scripture of a passage, especially when multiple imperatives are used in a short pericope, such as Ephesians 6:10-14. An imperative in Scripture is primarily a command, which means that it is not optional, especially if one desires to benefit from the command. Therefore, they should be taken seriously—and applied accordingly—along with the entire Bible if one desires maximum spiritual growth. Also, an imperative can be defined as essential or necessary rules, requirements, or obligations. The four imperatives Paul used here are: *be strong* (v.10), *put on* (v.11), *take up* (v. 13), and *stand firm* (v.14).[191]

Paul began by telling us to be strong in the Lord and the strength of His might (v. 10). The goal was for us to depend on God's strength and

---

191   Cleon L. Rogers, and Cleon Rogers III. *The New Linguistic and Exegetical Key to the Greek New Testament*. (Grand Rapids: Zondervan Publishing House, 1998), 446.

power and not man's, to endure the challenges of life. The phrase "put on the full armor of God" implied a sense of urgency—which meant to put it on now and never take it off (v. 10). If we obeyed these simple commands, it would allow us to stand firm against the devil's schemes (v. 11).[192] Our struggle is not against flesh and blood (human beings, regardless of race or ethnicity), but against rulers, against powers, against world forces of this darkness, against the spiritual forces of wickedness in the heavenly places (which is a long explanation for the devil and all of his entourage of evil spiritual forces).[193]

Paul made it evident that the equipment we need to wear daily was of extreme importance, which is why he used the conjunction "therefore" to continue to strengthen his argument. "Take up the full armor of God" is an important command the Lord provides so that we will be able to resist in the evil day (the day Satan attacks), and when we have done everything to stand, to keep standing firm—which means we are never to give up our position of advantage in Christ.[194]

In verses 14-17, Paul explained the six pieces of spiritual armor that provide every believer the ability to live an abundant and effective life, which are the *belt of truth,* the *breastplate of righteousness,* the *shield*

---

192   E.D. Radmacher, R.B. Allen and H.W. House. *Nelson's New Illustrated Bible Commentary.* (Nashville: Thomas Nelson Publishers), 1999, 1540. The whole armor of God is the believer's protection against evil and the Evil One. Paul presented the extended metaphor of the battle dress roughly according to the order in which the various pieces were put on. Wiles of the devil are Satan's subtle tricks to defeat Christians in spiritual warfare (2 Cor. 11:3).

193   Ibid. Our real battle is not with human cultists, false religionists, atheists, agnostics, and pseudo-Christians, but with the demonic beings working through them, of which even the flesh and blood opponents themselves are sometimes unaware.

194   M. Anders, *Galatians-Colossians,* Vol. 8. (Nashville: Broadman & Holman Publishers), 1999, 190. When we have obeyed all the instructions implicit in the full armor of God, we can resist Satan's attempts to deceive and destroy us. The day of evil is anytime during this era in history until Jesus returns. All days are evil in their potential and become evil in reality when Satan or his demons decide to use that day to attack you. The clear implication here is that, if the Christian has all his armor on, he has the ability to stand firm against Satan.

of faith, the *helmet of salvation,* the *shoes of the gospel,* and the *sword of the Spirit*—which is the Word of God.[195]

Can We Be Honest?

Perhaps, one of the best ways to express how many African Americans feel about racism in America was best summed up by the former coach of the Los Angeles Clippers professional basketball team and former National Basketball Association (NBA) player. While he was emotional and his voice cracking, Glen "Doc" Rivers stated, "It's amazing to me, why we keep loving this country, and this country does not love us back." Rivers, an African American, made this comment in August 2020 during the NBA playoffs. The media had asked him a question about Jacob Blake being shot in the back seven times by police in Wisconsin.[196] Rivers was right on the money with his candid but accurate assessment. Our history has told a nightmarish story about the plight of Blacks in America, which shouts loud and clear that the majority of white America has not appreciated us.

It appears to me that we are beloved as entertainers and athletes, but not as leaders, thinkers, educators, doctors, lawyers, scientists, or pastors, to name a few. If we are athletic and talented and can play a professional sport that can earn wealthy white millionaires and billionaires a lot more money, we are beloved by owners and fans alike. However, the moment we try to step into leadership roles and run an organization, regardless of whether it is at the local, state, or national level, we instantly get a lot of vitriol and resistance. Even in the NBA

---

195   W. W. Wiersbe. *Wiersbe's expository outlines on the New Testament.* (Wheaton: Victor Books), 1992, 555. These pieces of armor are for the believer's protection; the sword of the Spirit and prayer are weapons for attacking Satan's strongholds and defeating him. The Christian must fight spiritual enemies with spiritual weapons (2 Cor. 10:4), and the Word of God is the only sword we need. God's sword has life and power (Heb. 4:12) and never grows dull. Christians conquer as they understand God's Word, memorize it, and obey it.

196   Michael Pina, "Doc Rivers has been fighting racism all his life," *Yahoo,* 26 August 2020 [on-line]; accessed on 13 October 2020; available from Https://www.Yahoo.Com/Lifestyle/Doc-Rivers-Fighting-Racism-Life-153313551.Html; Internet.

and the National Football League (NFL), where the vast majority of players are Black, the leadership in those major sports is dismal at best. This does not just happen in professional sports; it also happens in many other areas of society, such as corporate America.[197]

Applications of Ephesians 6:10-17

Why do the various races of people on this earth continue to fight against one another instead of working in unity with one another?

Three Major Reasons:

1. We fail to follow Christ. (v.10)

   - Because we do not know Him (for the pardoning of our sins)
   - Because we are not willing to trust Him or obey Him, even if we know Him
   - Because we have convinced ourselves that we are okay without Him

2. We fail to wear God's armor of protection. (v.11)

   - Because there are Christians that somehow do not know God has spiritual armor for His children
   - Because we somehow want to try and walk with God on our terms

---

197   Jeanne Sahadi, "After years of talking about diversity, the number of black leaders at US Companies is still dismal," CNN Business, 2 June 2020; [on-line]; accessed on 13 October 2020; available from After years of talking about diversity, the number of black leaders at US companies is still dismal - CNN ; Internet. True corporate diversity can't be achieved unless it's reflected at the top. And given the persistent dearth of black professionals in power roles at major companies, corporate America has a long way to go. There's growing awareness of the need for diversity at all levels of the workplace -- not just because giving equal opportunities to all is the right thing to do, but because it helps companies better innovate and compete as US demographics and consumer habits change. Yet numerous studies show the number of black professionals on boards and in C-suite roles range from not great to dismal.

- Because we fail to put God first and keep Him first

3. **We fail to recognize who our real enemy is. (v.12)**
   - Because we are so busy fighting with other beliefs
   - Because the devil is winning the battle of keeping us confused
   - Because we are not familiar with God's Kingdom Agenda
   - Because even though we might be believers, we still are comfortable with racism or racist tendencies or ideas

What lessons should we learn from this passage about spiritual warfare?

1. **Satan and his demonic forces are real.** So, don't underestimate him or give him ammunition to use against you. (Note: Sin gives Satan ammunition).

2. **We face three enemies: the world, our flesh, and the devil.** In some cases, the three are so interwoven that it's difficult to tell them apart.

3. **Spiritual warfare is the devil's attempt to deceive us and divide us.** You make it much harder when you reject those that God places in your path to walk this journey with or give you Godly instruction from God's Word, such as the right pastor or church

4. **One of Satan's subtle strategies.** Entice us to operate in our natural strength, relying on our ability, without Christ's help. Satan's goal is to get us as believers to walk alone, without a church home, especially during a pandemic or crisis, without spiritual accountability, or without pastoral leadership, so he would then be able to manipulate your life. At that point, it would be easy because you will be outside the will of God

5. **We don't have to walk around spiritually naked.** God provides us spiritual armor for the spiritual battle. Although God provides us spiritual armor, we still must remain faithful to Jesus Christ to put it on, and keep it on.

CHAPTER 8

GOD'S ANSWER TO RACISM

The Diverse Multitude Of The Crowd

Now there were Jews living in Jerusalem, devout men from every nation under heaven. And when this sound occurred, the crowd came together, and were bewildered because each one of them was hearing them speak in his own language. They were amazed and astonished, saying, "Why, are not all these who are speaking Galileans And how is it that we each hear them in our own language to which we were born? Parthians and Medes and Elamites, and residents of Mesopotamia, Judea and Cappadocia, Pontus and Asia, Phrygia and Pamphylia, Egypt and the districts of Libya around Cyrene, and visitors from Rome, both Jews and proselytes, Cretans and Arabs—we hear them in our own tongues speaking of the mighty deeds of God." And they all continued in amazement and great perplexity, saying to one another, "What does this mean?" But others were mocking and saying, "They are full of sweet wine." (Acts 2:5-13)

Fifty-six years ago, on December 18, 1963, Dr. Martin Luther King, Jr. was the guest speaker at Western Michigan University in Kalamazoo, while during a Q&A session with students and faculty, he was asked the following question, "Don't you feel that integration can only be started and realized in the Christian church, not in schools or by other means?"[198] The student said that this would be a means of

---

198 "MLK at Western University Libraries," 8 June 2020 [on-line]; accessed on 17 September 2020; available from https://libguides.wmich.edu/mlkatwmu/

seeing just who are truly Christians. The question was asked to address segregation in America and the role of the Christian church. Dr, King responded with the following answer.

> *As a preacher, I would certainly have to agree with this. I must admit that I have gone through those moments when I was greatly disappointed with the church and what it has done in this period of social change. We must face the fact that in America, the church is still the most segregated major institution in America. At 11:00 on Sunday morning when we stand and sing and Christ has no east or west, we stand at the most segregated hour in this nation. This is tragic. Nobody of honesty can overlook this. Now, I'm sure that if the church had taken a stronger stand all along, we wouldn't have many of the problems that we have (today). The first way that the church can repent, the first way that it can move out into the arena of social reform is to remove the yoke of segregation from its own body. Now, I'm not saying that society must sit down and wait on a spiritual and moribund church as we've so often seen. I think it should have started in the church, but since it didn't start in the church, our society needed to move on. The church, itself, will stand under the judgment of God. Now that the mistake of the past has been made, I think that the opportunity of the future is to really go out and to transform American society, and where else is there a better place than in the institution that should serve as the moral guardian of the community. The institution should preach brotherhood and make it a reality within its own body.*

This was a really good question, but Dr. King's answer knocked the ball out of the park. I agree one hundred percent with Dr. King. If he were still alive today, Dr. King would be far more disappointed because the church (as a whole) remains quiet during the current period of racial unrest. Also, I agree that the church needs to repent for its role in slavery and segregation. As Dr. King stated, the church will be judged by God for not being what God created it to be, which

---

QandA; Internet. This transcript was the question and answer guide detailing Dr. Martin Luther King, Jr.'s, December 18, 1963, speech at Western Michigan University.

is supposed to be a reflection of His glory on this earth. The apostle Peter addressed this issue when he said, "For it is time for judgment to begin with the household of God; and if it begins with us first, what will be the outcome for those who do not obey the gospel of God?" (1 Peter 4:17) This passage is quite revealing because it lets America know that God will one day judge us for our sinful past—this includes slavery, which reveals our racist past that still affects us in the present. If America remains on the same course and does not change, racism will continue to be a big part of our future.

The Devastation Of Racism

Racism is a belief or doctrine that inherent differences among the various human races determine cultural or individual achievement, usually involving the idea that one's race is superior and has the right to rule others.[199] Since 1619, when the first African slaves arrived on American soil, racism has been entrenched in American culture, but it didn't have to be that way. Why is that the case? Because God long ago provided us with the answer to racism, when He gave up His only Son on the cross at Calvary, which established the church. Jesus came preaching a message of hope, unity, forgiveness, and love, which was possible through faith in Him. If only the early church in America had read, studied, and applied the Scriptures to their lives daily, our nation would have been in a better place from the beginning, especially as the nation became more racially diverse.

Could you imagine if Whites would have brought Africans to America, not as slaves in chains, but voluntarily as human beings to help build a racially diverse nation that placed God first, obeyed His Word, and loved their neighbor as they loved themselves? What a different trajectory this nation would have taken from the beginning! However, because that was not the case, and Whites did allow their new nation to be soiled by slavery, hatred, and mistreatment of Africans, America began with the impending judgment of God against it. White Christians in colonial America were the early church on our nation's soil, and not

---

199   Tony Evans, *Oneness Embraced: A Fresh Look At Reconciliation, The Kingdom, and Justice* (Chicago: Moody Press, 2011), 17

only did they fail God, but they also failed the nation. Since they called themselves Christians, they should have taken the time to study the beginning of the Christian church on *the day of Pentecost* [200] and what the remainder of the Bible has to say about the subject of racism, as well as what God expects from those who claim they are His children.

The Holy Spirit Makes The Difference

In Acts chapter 2:5-13, Luke describes what the early church was like in the Roman empire.[201] However, verses 1-4 allow us to put these verses into their proper context for how the chapter unfolds. Jesus' disciples gathered in the upper room, which included the women, Mary, the mother of Jesus, and His biological brothers (1:13-14). They obeyed Jesus' instructions and waited on the outpouring of the Holy Spirit. Chapter 2 began with that outpouring from heaven. Luke described a noise like the sound of a violent rushing wind, which filled the whole house where they were sitting. This day was the fulfillment of the prophet Joel's prophecy (Joel 2:28-29).

Moreover, God used this divine event to get the attention of the multitude of Jews that were present in Jerusalem to celebrate Pentecost. Also, God used the Jewish celebration of Pentecost to change history by birthing the Christian church.[202] Once the Holy Spirit came, there

---

200   Baker, W. H. *Evangelical Commentary on the Bible: Acts*, Vol. 3, (Grand Rapids: Baker Book House, 1995), 887. The day of Pentecost was also known as the Feast of Weeks and was commanded, along with six other holy days like Passover and the Feast of Tabernacles, in Leviticus 23:15–21. It was a festive time and tended to draw religious pilgrims from all over the world. This occasion provides a unique opportunity in which to proclaim the new message of the gospel.

201   Ken Anderson. *Roman and America – Comparing to the Ancient Roman Empire*, 5 May 2020 [On Line]; accessed on 17 September 2020; available from https://probe.org/rome-and-america/; Internet. Ironically, America mimics many sinful similarities to the Roman empire. Some similarities that played a significant role in the Rome's decline. 1. Decline of the family. 2. Spiritual decline. 3. American Elitism.

202   *Holman Illustrated Bible Handbook: Comprehensive Background Information for the Bible's 66 Books*. (Nashville: Holman Bible Publishers, 2012), 356. Acts opens by linking the book with the Gospel, Luke's "first narrative." Like the Gospel (Luke 1:3). The book is dedicated to Theophilus. The first

was enormous evidence of His presence. The 120 in the upper room were all filled with the Holy Spirit and began to speak with other tongues, as the Spirit gave them utterance.[203] It was these tongues that got the multitude's attention. However, these tongues were not ecstatic utterances or unintelligent sounds no one could understand. The way we know that is because of context. There are two words used here that help us understand what was going on. First is the Greek word *glossa*, which is translated tongue (v.4). Second is the Greek word *dialektos*, which is translated language (vs. 6, 8). We get our English word dialect from this word.

What the people heard was not what modern-day tongue speakers have been led to believe. This was not the ecstatic language Paul dealt with in Corinth (1 Cor 14:23).[204] Also, these verses described the multitude of races and ethnicities present for the outpouring of the Holy Spirit and the birth of the church. The Jews listed were from every nation under heaven. Although they were from outside Palestine, God brought them together for His divine purpose. Luke named fifteen different geographical locations and clearly stated that the citizens of those places heard Peter and the others declare God's wonderful works in languages they could understand.[205] The significance of Acts 2 is the multitude that was present from all over the Roman empire. What these Jews had in common was their religion, which was Judaism. However,

---

two chapters of Acts in many ways correspond to the first two chapters of the Gospel of Luke: Luke 1-2 dealing with the birth of the Savior, Acts 1-2 with the birth of the church. Just as Jesus was born of the Holy Spirit (Luke 1:35), the same Holy Spirit is the vital force in the life of the church. Acts 1 and 2 relate the coming of the Spirit to the church. Acts 1 deals with the events leading up to the Spirit's coming, and chapter 2 relates that coming at Pentecost. Without Pentecost there would been no further story in Acts.

203   J. B. Polhill. *Acts*, Vol. 26, (Nashville: Broadman & Holman Publishers, 1992), 97. The coming of the Spirit is described in three carefully constructed parallel statements, each pointing to an aspect of the event: a *sound* came … and it filled the house (v. 2); *tongues* appeared … and one sat on each of them (v. 3); they were filled with the Holy Spirit … and *began to speak* in other tongues (v. 4). The emphasis is on the objectivity of the event. It was audible, visible, and manifested itself in an outward demonstration of inspired speech

204   Ibid.

205   W.W. Wiersbe, *The Bible Exposition Commentary*, Vol. 1. (Wheaton: Victor Books, 1996), 408.

they were from a multitude of different races and ethnicities.[206] The crowd responded to what they were witnessing from the powerful move of the Holy Spirit. "And they all continued in amazement and great perplexity, saying to one another, "What does this mean?" But others were mocking and saying, "They are full of sweet wine" (vs. 13-14). Most were amazed, but some thought the disciples were drunk. However, Peter is led by the Holy Spirit, who preached one of the most powerful sermons about Jesus' life, death, burial, and Resurrection, in the entire Bible.

The Birth Of The Christian Church

Now when they heard this, they were pierced to the heart, and said to Peter and the rest of the apostles, "Brethren, what shall we do?" Peter said to them, "Repent, and each of you be baptized in the name of Jesus Christ for the forgiveness of your sins; and you will receive the gift of the Holy Spirit. For the promise is for you and your children and for all who are far off, as many as the Lord our God will call to Himself." And with many other words he solemnly testified and kept on exhorting them, saying, "Be saved from this perverse generation! So then, those who had received his word were baptized; and that day there were added about three thousand souls. They were continually devoting themselves to the apostles' teaching and to fellowship, to the breaking of bread, and to prayer. (Acts 2:37-42)

---

206 W. H. Mare, *New Testament Background Commentary: A New Dictionary of Words, Phrases and Situations in Bible Order* (Ross-shire, UK: Mentor Books, 2004), 148. The list of people from fifteen nations starts with one group to the East in the areas of modern day Iran and Iraq (Parthians, Medes, and Elamites, residents of Mesopotamia where Jews had been taken captive to Assyria and Babylon); and the list proceeds west to Judea; and then north to Asia Minor (Cappadocia, Pontus, Asia, Phrygia and Pamphylia); then to North Africa (Egypt, in which two districts of Alexandria were Jewish, and parts of Libya near Cyrene); then to Rome; and finally the list includes two widely separated areas, one, the island of Crete (a people thought of as seafarers) northwest of Jerusalem, and the other, Arabia (possibly a reference to Nabataean Jews and other areas of the Arabian Peninsula where Jews were living as far south as Yemen), located to the east and south of the city.

What transpired after Peter's powerful sermon is recorded in this section of the chapter. It says they were pierced to the heart, which means they were convicted of their sins—by the Holy Spirit. To prove they were moved by the message, they asked what shall they do. Peter responded by telling them to repent. This word is extremely important to the salvation of humanity. The Greek word is *mateneo*, which means to have a change of mind, will, or actions,[207] or as I like to say, to change your stinking thinking. As a man thinketh in his heart, so is he (Prov 23:7). What that tells us is, you will never change the way you live unless you change the way you think because our thought process determines our actions or behavior. So, when a person has truly repented, you will know because their behavior will change, which is related to Romans 12:2, "And be not conformed to this world: but be ye transformed by the renewing of your mind, that ye may prove what is the good, and acceptable, and perfect, will of God."

Peter's response was almost programmatic in that he presented them with four essentials of the conversion experience (v. 38): repentance, baptism in the name of Jesus Christ, the forgiveness of sins, and receipt of the Spirit.[208] From the multitude of Jews present at Pentecost, many of them responded, and the church was birthed at that moment. This is an extremely important revelation in this text because it lets us know that the first Christians came from all over the known world (Roman world) at that time and that the church was multicultural and multiracial.

Although not all of the multitude (at this time) accepted Christ as their personal Savior and Lord, approximately 3,000 of them did. How did the early church handle all the racial and ethnic diversity? "They were continually devoting themselves to the apostles' teaching and to fellowship, to the breaking of bread and to prayer" (v. 42). Because these racially diverse groups of new Christians surrendered to Jesus, we learn about their genuine commitment. Luke taught four

---

207   J.D. Barry, D. Mangum, D.R. Brown, M.S. Heiser, M. Custis, E. Ritzema, D. Bomar, *Faithlife Study Bible: Acts 2:38*. (Bellingham, WA: Lexham Press, 2016). Peter calls the people to believe that Jesus is the Messiah promised in the Old Testament.

208   J. B. Polhill, 116.

things that they devoted themselves to that helped bring them together and allowed the Christian church to grow. They devoted themselves to the apostle teachings, fellowship, breaking of bread, and prayer. If every Christian church today would apply these four principles and follow the early church's model, it would truly be the light of the world (Matthew 5:14-16) and help solve the problem of racism and racial division.

America Needs To Learn From The Early Church

How does Acts Chapter 2 relate to America's founding? We study history to learn from our past mistakes so that we don't repeat the same mistakes in the future. In this book, I researched America's sinful past, going back to 1619, when the first African slaves arrived, to the Trans-Atlantic Slave Trade, the Civil War, the Jim Crow era, the race riots, the KKK, the Civil Rights era, and the criminal justice system and police brutality, that continues to this day. Our history is painful, especially for people of color. However, it is time for America to have a reckoning with its past. One day, every American will have to stand before God and give an account of our sins, and how we treated others that God placed in our paths.

Based on the lifestyle we live, God will judge us for our actions. For many Americans, that encounter is not going to go too well because their actions were certainly not approved by God, and they never genuinely asked for forgiveness—and place their faith in Jesus Christ as Savior and Lord. America is very religious in every respect, just like Rome was in Paul's day, which he addressed this issue, "So Paul stood in the Areopagus and said, "Men of Athens, I see that you are very religious in all respects" (Romans 17:22). As Paul walked the streets of Athens, Greece, he was alarmed by the worship of idols he witnessed throughout the city (Rom. 17:16). Could you imagine if the apostle Paul walked the streets of America today? I would submit to you that his spirit would be even more deeply distressed than he was in Roman—because we are much more of an idol worshiping nation. But the sad thing is, we think we are a Christian nation, which will certainly bring a greater judgment from God. Paul witnessed religion at its best but still felt the need to proclaim God's truth to a group of men who believed they already had the truth, which they did not. Paul's message was simple: religion nor philosophy can save you, but Jesus can and will if you are willing to trust Him!

Now for the millions of Americans who have already passed, well they have made their bed and must lie in it. If they did not know the Lord Jesus as their personal Savior and Lord, well, they won't get a do-over—they will have to answer to God for their decisions and lifestyle, just like the rest of us. However, those of us still alive today have an opportunity to get our heart and life right with Jesus before it is too late. Furthermore, tomorrow is not promised! So, this moment may be all you have left. So, if today was your last day on this earth, where would you spend eternity? Smoking or non-smoking! Hell, or Heaven!

Application of Acts 2:5-13

What is God's answer to the sin, hatred, division, and racism in America and around the world?

The Day of Pentecost

1. **The Miracle (vs. 1-8)**

The outpouring of the Holy Spirit. God showed up to change the trajectory of human history. God's goal was, and still is, to turn man from his course of self-destruction and eternity to hell (Revelations 20:15).

2. **The Multitude (vs. 9-13)**

The multicultural, multiracial group of Jews from all over the Roman Empire met in Jerusalem on the Day of Pentecost. And because of the outpouring of the Holy Spirit, they were privileged to hear God's Word and be the first to be offered salvation among the multitude.

3. **The Message (vs. 14-36)**

From the beginning of time, the sins of all humanity played a crucial role in Jesus' death on the cross at Calvary (this includes my sins as well as yours). To pay the penalty required, for our sins, Jesus, the true Messiah, and only one qualified, to save us, was put to death voluntarily, but early, on Sunday morning, he got up with all power in His hand! In the process, defeating the bondage of death, hell, and the grave.

Now, if you are willing to trust your life to Jesus, as Savior and Lord, you can not only be forgiven for your sins, but you can live an abundant life in Christ as a kingdom citizen—just simply ask and repent.

4. The Mission (vs. 41-47)

The mission began with a unified body of Christ, including a multitude of races and ethnicities, to honor and glorify God so that they could reach the lost and disciple the saved! Today, the Christian church needs to follow that example, pick up that mantle, and continue Christ's mission (Matthew 28:19-20). The world is full of lost people, from every race and ethnicity, that do not know the Lord Jesus and are on their way to hell if they do not make a change before it is too late.

When the body of Christ today has chosen to remain divided and continue in separate houses of worship, solely based on race, and not always because of doctrine, it sends a loud message to God. It says that we do not agree with Your model or Your goal for unity. Why? Simply put, we don't care what you want God, we have our own goals, and like our model much better—it's just easier that way, and because of that, we are just going to take our chances with You in the end—says the current church around the world, especially in America.

Having acknowledged that, if there was ever a time that the Black Church, White Church, Asian Church, Hispanic Church, and others churches, need to put aside their differences and years of grievances, especially those based solely on race, and start working together, that time is right now, without delay! God united the Jews, Gentiles, and Samaritans then; therefore, that is God's model for His church today. God did not change His mind because we changed ours!

What should we learn from today's message?

1. The Church of Jesus Christ is God's answer to all of man's problems—including sin, hatred, division, and racism.
2. The Holy Spirit empowers us to get along with one another and love one another, and do God's Kingdom work together.
3. The Church must take the lead in showing agape love and unity to the lost world around us. Without the church taking the lead, no one else will be qualified and empowered by God to do so—because God created His church, the body of Christ, for that divine purpose, and to be a reflection of His glory.

CHAPTER 9

WHEN GRACE OVERCOMES RACE

The Samaritan Woman Meets Jesus

There came a woman of Samaria to draw water. Jesus *said to her, "Give Me a drink." For His disciples had gone away into the city to buy food. Therefore the Samaritan woman *said to Him, "How is it that You, being a Jew, ask me for a drink since I am a Samaritan woman?" (For Jews have no dealings with Samaritans.) Jesus answered and said to her, "If you knew the gift of God, and who it is who says to you, 'Give Me a drink,' you would have asked Him, and He would have given you living water." She said to Him, "Sir, You have nothing to draw with and the well is deep; where then do You get that living water? You are not greater than our father Jacob, are You, who gave us the well, and drank of it himself and his sons and his cattle?" Jesus answered and said to her, "Everyone who drinks of this water will thirst again; but whoever drinks of the water that I will give him shall never thirst; but the water that I will give him will become in him a well of water springing up to eternal life." The woman *said to Him, "Sir, give me this water, so I will not be thirsty nor come all the way here to draw." He said to her, "Go, call your husband and come here." The woman answered and said, "I have no husband." Jesus *said to her, "You have correctly said, 'I have no husband'; for you have had five husbands, and the one whom you now have is not your husband; this you have said truly." The woman *said to Him, "Sir, I perceive that You are a prophet. Our fathers worshiped in this *mountain, and you people say that in Jerusalem is the place where men ought to worship." Jesus said to her, "Woman, believe Me, an hour is coming when neither in this mountain nor in Jerusalem will you worship the Father. You worship what you do not know; we worship what we know, for salvation is from the Jews. But an hour is coming, and now is, when the true worshipers will worship the Father in spirit and truth; for such people the Father seeks to be His worshipers. God is spirit, and those who worship Him must worship in spirit and truth." The woman *said to Him, "I know that Messiah is coming (He who is called Christ); when that One comes, He will declare all things to us." Jesus *said to her, "I who speak to you am He." (John 4:7-26)*

The concept of grace unfolds gradually in Scripture. Its roots are found in the Old Testament Hebrew word *chen* describe the compassionate response of a superior to an inferior, suggesting that kindness, grace, or favor is undeserved. In this case, God is superior, and we are inferior to Him because He is sovereign, and we are not. However, we are not inferior to each other, regardless of race or ethnicity, because, once again, we are all created in God's image and likeness. Moses understood this when he prayed, "Now, therefore, I pray to You, if I have found favor in Your sight, let me know Your ways that I may know You, so that I may find favor in Your sight. Consider too, that this nation is Your people" (Exodus 33:13).[209] Moses recognized this principle because he knew that without God's favor and guidance, he as well as Israelites, would be in trouble.

A Further Understanding Of Grace

There is also another word in the Old Testament that plays a major role in God's relationship with those He has chosen. The Hebrew word *hessed* can also be translated as grace or loving-kindness. This word is best translated as covenantal love, which in its essence, is divine grace. It is the type of love that only a true believer in Yahweh in the Old

---

[209] Don Campbell, Wendell Johnston, John Walvoord, and John Witmer, *The Theological Workbook: The 200 Most Important Theological Terms and Their Relevance for Today*. (Nashville: Word Publishing, 2000), 147.

Testament and Christ in the New Testament can experience because it requires an intimate relationship. By the way, Christ is the Yahweh of the Old as well as New Testament because He is the great I AM.

In layman's terms, an example of a biblical covenant in the Old Testament was the agreement between God and the Israelites. God promised to love and protect them but required loyalty to His kingdom agenda in return—which was divine grace. However, the word covenant has often been misunderstood because it is treated as a mere contract. The difference is a covenant that God has made cannot be broken, but it can go unfulfilled by man, which often happened in Scripture, and continues to happen today. The point is God never reneges on His end, even if we renege on ours. However, we will be held accountable by God, for which we will be judged.

On the other hand, a man-made contract can be broken because both parties have equal grounds for creating the document or agreement. Therefore, at any time, either party is not pleased; for whatever reason, they can revoke. Unfortunately, this is how many marriages are treated in America. Instead, marriage should be treated as a covenant, which is what God created marriage to be. Instead, it is treated as a mere contract, which is why divorce happens so often.

In the New Testament, the concept of grace is fully developed. Our English word grace comes from the Greek word *charis*. Grace is often referred to as unmerited favor (meaning undeserved), but it can also be defined as kindness, leniency, compassion, forgiveness, or mercifulness. With the coming of Christ, grace took on its complete meaning (John 1:17).[210] In John Chapter 4, we find an important example of divine grace—regarding how Jesus dealt with the Samaritan woman at the well. In layman's terms, I like Tony Evans' definition of grace.

> *Theologians have developed a classic definition of this great concept called Grace. They define it as God's unmerited, or undeserved favor toward sinners. I define grace as the inexhaustible supply of God's goodness whereby He does for us what we could never do for ourselves. Grace has to do with the work of God whereby He*

---

[210] Ibid.

breaks into history to solve a problem that we could never solve by ourselves. Grace is "the gift of God."[211]

For by grace you have been saved through faith, and this is not of yourselves, it is the gift of God; not a result of works, so that no one may boast. For we are His workmanship, created in Christ Jesus for good works, which God prepared beforehand so that we would walk in them. [Ephesians 2:8-10]

Old preachers define grace by the following: God paid a debt He didn't owe because we owed a debt we could pay! Therefore, grace is not something we earn; it is something God freely gives—when we turn our heart and lives over to His will. However, once God extends grace to us, we should extend grace to others, even those that do not look like us. We do this by allowing God's unconditional love to flow through us by the power of the Holy Spirit working in us.

America Has Not Learned The Meaning Of Grace

Grace is not a word that can be applied to America as a nation. Throughout our history, any grace demonstrated was only applied to one race (Whites), but not to all others (like Blacks). Whites controlled all aspects of American society, including the Government: Legislative, Executive, and Judicial branches at every level, local, state, and national. Also, Whites control criminal justice, commerce and banking, education, housing, transportation, and aviation. As a result, Whites controlled grace in America. It might sound strange saying humans can control grace, but in the sense that they controlled the resources that everyone else needed, they controlled grace—human, not divine. When society lacks grace, it also lacks mercy and love as well.[212] Therefore, the absence of true reverence for God has led America to

---

211 Toney Evans. *Totally Saved: Understanding, Experiencing and Enjoying the Greatness of Your Salvation.* (Chicago: Moody Press), 110. 2002.

212 Ibid. In Ephesians 2:4-5 Paul pointed out the relationship of three important doctrinal words, love, mercy, and grace: "But because of his great love for us, God, who is rich in mercy, made us alive with Christ even when we were dead in transgressions—it is by grace you have been saved."

oppress its citizens, as well as enslave them, especially those that have been deemed less than human.

The word oppressed can be defined as burdened, dominated, cruel, persecuted, or demoralized, which exactly describes what African slaves were subjected to in America. Blacks were oppressed because they were under the complete control of Whites that held all the power and did not seek to use that power to make life better for the minority group. They used it to make the lives of Blacks worse. As a result, Blacks were powerless to defend themselves because all levels of government were used against them. Not only did the government turn their back on Blacks, so did American society.

To add insult to injury, the white church in America turned its back on slaves as well. Although many white churches in America allowed Blacks to attend services, Blacks were still not treated equally. Blacks were obligated to sit in the back of the church or the balcony—segregated from Whites. Blacks were not allowed to lead Whites in the church—therefore, Whites used the Bible to teach Blacks a version of the Bible that upheld their supremacy. Blacks were not allowed to participate in the Lord Supper with Whites, thus violating the biblical meaning of communion, which is first, a vertical relationship with God and a horizontal relationship with other believers.[213] Therefore, not only was this a form of racial oppression, but it also lacked grace. The key point here is this: the lack of God's grace in the hearts of white Christians (during and after slavery) was why the same racism outside the church made its way inside the church. Likewise, if a human being cannot be treated with dignity and humanity in the church—since all of mankind was created in the image of God—then he does not stand a chance of being treated equally in society.

In a quote by Randy Woodley, "Call it dehumanization, ethnocentrism, or cultural cannibalism—when one culture begins to lift itself as better than another, and it has the power to do so, any

---

[213] Michael O. Emerson and Christian Smith. *Divided by Faith*, 39. Almost immediately after the Civil War, before the formal institution of Jim Crow segregation, African Americans in frustration left the white churches in mass to form their own churches. Denied equal participation in the existing churches, "the move toward racially separate churches was not a matter of doctrinal agreement, but a protest against unequal and restrictive treatment.

act of deprivation can be, and has been 'justified.' And when such atrocities take place, Satan has a field day." [214] Woodley made these comments in a section of his book where he talked about the *cost of dehumanization*. He stated that dehumanization was a direct result of White condescension—the notion that one person or culture has more of a right to exist than another or than all others. Furthermore, he added, their haughtiness of attitude assumes superiority over the other person or culture.[215] I would argue that this still exists today but has morphed into white privilege—which again, shows a lack of grace.

Two Of The Greatest Tragedies In Our History

Without question, two of the greatest tragedies in the history of humanity were the Israelites in Egypt and Africans in America. Both groups faced very similar hardships. They both were held in bondage, against their will, and forced to be slaves in separate nations that were not their own. The inhumane way the Jews and Africans were treated; revealed just how evil mankind can be against its fellow man, especially when they do not have a personal relationship with our Savior and Lord. Therefore, we know there is a direct correlation between sinfulness in a nation and the absence of God in that nation.

When a nation does not know God, nor desires to walk with God, those that govern that nation are prone to oppress its citizens, as well as non-citizens, that live within their borders. What makes this even worse is when the people in charge use race, ethnicity, or gender to devalue a person's worth or importance as a human being. From American's founding as a nation, the oppression of everyone else that was not a white male of European descent was evident. Not even white European women were treated as equals. Subsequently, the Indigenous people that were here long before white Europeans arrived were called Indians because Christopher Columbus thought he had landed in India. What's sad is, the name stuck because white European men became the dominant race and have not relinquished

---

214   Randy Woodley. *Living in Color: Embracing God's Passion for Christ Diversity*, 23-24.

215   Ibid.

that title in America to this day. Therefore, everyone else that would eventually come to America, whether voluntarily or involuntarily, was forced to subjugate themselves to the will of the white majority. What this teaches us is that white Americans lacked the grace to properly deal with the racial diversity of a young nation, which has not changed to this very day.

School Is Now In

As we return to John Chapter 4, we find the perfect example of how a majority race should deal with a race in the minority. The relationship between Jews and Samaritans was non-existent because of their past. From the beginning of the Samaritan race, they were hated by the Jews as a people group. In 722 B.C., the Assyrians conquered the North Kingdom of Israel. At that time, the kingdom of Israel was divided into separate kingdoms (nations), which resulted from Solomon's heart being turned away from God by the ungodly foreign women he married. However, the divided monarchy did not come to pass until after his son Rehoboam became king.

The Assyrians took the various people they had conquered from various nations and placed them together in the land vacated by the defeated Jews while taking the Jews they wanted into captivity to Babylon. The few Jews left behind were viewed as less significant by the Babylonians, intermingled with these Gentile people groups (brought in), creating the Samaritans—half Jew and half Gentile race. As I have previously stated, the average Jew would go around Samaria when traveling to avoid encountering a Samaritan, even if it lengthened their journey. However, Jesus was different because He broke all kinds of social norms to accomplish the Father's will.

To avoid any distractions, Jesus sent His disciples into a nearby town to buy food. The Lord sat at the well to wait on a woman who was unaware that she had a divine appointment with the Messiah. When the woman arrived, Jesus immediately addressed her by asking her to provide Him a drink of water from the well. Surprised by His polite address, she responded by reminding Jesus of the norms between Jews and Samaritans—Jews had no dealings with Samaritans. Not concerned about man-made norms, Jesus responded by beginning a dialogue with the woman about divine grace. The phrase "gift of God" that John used as a reference to salvation—the pinnacle of divine grace. The phrase "living water" was a reference to the Holy Spirit—the One who dispenses that grace or salvation. This was why Jesus brought up the subject of water because He used it to talk to the woman about *living water*. Jesus often used this method of teaching in the New Testament. He would use ordinary everyday objects to teach spiritual lessons—and on this particular day, He took the Samaritan woman to school using objects she was very familiar with. The way the woman responded revealed that she did not understand spiritual things or divine grace. Her response to Jesus asking her for a drink revealed she was lost and in need of salvation.

The Samaritan woman wanted to know where was Jesus' bucket—because the well was very deep. Also, she wanted to know where He would get the water from, which He was speaking about. Again, Jesus talked about heavenly things, and she was stuck on earthly things. She asked Jesus about His identity and that He could not possibly be greater than their father Jacob.[216] This statement was interesting for several reasons. First, she was not aware of who she was talking to and that Jesus was certainly greater than Jacob because He existed before Jacob in eternity past. Second, she revealed that Samaritans followed certain teachings from the Torah that they would have learned from their Jewish side. Therefore, by the fact that she referred to Jacob as the father of the Samaritans (not just the Jews), she understood there was something significant about Jacob, even though she had not yet understood just how significant.

As school continued, Jesus now explained the difference between earthy water, the water at the well, and heavenly water, which again was a reference to the Holy Spirit—which meant eternal life or salvation. This sounded like a good idea to the woman. As such, she asked Jesus to give her some of this water, so that she would not have to take the long-hot journey from her home to the well outside the city. Once again, she was not there yet in her understanding. She still did not get Jesus' message, but Jesus did not give up on her. So, now, Jesus

---

216   Many of the Samaritans held Jacob in high regard, being half Jew.

turned up the heat by bringing up her husband—although He knew she did not have one at the time. Jesus went even deeper: He let her know that He knew everything about her home life. He told her that not only did she not have a husband, but that she had five of them in the past—which reminded her of her multiple divorces.

Jesus didn't stop there because He told her she was living in an ungodly relationship with a man that was not her husband—she was shacking up, which was against God's law. If you pay attention to how she responded, you notice how quickly she changed the subject because she did not want to talk about her miserable life. This was the main reason why she walked out to the well by herself in the heat of the day. Women were required to draw water for household duties such as cooking, cleaning, and bathing. Generally, women went out in the morning, and again, in the early evening, before sundown. The timing of her walk to the well revealed everything you need to know about her life. When she changed the subject, she began to talk about another subject about which she knew nothing: worship. However, she was right where Jesus wanted her to be.

Jesus (figuratively) took the woman by the hand to lead her to talk about spiritual things instead of earthly things. She said, "Our fathers worshiped in this mountain, and you people say that in Jerusalem is the place where men ought to worship" (v. 20). Her statement revealed the real problem. She thought worship was limited to time or place—like many people do today. Jesus responded, "Woman, believe Me, an hour is coming when neither in this mountain nor Jerusalem will you worship the Father. You worship what you do not know; we worship what we know, for salvation is from the Jews" (vs. 21-22). Jesus told her that she misunderstood the definition of worship and how worship worked. This was because the Samaritans did not know God, nor did they know the Messiah. Salvation came from the Jews because God designed His plan that way. Jesus chose to dwell in a Jewish body when He walked the earth. Thus salvation was from the Jews, or through a Jewish vessel that Jesus inhabited for the divine purpose of extending grace to humanity. Also, the Jews were saved first (Acts 2), then the Samaritans (Acts 8), then the Gentiles (Acts 10).

Now, we arrive at the climax of class: Jesus drove home His main point that He was building up to the whole time, "But an hour is coming, and now is, when the true worshipers will worship the Father in spirit and truth; for such people, the Father seeks to be His worshipers. God is spirit, and those who worship Him must worship in spirit and truth" (vs. 23-24). Jesus explained what true worship was all about: Him. To worship in *spirit and truth* revealed a new concept. God requires us to worship Him on His terms, not man's. Every person that has claimed they truly believe in Jesus as the Christ (Messiah) must worship Him 24/7. Also, they cannot limit their worship to time (Sunday morning only) or place (only at the church house).

Genuine worship is a lifestyle, not just a Sunday-only experience, whereby you live the rest of the week on your terms. The woman told Jesus what He had revealed was good, but when the Messiah comes, He will declare all things to us (Samaritans). This meant the Messiah would tell them even more about the kingdom of God. However, she was surprised when Jesus revealed His identity to her when He said, "I who speak to you am He." The woman was so moved because she finally got it; thus, she passed the class, so she left her waterpot, went back into town, and witnessed to a community that had ostracized her—due to her sinful past. This ended this session of school and allowed for a brief recess. However, school was not over because Jesus waited until the Samaritans came from her town to hear what He had to say. After Jesus schooled them too, many of them accepted Him and His message, just as the Samaritan woman had done. The outcome was divine grace overcame the human stumbling block of race!

Make America Great Again

How does the story of Jesus and the woman at the well relate to America and the problem with systemic racism? I am glad you asked, but are you sure you are ready for the answer? America has never allowed God's grace to overcome the division of race or racism. The history of those in power in America has lacked the grace necessary to take a stand against the culture of systemic racism. Furthermore, there have never been enough ordinary American white citizens to take a stand either and say enough is enough—since they are the majority by far. We would need them to have the same outrage that they have over the issue of abortion—without the violence but the energetic activism. Therefore, Whites can no longer just offer up more empty rhetoric but take decisive action against the problem to help eradicate systemic racism in America.

Unfortunately, the problem is most whites do not think there is a problem with systemic racism. As a result, they accuse Blacks of overplaying the "race card." This is rich, coming from the dominant race that has been the architect of black disenfranchisement, oppression, misery, and brutality since 1619. On behalf of all Blacks, I would submit to white folks that race is not a card we play; it is an experience we live. And until you live in black skin in a white America, you can't possibly understand what it's like for us daily, so stop guessing and stop judging—as though you get it when your actions (as a whole) say otherwise.

Again, you often hear people say how great America is as a nation. Ironically, you often hear politicians say this when they are running for office, while at the same time, they argue why they need to be elected to fix our broken country. Go figure! However, how great America is as a nation is a statement usually argued by Whites, but not so much by Black and Brown people in the country. The reason why is because many minorities do not view the country the same way because their life experiences are often very different from Whites. For instance, when Blacks hear the phrase "Make America Great Again,"[217] we hear something different than most Whites. Although many Blacks have made numerous strides in many areas, such as academia, music,

---

217 Ronald Reagan Blog. 1 May 2020 [on-line]; accessed on 21 September 2020; available from https://www.reagan.com/ronald-reagans-commitment-to-make-america-great-again; Internet. "Make America Great Again" has been everywhere in the last few years: on hats, billboards, T-shirts and everything in between. Many associate the phrase with President Donald Trump but, in fact, it has much older roots—with President Ronald Reagan. The Ronald Reagan campaign slogan "Make America Great Again" was first used at the Republican National Convention in July 1980, when the then-candidate accepted the Republican party's nomination for president. "For those who've abandoned hope," he said, "we'll restore hope and we'll welcome them into a great national crusade to make America great again." The legacy of Ronald Reagan prevails and is very much still relevant today.

education, arts and science, healthcare, athletics, government, and politics, to name a few, we still lag far behind whites in income, housing, education, employment, healthcare, and many other areas of life.

Furthermore, regardless of our achievements, we often do not receive the appreciation and recognition we deserve. Regardless of the fact, most African Americans are law-abiding citizens, we are still treated as criminals. Regardless of the fact, we can be in our neighborhoods and be stopped for walking or running while Black, driving while Black, or simply, just for being Black. Who else has to deal with that in America? Only, Brown people, but never White people, especially not under those same circumstances. Whites are still given the benefit of the doubt, even when they are guilty, not suspected or alleged.

So, when you say to an African American, "Make America Great Again," the response is: when has America ever been great for all Blacks, as it has been for Whites? What period in American history could you point to? The 366 years of the Transatlantic Slave Trade (16th-19th century);[218] American slavery from 1619 until the signing of the 13th Amendment in 1865; the Jim Crow era and Black Codes that followed slavery (1865-1877);[219] the Ku Klux Klan and how they terrorized Blacks for centuries (1866- onward);[220] the nearly 2,000 Black Americans lynched during Reconstruction (1865-1950);[221] Blacks still

---

218 "Transatlantic Slave Trade: Slavery and Remembrance" [on-line]; accessed on 21 September 2020; available from http://slaveryandremembrance.org/articles/; Internet.

219 National Geographic Resource Library. "The Black Codes And Jim Crow Laws." [on-line]; accessed on 21 September 2020; available from https://www.nationalgeographic.org/encyclopedia/black-codes-and-jim-crow-laws/; Internet. After the United States Civil War, state governments that had been part of the confederacy tried to limit the voting rights of black citizens and prevent contact between black and white citizens in public places.

220 National Geographic Resource Library. "The Ku Klux Klan" [on-line]; accessed on 21 September 2020; available from https://www.nationalgeographic.org/article/ku-klux-klan/. Internet. The Ku Klux Klan was founded at the end of the United States Civil War to repress the rights and freedoms of African Americans. It has used intimidation, violence, and murder to maintain white supremacy in Southern government and social life. Even after 150 years, it is still an active, domestic terrorist organization.

221 Alex Fox, "Nearly 2,000 Black Americans Were Lynched During Reconstruction," *Smithsonian Magazine*, 18 June 2020; [on-line]; accessed on

being treated as non-citizens even after the 14th Amendment was passed (1866); Blacks being denied the right to vote even after the 15th Amendment was passed (1869); Red Summer—the vicious attacks on Blacks during a period from late winter through early autumn (1919);[222] the Tulsa Race Massacre (1921); the Civil Rights Movement and the backlash and brutality from many whites (1960s & 70s); the attacks by police and citizens of Blacks; the Atlanta church bombings (1963); the murder of MLK (1963); the Tuskegee Syphilis Experiment (1932-1972);[223] the tough financial times of the 1980s, 90s, and 2000s; the Rodney King riots caused by police brutality (1992);[224] or the continued killing of unarmed Blacks at the hands of the police (Jim Crow era – present day); or the election of Donald J, Trump as President. His four years in the office earned him the title of the most racist President in American history, which he seemed to hold as a badge of honor. He welcomed the support of the white nationalists and white supremacists. Hate crimes against Black and Brown people increased dramatically during the Trump Administration.[225] Also, Trump's constant vitriol and division took its toll on the country—not to mention his cruel and unjust treatment of his predecessor, former President Barack Obama— which he did only because of Obama's skin color and the jealously of

---

25 November 2020; accessed from https:www.smithsonianmag.com/smart-news/nearly-2000-black-americans-were-lynched-during-reconstruction-180975120/; Internet.

222   Erik Ortiz, "Racial violence and a pandemic: How the Red Summer of 1919 relates to 2020." *NBC News*, 21 June, 2020 [on-line]; accessed on 21 September 2020; available from https://www.nbcnews.com/news/us-news/racial-violence-pandemic-how-red-summer-1919-relates-2020-n1231499; Internet.

223   Elizabeth Nix, "Tuskegee Experiment: The Infamous Syphilis Study," 16 May 2017 [on-line]; accessed on 21 September 2020; available from https://www.history.com/news/the-infamous-40-year-tuskegee-study; Internet. Known officially as the Tuskegee Study of Untreated Syphilis in the Negro Male, the study began at a time when there was no known treatment for the disease.

224   "Rodney King Biography," 2 April 2014 [on-line]; accessed on 21 September 2020; available from https://www.biography.com/crime-figure/rodney-king; Internet.

225   Frederick Reese, "As hate crime attacks increase in the Trump era," 5 July 2017 [on-line]; accessed on 21 September 2020; available from ; Internet.

his many achievements, and the admiration that many Americans have for him, as well as many people around the world.

Based on the history of the black experience in America, which is vastly different from white experience, African Americans are still waiting on America to be great to them as a whole for the first time and show us the appreciation and human dignity we all deserve. Furthermore, many of us who have been caught up in our criminal justice system, from law enforcement to the courts, would love to experience that level of grace often afforded to white Americans. However, because it is a hope and not a reality, we better understand why systemic racism continues in America.

Application of John 4:7-26

How does God display grace to a despised race?

The Woman of Samaria

1. **He shows up when you are least expected. (vs. 7-14)**

   This is why the Christian church in America needs to be united as one body of believers, and no longer separated along racial lines. It loses the power to act as one, whereby God is hindered from sending a revival.

2. **He offers you His plan out of your situation. (vs. 15-26)**

   As I have stated, God's plan for the church is to fulfill the Great Commission. However, racism and division hinder that plan. Because of the separation and division, the plan of salvation seems irrelevant to an unsaved society that does not see God as the answer because it does not see the church as relevant.

3. **He will use your story for His glory. (vs. 39-42)**

God uses the story of the deliverance of His children to be a living testimony of His unconditional love. However, Psalm 107:2 says, "let the redeemed of the Lord say so." We say so by our lifestyle and our speech and when necessary we used words! However, when the church remains divided along the lines of race, then so does America. When we are not saying so, we are saying no, to the lost around us.

What should we learn from Jesus' interaction with the woman at the well and how grace can overcome race?

1. **No one is out of God's reach to save them if they truly want to be saved.** Just like the woman at the well, all human beings are worth saving in the eyes of God. (Psalm 139)

2. **True worship of God is never limited to time nor place.**

    NOTE: How one worships is more important than where one worships. However, that does not mean Christians do not need a church to be actively involved in. During Covid-19, if not in-person, at least on-line. (Hebrew 10:25)

3. **What God thinks of you is far more important than what others think of you.** No one else is willing to die for our sins, but Jesus did on Calvary. (John 15:13)

4. **Your race or ethnicity does not have to be a barrier to knowing the God who created you.** The ground beneath the cross is level to all that would dare come to the cross for the forgiveness of sin. (John 3:16)

CHAPTER 10

CHRISTIAN ACCOUNTABILITY

Peter (Cephas) Opposed by Paul

But when Cephas came to Antioch, I opposed him to his face, because he stood condemned. For prior to the coming of certain men from James, he used to eat with the Gentiles; but when they came, he began to withdraw and hold himself aloof, fearing the party of the circumcision. The rest of the Jews joined him in hypocrisy, with the result that even Barnabas was carried away by their hypocrisy. But when I saw that they were not straightforward about the truth of the gospel, I said to Cephas in the presence of all, "If you, being a Jew, live like the Gentiles and not like the Jews, how is it that you compel the Gentiles to live like Jews? (Galatians 2:11-14)

Accountability can be defined as the act of being responsible for what you do and able to give a satisfactory reason for it.[226] It is well known that the secular society in America lacks accountability. In the winter of 1987, Nike was going through a big slump. They had just laid off 20 percent of their workforce. Keep in mind; this is before they became the corporate giant they are today. The company came up with a slogan that turned the fortunes of the company around. With obesity and procrastination becoming growing issues in American society, company leaders realized that there was untapped potential targeting universal fitness. From that point, "Just Do It" was born, and over the

---

[226] Cambridge Dictionary, [on-line]; accessed on 21 September 2020; available from https://dictionary.cambridge.org/dictionary/english/accountability; Internet.

next decade, Nike's sales increased by one thousand percent.[227] Nike's strategy succeeded because it became a household name. Today, Nike is the undisputed giant in the athletic shoe market. However, America adopted the "Just do it" slogan long before it was adopted by a shoe company.

The culture in America has been a "do as one pleases" culture, without regard to accountability, for a long time. Americans just don't like being told what to do, even if it is for their benefit. Case in point, the refusal of so many Americans to wear a mask in public during the contagious and deadly worldwide Covid-19 pandemic of 2020. As of the day I edited this chapter, there were 60,641,673 cases of Covid-19 worldwide and 12,818,629 cases in the U.S. Also, there were 1,426,394 deaths worldwide and 262,683 deaths in the U.S. from Covid-19. These numbers are not just statistics, but more importantly, they represent the lives of real people. A multitude of families now have an empty seat at the dinner table because a vital member of the family has unexpectantly been taken. Despite the serious health threat that ravaged the nation, I was appalled at the irresponsibility of my fellow Americans, who displayed a total disregard for not only their health but the health of those around them. Why? Because, for them, to wear a mask meant their civil liberties were violated. However, accountability is looking out for yourself and looking out for others as well, which is something we fail at miserably as a nation.

A President Who Lacks Accountability

Another definition for accountability is to be held responsible, liable, or answerable for one's actions.[228] Perhaps, the clearest example of this point is our current President, Donald Trump. According to an article by David Dayen, "When you tell someone they won't be punished

---

227 Riley Jones. Complex, "How Nike's 'Just Do It' Slogan Turned the Brand into a Household Name," 17 August 2015 [on line]; accessed on 21 September 2020; available from https://www.complex.com/sneakers/2015/08/nike-just-do-it-history; Internet.

228 Dictionary.com, [on-line]; accessed on 21 September 2020; available from https://www.dictionary.com/browse/accountability; Internet.

for their misconduct, they tend to keep doing it." [229] Unfortunately, Trump's lack of accountability began long before he ran for the office of President. Trump grew up as the "poster child" for white privilege. He attended prestigious private schools, as well as the college of his choice. He had carte blanche access to prestigious private clubs, politicians, corporate CEOs, including finance and banking, professional athletes, movie stars, and beauty pageants.

Trump never had to search for a job, apply for unemployment, worry about where he would live or his healthcare—like the average American. He has lived like the super-rich pretty much his entire life; therefore, he lacks empathy to understand the average American's plight. He has traveled in luxury wherever he has gone, whether by private jets or limousines. He didn't even have to worry about building a successful company from the ground up; he inherited the Trump Corporation from his father. He inherited hundreds of millions of dollars, which he repeatedly squandered through numerous business failures and bankruptcies.

The point being, Trump inherited everything he has ever owned, even his name. Somehow, even though Trump is a "wannabe emperor" that has no clothes, America looked at him and thought he would be a good president, despite his sinful character, abject failure as a businessman, or his lack of political, military, or government experience. As a pastor, I know the power of God to save because He saved me and uses me, despite my past. However, when a man says he does not have to ask God for forgiveness because he doesn't make mistakes, I would submit to you, don't trust that man—and definitely

---

229 David Dayen, The American Prospect: Ideas, Politics, and Power, "Trump's Impeachment and the Era of No Accountability." 24 September 2020 [on-line]; accessed on 21 September 2020; available from https://prospect.org/power/trump-impeachment-era-of-no-accountability/; Internet. Trump is Wells Fargo. He sought out dirt from foreign allies in the 2016 election. Nothing happened. He fired the FBI director before he could investigate the matter. Nothing happened. He used the presidency as a profit center for his hotels and resorts. Nothing happened. Protected by the backstop of Senate Republicans and the fecklessness of House Democrats, he knew that he could get away with whatever it took to stay in and profit from power. So, he called up the Ukrainian president, because why not

don't give him the keys to lead your country. "Oh snap!" We already did that! Huge mistake!

In 2016, when Trump was a presidential candidate, he was interviewed by CNN's Anderson Cooper. Cooper asked him if forgiveness was a central tenet in Trump's faith. He responded, by saying 'Why do I have to repent or ask for forgiveness if I am not making mistakes?'[230] Trump obviously does not read the Bible, nor obey it, because Romans 3:23 says, "For all have sinned and come short of the glory of God." Because of Trump's morally corrupt behavior and self-serving leadership style, it puzzles me why so many white evangelicals have devoted themselves with undying loyalty to a man that is the polar opposite of what they say they stand for, which is supposed to be Christ Jesus.

The Christian Church—The Enabler

Donald J. Trump has always done as he pleased and has not been held accountable to anyone for his actions, which has not changed, even since he has been President. What's surprising are all the enablers Trump has had throughout his entire life, not just since he took office. Perhaps, the worst enabler has not been his political party, the Republicans, but the Christian church. Many white evangelicals had supported Trump before he was elected, and since he has been in office—regardless of his behavior. A famous quote by Maya Angelou says, "When someone shows you who they are, believe them the first time." [231] Unfortunately, a large majority of America, including the

---

230 Ray Nohstine. The Christian Post. *"Trump: 'Why do I have to repent or ask for forgiveness if I am not making mistakes?'"* [on-line]; accessed on 15 October 2020; available from https://www.christianpost.com/news/trump-why-do-i-have-to-repent-or-ask-for-forgiveness-if-i-am-not-making-mistakes-video.html; Internet. Following Donald Trump's appearance, the previous week at the Family Leadership Summit in Iowa, CNN's Anderson Cooper sought out clarification on Trump's assertion that he's unsure if he ever asks God's forgiveness. Cooper used part of the interview to ask follow up questions for Trump in what some commentators believed were awkward comments he made regarding forgiveness and communion.

231 Dan Western, "50 Maya Angelou Quotes On Life And Death," [on-line]; accessed on 21 September 2020; available from https://wealthygorilla.com/23-maya-angelou-quotes-on-life-and-death/; Internet.

greater part of white evangelicals, didn't believe Trump the first time before running for president. Although Trump was exposed for who he was during the political primaries, the country voted him into office anyway. I guess, somehow, they thought he would change once he got in office. Hey Republicans! How has that worked out for you?

Trump has highjacked your party and turned it into a personality cult. Now you bow at his feet and fear him tweeting about you if you dare turn against him. I thought you were supposed to be the party of morals, character, and decency. Wasn't that the reason why you wanted President Bill Clinton kicked out of office, because of his moral failure with Monica Lewinski? Didn't you say he was no longer fit to hold the office of the presidency, not only because of what he did but for lying about it? My question to you, dear Republican party, where is that same outrage for a president that has done far worse than what Clinton did? I am in no way excusing what Clinton did because that was wrong as well. However, Trump has "trumped" Clinton in his sinful behavior—before he got in office, and since he has been in office.

America should expect more from its leaders, especially those that sit in the highest seat of our government. With a straight face, how can we point the finger at other world leaders that behave badly when our very own president makes them look not so bad, in comparison. What is rich and hypercritical is the worst president we have ever had when it comes to obeying the law, ran on a "law and order" platform for reelection. How absurd! When the man broke more laws and bent almost every governmental apparatus to his will. Trump caused extremely accomplished professional men and women to cower to him—those that had served government, military, and cooperate America. Contrary to Trump's cult followers' popular belief, the country is in the mess that it is in today because of him.

Furthermore, even when the country was doing better finally, it was doing so despite him, not because of him. Mainly for two reasons: First, Trump inherited an economy that was already on the upswing from the previous administration. Second, Trump was not concerned about what was best for America, only what was best for him and the Trump family. Everything he did was to either to line his pockets with taxpayer's money or dodge some legal, financial or pollical trouble. To some degree, it can be understood why America fell under Trump's spell—because, in some weird way, we have always been star-struck when it came to celebrities. However, for so many white evangelicals to be engulfed in that group is mind-boggling as well as disturbing. The church is not supposed to be "transactional"; it is supposed to be "transformational." "Therefore, I urge you, brethren, by the mercies of God, to present your bodies a living and holy sacrifice, acceptable to God, which is your spiritual service of worship. And do not be conformed to this world, but be transformed by the renewing of your mind, so that you may prove what the will of God is, that which is good and acceptable and perfect" (Romans 12:1-2).

If we were the Christian nation we claim to be, how did we vote for a man that is not only unsaved but is spiritually bankrupted as well. American has had plenty of presidents that were not Christians in the past, but, in the modern era, we have not had anyone like Trump—he is in a league of his own. He makes Richard Nixon look presidential. However, since Trump is a man that has no desire to ask God for forgiveness, by his admission, that makes him a very dangerous leader. A man who ridicules and maliciously attacks anyone who disagrees with him, even when he has been dead wrong, which was much of the time. A man who sided with our nation's enemies instead of believing all the professional men and women of our intelligence community. A man who cared more about his political career than he did the lives of Americans he swore an oath to protect. When Covid-19 was ramping up to overtake our country, Trump claimed it was a hoax and would go away on its own.

Trump even pushed back on reporters that told him that his racist supporters were dangerous, and we're encouraged by his rhetoric, such as the Proud Boys and white nationalists. His delays in the Covid-19 response cost hundreds of thousands of Americans their lives. To make matters worse, this man sat on the intelligence report at the beginning of 2020 that warned him about a dangerous pandemic headed to the U.S. He told the American public one thing but told rich investors another thing behind closed doors. Why? Because Trump cared more about Wall Street than he did about our street—where the average American lives. Why is any of this important to the argument that this book is making? More importantly, why is this important to us as a nation? The Bible provides countless examples of what happens when mankind is left to his own sinful devices and not held accountable for his actions.

Ahab was the king of the Northern Kingdom of Israel, and his evil wife Jezebel (1 Kings 16 and 21; and 2 Kings 9) were both clear examples of what happens when evil leadership is not held accountable. [232] Now Ahab was a mile past evil (labeled the worst king of Israel) and made no bones about it, but there was another king that should have known better—his name was Jehoshaphat. Although he was a good king, Jehoshaphat made some bad choices, and the worst was, aligning himself with Ahab, which almost cost him his life (2 Chron. 18:1-34). Also, Jehoshaphat gave his son Jehoram to Ahab's wicked daughter Athaliah, which took after her wicked mother, Jezebel. [233] King Ahab was evil and ruled by fear and intimidation, just like Donald Trump. However, in this story, white Evangelicals are like Jehoshaphat. They aligned themselves with Trump for political expediency, which means doing what is convenient rather than what is morally right. However, the Bible says, "Do not be deceived: 'Bad company corrupts good morals'" (1 Corinthians 15:33). When this verse talks about morals, it is talking about character. When the church aligns itself so closely with the government, it adopts a secular agenda to get its agenda, not God's. Instead of following Scripture and living out our Christian creed, we have been living out an American creed.

In a book by Michael Horton titled *Christless Christianity*, he made this exact point. Horton said we pursue the American Dream instead of our Christian faith.[234] Also, my former pastor, Dr. Tony Evans, put this

---

232   J. F. Walvoord, R. B. Zuck (Eds.), T.L. Constable, *The Bible Knowledge Commentary: 1 Kings, An Exposition of the Scriptures*, Vol. 1. (Wheaton: Victor Books, 1985), 522. Ahab ruled Israel from Samaria for 22 years (874–853 B.C.). He was the most wicked king Israel had experienced, even worse than his father Omri who was worse than all before him (v. 25). Ahab's wickedness consisted of perpetuating all the sins of Jeroboam; he even considered them trivial. In addition, Ahab married a pagan princess, Jezebel, who zealously tried to promote her depraved cult as the exclusive religion of Israel.

233   K. A. Mathews. *The Historical Books: Holman concise Bible Commentary*, (Nashville: Broadman & Holman Publishers), 1998, 167.

234   Michael Horton. *Christless Christianity: The Alternative Gospel of the*

more into perspective when he said, "For far too long Anglo Christians have wrapped the Christian faith in the American flag, often creating a civil religion that is foreign to the way God intended His church to function."[235] I believe this is what is going in our politics today. I address this point further in Chapter 12, *Religion and Politics*.

As I stated earlier, the church is supposed to be transformational, not transactional. However, because politics have taken on a greater role in our Christianity, we have not only lost accountability, but we have also lost our way. Furthermore, we have lost sight of what is truly Christian and confused it with what's American. Christians should hold their pastors and Bible teachers accountable to ensure that they preach and teach the Bible and do not use their pulpits as a platform for their political party. When the church loses its way and no longer represents Christ, then society is in trouble because the church is supposed to lead the way spiritually, not politically. Unfortunately, due to the state of the Christian church in America today, Christian accountability as well as Christian ethics both seem to be an oxymoron.

Christian Accountability

How does all of this apply to the Bible, and how should the church be different from secular society? The answer can be found in Galatians chapter 2 when the apostle Paul held the apostle Peter accountable for his hypocrisy. This encounter would have grabbed the attention of the Jews and Gentiles then, as it does for Christians today. By this time, Peter had walked with Jesus longer than did Paul. Also, Peter had been an apostle longer than Paul, which was the premier leadership position in the church.[236] Peter was the early chief leader and preacher that God used to advance the gospel up to this point. However, when

---

American Church. (Grand Rapids: Baker Books, 2008), 21.

235   Tony Evans, *Oneness Embraced*, 19.

236   W.W. Wiersbe, *Wiersbe's Expository Outlines on the Old Testament: Genesis*, (Wheaton: Victor Books, 1993), 518-519. In the first chapter, Paul proved that his Gospel and apostleship came directly from Christ, independent of the Twelve. His readers would naturally ask, "Then what was Paul's relationship to the Twelve and the Jerusalem church?" He answers that question in this chapter.

the outreach of the church turned to make a concerted effort to reach the Gentiles, Paul assumed that mantel.

In the Book of Galatians, one of Paul's main issues was how Gentiles were being treated in the church. The central message was all men are justified or made right before God in the same way. For Jews and Gentiles alike, salvation is by faith alone in Christ alone. Therefore, good works are insufficient for salvation because they are not a prerequisite for salvation. Paul made this crystal clear when he said, "For by grace you have been saved through faith; and that not of yourselves, it is the gift of God; not as a result of works, so that no one may boast" (Ephesians 2:8-9). Paul's point was, no man can ever get enough good grades for his conduct and character to earn salvation. The theme of the letter to the Ephesians was that faith in Christ freed us from the penalty of sin, not human efforts.[237] This is the central message of salvation and what led to the confrontation between two of the early church giants.

Galatians Chapter 2 picks up after Paul was already in Antioch, ministering to the Gentiles.[238] When Peter (Cephas) arrived, Paul opposed him, meaning he held him accountable for his actions. He did this to Peter's face and not behind his back. Paul could not let this go because of the serious ramifications the church would have had to endure going forward. Peter stood condemned because he was found guilty as charged. Paul said, before certain men (Judaizers) from James, the half-brother of Jesus, and leader of the church in Jerusalem, that Peter was guilty of hyposcrisy.

Peter was just fine with eating with Gentiles, without Jews present to scrutinize his actions. But when these Judaizers arrived, Peter purposely distanced himself from his Gentile eating buddies. Peter feared how his new close association with Gentiles would be viewed

---

237 W. C. Fields, H. F. Paschall, and H. H. Hobbs (Eds.), *The Teacher's Bible Commentary: Galatians,* (Nashville: Broadman and Holman Publishers, 1972), 741. Antioch was first evangelized by some of those Christians who were scattered abroad as a result of the persecution occasioned by Stephen's death. Almost from the beginning the church at Antioch seems to have been a mixed congregation of completed and converted Gentiles (Acts 11:19–21)

238 T. George, *Galatians,* Vol. 30. (Nashville: Broadman & Holman Publishers, 1994), 169.

back in Jerusalem. Paul understood this was more grave than simply breaking bread. Paul knew this was devastating to the new Gentile converts to Christ. It essentially created two classes of people in the church, Jews and Gentiles, which is what Jesus' death on the cross was designed to prevent. Without Paul being led by the Holy Spirit to intervene, there would have been "Gentile only" Christian churches as well as "Jewish only" Christian churches. In other words, the early church would have exhibited the same characteristics of division found in secular society today.

As previously stated, Jesus gave His life on the cross to provide salvation for Jews, Samaritans, and Gentiles and to unite them together as one family of faith or *body of Christ*. For either of these three groups to start their own churches, solely based on segregating from the other races, would have violated God's purpose for His church. Paul understood this important principle, which is why he asked Peter, "If you, being a Jew, live like the Gentiles and not like the Jews, how is it that you compel the Gentiles to live like Jews? This, of course, was the epidemy of hypocrisy. Unfortunately, the white church in early America played a pivotal role in why the church in America is divided along racial lines, even to this day. However, instead of the division being between Jews and Gentiles, it is between Blacks and Whites. Furthermore, the foundational division in America between Blacks and Whites has infected relationships with other races as well.

Paul was the type of leader the church needs today because he did not care who he offended when the gospel was on the line—although he did it in a Christian manner. He did not have a problem holding people accountable, especially when they claimed to be Christians. Therefore, anything that negatively affected the church, especially when someone, regardless of status, trampled on the Word of God. Paul would always take a stand for what was right so that he could advance the cause of Christ. Furthermore, Paul refused to align himself so closely with the Roman government that politics took precedent over the gospel for transactional reasons, which is exactly what many white evangelicals have done, notably in the age of Trump.

Application of Galatians 2:11-14

Why is it important for all Christians to be held accountable for their actions?

1. Our actions negatively impact those around us. (vs. 11-13)

As a pastor and retired military chaplain, I have heard countless stories of people leaving the church because of people's behavior, even from pastors and other church leaders, which was not Christ-like. Well, one of those stories really broke our hearts. A Hispanic woman, married to an African American Marine, arrived at the military base my wife and I were assigned. She told us about a really bad experience when her family first arrived at the base the previous year. She went to visit a church near the base. Being a committed Christian, her goal was to search for a new church home for her family. She arrived at the church about the same time service was about to start. An older white lady met her at the door, who was supposed to be a greater, but her greeting was not Christ-like. Realizing she was Hispanic, the white lady said, "You must be looking for your kind; well, that would be the church up the street." She was shocked and taken aback. Of course, she never returned because she was highly offended, and who could blame her. She could only think, what would it have been like if she had shown up with her African American husband and mixed kids. This experience still troubled her because she wiped away tears as she shared the racist experience. At that time, she still did not have a church home because the racist experience was still a stumbling block for her0.

2. Our negative actions hinder unity in the church. (vs. 14-17)

Years ago, when I was in seminary, my wife and I were interviewed to be the pastor of a new church plant, which would be sponsored by a Caucasian megachurch. They had already purchased a building and had another ministry that met at the location. The new church I pastored was racially diverse and primarily made up of White, Hispanic, and Black members. However, I quickly realized that these white people wanted me to be a figured head pastor, not lead the congregation. My first clash began early on when the main church sent white men and women to our location, not to join but to do as they pleased, without running it by me.

They instantly clashed with the members who joined the church because my wife and I were there. When I did not allow them to run over me as a pastor, they quit and went back to the main church and complained about my leadership. My wife and I tried our best to work with these white Christians, but they rejected me as the pastor no matter what we did. Despite their sabotage, the Lord still blessed that new church. We had some amazing worship. We were extremely glad to be reaching people from the community, regardless of the friction. One lady that came to the church, because my wife and I were there, was a nice Hispanic lady that used to attend worship in the same building when another church met there. Unfortunately, it dissolved, and afterward, the Caucasian megachurch purchased the building.

The Hispanic lady was a faithful member from the neighborhood. However, when she first started coming, she would walk to church on a walker, which would take her a while. So, my wife and I would pick her up for church, and then I asked some of the other members to help, which they did. She loved my wife and me and enjoyed me being her pastor, despite my race. Because they could not do as they pleased, the agitators turned the main church against me. So, the Executive Pastor from the main church came to the seminary and told me that they would appreciate it if I never returned to the new church. This happened in the middle of the week, so my wife and I did not even get a respectful send-off. However, I felt obligated to the members from the neighborhood to let them know. I went to visit the really nice Hispanic Christian lady that would come on her walker at her home.

When I drove up, she was in her front yard working on her flowers. Looking at my face, she knew something was wrong because I was often smiling when we hugged and greeted one another. I didn't want to beat around the bush, so I told her what happen, and that I would no longer be her pastor. Ironically, the first thing she said to me, with tears in her eyes, "Did they fire you because you are Black?" Somehow, she knew that! With tears rolling down her face, and my eyes tearing up as well, she said, "I am never going back there again!" I did not want to discourage her from attending, even though my wife and would no longer be there at the church. She had just gotten back into the church when we first met, and I did not want to discourage her, especially since she did not drive. I told her that they did hire me to be the pastor because of my race. However, I did not address why they fired me because we both already knew. By the way, she left the church as well. The actions of these White Christians directly, impacted in a way, not only my family but also the families of that new church.

3. Our negative actions hinder the gospel message from going forward. (vs. 18-21)

I often spend time on campus at my alma Mata mentoring students on the seminary campus. I was introduced to a white student who just began his Masters of Divinity, my master's degree. I asked him why he was pursuing that particular degree and what he planned to do with it. He told me he wanted to be a church planter or a chaplain in the Air Force. This got my attention because of my chaplain background and my church plant background. So, I offered to help mentor him.

He was married and had three children. I invited him and his family to join our church. While he did visit by himself, he never joined. As the years went by, I would wonder why he never accepted my invitation to bring his family to our church, especially with the areas he said he needed help in. I had the experience and wanted to help him and his family. While away on military deployment, I went to the campus to check on his wife and kids. She told me that they needed to find another church, but she would wait until her husband returned, which was still months away.

Well, she brought her kids to our church for about three or four weeks. However, after the first visit, she told me that she and her kids enjoyed our church, and in fact, it was the first time that her kids listened because they could understand the entire message, and they found it interesting, even on their level, the way it was explained. She was please by how they were treated; she said she would try to get her husband to come with them when he returned. I got the impression, based on her statements and the reaction of her children, our ministry was helping them to grow spiritually. So, when he returned from his deployment to the Middle East, I visited him to thank him for his service and welcome him home. Shortly after his return, we agreed to meet for breakfast. Based on our four-year interaction, it just didn't make sense to me why he continued to reject my help.

While sitting for breakfast in the restaurant, I asked him a simple question because nothing else made sense. I asked him was the fact that I am Black, even though our church is multiracial, the reason why he never wanted to bring his family to join our church. Ironically, he didn't hesitate; he said yes. I told him that I appreciated his honesty, but I was appalled at his answer. The sad thing is he did not realize his actions and response was racist. While our church has continued to preach the gospel, I strongly believe that he denied his family an opportunity for the gospel to go forward in their lives because he allowed race to get in his way when it was not an issue for his family.

What can we learn from Paul about why it is necessary to call out hypocrisy in the church?

1. **If we are supposed to represent God's glory to a fallen world, and we fail, how will the world see Christ?** If we do not reflect the glory of Christ, the world will lose its path to Christ, which is the responsibility of the church—to reach the lost and disciple the save.

2. **When the church lives like the world, it has the wrong impact on the world. God's grace means there are no second class-Christians.** If the church truly reflected racial harmony and racial diversity, as described by Scripture, the lost would see how God can do something man can't, and that is, bring people together.

3. **If the church lacks accountability, the church lacks the ability to be a church that God can use.** Standing up for the Gospel can be a lonely business because there are times you might have to stand alone. Accountability needs to be just as important in the church as availability.

4. **If the church remains divided racially, then it cannot be the example to lead the way of a nation that is divided racially.** The Bible describes the church as a light sitting upon a hill, and the world is pictured as a dark valley below. A big part of that darkness in America is racism, hate, and division. Therefore, the church is complicit when the world looks at the church and cannot tell the difference, even in the year 2020.

As Christians, we should always look for practical ways to have accountability and strive to achieve racial reconciliation in the body of Christ. We should be able to sit down as brothers and sisters in Christ have an honest conversation to address the issue of systemic racism in America and its effects on the Christian Church. One such method that is garnering a lot of attention today is what is known as the Critical Race Theory. However, this theory is very controversial in conservative Christian circles.

Critical Race Theory

An interesting theory that has been around for at least the last 40 years and gaining new tracking today is the critical race theory. To determine whether this theory is relevant to understanding the problem of systemic racism in America, I have included it in this section. So, what is critical race theory? In a book by Richard Delgado and Jean Stefancic, *Critical Race Theory*, they provide some answers to this question.

> *The critical race theory (CRT) movement is a collection of activists and scholars engaged in studying and transforming the relationship between race, racism, and power. The movement considers many of the same issues that conventional civil rights and ethnic studies discourses take up but places them under in a broader perspective that includes economics, history, setting, group and self-interests, and emotions and the unconscious. Unlike traditional civil rights discourse, which stresses incrementalism and step-by-step progress, critical race theory questions the very foundation of the liberal*

order, including equality theory, legal reasoning, Enlightenment rationalism, and neutral principles of constitutional law.[239]

The critical race theory resulted from lawyers, activists, and legal scholars across the country that sought new theories and strategies needed to combat racism. These educated individuals decided to debate the issue of racism in the legal realm and criminal justice system.[240] However, over the years, it has been expanded to look at systemic racism in other areas of American society. The goal of critical race theory is to understand inequality and racism in America. Also, critical race theory recognizes that structural racism is a part of American life and culture and challenges the beliefs that allow it to flourish.[241]

Critical race theory is a practice. It's an approach to grappling with a history of White supremacy that rejects the belief that what's in the past is in the past, and that the laws and systems that grow from that past are detached from it," said Kimberlé Crenshaw, a founding critical race theorist and a law professor at UCLA and Columbia universities.

In this article, Karimi stated that critical race theorists believed that racism is an everyday experience for most people of color. A large part of society has no interest in doing away with it because it benefits white elites and the (white) working class.[242] Also, she asked why is there so much resistance to the critical race theory? She said that critics have slammed the theory, with conservatives being some of the loudest voices against it, accusing it of poisoning the discussion on racism. She also contends that 2020 caused a resurgence of this theory with the deaths of George Floyd, Breonna Taylor, and other highly publicized killings of African Americans by police officers, which has led to a re-

---

239 Richard Delgado and Jean Stefancic. *Critical Race Theory*, Third Ed. (New York: New York University Press, 2017), 3.

240 Ibid, 4.

241 Faith Karimi, "What critical race theory is – and isn't," 1 October 2020 [on-line]; accessed on 30 December 2020; accessed from https://www.cnn.com/2020/10/01/critical race theory is -- and isn't - CNN; Internet.

242 Ibid.

examination of the nation's relationship with race. In our climate of racial unrest, the concept of critical race theory has taken on a new urgency among people calling for an examination of systemic racism—in part, through education such as teaching the 1619 project in schools and training.

The New York Times' 1619 Project is a Pulitzer Prize-winning project that reframes American history around the date of August 1619, when the first slave ship arrived on America's shores. President Trump said it should not be taught in schools because that is the religious right position that supports him. In September 2020, Trump even banned federal agencies from conducting racial sensitivity training related to critical race theory.[243] According to Karimi's article, she stated that the critics of the critical race theory claim that acknowledging America's history of racism is considered anti-patriotic and anti-American.[244]

In an article in Rebecca Bodenheimer, "What is Critical Race Theory? Definition, Principles, and Applications: A Challenge to the rhetoric of color-blindness," She provided a definition that connects critical race theory with the Civil Rights Movement.

Critical race theory (CRT) is a school of thought meant to emphasize the effects of race on one's social standing. It arose as a challenge to the idea that in the two decades since the Civil Rights Movement and associated legislation, racial inequality had been solved and affirmative action was no longer necessary. CRT continues to be an influential body of legal and academic literature that has made its way into more public, non-academic writing.[245]

The term "critical race theory" was coined by legal scholar Kimberlé Crenshaw in the late 1980s. The theory first emerged as a challenge to the idea that the United States had become a color-blind society where racial identity no longer influenced one's social or economic status.[246]

---

243 Ibid.

244 Ibid.

245 Rebecca Bodenheimer, "What is Critical Race Theory? Definition, Principles, and Applications: A Challenge to the rhetoric of color-blindness," 6 May 2019. [on-line]; accessed on 30 December 2020; accessed from Internet.

246 Ibid. CRT originated among legal scholars like Derrick Bell, Kimberlé

Those of us who live in black skin know that is patently false because we are constantly reminded somehow, shape, or form every day.

Critical race theory has not only impacted secular society, but it has also impacted Christianity in America. In a Christianity Today article by Kate Shellnut, *Southern Baptist Keep Quarreling Over Critical Race Theory*; she stated that the term "critical race theory" (CRT) is frequently ill-defined. According to scholars, it is an approach to racism that analyzes systems and biases embedded in social structures.

> *"Some in our ranks inappropriately use the label of 'CRT!' to avoid legitimate questions or as a cudgel to dismiss any discussion of discrimination. Many cannot even define what CRT is," tweeted SBC president J. D. Greear on Thursday. "If we in the SBC had shown as much sorrow for the painful legacy that sin has left as we show passion to decry CRT, we probably wouldn't be in this mess."*[247]

Additionally, Shellnut stated that to certain Southern Baptists, the SBC has not done enough to dismiss critical race theory, allowing secular thinking to overtake a biblical worldview. But for others in the SBC, the push to decry critical race theory distracts from what they see as more pertinent issues for their denomination in 2020, such as confronting racism. Also, she stated that Black leaders applying Scripture to racial issues or leading diversity initiatives at SBC seminaries have faced a backlash from more conservative members of the denomination who accuse them of succumbing to secular and Marxist ideologies.[248]

Crenshaw, and Richard Delgado, who argued that racism and white supremacy were defining elements of the American legal system—and of American society writ large—despite language related to "equal protection." Early proponents argued for a contextual, historicized analysis of the law that would challenge seemingly neutral concepts like meritocracy and objectivity, which, in practice, tend to reinforce white supremacy.

247   Kate Shellnut, "Southern Baptists Keep Quarreling Over Critical Race Theory," 17 December 2020. [on-line]; accessed on 31 December 2020; accessed from ; Internet.

248   Ibid. Tisby, the author of the bestselling book *The Color of Compromise*, referred to critical race theory as the "theological and ecclesiastical equivalent of the 'Red Scare.'" He said, "Slap anyone with the label 'Critical Race Theory,' and they automatically become enemies of the church."

Also, Shellnut documented the issue among Southern Baptist. She talked about the statement made by the six Southern Baptist Seminary presidents, which they issued in November of 2020. The seminary presidents stated that "affirmation of Critical Race Theory, Intersectionality and any version of Critical Theory" is incompatible with the Baptist Faith and Message, the denomination's core beliefs.[249] The problem was that during the Southern Baptist Convention (SBC) annual meeting in 2019, they approved a resolution that referred to CRT as "a set of analytical tools that explain how race has and continues to function in society" and clarified that it could only be employed as "subordinate to Scripture."[250] This was a logical conclusion because the SBC is constantly trying to add more racial diversity to their churches. Unfortunately, the SBC did an about-face when the six presidents voted down the issue of CRT.

In an article in the Christian Post by Leonardo Blair, *SBC wants to scrap resolution on critical race theory*, stated that Dwight McKissic Sr., Senior Pastor of Cornerstone Church, Arlington, Texas, retracted his support of the controversial statement from the SBC seminary heads that denounced racism and critical race theory. McKissic stated, "Initially, for the sake of unity and in the name of Christian charity, I was supportive of the statements released by the council of presidents and the resolutions committee. However, it then became apparent to me that these statements were merely paving the way for rescinding Resolution 9 at the upcoming annual meeting,"[251]

In 2019, the SBC passed Resolution 9, which officially denounced critical race theory (CRT). However, this resolution also declared that the ideas of CRT could conceivably be used "as analytical tools subordinate to Scripture.[252] The article also stated that Resolution 9 also

---

249 Ibid, Kate Shellnut.

250 Ibid.

251 Leonardo Blair, "SBC wants to scrap resolution on critical race theory, Pastor Dwight McKissic says," 17 December 2020. [on-line]; accessed on 31 December 2020; accessed from https://www.christianpost.com.news/SBC wants to scrap CRT resolution, Dwight McKissic says - The Christian Post; Internet.

252 Captain Cassidy, "The SBC's Battle Royale Over Critical Race Theory (CRT)," [on-line]; accessed on 31 December 2020; accessed from https//www.the SBC's Battle Royale Over Critical Race Theory (CRT) | Roll to Disbelieve: The Fight

decided that the denomination's leaders would be allowed to "carefully analyze how the information gleaned from these tools are employed to address social dynamics." At the same time, the resolution's writers warned churches and "institutions" needed to be super-careful not to "misuse" any "insights gained" from CRT. They do not define "misuse," but the word means *getting too pushy and wanting changes the top leaders don't approve of*. Many, like Mckissic, stated that the handling of Resolution 9 was a bewildering mess.

What it pretends to give with one hand, it more than takes away with the other. It provides no guidelines whatsoever for knowing what a "misuse" of "insights" might look like, nor how to handle racist SBC leaders who despise change almost as much as they hate human rights in general. It really looks like a Junior Chemist instruction manual from the 1950s, except nothing explosive, could ever come from this over-cautious mishmash. The whole resolution came about only because the SBC's leaders are getting a whole lot of negative press for their racism. It's an exercise in appeasing anti-racists while maintaining the status quo. I'm sure J.D. Greear, the SBC president, was thrilled with its wishy-washy flip-flopping.[253]

One of the biggest unintended consequences of the Southern Baptist Convention's mishandling of the critical race theory is that black pastors have started to leave the denomination, thus removing their churches from under its umbrella. For years, African American Christian pastors and seminary students have been looking for an avenue to have the discussion of racism in America with white evangelicals. However, with this latest decision by white evangelicals that run the denomination and the SBC seminaries, many black Christian alumni are very disappointed because we feel as though our voices do not matter to the powers that be that run everything. This point was made loud and clear in an article by Jean Hopfensperger; *Black pastor takes a*

---

for the Emperor's Scepter (patheos.com); Internet.

253   Ibid. Every time a fresh new scandal erupts from their leadership ranks, the SBC's top leaders swing into action — to unruffle the flocks' feathers enough to keep them tithing and parking their butts in pews. The SBC's leaders neither care about nor can even perceive the big picture. What they care about and perceive are the short-term effects of their damage-control efforts.

stand against Southern Baptist race statement. "The Rev. W. Seth Martin, the Brook Community Church pastor, belonged to the small minority of Southern Baptist clergy who are African American. He embraced its theology and looked beyond the denomination's historical association with slavery and racism — until now."[254] Also, in the article, Pastor Martin asked, "Why would they write this now?" asked Martin, whose decision has cast him in a national spotlight. "We've had the murder of George Floyd, Breonna Taylor, and continuous racial tensions. How can they talk about racial reconciliation and then do this?"[255]

In an article in the Religious Service News by Jim Wallis, *Southern Baptist seminary presidents double down on bad theology on race*; he stated that at a recent annual meeting, the six seminary presidents in the Southern Baptist Convention reasserted the SBC's dismissal of critical race theory, which examines the issues of embedded racism across institutions and culture in American society. Wallis also stated that the Southern Baptist leaders see the problem as bad sociology but that their statement reveals the bad theology that still haunts the denomination founded in support of slavery.[256]

> *The Southern Baptist statement's failure is biblical, not just sociological. Racism, in its many forms, is sin; indeed, it is America's original sin based on the lie, the myth, the ideology and*

---

254 Jean Hopfensperger, "Black pastor takes stand against Southern Baptist race statement," *StarTribune*, 30 December 2020. [on-line]; accessed on 30 December 2020; accessed from ; Internet. The controversy exploded after presidents of the six Southern Baptist seminaries issued a recent letter proclaiming that racial justice theories based on concepts such as white privilege and systemic racism were "incompatible" with the Baptist faith. Instead, the issue of race should be viewed through the lens of God, scripture and sin, the presidents' letter said.

255 Ibid. Martin broke away from the Southern Baptist Convention (SBC) last month, landing him in the heart of fresh turmoil sweeping through the nation's largest Protestant denomination over race.

256 Jim Wallis, "Southern Baptist seminary presidents double down on bad theology on race," 10 December 2020. [on-line]; accessed on 31 December 2020; accessed from Southern Baptist seminary presidents double down on bad theology on race (religionnews.com); Internet. CRT shows how white supremacy — the belief that some people are more valuable than other people because of their skin color — is not just a personal prejudice but a structural and societal practice in America.

> the idolatry of white superiority, or the assumption of whiteness as normative, and white privilege practiced through domination. To finally begin to understand how that sin of racism exercises itself both in human hearts and social systems — as we all saw in a white cop's knee pressed on a Black man's neck until he died, representative of all those systems — is important. But these seminary presidents wanted to attack sociology instead of facing theology at its core.[257]

Additionally, Wallis stated that the six SBC seminary presidents should have supported some type of mechanism to help the SBC address its racist past. If they had done so, it would have provided local SBC churches much-needed guidance. He added, imagine what these seminary presidents — entrusted with training their denomination's pastors and leaders — might have said if they'd chosen to confront the SBC's sinful history. The Southern Baptist seminary leaders could have called for their churches to begin preaching against white supremacy from their pulpits, and confess that the segregation of their churches exacerbates the racial separation within the body of Christ.[258] However, if they did, they would have had to acknowledge there was a problem with systemic racism in America, which still affects the Christian church.

Wallis also stated an important theological principle when he said that white supremacy assaults the image of God, throws away the *imago Dei*, and undermines God's purpose for humanity clearly stated in the first chapter of the Bible's Book of Genesis, to make *all* humankind in the "image" and "likeness" of God and have stewardship *together* over all the rest of God's creation. Therefore, white supremacy — which condones some people exercising violent dominion over other

---

257   Ibid.

258   Ibid. If these six seminary presidents had taken a bold stand, they could have acknowledged that any acceptance of racism in their political candidates is anti-Christ — especially reflecting on the election we just had. They could have prophetically called for removing Confederate statues and monuments that Black people in all their communities are forced to walk by every day.

people God created as equal — offends the Creator and is anti-God.[259] As many trained biblical scholars that exist under the SBC umbrella, at least, by now, one would think that these well-trained white evangelicals would have found a way to address the issue of systemic racism instead of ignoring or downplaying it.

Since the six SBC seminary school president's dismissed critical race theory on behalf of the whole denomination, why didn't they come up with their own theory based on Scripture? Furthermore, why do so many white conservatives not believe that systemic racism still exists in America? Why didn't the leadership of the SBC, along with these six presidents of the seminaries, invite African American pastors to sit down and discuss racism in America so that they could hear from our perspective, instead of deciding solely based on their conservative white America perspective? Why do these seminaries not allow their Black alumni to have a voice in these major decisions, especially those that involve us, our communities, and our churches?

Based on my research on this issue, the foundational principle that critical race theory advocates is America has a long history of racism that structurally exists in most, if not all, areas of our society. I do not understand why white Christians, who have never had to endure what Blacks have faced in America since 1619, as well as still must deal with today, so easily dismiss the racial struggles of their Christian brothers and sisters? If they do not agree with secular society on the issue, why don't they take our word for it as members of the Christian faith? If one carefully examines America's racist history (which I have done so repeatedly in this book), the obvious conclusion of the facts is that America definitely does have a systemic racism problem. Unfortunately, the incidents recorded in this book only represent a small portion of the systemic racism that people of color have had to endure ever since our ancestors were forced to board slave ships and brought to America in 1619.

---

259 Ibid.

CHAPTER 11

THE DANGERS OF IDOL WORSHIP

The King's Golden Image

Then Nebuchadnezzar in rage and anger gave orders to bring Shadrach, Meshach and Abed-nego; then these men were brought before the king. Nebuchadnezzar responded and said to them, "Is it true, Shadrach, Meshach and Abed-nego, that you do not serve my gods or worship the golden image that I have set up? Now if you are ready, at the moment you hear the sound of the horn, flute, lyre, trigon, psaltery and bagpipe and all kinds of music, to fall down and worship the image that I have made, very well. But if you do not worship, you will immediately be cast into the midst of a furnace of blazing fire; and what god is there who can deliver you out of my hands?" Shadrach, Meshach and Abed-nego replied to the king, "O Nebuchadnezzar, we do not need to give you an answer concerning this matter. If it be so, our God whom we serve is able to deliver us from the furnace of blazing fire; and He will deliver us out of your hand, O king. But even if He does not, let it be known to you, O king, that we are not going to serve your gods or worship the golden image that you have set up." (Daniel 3:13-18)

According to Exodus 20:4-5, "You shall not make for yourself a carved image or any likeness of anything that is in heaven above, or that is in the earth beneath, or that is in the water under the earth. You shall not bow down to them or serve them, for I the Lord your God am a jealous God, visiting the iniquity of the fathers on the children to the third and the fourth generation of those who hate me." Why did God command the Israelites not to erect statues or monuments that would become objects of worship? Because our God knew the sinful nature of man and the slippery slope it would cause. Also, in His foreknowledge, God knew that man would build statues or monuments to worship in place of Him.

An excellent example of this principle immediately transpired after God had delivered His people from bondage in Egypt. The Israelites built a golden calf at the foot of Mount Sinai, while Moses was up on top of the mountain intervening on their behalf before God—who had already displayed His covenantal love on behalf of His people. Furthermore, God knew that man would build statues of himself, or other men, as a form of deity to be worshiped. Although God forbade it, men have continued to build statues that dishonor God throughout the history of time. Often, man worships other men as well as man-made gods. You see it in government, entertainment, sports, education, and even in religion—which is why God never wanted this practice started because He knew where it would end up—the destruction of humanity.

God was so serious about this that He did not even want Israel to erect any statues or monuments of His image or likeness. God knew the sinful hearts and desires of mankind. God knew man would worship these man-made images of Him—in place of Him—whether made of wood, stone, gold, or whatever material man could get his hands on. However, despite God's clear objections to idol worship, man has erected statues since the *fall of man*. That does not mean all statues are monuments or wrong or sinful; it all depends on the purpose they were erected and what people do with them afterward. For instance, when Aaron was talked into creating the golden calf, he may have had good intentions, but how did that turn out? As the old cultural proverb goes, "The road to hell is paved with good intentions." And over the centuries, man has laid down a pretty good amount of asphalt!

These statues that man has constructed are not of God because they were set up to memorialize evil dictators or rulers such as the Caesar's of Rome, or in more modern time, Saddam Hussein when he was alive and ruled in Iraq, as well as Kim Jong Un in North Korea and Vladimir Putin of Russia. They all have ruled with an iron hand because they want to be feared and worshiped by their citizens. As history has proven, statues and memorials of mankind have only led to sin and the continued depravity of humanity.

History of Confederate Statues in America

According to the Southern Poverty Law Center, which maintains a list of the Confederate shrines, these memorials or statues are spread out over 31 states, plus the District of Columbia. Most Americans are unaware that many of these monuments were not erected until after the Civil War ended in 1865. During that time, commemorative markers of the Civil War tended to be memorials that mourned Confederate soldiers who had died.[260] However, what began as a reasonable expression of mourning someone that had died morphed into idol worship.[261] It also became hero-worship because, in some twisted way, traitors that killed Americans on American soul were hailed as heroes instead of traitors.

As a result of the Civil War, approximately 620,000 soldiers died from combat, accident, starvation, and disease. Two men who had fought for the Union Army provided these numbers in 1889, William F. Fox and Thomas Leonard Livermore. They developed these estimates by an exhaustive study using combat and casualty records generated by the armies over five years of fighting.[262] A recent study puts the number of dead as high as 850,000. Roughly 1,264,000 American soldiers have died in the nation's wars—620,000 in the Civil War and 644,000 in all

---

260   Becky Little, "How the US Got So Many Confederate Monuments?" 12 June 2020 [on-line]; accessed on 21 September 2020; available from https://www.history.com/news/how-the-u-s-got-so-many-confederate-monuments; Internet. These commemorations tell a national story. Surprisingly, early memorials were erected to mourn dead soldiers, and then they began to be erected to glorify leaders of the Confederacy like General Robert E. Lee, former President of the Confederacy, Jefferson Davis and General "Thomas Stonewall" Jackson, who were traitors of America, but now looked at as heroes.

261   Ibid.

262   American Battlefield Trust, "How so many soldiers died in the Civil War," [on-line]; accessed on 21 September 2020; available from https://www.battlefields.org/learn/articles/civil-war-facts#; Internet.

other conflicts. It was only recently, after the Vietnam War, that the number of American deaths in foreign wars eclipsed the number who died in the Civil War.[263] What's sad is, these casualties exceed our nation's loss in all its other wars combined—from the Revolutionary War, through Vietnam War, Korean Conflict, Desert Shield/Desert Storm, and to all current wars in Iraq and Afghanistan.

Ironically, Whites (mostly using taxpayer dollars) started to build Confederate monuments in large numbers to honor racist traitors who fought to uphold the institution of slavery. Many of these statues and monuments were built between the 1890s and 1950s, which coincides with the era of Jim Crow segregation. According to the Southern Poverty Law Center's research, the biggest spike was between 1900 and the 1920s, when race relations in America was at one of their lowest points in history.[264]

In addition to the 700 plus statues around the United States, what seems unthinkable is that there are Confederate statues in the halls of Congress and numerous schools named after these traitors throughout the nation. Finally, Confederate monuments are not just heirlooms or artifacts of a bygone era; because American taxpayers are still heavily investing in these tributes today. It recently came to light that over the past ten years, taxpayers have directed at least $40 million to Confederate monuments—which included statues, homes, parks, museums, libraries, and cemeteries—and even to Confederate heritage organizations.[265] It is a sad reality that in 2020, America is still paying for racism: culturally, politically, socially, and financially.

In addition to the numerous statues and monuments, we have several military bases in the U.S. named after many of these same

---

263   Military. "Memorial Day by the numbers: Casualties of every American War," [on-line]; accessed on 21 September 2020; available from https://www.military.com/memorial-day/how-many-us-militay-members-died-each-american-war.html; Internet.

264   Becky Little, "How the U.S. got so many Confederate monuments?" Internet.

265   Brian Palmer and Seth Freed Wessler, "The Cost of the Confederacy," *Smithsonian Magazine*, 1 December 2020 [on-line]; accessed on 21 September 2020; available from https://www.smithsonianmag.com/history/costs-confederacy-special-report-180970731/; Internet.

Confederate military men who were traitors and helped to divide the country to maintain the status quo of slavery. Fort Benning, Georgia; Fort Bragg, North Carolina; Fort Hood, Texas; Fort Polk, Louisiana; and Fort Rucker, Alabama, to name a few.[266] These traitors were responsible for the deaths of American military personnel, and we dishonor all Soldiers, Airmen, Sailors, Marines, and Coast Guardsmen, past and present, by having honorable men and women serve at bases that remind them every day of the traitors our country still honors—something is terribly wrong with that picture.

The Danger of Preserving Confederate Statues in America

One of the most dangerous organizations in American history that have terrorized millions of citizens for years was not born in the Middle East, nor did they give homage to Islam. Many of them have claimed to be Christians. Now that you are curious, to give you a hint, they terrorized Blacks, along with a few Whites that supported the equality of minorities. Of course, this group was the white supremacy group, the Ku Klux Klan. Fast forward to 2020; the KKK no longer wears sheets and hoods because they have been emboldened. Today, they no longer have to hide in the shadows—thanks to President Donald J. Trump—who has endorsed them because they support him. They are brave enough to show their faces during the day in large numbers in public to advance their cause of hate and white supremacy. Now they generally refer to themselves as "white nationalists," and their movement is called "white nationalism."[267] However, I will refer to

---

266 Alex Ward, "The racist history behind the 10 US Army facilities named after Confederate leaders." 9 June 2020 [on-line]; accessed on 21 September 2020; available from https://www.vox.com/2020/6/9/21285097/army-base-name-change-confederacy-marines-navy; Internet.

267 Carol M. Swain. *The New White Nationalism in America: Its Challenge to Integration*. (Cambridge: University Press, 2002), 13. Over the past ten years a new white racial advocacy movement had gained strength in the United States that poses a severe challenge to the ideals of an integrated society. Many of the leaders of this new movement, which is called "white nationalism" here, are different from the sorts of people we have come to associate with the traditional racist right in America.

them by their original name, white supremacist. However, their goals are the same, though their methods have changed.

In 2017, a 20-year-old named James Alex Fields Jr., affiliated with this racist group, revved up his Dodge Challenger, stepped on the gas, and plowed through a crowd that was peacefully protesting the removal of Confederate statues. Many of the protestors were severely injured—as they were toppled like bowling pins. However, instead of being rolled over by a bowling ball, it was a four-thousand-pound vehicle. Unfortunately, this incident cost young Heather Heyer, a Charlottesville resident, her life. She was mowed down by Field's vehicle that he used as a weapon, which was not accidental; it was intentional—due to utter hate. Although her mangled body was rushed to the hospital, she was pronounced dead upon arrival. To add insult to injury, Fields put his car in reverse, gunned the engine again, and backed up in his escape, hitting even more of the peaceful protestors. In addition to Heather Heyer being killed, 53 other innocent protestors were injured and survived the terrible ordeal. Field's was pulled over by the police a few blocks from the incident.[268]

Who would have thought all these years later that racist traitors from the Civil War era would still be impacting America, and innocent people still dying? Sadly, white supremacists are still impacting America, with support from the highest office of our government. After Heather Heyer's death, President Trump commented on the Charlottesville incident by defending James Field and all his white supremacist friends that support him; many of them were also present that day to terrorize the peaceful protestors as well. He responded by uttering his famous words, "There were very fine people on both sides."[269] In other words, Trump shamelessly equated the actions of

---

268   Justine Carissimo, "Woman Killed in Charlottesville, Virginia car attack identified," 13 August 2017 [on-line] accessed on 21 September 2020; available from https://www.cbsnews.com/news/heather-heyer-charlottesville-virginia-car-attack/; Internet. James A. Fields Jr., 20, of Maumee, Ohio, was taken into custody and charged with one count of second-degree murder, three counts of malicious wounding and one count of hit-and-run.

269   David Jackson, "Trumps defends response to Charlottesville violence, says he put it 'perfectly' with both sides remark," 1 June 2020 [on-line]; accessed on 21 September 2020; available from https://www.usatoday.com/story/news/politics/2019/04/26/trump-says-both-sides-charlottesville-remark-said-

the peaceful protesters, including Heather Heyer, with the racist white supremacist, including James Fields. Although they caused the death of an innocent young lady, hundreds of these racist men, along with a few women, marched with their faces exposed during the evening carrying torches and chanting, "Jews won't replace us!" The reason why Trump can make that statement is that he is their fearless leader, and they worship him; because his presence and high position in the office gives voice as well as motivation to their racism and hate. They see Trump as their last best hope of saving their white view of what they believe America should be. After Trump's election, white supremacists have come out of the woodwork like roaches. Unfortunately, this is what Trump meant when he said, "Make America Great Again," which has been the rallying call to white supremacists.

Whether to bestow honor on someone for evil actions, or heroic actions, erecting statues and monuments can lead to idol worship and a lack of humility among men. Moreover, putting famous athletes, musicians, actors, preachers, former or current presidents on a pedestal, where they do not belong, always leads to unintended consequences. Idol worship is sin, whether intentional or unintentional, which is why Christians should not participate in it—regardless of what the unsaved world around us chooses to bow down to daily. We should learn our lesson from Scripture and only bow down to Jesus.

Nebuchadnezzar's Statue

Throughout the history of humanity, man has built statues for political and religious reasons; to send a message to the people they have authority over. Since the beginning of time, man has allowed pride to cloud his judgment. The Bible warns us not to think more highly of ourselves than we ought, but rather think of ourselves with sober judgment (Romans12:2). In the Book of Daniel, we meet a dominant figure that allowed the false perception of himself to cloud his judgment. So, he built a statue that stood 90 feet tall and 9 feet

---

perfectly/3586024002/; Internet. President Donald Trump defended his widely criticized comments that there were fine people on "both sides" of the violent clashes in Charlottesville, Virginia, in 2017, saying the utterance was put "perfectly."

wide—for political and religious reasons. Many emperors and kings in Near Eastern culture saw themselves not just as earthly leaders; they wanted to be worshiped as deities. Nebuchadnezzar, the king of Babylon, which I will refer to as Neb, was no different.

In the Book of Jeremiah, we learn about how God allowed Neb to conquer His people due to their continued disobedience. God even called Neb His servant (Jeremiah 27:6-7). However, don't get it twisted! Neb never surrendered his life to God. So, he never became a true believer or follower of God. In Neb's case, "My servant" simply meant: God's vessel to bring about His divine plan concerning His people. (Always remember God uses whomever He pleases, saved as well as unsaved, to bring about His divine will). Because Neb conquered God's people, his pride got the best of him. This played a key role in him building his golden statue.

Neb had captured many nations during his reign, and in Chapter 3, he decided to flex his muscle. He summoned his multitude of leaders, from every branch of government, to attend a special ceremony to commemorate the statue he had set up. This included Shadrach, Meshach, and Abed-nego, three of the Hebrew young men captured from Judah. Neb assembled a huge orchestra for the occasion and gave the orders that the entire group of leaders were to bow down and worship his golden statue. If any of them refused, they were threatened with being thrown into a fiery furnace. When the music sounded, all the leaders fell on their faces and worshiped Neb's statue, except the three Hebrew boys. When Neb found out, he was enraged, but he gave the boys one last chance. Shadrach, Meshach, and Abed-nego responded with one of the most powerful confessions of faith in the entire Bible when they said, "O Nebuchadnezzar, we do not need to give you an answer concerning this matter. If it is so, our God whom we serve can deliver us from the furnace of blazing fire; and He will deliver us out of your hand, O king. But even if He does not, let it be known to you, O king, that we are not going to serve your gods or worship the golden image that you have set up" (vs. 16-18).[270]

---

270   S. R. Miller. *Daniel*, Vol. 18. (Nashville: Broadman & Holman Publishers, 1994), 124. Here is a pertinent lesson for believers today. Does God have all power? Yes. Is God able to deliver believers from all problems and trials? Yes. But does God deliver believers from all trials? No. God may allow trials to come into the lives of

Reluctantly, and being guided by rage, Neb had the Hebrew boys thrown into the furnace of blazing fire. To his amazement, Neb was astonished about what he saw going on inside the fiery furnace. He thought he was losing his mind, so he asked, "Was it not three men we cast bound into the midst of the fire?" They replied to the king, "Certainly, O king." He said, "Look! I see four men loosed and walking about in the midst of the fire without harm, and the appearance of the fourth is like a son of the gods!" (vs. 24-25) God moved in a mighty way to display His power over Neb and his statue, representing his so-called deity. Because of God's divine intervention, the Hebrew boys were not only rescued, but the Scripture says, "… In regard to these men that the fire had no effect on the bodies of these men nor was the hair of their head singed, nor were their trousers damaged, nor had the smell of fire even come upon them." (v. 27) [271] God intervened because His servants remained faithful to Him, despite being threatened with death by the government. This is a lesson for Christians today to never bow down to a leader in government who wants you to worship him or her as a god or goddess.

The Danger Of American Idols

So, how does this passage relate to America, and what role has Confederate statues and monuments played in continuing systemic racism? Here in the U.S., we are heavily into idol worship. Without question, we are starstruck as a nation. (This is how we allowed one of the biggest cultural idols in America to become president, which I will

---

his people to build character or for a number of other reasons (Rom 5). The purpose for trials may not always be understood, but God simply asks that his children trust him—even when it is not easy. As Job, who endured incredible suffering, exclaimed, "Though he slay me, yet will I hope in him" (Job 13:15). Although God does not guarantee that his followers will never suffer or experience death, he does promise always to be with them. In times of trial the believer's attitude should be that of these young men (3:17–18).

271   Ibid, 124. When the three came out of the fire, the other officials crowded around to examine them. There was no evidence that they had been in the furnace, for their bodies had not been burned (lit., "the fire had no power over their bodies"), their hair was not singed, their robes were not scorched, and there was not even any "smell of fire on them." All were convinced that they had witnessed a miracle.

return to later). That means we love our idols—although our idols do not stand 90 feet tall and nine feet wide, nor do we erect them out in the middle of nowhere, like Nebuchadnezzar, where no one can see them.

We flaunt our idols, and our idols crave attention—at least most of them. Our idols are often the size of the average man or woman because they are usually ordinary human beings that somehow became popular—in which we admire and idolize them afterward. Not only do we love our idols, but we also love creating new ones. Understanding the "idol worship," "pop culture" of America, on June 11, 2002, a brand-new show aired on the Fox network: American Idol. The show took ordinary citizens and turned many of them into household names as well as "pop culture icons." Carrie Underwood, Jennifer Hudson, Taylor Hicks, Kelly Clarkson, Ruben Studdard, Fantasia, David Archuleta, and Jordan Sparks, to name a few.

What was interesting about this show was many of the participates did not come in first place. However, they were able to use the American Idol platform to launch their careers. Remember, American Idol was created for entertainment, but it created human idols that millions of Americans and millions of people worldwide idolized, but not in a good way. It is okay to admire people and congratulate them for their success, but to idolize them—to the point—we worship them, which is specifically forbidden in Scripture. Unfortunately, that is exactly how we have behaved as a nation for centuries. Instead of desiring to become who God created us to be, we fantasize about being someone else, often mimicking their mannerisms, behaviors, and style in dress and appearance. A profound statement that sums up what is happening is this: we were all created by God to be an original, but most people die a copy—meaning they never discover God's divine purpose for their existence because they do not know personally the God that gave them life.

Political and military idols can be far more dangerous than someone who has a lot of followers because they have a great voice or an exceptional talent. The difference is a person with power and authority has the resources and mechanisms to impact people's lives in a greater and more significant way. For instance, when King Solomon's heart was turned away from God in his old age because of his many pagan wives' sinful influence, his sinfulness impacted the entire nation of Israel. Simply put, Solomon had a lot of influence on the people, and when he fell from grace, the nation fell as well because they kept their eyes on him and not on God.

Political and military leaders played a key role in the Confederate states that succeeded from the Union in 1861. They were so influential, because of their positions of power and authority, they convinced a significant number of ordinary citizens to join them in an attempt to overthrow the government. For instance, Jefferson Davis was a military man and the former Secretary of War. At the time of the Confederacy's succession, he was a Senator from the state of Mississippi. He was elected as the Confederate president. Alexander H. Stephens, the former Governor of Georgia and U.S. Congressman, became the Confederate's vice president. General Robert E. Lee, General Braxton Brag, and Lt. General Thomas "Stonewall" Jackson are just a few of the most senior officers that switched sides to lead the Confederate Army.[272]

> *The Confederate States of America was a collection of 11 states that seceded from the United States in 1860 following the election of President Abraham Lincoln. Led by Jefferson Davis and existing from 1861 to 1865, the Confederacy struggled for legitimacy and was never recognized as a sovereign nation. After suffering a crushing defeat in the Civil War, the Confederate States of America ceased to exist.*[273]

General Ulysses S. Grant was one of the key military officers for the Union Army that led to the defeat of the Confederate Army, and he used his popularity to become the 18th president of the U.S. The goal of the Confederate Army was twofold: First, to use military force to create an independent country they would control. Second, to allow the Confederate southern states to continue the inhumane institution of slavery, their bread, and butter.

---

272   History Channel, "*Confederate States of America*," 21 August 2018 [online] accessed on 16 October 2020; available from https://www.history.com/topics/american-civil-war/confederate-states-of-america; Internet.

273   Ibid.

Since they lost and could not have the whole slavery apparatus as before, they settled for "Plan B," which was Jim Crow. As a result, Confederate monuments were erected in America by Whites to send a loud message to Blacks. These statues were a way to remind Blacks of their place in society and keep them in servitude to Whites in America; by segregation, humiliation, and degradation. Whites built statues of white men that were traitors, who tried to overthrow our government for the sole purpose of reminding Blacks of slavery, and that they were still beneath Whites. Their disdain and racist attitudes toward Blacks were so strong, they were willing to destroy the country in the process (for their gain).

Researching this part of our sad history reminded me of the Republican party's visceral reaction to the election of Barack Obama as the first African American President in 2008. It was reported that the very night of the election, the senior leaders of the Republican party met in a secret meeting in Washington D.C. to discuss how they would sabotage Obama's Presidency to ensure he would fail.[274] Mitch McConnel, the Republican leader in the U.S. Senate, made it plain about their intentions when he said their primary goal was to ensure Obama was a one-term President—not to address the immediate needs of the country. The Republicans didn't care about the country—which was going through the worst financial crisis since the Great Depression at the time—they only cared about embarrassing and humiliating the black guy and his political party. Also, Republicans love to call people who do not agree with their tactics un-American or unpatriotic. However, I would argue, their hatred and racist reaction to Obama's Presidency and their goal to use the Legislative Branch of government to ensure his failure—regardless if Americans suffered in the process—is the textbook definition of un-American and un-patriotic.

The fact that in the year 2020, most of these Confederate statues are still standing tells you something about our country, and that is, racism is still okay in America. Many Whites defend these statues because they want to maintain white heritage, which does not make

---

[274] "GOP Top Goal: Make Obama a 1-Term President," NBC News, 4 November 2010 [on-line]; accessed on 28 November 2020; accessed from http// www.GOP leader's top goal: Make Obama 1-term president (nbcnews.com); Internet.

sense to anyone that understands the magnitude of how devastating slavery was (and still is to this very day) in America. For those racist statues and monuments to still exist is like someone breaking into your house and raping and killing your family, and you put a monument or statue of the perpetrator in front of your house as a memorial and reminder of the incident.

Application of Daniel 3:13-18

Why did God command Israel not to participate in idol worship?

1. Idol worship dishonors the God who created them and delivered them from bondage in Egypt.
2. Idol worship is giving glory to someone or something else that only belongs to God.
3. Idol worship causes man to demean himself, and thus, bring about God's judgment.
4. Idol worship causes man to become a being God never intended—an object to be worshiped.

What are the dangers of idol worship in a so-called Christian America?

1. Idol worship causes America to worship everything and everyone, but the God who created us. (vs. 1-7)
2. Idol worship causes America to pressure those that believe in God to act like those that do not. (vs. 8-18)
3. Idol worship causes America not to change or desire to do so, even when God reveals His glory to us. (vs. 19-30)

What are six dangerous idols that have consumed most American's lives?

1. Family and friends.

   "If anyone comes to Me, and does not hate his own father and mother and wife and children and brothers and sisters, yes, and even his own life, he cannot be My disciple. (Luke 14:26)

Most of us live our lives centered around our family and friends. Although family and friends are extremely important in the eyes of God, our loved ones were never given to us to take God's place. Family and friends (especially Christian ones) were given to us to enhance our walk with the Lord, hold us accountable to faith in Christ, and help us reach our God-given potential. If your life centers around your family or friends and has no room for Jesus, then your family or friends are first, not the Lord Jesus.

2. **Jobs and careers.**

> *"Whatever you do, do your work heartily, as for the Lord rather than for men." (Colossians 3:23)*

Most people spend so much time trying to earn a living or find meaningful employment, their job or career aspirations have become idols in the eyes of God. A job should be a blessing, but if it is not placed in the proper perspective, a job can become a curse, especially when your job keeps you from doing the will of God—like going to church and getting involved, tithing as well as Bible study, and growing spiritually. Only after putting Jesus first, can He teach you how to properly prioritize everything else in your life.

3. **Money and financial resources.**

> *"For the love of money is a root of all sorts of evil, and some by longing for it have wandered away from the faith and pierced themselves with many griefs." (1 Timothy 6:10)*

To most people money is everything, which is why they do just about anything to get it or keep it, no matter what sinful act they have to do. The Bible does not say money is evil, it says that money is the root of all evil. Money is an innate object that is not good or bad, it is neutral. What you do with it, or for it, can lead to bad things that can be very difficult to recover from.

4. **Power and influence.**

   "I can do all things through Christ which strengthened me." (Philippians 4:13)

   Most people that have worldly power and influence tend to abuse it because they use it to enrich themselves, and those around them; often to the detriment of others, especially those who are less fortunate. However, in Christ, we all have power and influence. However, we are to use our Holy Spirit's power and influence to glorify God.

5. **Material possessions.**

   "Do not store up for yourselves treasures on earth, where moth and rust destroy, and where thieves break in and steal. But store up for yourselves treasures in heaven, where neither moth nor rust destroys, and where thieves do not break in or steal; for where your treasure is, there your heart will be also. (Matthew 6:19)

   "No one can serve two masters; for either he will hate the one and love the other, or he will be devoted to one and despise the other. You cannot serve God and wealth." (Matthew 6:24)

   Our material possessions are given by God so that we may glorify Him. However, this does not include things we gain by some sinful or illegal means—that's the devil's doing. God opens doors for us and blesses us for our good and His glory. God also blesses us to be a blessing, not so that we can hoard everything for ourselves. To whom much is given, much is required. Therefore, we should never allow our material possessions to control us, or keep us from doing God's will.

6. **Success and failures.**

   This book of the law shall not depart from your mouth, but you shall meditate on it day and night, so that you may be careful to do according to all that is written in it; for then you will make your way prosperous, and then you will have success. (Joshua 1:9)

God's definition of success and failure is different from man's definition of those same terms. For instance, you could be a wealthy person that is viewed as a success in the eyes of the world, but still be a failure in the eyes of God—because you don't know Jesus. If you don't know Jesus, you will still be bankrupt in heaven, although you were rich on this earth. On the other hand, you can struggle financially your entire life, and be rich in heaven—because you do know Jesus as your personal Savior and Lord. This does not mean we should not strive for success; it just means we should strive for success God's way. God does not have a problem with us having things, He has a problem with things having us—meaning controlling us.

CHAPTER 12

RELIGION AND POLITICS

Jesus Before Pilate

Then they *led Jesus from Caiaphas into the Praetorium, and it was early; and they themselves did not enter into the Praetorium so that they would not be defiled, but might eat the Passover. Therefore Pilate went out to them and *said, "What accusation do you bring against this Man?" They answered and said to him, "If this Man were not an evildoer, we would not have delivered Him to you." So Pilate said to them, "Take Him yourselves, and judge Him according to your law." The Jews said to him, "We are not permitted to put anyone to death," to fulfill the word of Jesus which He spoke, signifying by what kind of death He was about to die.

Therefore Pilate entered again into the Praetorium, and summoned Jesus and said to Him, "Are You the King of the Jews?" Jesus answered, "Are you saying this on your own initiative, or did others tell you about Me?" Pilate answered, "I am not a Jew, am I? Your own nation and the chief priests delivered You to me; what have You done?" Jesus answered, "My kingdom is not of this world. If My kingdom were of this world, then My servants would be fighting so that I would not be handed over to the Jews; but as it is, My kingdom is not of this realm." Therefore Pilate said to Him, "So You are a king?" Jesus answered, "You say correctly that I am a king. For this I have been born, and for this I have come into the *world, to testify to the truth. Everyone who is of the truth hears My voice." Pilate *said to Him, "What is truth?"*

And when he had said this, he went out again to the Jews and *said to them, "I find no guilt in Him. But you have a custom that I release someone for you at the Passover; do you wish then that I release for you the King of the Jews?" So they cried out again, saying, "Not this Man, but Barabbas." Now Barabbas was a robber. (John 18:28-40)

Today, politics can be just as divisive in the church as racism and division. Therefore, what role should politics have in the Christian church? Should the church be so closely aligned or affiliated with a political party that it limits its effectiveness in preaching the gospel to all races? Should the Christian church hold political rallies in the house of God? Should the Christian church display a cult-like following toward a president just because they are all from the same political party? Should the church ever wrap itself around the American flag and place their politics on the same par as they do their religion? Should Americans claim they are Christians only because they are Americans? Should the litmus test of whether or not you are a Christian be based on whether or not you are a Democrat or a Republican? Should a political party act as though they corner the market on Christianity? These are all extremely important questions that I will address in this chapter.

Furthermore, every Christian pastor should answer these questions for their members as well because the church today has become increasingly political and less biblical. Furthermore, if pastors are excessively political and less biblical, members must hold their pastor accountable and not let them get away with preaching their opinion based on their political affiliation. If pastors refuse to be held accountable and continue to act as political pundits from the pulpit, instead of preaching the gospel of Jesus Christ, I encourage those members to find another church that preaches the Bible correctly.

Contrary to popular belief, Jesus was not a Democrat nor a Republican. So we as Christians must be careful not to try and represent the gospel message through the lenses of politics. Furthermore,

Christians should never use their political affiliation to hijack Christianity for their cause. According to my former pastor, Dr. Tony Evans, far too long, Anglo Christians have wrapped the Christian faith in the American flag, often creating a civil religion that is foreign to the way God intended His church to function.[275] In other words, there is a segment of the Republican party that has high-jacked Christianity for their benefit, as though it is an exclusive club for Republicans only. As such, they tend to treat Democrats as heathens and on their way to hell—at least, in their eyes—just because of their political party affiliation, not based on Scripture. Furthermore, some of these same Republicans elevate America's *founding fathers* to the level of the early *Church Fathers* in their arguments for the U.S. being founded as a Christian nation—which is a terrible precedent. On the other hand, some Democrats say similar things about Republicans because they blindly support President Trump. This is why so many Americans classify themselves as Independents and not aligned with either major political party. For the Independents, there is just too much partisan behavior and bickering and not enough willingness to work together for the good of the country.

While we have already acknowledged that the Christian church in America is fractured and divided along racial lines, some churches have taken that one step further by preaching a gospel that elevates its members—along the lines of race—acting as if they alone are God's chosen. This has led many white churches to preach a Caucasian-centric gospel, while many black churches preach an Afro-centric gospel. The problem is this false approach gives the impression that Jesus' death on the cross was for a specific race, only—which is heresy.

---

275   Tony Evans, *Oneness Embraced*, 19-20. Far too long Anglo Christians have wrapped the Christian faith in the American flag, often creating a civil religion that is foreign to the way God intended His church to function. Our nation's founding father's are frequently elevated to the level of church fathers in the arguments for the U.S. being founded as a Christian nation. While we should celebrate and affirm the Judeo-Christian worldview that influenced the framework for the founding of the nation, the church must also be careful to judge our nation's founder's failures to apply the principles of freedom that they were espousing to the area of race is a prominent reason why many minority individuals today are less than enthusiastic to join in with those in our nation who want to exalt or restore America's history and heritage.

Jesus Has No Political Affiliation

In a book by Tony Campolo titled, *Is Jesus a Republican or a Democrat?* the author employed a rhetorical title to make the important point of how Christianity has been politicized in America to the detriment of the church. Campolo talked about how the Republican party emphasizes individual responsibility, while the Democratic party emphasizes government responsibility.[276] Campolo stated that Republicans expect people not to blame others for their problems that are the result of their shortcomings or failures. Also, he said, Republicans come down especially hard on able-bodied men and women who unjustly collect welfare benefits, which I wholeheartedly agree with both positions. However, the government should never be the vehicle that is the one inflicting pain (or make it lawful for others to do so) or deliberately pass laws that hinder certain people groups from succeeding, which it has done to Blacks, in many ways, since 1619.

Many Republicans argue that the government is not responsible for people living in poverty, even if they are the entity that helps put them there. Also, Republicans believe the government treat all people groups equally, White as well as Black. On the other hand, Democrats adamantly disagree with Republicans in the role of government. Democrats argue that the government should not just be for the wealthy but all citizens. Also, Democrats have pointed out that so many people in this country have often been victimized by society's social structures that hinder them from achieving the American Dream, such as many African Americans.[277]

Ironically, the vast majority of white Americans tend to vote Republican. In contrast, the vast majority of black Americans tend to vote Democratic because they each tend to view life through the prism of their party's affiliation. What people often fail to realize, on both sides, is that people tend to hold political as well as religious views based on their life experiences. Therefore, Whites and Blacks have not had the same life experiences, so they view America differently. Based

---

276 Tony Campolo. *Is Jesus a Republican or a Democrat?: And 14 Other Polarizing Issues.* (Dallas: Word Publishing, 1995).

277 Ibid.

on the conflicting views of Republicans and Democrats, there has to be a balance, or at least a willingness to work together for the good of the country—especially if there is ever going to be some form of racial reconciliation, if not in secular society, hopefully in the church.

Do we have lazy people in America? Absolutely, but they are not just Black people; they are also, White, Asian, Hispanic, Native American, and others. However, Blacks have been stigmatized as the laziest people group in America, primarily because of a white supremacist view that has poisoned the minds of many white Americans (as well as others), especially when it is propagated by their beloved white politicians that lead their political party.[278]

The Bible And When Religion And Politics Collide

The good news is the Bible provides us clear directions on how to respond when religion and politics collide. Unfortunately, many Christians in American are not very good students of the Bible or Christian history, so they are unaware that politics during the Roman Empire was just as intense and divisive today in this country. The Pharisees and Sadducees were just as transactional as many Christians are today. In other words, these religious groups wanted a secular government to do their bidding, so they aligned themselves with the Roman Government, even if it meant they had to sell their souls to the devil. If certain officials in the government did what they wanted, they gave them their undying loyalty.

In John 18, Jesus was brought before Pilate, the Governor of Judah. The religious Jews were tired of Jesus, but they did not have the legal authority to put him to death by crucifixion. They needed the government to do their dirty work. What is also interesting about this passage is that during normal times, the Pharisees and Sadducees were at each other's throats. However, they found an equal foe that they hated more than they hated each other: Jesus. So, they led Jesus to the Praetorium, Pilate's governing headquarters and living quarters.

---

278   Ibram X. Kendi. *Stamped From the Beginning,* 465. President Ronald Reagan promoted the racist idea of "welfare queen," which was a trope against black women. However, this racist language was adopted into the public policy of the Republican party.

A large crowd had accompanied the religious establishment to Pilate's location. Because the Jewish Pentecost was near, the Jewish religious leaders refused to enter Pilate's home for fear of being unclean, by entering a Gentile's residence.

Pilate went back and forth between the two. He talked to Jesus inside and went outside to talk to the Jews from his balcony. Pilate did this about seven times. Pilate asked the Pharisees and Sadducees what their charges were against Jesus. They responded by telling Pilate, if Jesus were not guilty, they would not have bothered him (v. 30). They told Pilate, trust us, He's guilty! Take our word for it! Our word should be all the evidence you need, they retorted. Pilate told them, if Jesus was guilty, as they had proclaimed, he encouraged them to take Him and deal with Him according to their own law (v. 31). However, their selfish actions revealed their true motives. They did not want Jesus interrogated; they wanted Him crucified—which was only allowed to happen by the providence of God (v. 32).

Pilate went back in to question Jesus again. He asked Jesus if He was the King of the Jews (v. 34), to which He responded by asking Pilate about his faith in Him. Jesus said, "Are you saying this on your own initiative, or did others tell you about Me?" Pilate had an opportunity to acknowledge Jesus' true identity, but he dodged the question by saying he was not a Jew (v. 35).[279] What Pilate failed to realize was that he did not have to be a Jew to accept Jesus. However, God knew Pilate's stubborn heart and used it to fulfill His plan of salvation, which was to allow His Son to die on Calvary's Cross. Jesus told Pilate that His kingdom was not of this world—which meant His kingdom was heavenly (v. 36). Pilate asked Jesus if He was a King (because He said He had a kingdom), which was a logical conclusion.

---

279   John E. White and D. S. Dockery. *Holman Concise Bible Commentary: John*. (Nashville: Broadman & Holman Publishers), 1998, 486-487. This Gospel records three major conversations held between Jesus and an individual person who was being confronted with the truth and the claims of the gospel. In John 3 Nicodemus was a religious man who sought Jesus in order to pursue his spiritual questions. The Samaritan woman in John 4 was neither religious nor a skeptic but rather one who represented worldliness in its most common form. She was indifferent to the spiritual, living a life of moral self-indulgence. Pilate, however, is indicative of the modern secularist. Hardened to that which would speak to his soul, he was neither open nor inquisitive about the gospel.

Jesus told Pilate that He was not just a king, but He was the King because His kingdom was the Eternal Kingdom, not an earthly one (v. 37). However, Pilate did not fear God, so he did not care about heavenly things. So, Jesus' statements about heaven did not faze him. Pilate was only concerned about threats to Caesar's earthly kingdom, which in turn, would have threatened his position—if there had been a riot because of Jesus. To let him know he was in over his head, Jesus told Pilate that the purpose He came into the world was to testify to the truth and that everyone who was of the truth would hear His voice (v. 38). Jesus's answer was directed toward the Jews and the religious establishment, who had rejected Him, and the Roman Government that rejected Him as well, which included Pilate.

Jesus gave Pilate every opportunity to turn from his evil ways and not fall for the Jewish leaders' schemes, but again, he missed it. Pilate revealed where his heart was because he said to Jesus, "What is the truth?"[280] The sad reality was, Pilate had a divine encounter with "the Truth" but did not even recognize it. Based on how Jesus answered Pilate's questions, he did not view Jesus as a threat. So, Pilate knew Jesus was not guilty of any crime, but unfortunately, he continued to play along with the charade. Pilate went back out on his balcony to address the Jews and told them he found no fault in Jesus (v. 39).

Since Pilate refused to listen to Jesus, he could have, at least, listened to his wife. Pilate's wife had warned him not to have anything to do with the scheme against Jesus, which God warned her about in a dream (Matthew 27:19). As men often do, they refuse to listen to wise counsel, especially when it comes from their wife, which was the critical mistake Pilate made. In a last-ditch attempt to wash his hands of the situation and appease his conscience, Pilate offered the Jews a scapegoat. He offered to free Jesus in place of a known criminal named Barabbas. The Roman Government allowed for the swap of two

---

280   J. F. MacArthur, Jr. *The MacArthur study Bible: New American Standard Bible, John.* (Nashville: Thomas Nelson Publishers), 2006. What is truth? In response to Jesus' mention of "truth" in v. 37, Pilate responded rhetorically with cynicism, convinced that no answer existed to the question. The retort proved that he was not among those whom the Father had given to the Son, John made it clear that Jesus was not guilty of any sin or crime, thus exhibiting the severe injustice and guilt of both the Jews and Romans who executed Him.

prisoners during that time of the year, which was the rule Pilate tried to use to get himself out of the jam he allowed the Jews to put him in. Pilate assumed the Jews would ask for Jesus to be set free and for Barabbas to remain incarcerated, but it backfired.[281] The Jews said, not this man, but give us the criminal: Barabbas. Wow! How many times have men, women, boys, and girls chosen someone else over Jesus? Unfortunately, it happens all too often, even in the age of Covid-19 — when if there was ever a time, we need Jesus, that time is now!

The Jew's total rejection of Jesus was evident when they shouted, "Crucify Him! Crucify Him!" This is one of the saddest moments in the entire Scriptures. This is what transnationalism looks like in its ugliest form. The church aligned itself with the Roman Government to put Jesus to death on the cross. You would have thought the people would have learned their lesson, if not the world, at least, the church. However, the Christian church in America has not learned valuable lessons like these from Scripture. It somehow still insists on aligning itself with the U.S. Government to use the government to fulfill its agenda, even if it makes the church look political and not spiritual.

The Moral Majority

One could ask, when did white evangelicals become so political? Well, the answer is they always have been since they began to use evangelical as a designation. However, the modern-day version can be traced to Jerry Falwell.

> *In the mid-1960s, Jerry Falwell, a well-known fundamentalist pastor of Thomas Road Baptist Church in Lynchburg, Virginia, would have seemed an unlikely candidate to shepherd conservative Christians into mainstream politics. In an oft-quoted sermon he gave in 1965 titled "Ministers and Marchers," Falwell declared, "Preachers are not called to be politicians, but soul winners."*

---

281 W. W. Wiersbe. *Expository Outlines on the New Testament*, 262. In John 18:33 through 19:15, we read the sad record of Pilate's cowardly indecision. At least seven times Pilate went from the hall to the Jews outside, trying to work out a compromise. Pilate crucified Christ because he was a coward, "willing to content the people" (Mark 15:15). How many sinners will be in hell because they feared people and sought to please them!

> Delivered during the height of the civil rights movement, most observers interpreted Falwell's sentiments as a critique of the movement in general and of Martin Luther King Jr. specifically. By 1976, Falwell had completely flipped his position and his stance against mixing religion and politics and embarked on an "I Love America" rally tour. In a sermon delivered on the fourth of July, he made his new position clear: "This idea of religion and politics don't mix was invented by the devil to keep Christians from running their own country."[282]

Falwell did not just preach about his transformation to mix religion and politics; he took action to do something about it. According to Tisby, in 1979, Falwell met with other members of the emerging "New Right." This meeting included the conservative political activists Paul Weyrich and Robert Billings and the Christian right godfather, Edward McAteer. These three men helped rouse the religious right into a potent pollical force and founded the Moral Majority as the vehicle.[283] The first test of their political might was that they organized just in time to support the man who would become the darling of the Religious Right, Ronald Reagan. Ironically, Reagan had been a Hollywood actor-turned-politician and would not have seemed that he would have been their choice because he had supported a liberal pro-abortion law when he was governor of California. However, Reagan's charisma got their attention and acceptance when he adopted the religious rights talking points into his campaign. Perhaps, many conservatives and non-conservatives believed what sealed the deal was Reagan's speech at the First Baptist Church in Dallas in early 1980.

Reagan all but sealed the white conservative Christian support for his run for the presidency when he said, "I know this is a non-partisan gathering, so I know you can't endorse me, but I want you to know I endorse you and what you are doing."[284] Ironically, in the 1980

---

282   Jemar Tisby. The *Color of Compromise*, 166.

283   Ibid. within a few years, the Moral Majority had an annual budget of $6 million, and its publication, Moral Majority Report, went to 840,00 households, with hundreds of Christian radio stations carrying their daily commentary, 166-167.

284   Ibid, 167.

presidential election, Reagan won the electoral college in a landslide of 489 to 49—one of the most lopsided wins in American presidential history. Reagan's alignment with the *Religious Right* movement proved to be a winning combination. He carried all the Sunbelt states and all the former Confederacy states, except Georgia, the home state of the Democratic challenger, Jimmy Carter.[285]

So, the question was asked, what did the conservative Christians support when they voted for Ronald Reagan?

A brief glimpse of his actions and policies demonstrates that in throwing their electoral power behind this charismatic politician, they also bolstered several stances that could be perceived as anti-black. Reagan did not shy away from publicly aligning himself with racists or from using racially coded language in his appeal to white voters. As historian Joseph Crespino relates, Reagan began his 1980 presidential campaign at an annual fair in Neshoba County, Mississippi, wherein 1964, three civil rights workers—James Chaney, Mickey Schwerner, and Andrew Goodman—had disappeared. After a search that lasted all summer and attracted national attention, an anonymous tip led investigators to an earthen dam where the bodies of the three young men were buried. They had each been shot by a white supremacist member of the KKK and local law enforcement officers who were outraged by the presence of "outside agitators" during Freedom Summer, a movement to register black voters in Mississippi.[286]

According to Tisby, in Reagan, conservative Christians got someone who was not afraid to stoke racial tensions and play to his base, including some racist whites. When Regan spoke at the Neshoba Country Fair, even though it had been years later since the KKK killed Chaney, Schwerner, and Goodman, that heinous crime was a fresh memory, especially among African Americans. However, Reagan chose the annual fair for political reasons and used words familiar with Mississippi segregationists, who believed the federal government should stop disrupting the states' social affairs. In other words, if a state

---

285 Ibid.

286 Ibid, 168.

wanted to be racist, that was not the business of the federal government to intervene.

Republicans wanted the votes in Mississippi, so they assisted Reagan in tailoring his speech that day to appeal to "George Wallace inclined voters (referring to the failed 1968 third-party presidential candidate who opposed black civil rights." Reagan promised the crowd that if he were elected, he would restore to states and local governments the power that properly belongs to them. [287] Reagan's charisma and commitment to support states' rights all but sealed the religious right support behind Reagan for the White House. Also, so that he could push their agenda. Since that time, white evangelicals have relied on their political power and financial strength to influence the outcome of local, state, and national elections.

Unfortunately, the religious right's influence on the Republican party has driven a greater divide between Blacks and Whites, especially among Christians. This is because their white agenda is good for them, but not for people of color. For instance, most white evangelicals view the Black Lives Matter movement as a cult or terrorist organization, which further divides Whites and Blacks. Instead of trying to understand the difficulty for African Americans and why we feel that law enforcement and the criminal justice system are stacked against us, many Whites continue to complain about any method we choose to draw attention to the racism we still face in this day and time.

Case in point, most white evangelicals view Colin Kaepernick, the former quarterback for the San Francisco 49ers football team, either as a traitor, ungrateful liberal, or un-America, but certainly not a patriot. Kaepernick drew national attention when he decided to kneel during the National Anthem before a football game to protest police brutality against African Americans silently. Kaepernick initially would stand with his fist raised, but a retired Army Green Beret name Nate Boyer convinced him to kneel during the national anthem. Boyer explained to Kaepernick the significance of kneeling in military terms to show honor or respect. As a result, Kaepernick began to kneel during his peaceful protest. Every conservative media outlet blasted Kaepernick for his actions, and many continue to do so to this very day.

---

287   Ibid.

His kneeling protest cost him his livelihood of playing professional football. After Kaepernick's contract ended, the 49ers refused to resign him, and no other NFL team has dared to sign him as well, although he is a very talented and capable quarterback. Those white billionaire owners refused to go near Kaepernick for simply kneeling because of the toxic political climate around the issue. Ironically, these same billionaires will sign former players that have been kicked out of the league for a variety of reasons such as performance-enhancing drugs, gun charges or violations, convicted and spending time in jail for a dogfighting ring, drug or alcohol abuse, spousal or child abuse, or any other type of domestic violence, or anger management issues, but silently kneeling was unforgivable.

As long as these rich white owners think they have a better chance of winning, they normally do not care what the background of the coach or athlete has done, but for racial reasons, they cared about what Kaepernick did. Oddly, when Black folk get upset about something in America, it does not matter (at least not to the majority of Whites), but when white folk gets upset about something, it can cause even white billionaires to stop in their tracks, even to go against their own interests, especially if it brings them some political backlash.

The Elephant In The Room

Allow me to make this plain; there is nothing wrong with wanting conservative judges to help push Christian principles through the courts, impacting secular society in a godly way. However, as a Christian pastor, I don't believe one should ever align themselves with such a destructive, immoral, and incompetent human being to lead them, like President Donald Trump. A man that is so depraved and verbally abusive that you allow him to destroy everything else in the process that you once said you cared about. Loyal Republican supporters of Trump failed to realize what the rest of America had witnessed for the entire four years of his Presidency. The man they unleashed on America, by voting him into the highest office in the world, with all that power, was like a bull in a China shop. They watched him demolish everything in sight, including many of the things they claimed to treasure—in the past. It was not just that millions of unsaved Americans voted for Trump, but a vast majority of white Evangelicals did as well. Once again, without the white Evangelical vote, Trump would never become the President.

True Christians should never give up their morals, spiritual identity, and godly character to align themselves so closely with the government that its agenda becomes the church's agenda, and not God's kingdom agenda. In the age of Trumpism (the cult-like following of Trump), the influence of politics on the Christian church has caused the Great Commission to become the "great omission." Why? Because controlling a secular government has taken precedence over saving souls. What is lost in all of this is the fact that you cannot regulate morality! We have a ton of laws on the books in America, but that still does not stop people from breaking the law. I am by no means advocating for a lawless society, but I am advocating for the church to get back to God's business, which is to reach the lost and disciple the saved—and not making the church's main focus the control of the U.S. Government.

Having said all of that, now let's address the elephant in the room in a more precise way that gets to the heart of the matter. Two issues are paramount to evangelicals: abortion and homosexuality. The Bible clarifies that both issues are sinful, but so are a host of many others. However, evangelicals place abortion and homosexuality on a pedestal above all other sins and treat them with absolute disdain, while not holding other sins in the same vein. Before Trumpism, evangelicals also cared about other important Christian principles such as leadership, character, morality, decency, the faithfulness of a man to his wife, and that he was not self-centered or a narcissist. However, since Trumpism, many white evangelicals changed their views on these issues or were willing to give their fearless leader Trump a past, I order that they could use him to further their agenda. Abortion and homosexuality are both sins, not because a man says so, but because God says so. First, God gives life, and because He alone is sovereign, He is the only one with the legitimate authority to take life—without it being a sin, because He alone makes all the rules. This is why God told us, "You shall not murder," [288] which is the sixth of the Ten Commandments (Exodus 20:13). "You shall not" is a prohibition, not a suggestion. In the Bible, this is a command with a very strong emphasis on what "not to do" because God said so, full stop! Most Americans would agree murder is wrong, but depending on the situation, there are those that waffle on their answer, which is why there are people, including Christians, that do not believe abortion is murder or a sin. How do we know that life begins at conception and not just at birth? The gift of life is not a man-made invention; it is a divine gift from God.

> *"Before I formed you in the womb, I knew you, and before you were born, I consecrated you; I have appointed you a prophet to the nations." (Jeremiah 1:5)* [289]

Jeremiah reveals a principle about humanity, and that is, our purpose for existence is not by accident; it is by God's divine plan, which began when our life began, which is in the womb-at the very moment of conception, not at birth. The Psalmist also makes this clear.

> *"For You formed my inward parts; You wove me in my mother's womb. I will give thanks to You, for I am fearfully and wonderfully*

---

288   E.D. Radmacher, R.B. Allen, & H.W. House. *Nelson's New Illustrated Bible Commentary: Exodus.* (Nashville: Nelson Publishers, 1999), 123. The sixth commandment, you shall not murder, did not forbid all taking of life, for the Law itself included provisions for capital punishment (21:15–17, 23) as well as warfare (17:8–16). The deliberate murder of another person (outside the legitimate provisions of capital punishment or war) flagrantly violated the sanctity of life. This included murder committed by officers of the state (read the story of Naboth, 1 Kin. 21). The first murder recorded in the Bible was the killing of Abel by Cain (Gen. 4:8–14). Indeed, the death of Jesus, based on false charges and an illegal trial, was the most horrible murder of all time!

289   Walvoord John F, Roy B. Zuck, *The Bible Knowledge Commentary: An Exposition of the Scriptures, Jeremiah*, Vol. 1. (Wheaton: Victor Books, 1985), 1130. God's call of Jeremiah as a prophet, though brief, contained a message designed to motivate him for his task. God revealed that His selection of Jeremiah as a prophet had occurred before he had even been formed ... in the womb. The word knew (yā→a') means far more than intellectual knowledge. It was used of the intimate relations experienced by a husband and wife ("lay," Gen. 4:1) and conveyed the sense of a close personal relationship ("chosen," Amos 3:2) and protection ("watches over," Ps. 1:6). Before Jeremiah was conceived God had singled him out to be His spokesman to Israel.

made; Wonderful are Your works, and my soul knows it very well. (Psalm 139:13-14)

The Psalmist affirms Jeremiah's argument of life beginning in the womb. This is a Psalm of David that proclaims the Omnipresence and Omniscience of God and explains how He is intimately involved in humanity: before, during, and after conception. Furthermore, only God decides when life is conceived or taken. However, a life taken on man's terms, regardless of the method, whether murder, homicide, or abortion, the person causing the action has to answer to God for their actions.

"You shall not lie with a male as one lies with a female; it is an abomination." (Leviticus 18:22)

When God gave Moses this command, it was so that he would inform the Israelites of what He required of them, especially as they were about to enter the land of Canaan—where this sort of sinful behavior permeated throughout the Canaanite society. This is why God dealt so harshly with them because this behavior is an abomination or disgrace to Him.

"And the men likewise gave up natural relations with women and were consumed with passion for one another, men committing shameless acts with men and receiving in themselves the due penalty for their error." (Romans 1:27)

The apostle Paul was well versed in the Old Testament, including Leviticus. When he wrote this to the church in Rome, he was aware of the sin of homosexuality prevalent in Roman society, just as it was in the Canaanite society. In this verse, Paul described the downward spiral of humanity and how homosexuality played a significant role in it. He also explained God's penalty of eternal judgment for those that practice such behavior.

Or do you not know that the unrighteous will not inherit the kingdom of God? Do not be deceived; neither the sexually immoral, nor idolaters, nor adulterers, nor homosexuals, nor thieves,

> *nor the greedy, nor those habitually drunk, nor verbal abusers, nor swindlers, will inherit the kingdom of God. (1 Corinthians 6:9-10)*

The city of Corinth was part of the Roman Empire at the time. Therefore, the same sinful issues that plagued other parts of the Empire were also prevalent in Corinth, including homosexuality, which is why Paul addressed the issue to the church in this letter. He made it clear that no homosexuals will inherit the kingdom of God, which meant that no person that practices that behavior is going to heaven unless they repent. Paul told the church to do this in his letter to Rome, which included Corinth (Romans 10:9-10).

In this passage of 1st Corinthians, eight other sins are mentioned, in addition to homosexuality. However, it is ironic how Christians tend to blast one type of sinner on the list, the homosexual, but give a pass to the other eight sinners—when none of them deserve it. Again, this is why I do not understand why white evangelicals support President Trump when he covers at least seven of the nine categories of sins on the list and does it open with no shame. Other than drunkenness and homosexuality, he does everything else.

In the capacity of a pastor as well as a military chaplain (now retired), there were numerous times that I had to counsel someone that struggled with the sin of homosexuality and the sin of already having an abortion (and the devastating impact it had on their life), or contemplating having an abortion for various reasons. Although I strongly disagree with both of these issues—because of my strong Christian values, based on Scripture—I could still effectively minister to each of these individuals. By God's grace, I was even able to lead some of them to genuine faith in Christ. Yet, I did not act as though I was their judge, jury, and executioner, which caused them to come and talk to me. After listening to their issues, I was glad to share the redemptive story of Jesus Christ as Savior and Lord on a level they could relate to. Sometimes I would share my struggles in life and how God brought me out by His grace and was able to use me in a mighty way—even though my struggles were different than theirs (Romans 3:23).

I understood the way I treated them was going to be their view of a Christian pastor, perhaps for the rest of their life—since many people I have encountered had never had a close encounter with a minister of the gospel. If I came across the wrong way, I could have caused them to never seek guidance again from another Christian, less known, a pastor. Furthermore, neither abortion nor homosexuality is an unpardonable sin, but neither are any of the other eight sins on the list, in the eyes of God. However, the Republican party treats homosexuality and abortion as though they are unforgivable, so they get elevated above any other sin. If the Christian church displayed humility and a Christ-like attitude toward those trapped in the vise of homosexuality or any other sin, they could be a better vessel to reach these individuals with the gospel message..

What Does Evangelical Even Mean These Days?

It is often said, perception is not necessarily reality. However, perception can be a big influence even if it does not match reality. Case in point, based on the name, evangelicals are supposed to be true Christians that believe in the following: The Bible is the authoritative word of God; the emphasis of salvation based on the atoning death of Christ through personal conversion; the significance of baptism by emersion; and the importance of preaching the Bible correctly. Therefore, the perception is that these characteristics define evangelicals in theory, but not always in practice or reality. Why? Because a vast majority of white evangelical's reality is mired in politics and social issues. This point is made in Emerson and Smith's book, Divided by Faith, which I have quoted from throughout my book.

> *Evangelicals believe in "engaged orthodoxy." By engaged orthodoxy, we mean taking the conservative faith beyond its boundaries of evangelical subculture and engaging the larger culture and society. To be sure, for many non-evangelical Americans, this is controversial. For evangelicals, however, this engaged orthodoxy is part of their very identity. Evangelicals*

> want their traditional faith to offer solutions to pressing social problems, such as race relations.[290]

Emerson and Smith make a great point about white evangelicals' desire to engage social problems and race relations. Unfortunately, they fail to realize that they are part of the problem, not the solution. Their blinders hinder them from being a voice of reason. As a result, their positions on social problems and race relations negatively affect their relationship between black evangelicals and other black Christians. Ironically, only 10 percent of African American Christians identify themselves as evangelical, even though many would agree with the fundamental tenants of evangelicalism. They just don't agree with how it is practiced among many white conservatives, perhaps, because the vast majority of African American Christians view evangelicalism as a conservative Caucasian Christian movement whose agenda does not include or benefit people of color.

Additionally, it is because most of the white evangelical's energy and effort seems to be to push a conservative white America's agenda and lacks concern for the lives of Blacks. This has caused black Christians to promote their political agenda by joining liberal causes that enhance people of color's lives. The problem with this tug of war is that it has caused both black and white Christians to take their eyes off what's most important: the redemptive story of Jesus Christ. That does not mean social issues in America are not important. Still, they are not more important than a personal relationship with Jesus Christ as Savior and Lord, especially for a country mired in sin.

Both White and Black Christians are concerned about social issues, and they both fight for what they believe in. The contrast is they tend to focus on different issues, which only adds to the division along racial lines. Whites and Blacks just do not view life through the same lenses. I would argue that culture wars and systemic racism have a lot to do with that. Blacks have to deal with systemic racism issues daily. Therefore, our life experiences are lived within that prism. However, many white evangelicals do not believe systemic racism exists today, thus downplaying the issue and hindering racial reconciliation.

---

290   Michael O. Emerson and Christian Smith. *Divided by Faith*, 3.

Whites created the foundation for America, and they are the majority race that has controlled the direction of America since its beginning. As such, their life experiences are different. They never faced slavery, Jim Crow, being lynched, or law enforcement and court system that singles them out just because of their race. So, when white evangelicals speak about the plight of African Americans, it is often from a skewed viewpoint. This is why many white evangelicals so easily dismiss the Black Lives Matter movement without first trying to understand the premise of their arguments. I would venture to believe that if the roles of Whites and Blacks were reversed in America, and Blacks were the dominant group and treated Whites exactly how we have been treated since 1619, there would more than likely be an aggressive "White Lives Matter" movement thriving today. Also, I would venture to say that the premise of the white movement would probably read as follows:

> *#WhiteLivesMatter was founded in 2020 in response to the acquittal of little Billy Martin murderer at the hands of a black vigilante "wannabe" cop. White Lives Matter Global Network Foundation, Inc. is a global organization in the US, UK, and Canada, whose mission is to eradicate black supremacy and build local power to intervene in violence inflicted on White communities by the state and vigilantes. By combating and countering acts of violence, creating space for White imagination and innovation, and centering White joy, we are winning immediate improvements in our lives.*[291]

This statement was taken from the official Black Lives Matter website. I meant no disrespect to the founders of this movement by editing their statement to make a valid point. The fundamental structure of the paragraph is the same. The only difference is, I purposely edited it, and substituted "black" with "white," and changed the name of Trayvon Martin to little Billy Martin, and described Trayvon's killer as a black vigilante "wannabe" cop, which is a reference to George Zimmerman. Therefore, if the premise of my argument stands, what

---

[291] Black Lives Matter. [on-line]; accessed on 30 December 2020; accessed from www://blacklivesmatter.com/about/:Internet.

would white evangelicals disagree with in the following paragraphs, if again, they were the minority group striving for equality in a black America?

White people are expansive. We are a collective of liberators who believe in an inclusive and spacious movement. We also believe that to win and bring as many people with us along the way; we must move beyond the narrow nationalism that is all too prevalent in White communities. We must ensure we are building a movement that brings all of us to the front.

White people affirm the lives of white queer and trans folks, disabled folks, undocumented folks, folks with records, women, and all-white lives along the gender spectrum. Our network centers on those who have been marginalized within White liberation movements.

White people are working for a world where white lives are no longer systematically targeted for demise.

White people affirm our humanity, our contributions to this society, and our resilience in the face of deadly oppression.

These four paragraphs were also taken from the Black Lives Matter website.[292] The only editing was changing "We" and replacing it with "White people" and replacing "black" with "white." As it relates to the content of these paragraphs, if white people were brought to America during the slave trade, and instead of it being Africans, what if it had been white Europeans instead? And what if white Europeans had been purchased by Africans and brought to a black America on inhumane slave ships and forced into slavery?

What if white people were forced to endure 100 years of Jim Crow, only after having to endure 246 years of brutal slavery? Also, what if it was white people that had to fight for their citizenship, the right to vote, and had to be subjected to a Civil War that was fought to keep them enslaved?

What if white people had to endure a Black KKK that began in 1865 and was still around today (mostly known as black nationalist)?

What if white people had to endure being repeatedly lynched by black people, discriminated against with unfair housing and schools, and were constantly targeted by the police?

---

292   Ibid.

What if white men had to endure years of police brutality, including constantly being shot or brutalized, and disproportionately incarcerated, even though white people were the third largest people group in America?

What if white women had to endure a black society that constantly disrespected and mistreated them going back to 1619.

What if white women were the ones constantly disrespected and degraded by society simply because they were white women, to include being labeled by the President of the United States as "welfare queens" because it excited his base, while corporate America used their white image in a racist manner on pancake bottles and packages to make hundreds of millions of dollars off that image?

What if white teenaged girls had to face an "adultification bias"[293] and were treated as white adult women and not as kids? As a result, they were not protected by society as innocent children, but faced harsh criticism, treated as angry or aggressive trouble makers when simply asking an adult black authority figure why they are being singled out.

What if white girls and teenagers were called ugly and treated as inferior because of their skin color and hair texture and made to feel less than because society only valued blackness?

---

293 P. R. Locket, "A New Report shows how racism and bias deny black girls their childhood," 16 May 2019. [on-line]; accessed on 30 December 2020, accessed from https://www.vox.com/new report shows how racism and bias deny black girls their childhoods - Vox; Internet. It's long been suspected that black girls are perceived as more adult-like and less innocent than white girls in school and other environments, and a new report offers further confirmation that this is the case. Researchers with the Initiative on Gender Justice and Opportunity at Georgetown Law's Center on Poverty and Inequality spoke directly to black girls and women across the country about how they are forced to deal with harmful perceptions — like that black girls are more mature and less in need of protection than other students — from a young age. This phenomenon, which the researchers refer to as "adultification bias," was examined in a 2017 report from the same team. The latest report builds on those findings by including the lived experiences of black women and girls. It's also worth noting that many of the women cited in the report recalled dealing with the same sorts of issues in their childhoods, showing that this is far from a new problem. According to participants in the Georgetown study, which was released on Wednesday, "when Black girls express strong or contrary views, adults view them as challenging authority or, more fundamentally, simply assume a girl's character is just plain 'bad.'"

What if white teenaged boys had to endure "stop and frisk" and constantly be racially profiled for simply being out in public and being white?

What if white young men had to endure being the first ones' police came after when a crime happened in their vicinity, even though they were innocent?

What if police kept white male teenagers in an interrogation room for seven hours or more and threatened them until they gave false confessions about brutally raping and killing a black woman they had never met, and police used those same false confessions to lock them up for years as adults, without a shred of evidence tying them to the crime?

What if white people had to endure longer prison sentences for committed similar crimes to black people, and the only reason they did, was because of their skin color?

What if white people had to endure an education system that discriminated against them because of their race, and that all the prestigious colleges and universities were black, and the only way you could possibly get a shot was because of something called white affirmative action?

What if the U.S. Constitution said that white people were 3/5's a person?

What if Chief Justice Roger Taney and the entire Supreme Court had been made up of black men in 1857, and Dred Scott had been a white man, and they concluded that white people had no standing in federal court because of the U.S. Constitution did not apply to the white people?

What if the roles were reversed, and Trayvon Martin had been a white teenager trying to defend himself against an overzealous out-of-control vagility "wannabe" cop, would Zimmerman still have been found innocent?

These are a lot of "what ifs," but if we were living in an alternate reality, and the roles were reversed between black people and white people in America, and there was such a thing as black supremacy, instead of white supremacy, and white people had to endure systemic racism since 1619, Whites would then truly understand the plight of

Blacks in America, as well as be far more sympathetic. I am convinced that white evangelicals would be forced to look at the issue of systemic racism from a different perspective because only after walking in another man's shoes can you properly judge why he feels the way he does about the way he and his people have been mistreated for centuries. However, white evangelicals insist on making that judgment about black people without properly understanding the whole black experience in American since 1619.

Many white evangelicals falsely judge African Americans without showing any Christian compassion in at least trying to understand our unique experiences, instead of constantly downplaying those experiences and claiming we overplay the "race card," when we simply want you to stop mistreating us and our black families. Finally, for some strange reason, white America insists on continuing to view the experiences of all non-whites in America through their white psychological, criminological, biological, and sociological construct, which is why they so often misunderstand other races. In other words, they do not see us as we really are (or how God made us); they only see us as what they think or picture we are (not of God), according to their white American dominant perspective. Many whites may disagree with this assessment, but American history since 1619, along with my own 57 years of personal life experiences in America, as well as the countless other Blacks, past and present, would say otherwise. As it is often said, you are entitled to your own opinion, but you are not titled to your own facts!

As I stated, many white evangelicals are adamantly opposed to the Black Lives Matter movement. However, when you examine the focus of this movement, based on their website, there are two areas that white evangelicals disagree with, based on their stance on social issues. The mention of homosexuals or transgender, and undocumented Hispanics. These are non-starters for white evangelicals, and if you include them in anything you want them to support, you have no chance at all for religious or political reasons. However, when it comes to the other points made from the Black Lives Matter movement website, these should be something that white evangelicals can relate to, especially if the roles were reversed.

I would venture to say that many white evangelicals that oppose Black Lives Matter, do so for religious reasons, more than political reasons. However, because these two issues have been so closely entangled in evangelical circles, it is often hard to tell which is which. Many white conservatives predominately or exclusively consume numerous hours of conservative news and media outlets for their information daily, which is why they have a very negative view of Black Lives Matter, and black people in general, because that is how we are portrayed, no matter what we do, even if one of us happens to become the President or Vice President of the United States. Those conservative news outlets portray African Americans as frauds. We are only scamming white America. The only way we can do anything better than they can, in life or an election, is if we lie, cheat, or steal. Unfortunately, these conservative news outlet's listeners believe these false characterizations no matter how far-fetched they may be. In addition, conservative white politicians that want to either get elected or remain in office, spout the same "fake news." (And many Whites still won't admit that systemic racism is not alive and well in America).

By their actions, the majority of white evangelicals don't seem to care about the enormous number of unnecessary shootings of unarmed black men by police officers. In fact, black men are always portrayed as worthless thuggish criminals, never as human beings. Simultaneously, the police officers are always treated as patriots or heroes, even after shooting and an unarmed black person or kneeling on his neck for 8 minutes and 47 seconds until he expires.

White evangelicals say they are all about preserving the family, which is why they fight so hard against abortions, but they do not share the same concern for preserving the black family. So how is it that there never seems to be the same outrage by white evangelicals for a black life that is taken unjustly in America—as they do a child that is wrongly terminated by an abortion. Shouldn't a human life matter after it is born, and not just when it is in the womb? Shouldn't that same life matter, regardless of the race or age of the individual? Shouldn't murder matter regardless if it takes place before birth or after the child grew and became a teenager or adult? For a true Christian, these questions should be rhetorical and have the obvious biblical answer, yes, definitely, or absolutely! Unfortunately, for many white Christians, their complicity of silence, lack of outrage, and refusing to stand and hold a Black Lives Matter sign during a protest, in the front of the line with Blacks, that are so sick of being sick and tired, because of the same old racism in America, says otherwise. If protesting in the streets of America, and holding a sign affirming the rights, dignity, and humanity of someone that does not look like you, in public, for all the world to see, is not your thing, how about just taking a stand for human decency when your president goes off the rails (as he often does regularly), and says and does racist things, can you say something then?

How about when Fox News applauds and glamorizes Trump's racism, can you show some outrage then? How about when a white nationalist's racist young man ran down innocent protestors with his vehicle because they were peacefully marching against confederate statues, and many innocent people were seriously injured, and a young white woman died? Where was your outrage? Where were your signs protesting the death of Heather Heyer at the home and workplace of white nationalists, as you do with the abortion doctors? If that was not bad enough, where was the outrage of white evangelicals when President Trump stood on national television, siding with those same racist white nationalists, when he said there were very fine people on both sides, including James Alex Fields Jr, who ran her down in the street like a dog?

If white evangelicals are not going to show any outrage when Blacks are being constantly humiliated, disparaged, mistreated, falsely accused, and dehumanized in America, why does Black Lives Matter enrage you so? Why are you so against a movement that only started because of what you failed to want to be outraged about—the constant killing of unarmed black men in America? I look at it this way; it took decades for many white evangelicals not to hate and wish ill will against the Civil Rights Movement of the 1960s and to acknowledge Rev. Dr. Martin Luther King Jr. as an American hero and patriot for his non-violent stance and push for racial equality. I guess it will take a lot longer for white evangelicals to say the same thing about Black Lives Matter if they ever do.

The social issues that black Christians get energized about impact our everyday lives, such as police brutality, black incarceration, Black Lives Matter, systemic racism, having adequate healthcare and educational opportunities, an economy that works for us, and better job opportunities. Although white Christians share in some of these same issues, the social issues they get energized about are narrowed toward conservative issues such as anything having to do with homosexuality, whether transgender or same-sex marriage issues, repealing Obama Care, or abortion. While black pastors tend to focus more on their congregations and their local communities, and even, for some, local politics, white pastors tend to focus more on national politics and the use of government, especially the federal courts, to further their agenda. Their goal is to push social issues that are important to them by using their political muscle, so they are willing to soil their reputation and good standing in the community by tying themselves to unscrupulous politicians like Trump and others in the Republican party. Therefore, for many Americans, the name evangelical does not mean Christ-like. They are not viewed as people pushing Christ's agenda; they are viewed as pushing a political agenda.

I have many white evangelical friends that are wonderful godly people, but I do not hear enough of them pushing back against the direction of their movement and how it is only alienating their black Christian brothers and sisters. Their silence makes them complicit in the whole evangelical movement's actions, whether they agree with what's going on or not. Unless they are willing to take a stand and speak out boldly, nobody will know they disagree. Unless they are willing to reach out to their black Christian brothers and sisters, who are hurt by the current climate of political Christianity in America and find common ground in Christ, the divide between black and white Christians will continue to expand.

As people of the Bible, I appeal to my white evangelical brothers and sisters with Scripture.

> *Romans 12:5, "So we, though many, are one body in Christ, and individually members one of another" ESV.*

According to Romans 12, when our heavenly Father looks down on us, He does not see a "White church" or "Black Church" or "Asian Church" or "Hispanic Church." God sees the multiracial multiethnic body of Christ He sent His Son Jesus to die for on Calvary's cross. However, we do not act as members of one another. Unfortunately, our attitude seems to be, you reach your race, and I will reach my race, and I don't need you, and you don't need me. With that attitude, we have a lot to learn about truly loving one another in Christ. Also, we have allowed the sin of racism and cultural division to cause us not to want anything to do with each other because of our bad history, as though God doesn't notice. This is wrong on so many levels, but prayerfully, we will make some progress before Christ returns.

Micah 6:8b, "What does the LORD require of you but to do justice, and to love kindness, and to walk humbly with your God?" ESV.

This command was not written to non-Christians, but to the entire body of Christ, regardless of race, ethnicity, or gender, as well as to those who are the majority group and those who are in the minority groups in America. But we, as Christians, have failed one another in America. Justice is not administered equally in this country, and those in the majority remain silent and blame minorities when we speak out against the ill-treatment by protesting peacefully. Also, the Christian church has failed to lead by example by showing loving kindness to one another so that the unsaved world can see Christ in action—working through His multiracial multiethnic children. As a result, the unsaved world cannot learn from us what Jesus meant when He told us to love one another.

Due to the lack of Christ-like love and unity coming from the church in America, it has played a role in systemic racism continuing. That is unacceptable because God answered His church, but we fail to implement it by simply obeying His Word. Thus, we fail to stand united as one body of believers, utilizing our God-given authority and Holy Ghost power to make the necessary changes for the glory of God. Furthermore, we do not walk humbly with God because we openly boast about our support for policies that endanger the lives of others that do not look like us, such as giving hearty approval to take away healthcare from the less fortunate, while at the same time giving a thumbs up to giving tax breaks to the wealthiest among us. Something is definitely wrong with that picture! As Christians, shouldn't we be more concerned for the less fortunate among us?

> *John 13:34-35, "A new commandment I give to you, that you love one another: just as I have loved you, you also are to love one another. By this, all people will know that you are my disciples if you have love for one another." ESV.*

As Christians, we violate this command as well because, again, our actions prove we do not love one another. When you truly love someone, you learn who they really are and share in their hurts, pains, sufferings, and struggles. When they hurt, you hurt, and you do everything within your God-given abilities to help ease the burden, and even if you can't do anything but pray, you still stand with them anyway—encouraging them with the Word of God. This passage was not a suggestion; it was a command. It was not optional; it was mandatory for Jesus' followers then, and it is still binding upon us as His followers today. However, the picture we have given to the unsaved world around us is that the Christian church is no better off than secular society, as far as being dysfunctional and having an uncaring heart. If we continue to act as though we do not care about each other because of skin color, how are we ever going to convince non-believers we care about them and are concerned about their souls.

> *1 Corinthians 16:13-14, "Be watchful, stand firm in the faith, act like men, be strong. Let all that you do be done in love." ESV.*

Again, when you truly love someone, there are things you do not deliberately do to them. You do not mistreat them, you do not take advantage of them, and you do use them for personal gain. You do not sell them out because you disagree with them on political, cultural, or social issues. You love them no matter what, despite your differences, not just because a preacher said so, but more importantly because God said so. Once again, we fail as Christians because our actions are often self-seeking and self-serving. The true test of genuine love is not when you can love those in your own house, church, or political party, but when you can love your neighbor, who is different from you in every way possible, as you love yourself. When you care about their plight in life, you are willing to consider that when you support an agenda that may be harmful or detrimental to them. Your love for Christ, and your Christian love for your brother, will cause you to reverse course, even if it cost you political standing with those whose heart has not been moved by God like yours.

Based on a simple understanding of Scriptures on racial reconciliation, if these principles were applied, the Christian church in America could achieve racial reconciliation, especially if we stop allowing political, cultural, and social issues to get in the way.

Being More Politically Driven Than Spiritually Driven

Why is the subject of politics an important and necessary debate for the church to have? Because many believers are more likely to be informed by a political party or ideology than a Christian perspective on the nature and purpose of government.[294] Furthermore, in many pulpits in America, a political message has replaced the gospel message. Today, Christians are far more engaged in the political debate than they have been in the past. Many tune in to political shows on TV and radio in an attempt to stay informed. The problem is when political views rise to the height of Scripture, and one political party is seen as God's party over the other party. When that happens, the church becomes a place where politics becomes a religion—and Christianity becomes a tool to control the government. Unfortunately, when politics collides with Christianity and Christianity takes a back seat, America gets a twisted view of Scripture and the role of the church. As a result, people are led astray, and family relationships between the races suffer. Instead of America being united, the country is divided. Instead of the church being united, politics is dividing it. This is where the gospel of Jesus Christ should transcend politics.

---

294 Timothy J. Demy & Gary P. Stewart. *Politics and Public Policy A Christian Response: Crucial Considerations for Governing Life*. (Grand Rapids: Kregal Publications), 2000. 23.

Pastors must resist the temptation to get so caught up in the political discourse; they preach politics from their pulpits instead of the truth of the gospel. This does not mean a pastor should never mention what is going on in our government from the pulpit. However, a pastor must first do a proper exegesis of the text and employ careful hermeneutics so they do not use the Bible to prop up their own personal or political views. Many people take their politics just as seriously as they do their religion. And for some, they are the same—because America is believed to be God's country, which implies that God approves of the many sins we are guilty of as a nation. However, politics by itself is not necessarily a bad thing. In a democratic society, politics are needed in the realm of government. However, in the realm of Christ, politics can, and often does, cause great division in the church, especially when Christians wrap their theology around the American flag. Furthermore, division in the church intensifies when Christians align themselves so closely with a particular political party that the gospel is hijacked by that party, as though the party speaks exclusively for God. A believer that supports a different political party should not be treated as less than a Christian and told they do not believe in American "exceptionalism" (which is not a biblical commandment) because of their party affiliation.

The problem with the idea of American exceptionalism is when our political views are intertwined with our Christian views—to the degree—they become one and the same. When patriotism is interconnected with worship, the result is a twisted view of biblical doctrine.

The Christian church in America must resist the temptation of allowing its political views to become the centerpiece of its message instead of the gospel of Jesus Christ that speaks a powerful message on racial reconciliation, forgiveness, love, and grace.

Application of John 18:28-40

What are the dangers when religion uses politics to push its own agenda?

Jesus before Pilate

1. **When religion uses politics to push its own agenda, the world loses sight of who Jesus really is. (18:28-30)**

    This is a major problem in America because of the influence of politics on the church. Many people have been seriously turned off because the church has been too entrenched in politics, especially our younger generation. Therefore, unsaved people do not need an excuse to reject God, so the church should not give them any.

2. **When religion uses politics to push its own agenda, the government is guilty before God in how it responds. (18:31-35)**

    Today, many Americans hate our brand of conflict-ridden politics. However, the church has become guilty by association because of its desire to play politics.

3. **When religion uses politics to push its own agenda, God's truth is lost. (18:36-38)**

    When the unsaved look at the church, they do not see the church; instead, they see a political party.

4. **When religion uses politics to push its own agenda, people will always make the wrong choices. (vs. 39-40)**

    Sadly, due to their lack of spiritual growth, many Christians see their church's alignment in politics as God's agenda, even though it is not.

CHAPTER 13

THE STAIN OF SLAVERY ON AMERICA

Plea for Onesimus, a Free Man

I appeal to you for my child Onesimus, whom I have begotten in my imprisonment, who formerly was useless to you, but now is useful both to you and to me. I have sent him back to you in person, that is, sending my very heart, whom I wished to keep with me, so that on your behalf he might minister to me in my imprisonment for the gospel; but without your consent I did not want to do anything, so that your goodness would not be, in effect, by compulsion but of your own free will. For perhaps he was for this reason separated from you for a while, that you would have him back forever, no longer as a slave, but more than a slave, a beloved brother, especially to me, but how much more to you, both in the flesh and in the Lord. If then you regard me a partner, accept him as you would me. But if he has wronged you in any way or owes you anything, charge that to my account; I, Paul, am writing this with my own hand, I will repay it (not to mention to you that you owe to me even your own self as well). Yes, brother, let me benefit from you in the Lord; refresh my heart in Christ. Having confidence in your obedience, I write to you, since I know that you will do even more than what I say. (Philemon 1:10-21)

2019 marked the 400th year since the first slaves arrived on American soil in Jamestown, Virginia, in 1619. Even after the Thirteenth Amendment was passed in 1865 and slavery was abolished in the U.S., a new form of slavery continued through Jim Crow laws and Black Codes. These rules were a series of oppressive laws and maneuvers specifically designed to ensure Blacks remained subservient to Whites. After slavery ended, Reconstruction was supposed to protect the rights of Blacks, which is why the Thirteenth, Fourteenth, and Fifteenth Amendments were passed.[295] However, Jim Crow laws took a sledgehammer to the Constitution, at least parts designed to protect Black rights. Although the amendments remained on the books, the force they should have had to help Blacks was severely diminished.[296] This allowed local city governments to pass laws to supersede the Constitution. These laws were safeguarded by a collection of state and local statutes that legalized racial segregation. Therefore, Whites, in authority, succeeded in their goals to marginalize Blacks while at the same time making their lives miserable, which only added to the stain of slavery on America.

Blackface: The Birth of An American Stereotype

It is often said that truth is stranger than fiction. It was certainly the case when a minstrel show character became the surname for some of the most racist laws following the most racist period in American history—which was slavery. A white performer named Thomas Dartmouth Rice portrayed a fictional character he named Jim Crow.[297]

---

295   National Construction Center, "The Reconstruction Amendments," [on-line]; accessed on 22 September 2020; available from https://constitutioncenter.org/learn/educational-resources/historical-documents/the-reconstruction-amendments; Internet.

296   National Geographic Resource Library, "The Black Codes and Jim Crow Laws," [on-line]; accessed on 21 September 2020; available from Https://www.Nationalgeographic.Org/Encyclopedia/Black-Codes-And-Jim-Crow-Laws; Internet.

297   Smithsonian. Blackface: The Birth of An American Stereotype [on-line]; Accessed on 21 September 2020; available from https://nmaahc.si.edu/blog-post/blackface-birth-american-stereotype. Internet. The first minstrel shows were performed in 1830s New York by white performers with blackened faces (most used burnt cork or shoe polish) and tattered clothing who imitated and mimicked enslaved Africans on Southern plantations. These performances characterized blacks as lazy, ignorant, superstitious, hypersexual, and prone to thievery and cowardice. Thomas Dartmouth Rice, known as the "Father

His act drew large white crowds as he mocked Blacks while wearing a painted-on blackface mask and tattered clothing. His language was a stereotypical black dialect. Rice performed a mocked song and dance routine that he claimed he learned from a slave. However, Rice simply played into the stereotype about White sentiment toward Blacks. His stage act portrayed Blacks as buffoons with low intelligence.

> *The portrayal of blackface—when people darken their skin with shoe polish, greasepaint, or burnt cork and paint on enlarged lips and other exaggerated features, is steeped in centuries of racism. It peaked in popularity during an era in the United States when demands for civil rights by recently emancipated slaves triggered racial hostility. And today, because of blackface's historic use to denigrate people of African descent, its continued use is still considered racist.*[298]

Thomas Dartmouth Rice was not alone in his negative and demeaning portrayal of Blacks. Many other white performers in blackface played characters that perpetuated a range of negative stereotypes about African Americans, including being lazy, ignorant, superstitious, hypersexual, criminal, or cowardly.[299] Ironically, blackface was such a tremendous success in theaters; the film industry got in on the action. *The Birth of a Nation* was a blockbuster movie released in 1915 in America. Although it was a silent film, it spoke volumes nationwide. The movie essentially revealed the openly racist attitudes of white America at the time—and in many ways, continues to this day. The movie was so bad in its depiction of Blacks; it was labeled

---

of Minstrelsy," developed the first popularly known blackface character, "Jim Crow" in 1830. By 1845, the popularity of the minstrel had spawned an entertainment subindustry, manufacturing songs and sheet music, makeup, costumes, as well as a ready-set of stereotypes upon which to build new performances.

298   Alexis Clark, "How the History of Blackface is Rooted in Racism," 15 February 2020 [on-line]; accessed on 21 September 2020; available from https://www.history.com/news/blackface-history-racism-origins; Internet. Blackface began in the US after the Civil War as white performers played characters that demeaned and dehumanized African Americans.

299   Ibid.

the most racist movie ever.[300] The movie's problem was not the acting but the film's storyline, which depicted white actors in blackface that demeaned Blacks. The movie portrayed defeated white Southerners being terrorized (and even disenfranchised from voting) by illiterate, corrupt, and foul-mouthed former slaves (whites in blackface) seeking interracial marriage.[301]

The movie essentially reversed the roles of Blacks and Whites. Therefore, making Blacks the villain, which was applauded by Whites. *The Birth of a Nation* was essentially three hours of racist propaganda — starting with the Civil War and ending with the Ku Klux Klan riding in to save the South from black rule during the Reconstruction era.[302] Although the birth of a nation was pure fiction, it was spot-on with white sentiment toward Blacks.

To treat people badly is one thing, but to mock the results of your horrendous treatment for your own amusement, is not only inhumane, but it is also extremely evil. This was just another way Whites reminded Blacks of their place, which is another stain on America. However, I do not believe that these Whites will fare well when they stand before God to answer for their actions.

---

300   Lou Lumenick, "New York Post. Why 'Birth of a nation' is still the most racist movie ever," 7 February 2015 [on-line]; accessed on 23 September 2020; available from https://nypost.com/2015/02/07/why-birth-of-a-nation-is-still-the-most-controversial-movie-ever/; Internet. Based on a play by Thomas Dixon so notoriously racist it had been banned in several places, "The Birth of a Nation" mirrored the attitudes of Griffith, a fellow Southerner who raised an unprecedented $100,000 (outside the nascent Hollywood studio system) for a three-hour spectacular at a time when few American movies ran longer than 20 minutes.

301   Ibid.

302   "100 Years Later, What's the Legacy of 'Birth of a Nation," *NPR*, 8 February 2020 [on-line]; accessed on 23 September 2020; available from https://www.npr.org/sections/codeswitch/2015/02/08/383279630/100-years-later-whats-the-legacy-of-birth-of-a-nation; Internet. "[Griffith] portrayed the emancipated slaves as heathens, as unworthy of being free, as uncivilized, as primarily concerned with passing laws so they could marry white women and prey on them," Dick Lehr, author of *The Birth of a Nation: How a Legendary Filmmaker and a Crusading Editor Reignited America's Civil War*, tells NPR's Arun Rath.

The Black Codes and Jim Crow Laws

In many ways, it is hard to believe that Jim Crow laws were allowed to exist for almost 100 years, from the post-Civil War era until 1968. These laws were extremely effective in ostracizing African Americans by denying them the ability to depart their poverty: having adequate education, better housing, employment that paid a living wage, decent healthcare, and the right to vote. To enforce Jim Crow laws, African Americans were arrested, jailed, fined, and manipulated. They also faced threats, violence, and even death. In 1865, the Thirteenth Amendment was ratified, and shortly after that, Jim Crow laws began to spring up all over the country. In addition to Jim Crow laws, many state and local governments instituted "Black Codes." These laws specified when, where, and how formerly enslaved people could work and how much they could be compensated.[303] The South, the major loser to the ratification of the Thirteenth Amendment, was a major player in pushing "Black Codes" as a way to retaliate against losing the Civil War, as well as losing years of free labor. The Black Codes were a legal way to return African Americans to a form of slavery called indentured servitude. The Black Codes were designed to take voting rights away, to control where they lived, how they traveled, and to seize their children for labor purposes.[304] Again, to add insult to injury, the legal system was stacked against Black citizens because it allowed former Confederate soldiers to work as police and judges. This made it difficult for African Americans to win court cases and ensured they were subjected to Black Codes. These codes worked in conjunction with labor camps for the incarcerated, where prisoners were treated as enslaved people. Black offenders typically received longer sentences than white offenders, and because of the grueling work, Blacks often did not live out their entire sentence.[305]

---

303 History Channel, "Jim Crow Laws," 19 August 2020 [on-line]; accessed on 21 September 2020; available from https://www.history.com/topics/early-20th-century-us/jim-crow-laws; Internet. After the United States Civil War, state governments that had been part of the Confederacy tried to limit the voting rights of black citizens and prevent contact between black and white citizens in public places.

304 Ibid.

305 Ibid.

Jim Crow was more than a series of rigid anti-black laws. It was a way of life. Under Jim Crow, African Americans were relegated to the status of second-class citizens. Jim Crow represented the legitimization of anti-black racism and extremely cruel treatment. Jim Crow looked to preserve white supremacy and white privilege through the law after the South lost the Civil War. In-state after-state, in America, white supremacy was forged through Jim Crow laws, replacing the old laws of slavery with new laws of segregation and prejudice. Legally, Whites could no longer own Blacks as property, but through a new evil scheme, they learned how to control their lives just the same. Jim Crow laws segregated African Americans and White Americans in every way they possibly could: in schools, restaurants, public transportation, restrooms, cemeteries, hospitals, and that only lists a few examples.

It's sad to say, the U.S. Supreme Court upheld the Jim Crow laws, which made them legal in the United States. This had a direct impact on African Americans and was why the Civil Rights Movement, led by Dr. Martin Luther King Jr., was necessary. White sentiment in America in 1963 was to uphold segregation. Perhaps, there was no bigger voice for racism and white supremacy than Governor George Wallace of Alabama. In his inaugural address in January of that same year, Wallace made the following statement, "I draw the line in the dust and toss the gauntlet before the feet of tyranny, and I say, segregation now, segregation tomorrow, segregation forever." [306] This was labeled as Wallace's segregation speech.

In April of that same year, Rev. Dr. Martin Luther King Jr., along with Reverend Fred Shuttlesworth, and Reverend Ralph D. Abernathy, began a campaign for desegregation in Birmingham, which was viewed by the black community as the most racist big city in the South.[307] To combat racism and segregation, Dr. King traveled around the country, from Washington to Atlanta, back to Atlanta, and then onto a California tour—to raise money and preach against segregation.[308] In that same

---

306   Robert Edgerton. *Hidden Heroism: Black Soldiers in American Wars*, 175.

307   Ibid.

308   Taylor Branch. Pillar of Fire: American in the King Years 1963-1965. (New York: Simon & Schuster, 1988), 291.

year, Dr. King gave his famous "I Have a Dream speech," during the march on Washington D.C. The contrasting speeches that year, by King and Wallace, gave the pulse between most Blacks and Whites in the country. Therefore, King's speech resonated with Blacks, while Wallace's speech resonated with Whites, which showed the country's divide.

Paul's Response to Slavery

The book of Philemon is an epistle that addresses slavery from a Christian perspective. Ironically, the apostle Paul wrote this letter while incarcerated by the Roman Government. Philemon is one of four prison epistles Paul wrote.[309] So, Paul understood, to some degree, what it felt like to be held in bondage. In Paul's epistles, he would often refer to himself as a *doulos*, the Greek word for slave or bondservant. However, he never said he was a *doulos* for the Roman government but called himself a *doulos* for Christ, which was very significant in understanding Pauline theology.

The major characters in this short book of the Bible are Philemon and Onesimus. Philemon was a dear friend of Paul since the time he led Philemon to faith in Christ. Philemon lived in Colossae, and he was a wealthy man since he owned slaves and had a house large enough to accommodate church meetings. Onesimus, a slave of Philemon, ran away from his master, probably robbing him in the process (v. 18).[310] The purpose of Paul's writing was to make it possible for Onesimus to return to his master by appealing to Philemon's Christian character. Therefore, this is an intimate letter from the apostle Paul to his dear friend Philemon.[311] At this point, Onesimus is not the same man that fled, but he probably took something of value from his master before he left and ran away, he fled to Rome. While there, Onesimus ran into Paul, who led him to faith in Christ. Paul asked Philemon to receive his

---

309   Tony Evans. *Tony Evans Bible Commentary*. (Nashville: Holman Publishing, 2019), 1307.

310   D.A. Carson, Douglas J. Moo, and Leon Morris, *An Introduction to The New Testament*. (Grand Rapids: Zondervan Publishing House), 1992, 388.

311   Tony Evans, Bible Commentary, 1307.

slave back not as property but as a Christian brother. Paul's letter urges grace and forgiveness, reconciliation, and renewed relationship based upon Christ.

Paul led these two men to faith in Christ, so he had a heart-felt concern about the outcome. Paul, being an apostle, could have simply ordered Philemon to do the right thing, as it related to Onesimus. However, he appealed to Philemon's Christian heart. Paul says, "I appeal to you for my child Onesimus whom I have begotten in my imprisonment" (vs. 10). Although Onesimus was a grown man, Paul referred to him as "my child." Paul considered Onesimus a spiritual son-in Christ, which was a closer bond than if Paul had been like a biological father. Paul told Philemon that Onesimus was useless to him in the past, but now, because of his faith in Christ, he would be useful to them both. (It is amazing what a life-changing conversion to Christ can do in a human being's life). Paul wasn't saying Onesimus was a nobody because he was a slave. He was saying what a difference the Holy Spirit makes in the life of a true believer. All human beings are useless, outside a personal relationship with Jesus Christ as Savior and Lord, whether slave or free, rich or poor, male or female, or Black, White, Asian or Hispanic.

What may be confusing to modern Bible readers was that Paul sent Onesimus back to Philemon, his slave owner, while at the same time, he stated that Onesimus was his heart. The statement *his heart* meant Paul loved Onesimus with the love of Christ, as well as a biological father. Paul took a risk by sending Onesimus back to Philemon because, according to Roman law, an owner could severely punish or even, execute, a runaway slave. Also, anyone who harbored a runaway slave could be charged as well. Even so, Paul sent Onesimus back to Colossae with Tychicus, along with this letter.[312]

Although Onesimus was useful to Paul's ministry, he wanted to allow Philemon to display genuine Christian love in a unique situation while he was in chains. Again, Paul could have flexed his apostolic authority and not only commanded Philemon to forgive Onesimus and

---

312   J.D. Barry, D. Mangum, D.R. Brown, M.S. Heiser, M. Custis, E. Ritzema, D. Bomar, *Faithlife Study Bible, Philemon 1.* (Bellingham: Lexham Press, 2016).

to receive him back as well. However, this would not have allowed the opportunity for both men to apply their faith in what was a challenging situation. For one thing, it would not have helped Philemon to grow in grace or gain a real blessing from the experience.[313] Paul's language to his dear friend Philemon revealed his concern for both men to continue to grow in their walk with the Lord and not to allow this situation to be a hindrance to their faith. At the same time, Paul viewed this situation from a perspective of God's divine providence, when he told Philemon that perhaps it was for this reason (Onesimus' conversion experience) that Onesimus was separated from him for a while so that he could have him back forever (v. 15). To have him back forever meant that Onesimus would be his brother-in-Christ forever—although Onesimus would probably not always be his slave. Paul goes on to say, accept Onesimus as you would me. This again revealed Paul's close relationship with Philemon. Paul said, "But if he has wronged you in any way or owes you anything, charge that to my account."

Paul acknowledged that Onesimus likely owed a debt to Philemon but took the obligation upon himself.[314] What a friend to have that loves you enough, he is willing to pay your debts. Paul knew Onesimus didn't have any money, and because he ran away from Philemon, that debt had increased. Even though Onesimus owed Philemon, Philemon owed Paul more because he was the very reason Philemon knew the Lord. Also, Paul realized that he, as well as Philemon and Onesimus, were both indebted to Christ. Therefore, all three men were equal in Christ because the ground at the foot of the cross is level: to all who would dare place their faith in Jesus Christ as Savior and Lord, whether slave or free.

Paul's letter to Philemon is a manuscript on how we can deal with the stain of sin on America and how to deal with the issue of being an unforgiving nation. So, the question could be asked, why didn't the apostle Paul just order Philemon not to have anything to do with the evils of slavery since slavery is incompatible with Scripture? I believe for two reasons. First, Paul understood the world in his day and that

---

313   W.W. Wiersbe, *Wiersbe's Expository Outlines on the Old Testament: Philemon*, (Wheaton: Victor Books, 1993), 670–671.

314   Ibid.

slavery was an acceptable practice. However, Christians should not conform to the world but be transformed by the renewing of their mind (Romans 12:1-2). Paul understood that if a person's mind was truly transformed (by the Word of God), you won't have to order them to obey; you just have to allow the Holy Spirit to work.

Second, Paul allowed the Holy Spirit to work to deal with not only Philemon but Onesimus as well. Therefore, even if slavery continued to be the law of the land, it would not be the law that led someone that had been set free in Christ. So, it was not about our status in life for Paul but our position in Christ. Paul knew that if someone like him—a former persecutor of the church and now a faithful follower of Christ and a builder of the church—could be transformed, he realized that so could a slave owner like Philemon and a slave like Onesimus. What a better place America could be if we all, Black, White, Asian, Hispanic, Native, and others, practiced the principles of love and forgiveness revealed in Paul's epistle to Philemon. Systemic racism would never have taken hold in America if America was Christian from its founding and followed correct biblical teaching.

Application of Philemon 1:10-21

Instead of commanding Philemon to forgive Onesimus, why did Paul appeal to his faith in Christ instead? By doing so, Paul understood three things:

1. **Paul understood the <u>spiritual character</u> of one who forgives (vs. 4-7).**

In Paul's eyes, for a person to claim they are a Christian and unwilling to forgive would have been unthinkable.[315] This is why Paul knew if he challenged Philemon to do the right thing, based on his Christian character and love of Christ that Onesimus would be treated as a brother in the Lord and no longer as a slave. Therefore, Paul teaches

---

315   J. F. MacArthur, *Philemon*, 226.

us that you do not have to make a genuine Christian behave as a child of God because it is already a big part of their Christian character.

2. **Paul understood the <u>spiritual actions</u> of one who forgives (vs. 8-18).**[316]

In response to a question by the Pharisees about the greatest commandment in the Law, Jesus said, "'You shall love the Lord your God with all your heart, and with all your soul, and with all your mind.' This is the great and foremost commandment. The second is like it, 'You shall love your neighbor as yourself'" [Matthew 22:37-39]. This passage applies to how Paul challenged Philemon. Paul knew that Philemon loved the Lord, but he had to prove it by showing he also loved his neighbor, Onesimus.

3. **Paul understood the <u>spiritual motivation</u> of one who forgives (vs. 19-25).**

In this passage, there are six motives for forgiving others: the recognition of unpayable debt, the possibility of being a blessing, the necessity of obedience, the acknowledgment of accountability, the importance of maintaining fellowship, and the requirement of grace.[317]

What can we learn from Paul about why it is necessary to forgive in order to heal race relations in America? [Hard lessons learned]

1. Failure to forgive imprisoning us in the past.
2. Unforgiveness produces bitterness and hatred.
3. Unforgiveness gives Satan an open door.
4. Unforgiveness hinders fellowship with God and spiritual growth.
5. Unforgiveness gives the sin of racism fuel in which to thrive.

316　Ibid.

317　Ibid.

CHAPTER 14

GOD'S ROLE FOR GOVERNMENT

A Christian's duty to the State

Every person is to be in subjection to the governing authorities. For there is no authority except from God, and those which exist are established by God. Therefore whoever resists authority has opposed the ordinance of God; and they who have opposed will receive condemnation upon themselves. For rulers are not a cause of fear for good behavior, but for evil. Do you want to have no fear of authority? Do what is good and you will have praise from the same; for it is a minister of God to you for good. But if you do what is evil, be afraid; for it does not bear the sword for nothing; for it is a minister of God, an avenger who brings wrath on the one who practices evil. Therefore it is necessary to be in subjection, not only because of wrath, but also for conscience' sake. For because of this you also pay taxes, for rulers are servants of God, devoting themselves to this very thing. Render to all what is due them: tax to whom tax is due; custom to whom custom; fear to whom fear; honor to whom honor. (Romans 13:1-7)

The apostle Paul lived at a very dangerous time for all true Christians due to severe persecution. Rome was the seat of government for much of the known world because of sheer dominance and the ability to topple nations at their will. Therefore, the apostle Paul penned this epistle to provide the church guidance in operating in a secular society led by non-believers and populated with mostly non-believers.

> *These seven verses contain the clearest and most specific New Testament teaching on the Christian's responsibility to civil authority. Every Christian, no matter what form of government he lives under, is under command from the Lord to maintain proper and useful submission to that government for the sake of leading a peaceful life and having an effective witness. This recurring theme of submission to society's controlling power is nowhere more forcefully dealt with than here.[318]*

The president or leader of the nation in Rome was called emperors, and most, if not all, of them, were evil men that wanted to be treated as deities. When the Roman Empire conquered a nation, they would expand their territory by annexing the country and placing garrisons of soldiers in that territory to enforce Roman law. Territories that once belonged to the nation of Israel were also dominated by the Rome Empire. Therefore, the Jews hated the Roman government because they despised being under the rule of a heathen nation. The Jews missed the days of the reigns of David and Solomon—when Israel was the most feared nation on the planet—primarily because Yahweh fought for them and protected them. So, the Jews, once again, yearned to be a sovereign nation.

Within the context of that background, Paul wrote this epistle to encourage all Christians, especially Jews—which is why he says, "Every person is to be in subjection to the governing authorities." "Every person" meant all persons, saved as well as unsaved, Jews as well as Gentiles. "To be in subjection" meant to obey the laws of the state unless those laws violated God's laws. Paul goes on to explain why when he says, "For there is no authority except from God, and God establishes those which exist." [319] Whether we agree with it or not,

---

318 J. F. MacArthur. *Romans*, Vol. 2. (Chicago: Moody Press, 1991), 205-206.

319 G. R. Osborne. *Romans*. (Downers Grove: InterVarsity Press, 2004), 341. How do we relate to our increasingly secular government and culture? Is it correct to say that when a government begins to turn evil, the Christian is obligated to oppose it and to refuse to support it? We must remember that when Paul was writing this, Nero was on the Roman throne. While he had not yet turned into the evil anti-Christian emperor he was to become, there were definitely signs of anti-Christian activity in the empire. So, Paul is not writing

every leader, of every nation, throughout human history, has only been in place because God allowed them to be. No matter if these leaders were good or evil, God allowed them to reign to serve His overall plan.

This passage is another example of God's sovereignty and how He alone controls world events. So, regardless of how much the Jews hated the Roman Government, Paul encouraged all Christians to be law-abiding citizens—reflecting God's glory in the process. Paul referred to the Roman Government as a minister of God for the good of His people. In a fallen world, law and order are needed. So, God gave the government the authority to bring wrath or discipline to those who practiced evil (v.4). Paul went on to tell us why we should submit to the governing authorities. He stated, "not only because of wrath but also for conscience sake" (v. 5). With this statement, Paul moved a bit higher in what should be our motivation as true Christians. Any citizen can obey the law because of fear of punishment, but a Christian ought to obey because of conscience.[320] Wrath had to do with God's judgment for wrongdoing, which an obedient Christian does not have to worry about.

On the other hand, for conscience's sake had to do with having a clear conscience because our behavior glorifies God. When a faithful believer in Christ does something wrong, they will automatically be troubled by their conscience because the Holy Spirit will convict them. Furthermore, an obedient Christian has a clear conscience because they know their actions are right and just. Paul summed up his argument when he said, "Render to all what is due them: tax to whom tax is due; custom to whom custom; fear to whom fear; honor to whom honor reason." [321] According to Paul's message, the government has a

---

this under the kind of government many of us have grown up under, and he still calls upon people to submit.

320   W.W. Wiersbe. *The Bible Exposition Commentary.* Vol. 1. (Wheaton: Victor Books), 1996, 557.

321   J. F. Walvoord & R. B. Zuck, Vol. 2, *The Bible Knowledge Commentary: Romans*, 490. A Christian's responsibility to civil authorities involves more than obedience (vv. 1, 5). It also includes support by paying taxes (cf. Matt. 22:21). This is because the leaders, as God's servants (cf. Rom. 13:4), are supposed to give their full time to governing and need support through taxes from citizens, Christians included. So, a Christian ought to give everyone what he owes him (lit., "repay everyone his dues"), whether substance (taxes and revenue) or

right to function because it was established to be God's instrument, and the leaders are God's servants.

Christians have been called *out of this world* (John 15:18 and 17:14), but they still have responsibilities to the state or government. The best citizen ought to be a Christian citizen. Though the church is not to get involved in party politics that lead to division, individual believers certainly should use their God-given privileges as citizens to see to it that the best leaders are elected, and the best laws are enacted and enforced justly.[322] However, believers should never place their commitment to a particular political party above their allegiance to Christ, especially if they are truly Christians and not just in name only. Second, Christians must never neglect the gospel of Jesus Christ to push the agenda of a particular political party. Third, Christians should never become bad citizens because the party they support is not in power.

Paul's Reasons Why We Should Obey Human Government?

(Romans 13)

1. On account of God's wrath. (vs. 1-3)

God not only disciplines the unsaved, but he also disciplines the saved—which belong to Him. The Bible says, "Judgment begins with the household of faith." [Isaiah 40:5] This knowledge should cause Christians to pause before they desire to sin against God.

2. On account of a clear conscience. (vs. 5–7)

Our conscience plays a huge role in our daily decisions, whether saved or unsaved. However, for an obedient Christian, living in guilt because of some sin is not an option because of their genuine commitment to Christ. However, for the unsaved, they have no conscience because

---

respect and honor.

322   W.W. Wiersbe. *The Bible Exposition Commentary*, 402.

their sinful actions do not bother them enough to want to change—if it did, they would turn to Jesus for deliverance.

3. On account of Christian love. (vs. 8-10)

For a genuine Christian, the love of God naturally flows through them, whereby it is visible and received to all that cross their path. As a result, they strive to be law-abiding citizens for the glory of Christ.

4. On account of Christ's sacrifice. (v. 14)

Genuine Christians understand Jesus' sacrifice on Calvary's Cross on their behalf. Therefore, based on what He did for us, they want to give their all to Him, which includes obeying the laws of human government.

The apostle Paul wrote seven epistles and found within these writings are valuable nuggets for understanding the power of the State and the power of the Church. In Romans 13, Paul addressed the power of the State, but in 1 Corinthians 10:3-4, he addressed the power of the Church.

> *"For though we walk in the flesh, we do not war according to the flesh, for the weapons of our warfare are not of the flesh, but divinely powerful for the destruction of fortresses."*

To walk in the flesh refers to how we live our lives in human bodies. When Paul says that *we do not war according to the flesh*, he is reminding us that we do not fight a spiritual battle, which we are all in, whether saved or unsaved, by using physical means or human instruments. The fact that we have *weapons of warfare* acknowledges that we are in a spiritual battle with a real enemy that is crafty—referring to Satan. *Divinely powerful* (meaning Holy Spirit's power) lets us know that we are not powerless. However, this power is not just for possession; it has a purpose because Paul says, "for the destruction of fortresses" (spiritual strongholds or bondages). What this passage teaches us is that the church and the state are empowered differently by God. The state (government) is a physical institution and fights by using physical means. On the other hand, the church is a spiritual institution, so it fights or battles by spiritual means—such as prayer, worship, fellowship, and preaching and teaching the Word of God. Although the church and government have different functions, the government still has an important God-given role.

> *In the ultimate exercise of authority, direction, and justice, government rests in the hands of God, the Sovereign Creator and Ruler of the universe (Exod. 15:18; 1 Chron. 29:11-12; 2 Chron. 20:6; Ps. 10:16; 22; 28). God did not create the physical universe to operate by inherent laws, while He served as an absent landlord (Col. 1;17; Heb. 1:3), nor did He create people to be autonomous. God is continually working both directly and providentially to fulfill His eternal plan (Eph. 1:11; 3:11) for His glory. God uses both spiritual and human agents, but He remains in ultimate authority and control.*[323]

Although it may not always seem that way to us, God still has ultimate authority and control over world events. Likewise, God also controls world governments to bring about His divine plan. For example, in God's timing, He moved heaven and earth to manipulate events to usher His Son, Jesus (the Messiah) into the world. In the world, God controlled what government would be in place when Jesus arrived. This was not only the case in the New Testament but also in the Old Testament.

> *The foundation for authority and government on the human level was established after the Flood by God's pronouncement to Noah about the sanctity of human life, because "in the image of God has God made man" (Gen, 9:6). As a result, He said, "And from each man, too, I will demand an accounting for the life of fellow man" (9:5). Human government was undoubtedly established to carry out this objective.*[324]

Finally, one of the main points that the book of Romans revealed was that God created three great covenants to provide structure, law and order, and a foundation for an obedient society to thrive and

---

323 Don Campbell, Wendell Johnston, John Walvoord, and John Witmer, *The Theological Workbook*. 144.

324 Ibid.

function in an orderly society.[325] What we might call institutions, the Bible calls covenants. However, the Bible also has revealed what happens when these institutions serve man's interest and not God's interest—for which they were created.

Why Americans Hate Government?

In America today, many people hate government, mainly because it is so dysfunctional or favors some citizens. Sometimes, this is based on wealth, and at other times, it is based on race. Also, the division between Democrats and Republicans across all government levels is another major cause for this dysfunction. People hate government because they hate the state of politics, and since they are both viewed as mutually exclusive, their hate for one means a disdain for the other. This dysfunction has caused chaos and division throughout the entire country between Democrats, Republicans, and Independents. However, no matter how bad or dysfunctional government may be, the Bible has taught us that God has a divine purpose for creating government covenant.

Because sin is a reality in human culture, Paul knew that it would be to the advantage of Christians to be sheltered by the civil authorities from the effects of sin in society—especially in light of the likelihood of the escalation of sin, as the present age drew to a close. Therefore, what seems contradictory at first—for believers in Christ to submit themselves to pagan "lords"—is really for the believers' good.[326] Since God has placed government rulers or leaders over us, we should submit to the governing authority—unless those in authority want us to violate

---

325   W. W. Wiersbe. *The Bible Exposition Commentary*, 556. God created the family, government, and the church. God has established three institutions: the home (Gen. 2:18–25), government (Gen. 9:1–17), and the church (Acts 2). Paul was writing to believers at the very heart of the Roman Empire. As yet, the great persecutions had not started, but were on the way. Christianity was still considered a Jewish sect, and the Jewish religion was approved by Rome. But the day would come when it would be very difficult, if not impossible, for a Christian to be loyal to the emperor. He could not drop incense on the altar and affirm, "Caesar is god!"

326   K Boa & W. Kruidenier. *Romans*, Vol. 6. (Nashville, TN: Broadman & Holman Publishers, 2000), 391-392.

God's Word. However, we do not get to pick and choose whether we obey depending on the political party affiliation of the person in authority. The unsaved can do that and suffer whatever consequences that result, but for the true Christian, we obey because that is not only what the law requires, it is what God requires.

The Early Church Conflict with the State

Most Christians today do not realize that Christianity was not birthed in a vacuum. The Roman Government was in full bloom during the time Jesus lived, bled, and died—and it was God's providential hand that made it play out that way. Many people complain about our government in America, especially when they feel it infringes on their religious freedoms. However, the early church did not expect the Roman Government to provide them religious freedoms. Like in America, under the Roman Empire, there were many religions, not just Christianity.

When Christianity arrived on the scene, the Roman was already a very chaotic and polytheistic world, whereby people believed in a multitude of gods. Also, Roman emperors were treated as deities—although they were mere men with big egos and the sinful desire to be worshiped. Therefore, the Roman Government didn't care what religion you followed, as long as you bowed to Caesar as lord. In such a sinful society, Jesus's disciples did not fear the government but instead sought to carry out God's divine will, despite harassment and threats of death. Also, many of the early church leaders were martyred because of their faith.[327] In the midst of this environment, Paul wrote to encourage the church in Rome, which is the book of Romans. However,

---

327 Justo L. Gonzalez. *The History of Christianity: The Early Church to the Dawn of the Reformation*, Vol. 1. (New York: Harper Collins Publishers, 1984), 33-35. The persecution by the Roman Emperor Nero against Christians was brutal. He set fire to part of the city of Rome and blamed Christians—although it was found out that he did it. Before killing Christians, Nero used them to amuse the people. Some were dressed in furs, to be killed by dogs. Others were crucified. Still others were set on fire early in the night, so that they might illuminate it. Nero opened his own gardens for these shows, and in the circus he himself became a spectacle, for he mingled with the people dressed as a charioteer, or he rode in his chariot.

Paul specifically addressed the Christian's responsibility to obey government authorities placed over them—because all authorities are put in place by God. Now, I want to address how America has struggled with the subject of God's role and the government.

Separation of Church and State

The First Amendment to the United States Constitution, with its provisions, that "Congress shall make no laws respecting an establishment of religion, or prohibiting the free exercise thereof," took effect in 1791. At the time, five of the nation's fourteen states (Vermont joined the Union in 1791) provided for tax support for ministers, and those five plus seven others maintained religious tests for state office. Only Virginia and Rhode Island enjoyed the sort of "separation of church and state" that Americans now take for granted—government providing no tax money for churches and posing no religious conditions for participation in public life. With less than a handful of exceptions, even the defenders of religious liberty in Rhode Island and Virginia did not object when Congress or the president proclaimed national days of prayer, when the federal government began its meetings in prayer, or when the military chaplains were appointed and funded by law.[328]

The Revolutionary War was fought so that the original *Thirteen Colonies* could free themselves from the tyranny of England. The uniqueness of England is that church and state are intertwined.[329]

---

328   Mark A. Noll. *A History of Christianity in the United States and Canada.* (Grand Rapids: William B. Eerdmans Publishing Company, 1992), 144.

329   History Channel, "Church of England." [on-line]; accessed on 19 October 2020; available from https://www.history.com/topics/british-history/church-of-england/; Internet. The Church of England, or Anglican Church, is the primary state church in England, where the concepts of church and state are linked. The Church of England is considered the original church of the Anglican Communion, which represents over 85 million people in more than 165 countries. While the Church upholds many of the customs of Roman Catholicism, it also embraces fundamental ideas adopted during the Protestant Reformation. In recent years, the Church of England has been viewed as one of the more progressive sects of Christianity and is known for its relatively

First, England (Great Britain) has a monarchy-style government that rules the country. The King or Queen of England is the head of the church and the state. However, a Prime Minister is appointed to lead the government, and the Archbishop of Canterbury leads the church (Anglican). Many state laws and religious laws were intertwined in the 17th century, and many remain that way to this day. After discovering the *New World*, and the colonization, many Europeans fled England not just for freedom of religion but also for freedom from religion. Because of what our *Founding Fathers* experienced in England, they came up with the clause "separation of church and state." The First Amendment rests upon the concept of a secular state. The government is denied jurisdiction over religious affairs, and upon the recognition of America as a pluralistic society, in which "the free exercise of religion" is assured to all religions equally under the law. Therefore, the Constitution allows others to worship in America, even if they are not of the Christian faith.[330]

A Democracy vs. a Theocracy

The difference between America's founding and the nation of Israel is that one was founded as a democracy—ruled by men, and the other was founded as a theocracy—meaning ruled by God.[331] God created Israel to be a true theocracy, based solely on Yahweh being worshiped as their King, obeying all His commands. Israel was not supposed

---

liberal policies, such as allowing the ordination of women and gay priests.

330 Daniel G Reid, Robert D. Linder, Bruce L. Shelley, and Harry S. Scott. *Dictionary of Christianity in America: A Comprehensive Resource on the Religious Impulse that Shaped a Continent*. (Downers Grove: InterVarsity Press, 1990), 268. The concept of the secular state is not born out of hostility toward religion, for hostility toward religion is irreconcilable with the very nature of a secular state, and therefore, has been so declared as irreconcilable with the American tradition in church and state. America is a secular society state, a free society, in which neither religion, nor irreligion enjoys any official status, but one in which the attitude of government toward religion is, in words of the Supreme Court, one of "benevolent neutrality." As the separation of church and state is regarded as the guarantee of religious liberty, so the secular state is the legal basis of the pluralistic society.

331 Ibid, 1169.

to have any competing gods for Yahweh's place. However, Israel miserably failed because they turned away from God and followed all of the false man-made gods of the ungodly people and nations around them, which they aligned themselves with.[332]

That leads us to examine America. Can a nation that is not a theocracy, that allows anyone to worship or believe as they choose, or not choose to follow any belief at all, and still be a Christian nation? In a book by Daryl Cornett, he addressed this question. He stated, "The story of America is not Christian or secular, but Christian and secular. The real debate ultimately rests on which one at the crucial years of the founding remains the focus. The interpretation suffers from the lack of acknowledgment of non-religious ideas impacting the first Americans' minds and actions." [333] I would counter Cornett's argument by inserting non-Christian for non-religious because Christianity and religion are not mutually exclusive.

I would argue that Christianity in early America and throughout the time of slavery, Jim Crow, the Civil Rights Era, and even up until today has been hypocritical. In a book by David Kinnaman, titled *Un-Christian*, he asked how Christians acquired a hypercritical image in America today?[334] Before I answer his question for today, I will address the issue when the hypocrisy first began. First, the hypocrisy of the so-called Christian American hinges on two issues that sunk the nation's reputation from the beginning: white supremacy and the institution of slavery. For a predominately White country then (and remains that way today) and claimed to be a Christian nation—or at least, claimed to be influenced by Christianity, at best, it missed the mark by a longshot. I would argue that the treatment of Blacks from Africa set the tone for what the soul of America would be then and still plagues the nation to this day. Second, racism based on white supremacy (as well as fueling

---

332 John Bright. *A History of Israel*, Third Edition. (Philadelphia: Westminster Press, 1972), 269; 329-331.

333 Daryl C. Cornett. *Christian America?* (Nashville: B&H Publishing Group, 2011), 256. The story of America is not Christian or secular, but Christian and secular. Cornett argued America is partly Christian, a nation shaped by a blend of religious and non-religious tendencies.

334 David Kinnaman. *Un-Christian: What a new generation really thinks about Christianity*. (Grand Rapids: Baker Books, 2007), 46.

racism) does not go away just become time passes, especially if it is never really addressed by the dominant white race that caused it. So, the answer to Kinnaman's question about how did America acquire the image of hypocrisy, well, that happened in 1619 and was reaffirmed in our Constitution and played out in the lives of Caucasian Americans against African Americans for centuries. When our white Founding Fathers said, "We hold these truths to be self-evident, that all men are created equal, that they are endowed, by their Creator, with certain unalienable Rights, that among these are Life, Liberty, and the pursuit of Happiness." In that same Constitution, they added the three-fifths clause as a compromise between the Northern and Southern states, which was done to appease the South so that they would agree to sign the document. This allowed three-fifths of the slave population would be counted for determining direct taxation and representation in the House of Representatives.[335] Their bad decision led to the stain on America that has made race relations between Blacks and Whites irreparable unless God intervenes. The reason why is because we have had all these years to fix it, but we are more divided now than we have ever been in the history of race relations—with no end in sight, especially in the age of Trump.

White Grievance

I would submit that Trump understood white anger and sentiment in America and played it for all it was worth. For African Americans, we know why many of us are still upset, which many of those reasons are covered in this book. However, what Trump has done, and I might add successfully, is that he has turned the attention away from the real problems (covered in this book). Trump has tapped into what is known as "white grievance."[336] Trump never would have become President of

---

335 "Three-fifths Compromise: United States history," [on-line]; accessed on 19 October 2020; accessed from https://www.britannica.com/topic/three-fifths-compromise; Internet.

336 Michelle Goldberg, "Trump's Re-election Message Is White Grievance: Republicans in D.C. just pretend not to see it, *New York Times*, 2 July 2020. [on-line]; accessed on 20 November 2020; accessed from https://www.opinion/trump's-re-election-message-is-white grievance - The New

the United States if he had not gone down that road, otherwise, he had no shot in politics. As an avid television watcher, Trump witnessed how a portion of the country responded to Sarah Palin—when she was selected by John McCain on the Republican ticket as Vice President in 2008. Palin's rhetoric against then Presidential candidate Barack Obama was way over the top and very racist.

Nevertheless, it was very effective with the white base of the Republican party.[337] Palin emphasized Obama's race and his pastor's race back in Chicago, the Rev. Jeremiah Wright. Wright had some fiery sermons about controversial issues in America, including racism and our government's dysfunction on the local and world's stage. However, one of Wright's sermons became national news; it reenforced the white stereotype against African Americans and our pastors. Pastor Wright used some profanity in a sermon that condemned American's behavior. This allowed white Republicans to characterize Obama as too radical because his pastor made the remarks. However, many white evangelical pastors have criticized America as well. In fact, they have made some of the same arguments against America that Pastor Wright made; they just said it differently.

Interestingly, Whites can criticize America (on the regular), but not Blacks. When we do it, we are labeled as un-American or unpatriotic and told we hate the country—even we have served in the military and fought for the country. (This is another example of "white privilege.") It was about the time when Palin had her 15 minutes of fame that Trump began to push "birtherism," which was his false attack on Obama's citizenship. With his racist efforts, Trump convinced millions

---

York Times (nytimes.com); Internet. But Trump understands that he became a significant political figure by spreading the racist lie that Barack Obama was really born in Kenya. He launched his history-making presidential bid with a speech calling Mexican immigrants and rapists, and adopted a slogan, "America First," previously associated with the raging anti-Semite Charles Lindbergh. Throughout the 2016 campaign, he won the invaluable prize of earned media with escalating racist provocations, which his supporters relished and which captivated cable news.

337   Johnathan Martin, "Palin Electrifies Conservative." *Politico*, 31 August 2008, [on-line]; accessed on 30 November 2020; accessed from //www.Palin electrifies conservative base - POLITICOBack ButtonSearch IconFilter Icon; Internet.

of white Americans that Obama was born in Kenya, Africa, which many Republicans still believe today. The goal was to label Obama as an illegitimate President. Many Whites, including Christians, hated the fact that a black man was in the White House. Therefore, it was easy for white Americans to jump on Trump's racism bandwagon.

Trump did not invent "white grievance" politics, but he learned how to use it to his advantage. Trump has convinced many whites to complain because, in their mind, it is because of Blacks and Hispanics that the country is the mess that it is in. In their mind, it is our fault, and they take no blame. Therefore, it was easy for Trump to resurrect Ronald Reagan's slogan "Make American Great Again" to get him into office and Richard Nixon's slogan, "Law and Order President," in an attempt to get him reelected, but he failed miserably. However, over 80 million American voters said no thanks to Trump's second term in office on November 3, 2020. However, many people still have underestimated Trump's ability to sell his brand of politics because he had over 73 million votes in the 2020 Presidential Election—the second most votes by any other candidate, Democrat or Republican.

America's Beginning

When our Founding Fathers set up our form of government, they decided they did not want to be led by a king or monarchy—like where they had come from in England. This was because they saw how powerless people were when led by a monarchy—meaning a king or queen. So, they decided to create a three-tier system of government, which equally distributed that power.

Our founders created three co-equal branches in this new government, whereby each branch had checks and balances over the other. This was done to avoid ever having a single dictator or ruler—although President Trump has challenged that like no other president before him—Richard Nixon behaved better, believe it or not. These three levels of government the founders created were Legislative, Executive, and Judicial. In their basic function, the Legislative Branch makes laws. The Executive Branch enforces laws, and the Judicial Branch determines whether or not a law is constitutional.

Although we have many judicial or court system levels, the Supreme Court has nine justices or judges—appointed for life. These justices are the final court of appeals in all matters concerning the law or the Constitution—that means the Supreme Court is the highest court in the United States. Therefore, when the Supreme Court renders its rulings, they are final and cannot be appealed. However, the Supreme Court can overturn previous rulings with a simple majority decision of the High Court justices. Unfortunately, with all that power comes responsibility. The Supreme Court has had numerous rulings or final legal decisions throughout the 244 years of our nation's history. Although one could argue whether or not many of these decisions were constitutional, they could definitely argue the Bible did not support them, nor did they apply basic decency and fairness.

As I have already stated, many people in America claim the United States was founded as a Christian nation. If that were true, how could a Christian Supreme Court make such un-Christian rulings against black people? These racists rulings helped perpetuate white supremacy in America, which has not only allowed racism to thrive but built the foundation that still affects all aspects of American life to this day. By the way, this is the textbook definition of systemic racism.

Once Again, the preamble to our U.S. Continuation states, *We hold these truths to be self-evident, that all men are created equal, and that they are endowed by their Creator with certain unalienable Rights, that among these are Life, Liberty and the pursuit of Happiness*. The reason why I keep reiterating this point from our Constitution is that it is paramount to the argument of how America became so racially divided—the U.S. Government made racism legal. However, someone forgot to tell our U.S. Supreme Court to read the very *Constitution* they were supposed to uphold. How do we know they had a biased interpretation? Because the Supreme Court has a history of making some of the worst rulings imaginable, which proved they did not believe all men were created equal in the eyes of God. However, maybe they did understand what they were doing, and it is the rest of us that have gotten it wrong all these years. Maybe it was minorities who thought the Constitution was on our side but have been sadly mistaken.

The High Court Made Racism In America Legal

There are at least five U.S. Supreme Court rulings that have not only led to the continued problems in America between Blacks and Whites today, but they help set the foundation for systemic racism that has plagued our country from the beginning.

Dred Scott v. Sandford (1856)

The Dred Scott decision held that Blacks could not become citizens of the United States solely based on race. What is sad was, Blacks were forced to build a country they could not legally become a part of as citizens. This Supreme Court decision triggered the Civil War, which led to over 600,000 Americans dying on a multitude of battlefields around the country. This case is discussed in greater detail in Chapter 2.

Pace v. Alabama (1883)

In 1883 Alabama, *interracial marriage* meant two to seven years of hard labor in a state penitentiary. When a black man named Tony Pace and a white woman named Mary Cox challenged the law, the Supreme Court upheld it—on the grounds that the law, since it prevented Whites from marrying Blacks and Blacks from marrying whites, was race-neutral and did not violate the Fourteenth Amendment. The ruling was finally overturned in the Supreme Court case *Loving v. Virginia* (1967).

The Civil Rights Cases (1883)

The Civil Rights Act, which mandated an end to racial segregation in public accommodations, has actually passed twice in U.S. history. Once in 1875, and again in 1964. We don't hear much about the 1875 version because it was struck down by the Supreme Court in the Civil Rights Cases ruling of 1883, which were made up of five separate challenges to the 1875 Civil Rights Act. Had the Supreme Court simply upheld the 1875 civil rights bill, U.S. Civil Rights history may have been dramatically different.

Plessy v. Ferguson (1896)

Plessy v. Ferguson was a landmark 1896 U.S. Supreme Court decision that upheld racial segregation's constitutionality—under the "separate but equal" doctrine. The case stemmed from an 1892 incident in which an African American train passenger named Homer Plessy refused to sit in the car for Blacks. Rejecting Plessy's argument that his constitutional rights were violated, the Supreme Court ruled that a law that "implies merely a legal distinction" between Whites and Blacks was not unconstitutional. (This ruling basically made the 13th, 14th, and 15th Amendments powerless). As a result, restrictive Jim Crow legislation, and separate public accommodations based on race, became commonplace in America. This case is covered in greater detail in Chapter 3.

Cumming v. Richmond (1899)

When three black families in Richmond County, Virginia, faced the closing of the area's only black public high school, they petitioned the High Court to allow their children to finish their education at the white high school instead. It only took the Supreme Court three years to violate its own "separate but equal" standard by establishing that if there was no suitable Black school in a particular district, black students would simply have to do without an education. In other words, these black high school students were told they could not continue their education because racism was legal in America's education system.

Although there are many other examples, these five Supreme Court cases set the tone for how America has treated African Americans since its beginning. Furthermore, with the Supreme Court's help, *white supremacy* and *white nationalism* have been a big part of American culture for years, which has upheld systemic racism. Many people fail to realize that when you build something on a racist foundation, it does not change because you may change a few laws along the way, especially if those laws are changed or updated by the same dominant race that created the original laws. Furthermore, it never allows for racial healing and reconciliation when the dominant race (by numbers) has only made half-hearted empty apologies throughout the years but has never made amends for all the wrong they have caused Blacks, especially when they are directly responsible for the plight of many Blacks today. Whites cannot blame Blacks because they can't seem to get up off the mat, since they are the reason why they are knocked out on the mat in the first place—as well as creating new mats every year.

A Memorable Illustration

Say you finally save enough money to put a down payment on a new home, and after months of searching, you finally get the break you were looking for. You find a home for sale in a nice neighborhood. The yard has been resodded, along with new trees, hedges and flowers. The exterior of the house has been upgraded, and the entire interior of the house has been redone, including all new hardwood floors and carpet; new drywall covering all the walls and ceilings; a fresh coat of paint throughout the whole house; and brand-new appliances.

After closing on the house and finally moving in, you get a visit from some of your new neighbors to welcome you to the neighborhood. After exchanging some pleasantries, you gladly give your neighbors a grand tour of your new home that you are so proud to own. After the tour, your neighbors turn to you and say, we are amazed how well the realty company was able to clean up all the blood, the stains on the walls and floors, and fix the multitude of bullet holes that had previously ravaged the house. It's no wonder you got this house so cheap, you are told.

You turn to your neighbors, with a look of shock and horror, as to say, what are you talking about? Well, the previous owner was a mass murderer—who is now in prison serving at least ten life sentences, they continued. We are surprised he survived because when they came to arrest him, there was an intense standoff, which ended in a blaze of gunfire before they were finally able to take him into custody. The house was shot up with bullets and in bad shape. By the way, that was more than fifteen years ago, which is why you probably never heard about it. They were going to tear the house down because the man's family didn't think anyone would ever want to live here after what happened—they certainly didn't. You see, there were more than 50 bodies found buried on this property, half of them buried in the walls and floors of this house, and about half in the yard—front as well as back. Also, we were told by the contractors that there were bodies buried in the floor of the basement, but because they thought the house would be torn down, they were never removed. By the way, the police never knew there were bodies in the floor of the basement. So, they would not have to tear the house down, the contractors simply placed a new concrete floor over the top of the old floor. Also, the contractors never removed the old walls or floors; they simply covered up the devastation with new materials. We must say, you can't even tell. The contractors did an outstanding job remodeling. It doesn't even look or smell the same. This house was on the market for over ten years. We guess if enough time went by, they thought some unsuspecting fool would come and buy it without knowing its history, and because you are here, we guess they were right.

The moral of this story is, you can clean something up and attempt to make it look good on the surface, but it does not mean anything if the underlying problem is never dealt with and only covered up or ignored—which is what America has done with the stain of racism that still plagues us to this very day.

CHAPTER 15

IT'S ALL IN A NAME

The Four Hebrew Boys

> *Then the king ordered Ashpenaz, the chief of his officials, to bring in some of the sons of Israel, including some of the royal family and of the nobles, youths in whom was no defect, who were good-looking, showing intelligence in every branch of wisdom, endowed with understanding and discerning knowledge, and who had ability for serving in the king's court; and he ordered him to teach them the literature and language of the Chaldeans. The king appointed for them a daily ration from the king's choice food and from the wine which he drank, and appointed that they should be educated three years, at the end of which they were to enter the king's personal service. Now among them from the sons of Judah were Daniel, Hananiah, Mishael and Azariah. Then the commander of the officials assigned new names to them; and to Daniel he assigned the name Belteshazzar, to Hananiah Shadrach, to Mishael Meshach and to Azariah Abed-nego. (Daniels 1:3-7)*

Let's face it, since the Fall of Man, the absolute cruelty that mankind has perpetrated against itself, year after year, is not only heartbreaking, but it is a total travesty. Perhaps no other event in human history reveals the depravity of mankind like the Transatlantic Slave Trade.[338] How

---

[338] Isabel Wilkerson, *Caste: The Origins of Our Discontents*, 145. In the U.S., African American, denied pay for their labors during slavery and barely paid afterward in the twentieth century, were whipped or lynched for stealing food, for the accusation of stealing seventy-five cents, for trying to stand up for themselves or appearing to question a person in the dominate caste.

could human beings treat other human beings with such disdain and hatred, especially when all of mankind was created in the image and likeness of God? The Transatlantic Slave Trade enslaved Black people from Africa. It caused them to endure a series of catastrophic events that, by design, severed them from their home, family, livelihood, and everything else familiar.[339]

The Trans-Atlantic Slave Trade was not just a series of numerous horrific voyages for African slaves. It was an enormous business operation with many moving parts for trading, buying, and selling goods. Remarkably, human beings were traded, bought, and sold as a commodity. The fact that this human travesty lasted for 366 years is unthinkable. European slavers loaded approximately 12.5 million Africans onto Atlantic slave ships, whereby about 11 million survived the Middle Passage to landfall and life in the Americas. Unfortunately, over a million and a half Africans died just on the journey alone.[340] It was not until January 1808 when a new United States federal law made it illegal to import slaves from Africa. The law devastated Charleston, South Carolina, because slavery was a cash cow for the city and the white men that brokered the trades. The day the law was enacted, it marked the end—the permanent, legal closure—of the Trans-Atlantic slave trade into our country. Unfortunately, this did not end the practice of slavery.

The practice of slavery continued to be legal in much of the U.S. until 1865. Sorry to say, enslaved Blacks continued to be bought and sold within the Southern states, but in January 1808, the legal flow of new Africans into this country stopped forever.[341] While white American enslavement of Blacks was abolished in the mid-nineteenth

---

339 "Transatlantic Slave Trade," *Slavery and Remembrance* [on-line]; accessed on 25 September 2020; available from http://slaveryandremembrance.org/articles/article/?id=A0002; Internet.

340 Ibid.

341 Ibid. The traffic of importing Africans through the port of Charleston officially ended in January 1808, after 137 years of turbulent activity, but the practice of slavery continued in the Charleston area until late February, 1865. Some African captives were undoubtedly smuggled onto America's shores during the first half of the nineteenth-century, but such events represent isolated aberrations from the law that are nearly impossible to document.

century, the scars from this long period of forced labor have not healed and hinder the growth and development of modern democracy to this day.[342] Furthermore, since slavery ended in 1865, not only have African Americans not been able to shake the stigma of slavery as well as still being viewed by many Whites as the "N" word, the damage of the caste system of systemic racism has had a lasting impact.

A Memorable Illustration

To put slavery in a context you could understand, what if some heavily armed men came to your home, forced themselves in, slapped you around, threaten they'll kill you if you didn't cooperate, took everything you had of value, and then kidnapped you and your family? Although you were taken in broad daylight, no one came to your rescue, and no matter how much you and your family screamed, your cries went unanswered. You are placed into a vehicle and driven to the coast, where a large ship awaits. You are taken aboard, placed into the bottom of a crowded ship with poor ventilation. To your amazement, 600 other people look just like you, chained together for a 4,000-mile trip, which will take about four months to complete the journey to a new country across the Atlantic Ocean.

Throughout your long voyage, you were not even treated as human but more like a caged animal. You were chained to the person next to you throughout your voyage. By the way, you were only given one or two meals a day with water, but not something you would fix for yourself, but something you would feed a pet. When you had to go to the bathroom, you were forced to use it on yourself. Now multiply that times everyone crowded into the bottom of that ship with you, which at some point or another, having to use the restroom multiple times during that voyage. Could you imagine the smell? Could you imagine

---

342   Angela Thompsell, "Timeline of the Trans-Atlantic Slave Trade," 19 June 2019. [on-line]; accessed on 25 September 2020; available from https://www.thoughtco.com/trans-atlantic-slave-trade-timeline-4156303: Internet. The slave trade in the Americas began in the 15th century when the European colonial forces in Britain, France, Spain, Portugal, and the Netherlands forcibly stole people from their homes in Africa to do the hard labor that it took to power the economic engine of the New World.

the sheer horror and Post Traumatic Stress Disorder (PTSD) you would have to endure, just like other African slaves endured before you? Also, could you imagine the sickness and disease that would spread among those captured with you? This is why so many African slaves died along the journey—only to have their bodies thrown overboard into the ocean and not even given a proper burial.

When you finally arrived at your new destination, you were greeted with vile language, disrespected, and even whipped—just for showing up. You are hosed down with water in public while standing naked with strangers looking at you. You are placed on an auction block, while other people you have never met bid for you, as though you were cattle. After the highest bidder purchased you as their property, you are placed into a vehicle and taken to a plantation out in the middle of nowhere. To add to your misery, your family members were purchased by a different owner. As a result, that was the last time you laid eyes on your loved ones. When you arrived at your new home, you were greeted with a welcome beating to show you who's in charge and to remind you that you were no longer free but a slave.

You are not asked your name because your slave owner gave you the name he wanted you to answer to. You are assigned to a crowded sleeping cabin that was already full of other slaves. You are told this is now your reality, and you are expected to work like a dog the rest of your life, and there is nothing you can do about it. While all of this is going on, you have to deal with being separated from your family, the loss of your friends and community, and more importantly, you have lost everything that meant anything to you. As a man, you are stripped of your manhood, identity, heritage, self-esteem, dignity, and faith. You are no longer treated as a man but like a dog with zero rights. If you happened to be a female slave, you are treated far worse. You are sexually harassed and raped repeatedly. As a woman, you are used as a breeding machine, especially if you arrived after 1808 when Congress ended America's participation in the Trans-Atlantic Slave Trade. Since slave owners could no longer purchase slaves kidnapped from Africa, as a female slave, you were forced to produce numerous slave children for your owners. As a result, the burden fell to you as a black woman in America to enhance the slave population. After your first night in the New World, you go to sleep, finally, after working from sun up to sundown. You hope this was only a nightmare, but you wake up feeling as though you have been placed into the twilight zone because your horrible experience is real.

Trusting God Even While In Bondage

In the book of Daniel, the Jews were taken hostage into captivity in Babylon. In 586 B.C, King Nebuchadnezzar tore down the walls of Jerusalem and destroyed the temple. He carried off most of the Jews, at least the significant ones, and placed them under his rule. It was common for the Babylonians to take some young, intelligent captives and train them to serve in government. In the first chapter of Daniel, Nebuchadnezzar ordered Ashpenaz, his chief official, to bring in some of the sons of Israel, with the emphasis on those from the royal family and nobles (v. 3). Specifically, those that had intelligence in every branch of wisdom, young men with discerning knowledge, and the ability to serve in the king's court (v. 4).

Once chosen, the young men were appointed daily rations of food and wine from the king's table and given a three-year education in Babylonian law and culture. Once completed, these young men were placed in government roles to serve Nebuchadnezzar (v. 5). Four prominent Jewish young men took center stage and played a major role in God's agenda throughout the book. These four were Daniel, the leader of the group, Hananiah, Mishael, and Azariah (v. 6). The next verse was key because it set the stage for how the Babylonians sought to control their subjects. "Then the commander of the officials assigned new names to them; and to Daniel, he assigned the name Belteshazzar, to Hananiah Shadrach, to Mishael Meshach, and Azariah Abed-nego" (v. 7). The change of the names of the four Hebrew boys was a significant event in the life of devout Jewish followers of God, but it is often misunderstood by modern Bible readers.

Understanding African Names From Nigerian Members Of Our Church

What was the significance of the Babylonians changing the names of the four Hebrew boys? For years I have read and studied this passage, preached on it many times, and even taught the book of Daniel as a Bible college professor. However, I gained good insight into this passage when Nigerian families attending seminary from my alma mater, at Southwestern Baptist Theological Seminary, joined our church. Our church has been tremendously blessed with the presence of Rev. Samson Aremu (my prince charming), his wife Ruth, their son Emanuel, and their two daughters, Mary and Abigail; Min. Paul Adegoke (the king has been Exalted), his wife Elizabeth, and their son Enoch; and Rev. Victor Adebiyi (royal one), wife Olutayo, their son Oluwasemiloore (the Lord has been good to me), and their daughter Oluwadamilola (the Lord honors me).[343] These Nigerian families make a huge difference in our lives and church. As these faithful men of God study to complete their Ph.D. programs, they have been a tremendous asset to our staff and ministries.

When Americans have children, we tend to choose names for various reasons, but not necessarily because of meaning or purpose. Many Americans name their kids after a relative, a state, flower, season, someone famous, or someone for sentimental reasons. Also, we tend to use names that are popular or whatever sounds good at the moment. As a result, many kids grow up adopting nicknames because they are embarrassed by what their parents thought of them at birth. However, I found that is not what Africans do. In fact, to them, to follow American culture, along the lines of naming their children, would be nonsensical. In Africa, a name is not just a label like it is in America. In Africa, names are tied to the destiny or divine purpose, as well as the character of their children. For instance, one of the key members of our pastoral staff is Rev. Samson Aremu. The following is a list of his family and their American names, as well as their Nigerian names.

---

343   These dedicated Nigerian families use names in a very significant way. To each the them their names matter because their names reflect God's calling and presence in their lives. Their names also remind them how their destiny in Christ.

- **Samson**. His Nigerian name is Oluwaseun (O-lu-was-se-un), which means "Thanks be to God."
- **Ruth** (wife). Her Nigerian name is Oluwabanke (O-lu-wa-ban-ke), which means "God helps me care for her."
- **Emmanuel** (son). His Nigerian name is Oluwanifemi (O-lu-wa-ni-fem-mi), which means "God loves me."
- **Mary** (daughter). Her Nigerian name is Oluwadarasimi (O-lu-wa-da-ra-si-mi), which means "God is good to me."
- **Abigail** (daughter). Her Nigerian name is Fiyinfoluwa (Fi-yin-fo-lu-wa): "Give praise to God."

The Aremu family names reveal their faith in God, which is Jesus Christ our Savior and Lord. So, when their name is called, they automatically are reminded of God's awesome presence in their lives. So, no matter how difficult things might get, they are reminded every day that they are Kingdom kids. Another important point that is notable about this family is that even their names in English are biblical. I talked to Rev. Samson and his wife Ruth about the importance of this subject, and they helped me understand Daniel Chapter 1. Among Christians in Africa, it is common for them to adopt an English name from the Bible because outside of their country, their names are often too hard to pronounce. However, Africans who do not consider themselves Christians still follow the same practice and assign their kids names tied to their purpose or destiny, even if it is not for religious reasons.

In Jewish culture, they followed the same cultural standards as Africans, as it relates to naming their children, which was also based on destiny or divine purpose, as well as character. It was not by accident that out of all the youth chosen to work in Nebuchadnezzar's court, there happened to be four young Hebrew men that God could count on to fulfill His divine plan in a sinful nation. The names of these four Hebrew boys revealed more about them than simply what they were called. Their names tied them to the God of Israel.

- Daniel. His name means "God has judged or God is my judge." His name was changed to the Babylonian, Belteshazzar—which means "Lady, protect the king."

- Hananiah. His name means "Yahweh has been gracious." His name was changed to the Babylonian, Shadrach—which means "I am fearful (of a god)."
- Mishael. His name means "Who is what God is." His name was changed to the Babylonian name Meshach—which means "I am despised, contemptible, humble (before my god)."
- Azariah. His name means "Yahweh has helped (me)." His name was changed to Abednego—which means servant of Nebo—the Babylonian god of writing and vegetation.

What's in a name? When it comes to God's children, obviously everything. Changing a person's name was a sign of having power and authority over that person. Conquering nations often did this to their captives to make them more a part of their new culture.

The Aremu family's Nigerian culture helped our church to understand better the captivity of the Jews in Babylon, as well as the significance of their names being changed. So, there are four significant reasons why the Babylonians changed the names of the four Hebrew boys.

To Strip Them of Their Identity. (Individuality, uniqueness, personality, character)

If you want to know what it is like to struggle with identity or to have an "identity crisis," look no further than our youth in this country today. Because they lack identity, they strive to create one, often based on feelings, emotions, peer pressure, or Satan's manipulation. Just look at their groom and dress (or lack thereof), choice of friends, music, cult religions, and demonic activity. Also, they are enamored with tattoos and body piercings. In the extreme, you see youth joining gangs, using drugs, or struggling with gender identity—which is why you have kids at younger and younger ages accepting transgender language or homosexual lifestyles. Also, youth are often influenced by the behavior of adults that struggle with their identity. They also are heavily influenced by television and social media.

In the eyes of God, identity is not something you create. It is something God creates in you. However, when you refuse to accept who God created you because you do not know your divine purpose because you do not know Jesus Christ as Savior Lord. (Psalm 139)

To Strip Them of Their Heritage. (Inheritance, legacy, birthright, culture)

When Jacob stole Esau's birthright (by trickery), he stole something he could not use because he had to flee for his life. If you recall, his mother Rachel helped him concoct a plan to trick Isaac into blessing the wrong son, in his old age, when he was blind. Well, the plan worked, but Jacob ended up fleeing to live with Rachel's brother Laban—who was better at the craft of deception than he was. Because of Jacob's actions, for over 20 years, he was denied his inheritance, legacy, birthright, and culture. It was not until he gathered his family together to head back to Jerusalem that his life was changed—for the purpose God created him. God met Jacob at the Jabbok River and wrestled with him. Jacob told God that he was not going to let him go until He blessed him. So that Jacob would fully submit and stop wrestling with the Lord, God reached down a touched the socket of Jacob's thigh, thus dislocating it. To stand, Jacob grabbed onto God to lean on Him, which was symbolic of trusting Him. The good news didn't stop there. God changed Jacob's name to Israel. This was extremely important because the name change allowed Jacob to finally access his inheritance, legacy, birthright, and culture. (Genesis 32:22)

To Strip Them of Their Destiny. (purpose, calling, vocation, future)

First of all, every human being born on this earth (from the beginning of time until the end of time) is born with destiny or purpose. If not, God would not have created you or me. [Jeremiah 1:5]. Second, the vast majority of human beings die without ever reaching their destiny or fulfilling their God-given purpose. Why? Because they reject God's only path that leads to not only to heaven but our purpose on this earth. Jesus is the only way to that path!

To Strip Them of Their Faith. (trust, reliance, conviction, beliefs, confidence, assurance)

For a Jew, especially for one committed to Yahweh, their faith meant more to them than anything else. Why? Because they knew without a personal relationship with God, their life was meaningful—just like the rest of the world that did not know Him. Therefore, if you are stripped of your faith in Jesus Christ as Savior and Lord, you have no identity, or heritage, or destiny. As a result, you would be just like the vast majority of the world's population and on your way to hell. (Hebrews 11:6)

12 Years A Slave

It is said that history often repeats itself. In the case of slavery in America, it is obvious. One of the first significant things that slave owners did after they purchased African slaves was changed their names. This was significant because of all the reasons already stated. Slaves were beaten ferociously to break their will and get them to accept the slave master's plan as well as their slave name. My wife and I recently watched the movie *Twelve Years a Slave*. Although it was heartbreaking to watch, we sat through it, not for entertainment but education.

The movie was interesting because it told the true story of Solomon Northup, who was also the author of the book, which bears the same title as the movie. Northup was born in the free state of New York in 1808 as a free man. Although he was educated and lived a peaceful life, in his own home, with his wife and children, he was kidnapped and sold into slavery in 1841. As I have already stated, the U.S. Government ended its involvement in the Trans-Atlantic Slave Trade in 1808. One of the negative results of that important congressional legislation was that many Whites sought to continue slavery by any means necessary.

As a result, Whites would kidnap free African Americans from the North and illegally transport them to the South, which placed many of them into the bondage of slavery for the first time in their lives. Regrettably, Northup's horrendous ordeal lasted twelve years. After being kidnapped, Northup's first slave owner, William Ford, changed his name to a slave name, which was Platt.³⁴⁴ Ironically, Platt means a plot of land or piece of ground, while Solomon is from the Hebrew word shalom, which means peace. Therefore, in the eyes of Solomon's slave master, he was not a man, but a piece of dirt, which is why it's all in a name matters, especially when it comes to value and worth.

Somehow, Northup endured being enslaved until January 1853. Northup kept a journal where he documented his ordeal, which provided him the first-hand material for his novel, *Twelve Years a Slave*. As I watched this movie, it saddened and angered me at the same time. My wife and I both shed tears because we were reminded of what our ancestors had to endure at the hands of a nation that allowed racism to flourish. Also, the movie reminded me of the plight of Blacks in America and what we have endured at the hands of Whites for years, including by those that claimed they were Christians. In my opinion, this is the saddest part of our history in America.

Whites began Christian churches in America early on in the Thirteen Colonies.³⁴⁵ How could white Christians be so instrumental in the racist system of slavery in America?³⁴⁶ How could white pastors

---

344   Isabel Wilkerson, *Caste: The Origins of Discontent*, 143. Upon their arrival at the auction blocks and labor camps of the American South, Africans were stripped of their given names and forced to respond to new ones, as would a dog to a new owner, often mocking names like Caesar or Samson or Dred. They were stripped of their past lives and identities as Yoruba or Asante or Igbo, as the son of a fisherman, nephew of the village priest, or daughter of a midwife. Decades after, Jews were stripped of their given and surnames and forced to memorize the prison numbers assigned them in the concentration camps of Hitler.

345   Mark A. Noll, Nathan O. Hatch and George M. Marsden. *The Search for Christian America*, 7. Almost as soon as there where European settlers in North America, there were also several varieties of Christianity, Protestants as well as Catholics.

346   Jemar Tisby, *The Color of Compromise*. Racial segregation in Christian churches occurred in the eighteenth century in large part because white believers did not oppose the enslavement of African persons. Instead, Christians sought to reform slavery and evangelize the enslaved. In the process, the learned to rationalize the continued existence of slavery. Many white Christians comforted themselves with the myth that slavery allowed them to more adequately care for the material and spiritual needs of enslaved Africans.

preach racist sermons to their congregations that used the Bible (out of context) to uphold slavery? Why, after all these years, don't our Christian Seminaries and Bible colleges set the record straight when teaching their students church history? In all my years of attending Bible college and seminary training, I do not ever recall any of my professors dealing with the sin of racism in America, even in my church history courses where we covered Christianity in early America.

As I look back at our nation's history, the position of many white Christians is perhaps the most disappointing and disturbing. If white Christians had taken a bold stand for Christ and followed the correct teachings of Scripture, slavery would not have taken root in the colonies they founded or were instrumental in developing. How the early church in America essentially agreed with slavery and racism is one of the most difficult things for African Americans to fathom, which is why I believe many Blacks reject Christianity because they view it as a "white man's" religion. One of my close friends, when I was growing up in East St. Louis and graduated from high school in 1981, named Mabry, became a devout Muslim because that's how he felt about Christianity. Based on our past and our continued struggles with systemic racism, it inspired me to write this book from the perspective of a dedicated Christian pastor that happens to be an African American.

It's All In A Name is the title of this chapter. It speaks volumes to how for years African Americans or Africans, and all other Blacks from other countries, that have lived in this country, whether as citizens or on a visa, have been disrespected by Whites by calling them derogatory names, which the worst was being called the "N" word or some variation of that name.[347] It does not seem to matter to some Whites what Blacks do, and no matter how successful we become, we are still the "N" word in the eyes of many Whites today, even if we become President of the United States., such as Barack Obama.

---

347 Nathaniel T. Powell. "Implementing the USAF's Chaplaincy Model of Racial Diversity," 44. Although the institution of slavery in America ended more than 100 years ago, the harmful effects still linger. For example, a retired U.S. Navy veteran named William S. Fortner referred to President Obama as the "Tragic Negro" because of the way he has governed as the nation's leader concerning fiscal policies. The term "Negro" is inflammatory, derogatory, and racist, which is why it is not often used today to describe African-Americans.

As I have said before, as a devout Christian that continues to read and study my Bible daily, I realize that any person or people group can be a tool for Satan. Ephesians 6:12 reminds us that our struggle is not against flesh and blood, but against the rulers, against the powers, against the world forces of this darkness, against the spiritual forces of wickedness in the heavenly places. So, I realize that since the fall of man, Satan has mastered pitting people against each other, especially along the lines of race. Therefore, I understand why unsaved Whites fell for Satan's manipulation and went all-in on racism and slavery. Still, for the life of me, I cannot understand why white Christians allowed themselves to be Satan's vessels as well. Using the Bible as a guide, the only conclusion that one could come to is that they were either not truly saved or were just really a bad example at best.

Application of Daniel 1:3-7

What are the same things that the Babylonians tried to do to Daniel, Hananiah, Mishal, and Azariah, that the devil tries to do to Christians today?

- He wants to strip us of our identity (our character in Christ).
- He wants to strip us of our heritage (our blessings in Christ).
- He wants to strip us of our faith (our trust in Christ).
- He wants to strip us of our destiny (our purpose in Christ).

Therefore, if America is ever going to get past our problem with systemic racism, we will have to stop being tools for Satan. Furthermore, those of us that are truly Christians are going to have to come out of our comfort zones and be willing to reach out to others that do not look like us to advance the cause of Christ. Christians from every walk of life in America will have to turn away from division, especially along racial lines, and be willing to be a true light for Christ. As Rev. Jimmy Ingram, one of the faithful trusted senior ministers of our church for years, often says, "There certainly is no shortage of customers." This is one of his favorite sayings—as it relates to outreach and evangelism. Jesus said something very similar when He proclaimed, "Seeing the people, He felt compassion for them because they were distressed and dispirited like sheep without a shepherd" (Matthew 9:36). Therefore, as servants of God, called by God, regardless of race or ethnicity, we have plenty of customers to serve and reach for the glory of God. Finally, if we never acknowledge there is a problem or refuse to use our God-given gifts to help solve the problem—as one multiracial unified body of Christ— then our beloved country will continue to struggle with systemic racism. If we accept the status quo by doing nothing, allowing it to continue as the norm, then the Christian church in America will never be what God created it to be. But one thing is for sure, Black, White, Asian, Hispanic, Native, and others will have to answer to God why we failed to follow His Bible blueprint to deal with the sin of America.

CHAPTER 16

WHEN YOUR SKIN BECOMES THE PROBLEM

The murmuring of Miriam and Aaron

> *Then Miriam and Aaron spoke against Moses because of the Cushite woman whom he had married (for he had married a Cushite woman); and they said, "Has the Lord indeed spoken only through Moses? Has He not spoken through us as well?" And the Lord heard it. (Now the man Moses was very humble, more than any man who was on the face of the earth.) Suddenly the Lord said to Moses and Aaron and to Miriam, "You three come out to the tent of meeting." So, the three of them came out. Then the Lord came down in a pillar of cloud and stood at the doorway of the tent, and He called Aaron and Miriam. When they had both come forward, He said, "Hear now My words: If there is a prophet among you, I, the Lord, shall make Myself known to him in a vision. I shall speak with him in a dream. "Not so, with My servant Moses, He is faithful in all My household; 8 With him I speak mouth to mouth, even openly, and not in dark sayings, and he beholds the form of the Lord. Why then were you not afraid to speak against My servant, against Moses?" 9 So the anger of the Lord burned against them and He departed. 10 But when the cloud had withdrawn from over the tent, behold, Miriam was leprous, as white as snow. As Aaron turned toward Miriam, behold, she was leprous. [Numbers 12:1-8]*

Often when we talk about the history of slavery in America, we focus on the treatment of black men and how they were whipped, beaten, disfigured, abused, humiliated, oppressed, dishonored, and even lynched. Black men were often sleep deprived because they were forced to work long hours, from sun up to sundown. At the same time, African men have always been proud of their heritage. However, to maintain slavery and dominate them, they were stripped of their dignity, stripped of their heritage, stripped of their identity, and stripped of their faith. Whites constantly dishonored black men to treat them as less than human, primarily because they were not viewed as human. White men did just about any cruel and unusual punishment designed to hold black men in a perpetual state of servitude, even after slavery ended. However, as bad as black men were treated, an argument can be made that black women were treated far worse.

> *The abjection of slavery took an added dimension when women were concerned. They were the victims of sexual abuse, from harassment to forced prostitution, and from breeding to rape. Rape by sailors on the slave ships, and rape by overseers, slaveholders, and their sons in the Americas was a persistent threat to all, a horrific reality to many. Used, like it continues to be used today, as a weapon of terror, rape was meant to assert power over and demean not only the women, but also their fathers, brothers, husbands, and sons, who were reminded daily that they were considered less than men since they could not protect their womenfolk. Breeding through compulsion or incentives was another appalling feature of the gender-based violence and exploitation women had to endure. Overall, the sexual abuse of women was part of the larger attempt at demoralization and submission of the entire community.*[348]

Since slavery ended in America, there have been numerous books, dissertations, and articles written on the subject. The tremendous research these individuals and scholars undertook is commendable. However, having someone present during the time of slavery to tell the story is far more valuable. The good news is there are first-hand accounts of just how bad it was for black women during slavery in

---

348   Sylviane Diouf, "Remembering the Women of Slavery," *New York Library*, 27 March 2015. [on-line]; accessed on 13 Nov 2020; accessed from https://www.nypl.org/blog/2015/03/27/remembering-women-slavery; Internet.

America. One such account was the very compelling story of Harriet Jacobs.

Incidents In The Life Of A Slave Girl

Many slaves, once freed, wrote about their experiences, which were called slave journals or diaries. A black woman named Harriet Jacobs, who was born into slavery in North Carolina, was a first-hand eyewitness of what it was like for black women during slavery. Harriet Jacobs was born on February 11, 1813, and died on March 7, 1897. Her story was one of the first of its kind that revealed the struggles of how the average black woman suffered. Although born a slave, she was able to earn her freedom and became an American writer, abolitionist speaker, and reformer. Her biggest contribution that brought her notoriety was a book she published under the pseudonym, Linda Brent. *Incidents in the Life of a Slave Girl* was one of the first autobiographical narratives about the struggle for freedom by female slaves and the sexual abuses they endured.[349]

Harriet's life provides insight into what it was like for Blacks when their lives were intertwined with Whites in the South. There was a dynamic to slavery that impacted race relations in America, in a way that has often been overlooked, but was evident in the life of a brave black woman that dared to tell her story in a book—which provided these details. According to the book, Elijah Knox, Harriet's father, was said to be the son of an enslaved black woman, Athena Knox, and a white farmer, Henry Jacobs. Harriet was born a slave in Edmonton, North Carolina, and had a brother named John S. Jacobs.[350] Harriet and John's parents were both slaves but owned by different white men. Harriet's father, Elijah, was an enslaved black carpenter owned by Dr. Andrew Knox, from which Elijah received his last name.

However, Harriet and John inherited the status of "slave" from their mother, Delilah Horniblow,[351] an enslaved black woman held by

---

349   Harriet Jacobs. *Incidents in the Life of A Slave Girl*. (Great Britain: Coda Books, 2012), 6.

350   Ibid.

351   Isabel Wilkerson, *Cast: Origins of Discontent*, 105. The Virginia

John Horniblow, a tavern owner. Harriet lived with her mother until Delilah's death around 1819, when Harriet was six. Then she lived with her mother's mistress, Margaret Horniblow, who taught Harriet to read, write and sow.[352] After Margaret died in 1825, Harriet was 12-years-old and was willed to Margaret's 5-year-old niece. However, the niece's father, Dr. James Norcom, intervened and became Harriet's de facto master. Norcom sexually harassed Harriet from age twelve until she was twenty-four. He refused to allow Harriet to marry, regardless of the man's status.

In an attempt to escape Norcom's sexual harassment and years of sexual abuse, Harriet began a consensual sexual relationship with a white lawyer, Samuel Sawyer, who became a member of the U.S. House of Representatives. Harriet and Samuel had two children, Joseph and Louisa. However, the children inherited their mother's slave status because Norcom still owned her. As a result, her children became Norcom's property by default because he still owned Harriet. Unfortunately, Norcom used Harriet's children as leverage for sexual favors. If she refused, he threatened to sell her children. By 1835, when she was twenty-four, her domestic situation became so unbearable that Harriet escaped with her children. She lived for seven years in her grandmother's attic before she escaped to Philadelphia and then to New York. Her children's father, Samuel, purchased the children he shared with Harriet and set them free. The children were left behind in the South when Harriet headed North.[353]

As a writer, Harriet Jacobs tried to appeal to white women and northern abolitionists. The goal was to expose the horrors of slavery from a non-white perspective by appealing to a more sympathetic audience. Unfortunately, the vast majority of American history, especially as it relates to White's treatment of Blacks, was written by the dominant white race that controlled the narrative, as well as all

---

Assembly declared the status of all people born in the colony. "Whereas, some doubts have arisen whether children got by an Englishman upon a negro woman should be slave or free," the Assembly declared all children born in this country shall be held bond or free only according the condition (status) of the mother."

352   Harriet Jacobs. *Incidents*, 6.

353   Ibid.

levels of government and journalism outlets. However, Harriet, as a black woman, was able to defy the odds during slavery. Harriet wrote about systemic racism in her book, which was derived from her personal experiences. Ironically, she was the first black woman to write a fugitive slave narrative in the U.S., in 1860. For years, Harriet's work was credited to a white abolitionist named Lydia Maria Child. [354]

> *Praised by the antislavery press in the United States and Great Britain, Incidents was quickly overshadowed by the gathering clouds of Civil War in America. Never reprinted in Jacob's lifetime, it remained in obscurity, until the Civil Rights and Women's Movements of the 1960s and 1970s. which spurred a reprint of Incidents in 1973. Not until the extensive archival work of Jean Fagan Yellin did Incidents begin to take its place as a major African American slave narrative. Published in Yellin's admirable edition of* Incidents in the Life of a Slave Girl *(Harvard University Press, 1987), Jacob's correspondence with Child helps lay to rest the long-standing charge against* Incidents *that it was, at worst, fiction, and best, the product of Child's pen, not Jacobs's. Child's letters to Jacobs and others make clear that her role as editor was no more than she acknowledged in her introduction to* Incidents: *to ensure the orderly arrangement and directness of the narrative, without adding anything to the text or altering in any significant way, to allow Jacob's manner of recounting her story.*[355]

In Harriet Jacob's first-hand account—during slavery—the black African woman was deemed as an object of economic usefulness. At the same time, black female slaves were also treated as an object of sexual abuse by white slave owners. Unfortunately, black women were viewed by many whites as sexually immoral and loose. As a result, they were raped and abused repeatedly, at the slave master's will. Harriet's book provides insight into the sexual exploitation of black women and what they endured during slavery. She noted the brutalization

---

354 William L. Andrews, "Harriet A. Jacob (Harriet Ann) 1813-1897," [online]; accessed on 25 September 2020; available from https://docsouth.unc.edu/fpn/jacobs/bio.html; Internet.

355 Ibid.

of black girls and women by white slave-masters, who justified their cruelty by viewing black women as sexual savages. Ironically, many white women hated black women because their husbands found them sexually desirable. Black women were extremely vulnerable during slavery because they lacked the physical strength and legal standing to fight off their white male attackers. Unlike black men, that suffered more of a physical burden, black women suffered a double burden. Black women were continuously stripped, beaten, raped, and forced to 'breed' more children to keep the slave system going. As a result, black women suffered far worse than black men because of their sexual vulnerability.[356]

A black slave was the property of their white slave owner and could be treated any way that pleased the owner. Not only did black female slaves have to endure the abuse and rape from their white owners, but they also had to deal with the abuse from the slave owner's wife, who blamed the black woman for what their husbands did, for which the black women had no control over. This was portrayed in the movie 12 Years A Slave. A young black female slave named Patsey was the mistress of slave owner Edwin Epps. Although Epps had a sexual relationship, with Patsey, at his will, his wife severely abused her for his behavior, even demanding him to beat Patsey with a whip until her back was open and bleeding profusely in one of the scenes.

Although there were Colonial laws at that time regarding rape, they did not apply to black female slaves.[357] The laws protected white males from any forms of abuse they perpetrated against black female slaves. Therefore, black slave women were unable to defend themselves

---

[356] Annie Nakao, "Her tale was brutal, sexual. No one believed a slave woman could be so literate. But now Harriet Jacobs has reclaimed her name," 23 June 2004 [on-line] accessed on 24 October 2020; accessed from https://www.sfgate.com/entertainment/article/Her-tale-was-brutal-sexual-No-one-believed-a-2747114.php; Internet.

[357] Isabel Wilkerson, *Caste: The Origins of Discontent*, 153. The crimes of homicide, of rape, and of assault and battery were felonies in the slave era as they are today in any civil society. They were seen as wrong, immoral, reprehensible, and worthy to be inflicted on the black body. Thus twelve generations of African-Americans faced the ever-present danger of assault and battery or worse, every day of their lives during the quarter millennium of enslavement.

from the constant abuses of white males. Because they were property, according to the law, they had no right to complain. If a black slave woman complained and accused her slave master of rape, she would be subjected to even more beatings, rape, and abuse, not only by her master but the master's wife as well. Besides, not only did black slave women have to take care of their own children, they were forced to take care of their master's children, for the master's wives as well. Also, they were forced to put the master's kids above their own.

Slave owners often allowed their slaves to get married on their plantations, albeit according to African customs, not American law. Also, slaves were allowed to raise families. However, according to the Constitution, these marriages or families were not legal because slaves had no rights under American law. These slave marriages were simply "plantation marriages" because they were not legally binding. Therefore, when white slave owners wanted to break up a slave family, it was his prerogative, by law.

Moreover, this did not stop white slave owners from raping married female slaves and their daughters, and there was nothing that a black male slave could do about his master forcing himself on his wife or daughters. If he did challenge his white owner, he faced being beaten, disfigured, lynched, or sold to another plantation, even out of state. The bottom line was, the white slave owner held all the cards, and everything he did was to benefit himself.

> *Within this system, white slaveholders made all the decisions: They determined whether and when enslaved people could wed. They split them apart when finances dictated. They sometimes chose who would marry who. Or brazenly violated enslaved couples' marriages by forcing the women to serve as their own concubines. And those in political power set laws that made it exceedingly difficult for freed black people to reside for long near their still-enslaved families without being sucked back into the harrowing state of bondage themselves.*[358]

---

[358] Tera W. Hunter, "Enslaved Couples Faced Wrenching Separations, or Even Choosing Family Over Freedom," *History channel*, 20 September 2019 [on-line]: accessed on 19 November 2020; accessed from https://www.history.com/news/african-american-slavery-marriage-family-separation; Internet.

In the Bible, marriage is sacred; therefore, it should be treated in the highest regard because it is not a man-made institution—it is a divine covenant. Then, how could white Christians during slavery treat marriage so flippant?

> *Since marriage was both a civil right and a religious rite afforded only to those with legal standing, enslaved people, who had no recognizable standing in society, could not make contracts of any kind. Their marriages were neither legally binding, nor sanctified by the Christian church, which routinely allowed one of its holiest rites to be tarnished by power, money, and whim. Property owners were its leading constituents, and their rights prevailed over human rights. So enslaved people were forced to settle for conditional unions that could be torn asunder at any time.*[359]

Today, white evangelicals always harp on the deterioration of the family in America, which there is some truth to their argument. However, they often aim their scorn toward the African American family, not the Caucasian family, which has just as many issues, if not more, by sheer population numbers. White evangelicals primarily blame black men for the condition of their families, and they agreed with their hero, former President, and one-time leader of the Republican party, Ronald Reagan. They falsely labeled black women as "welfare queens," which is a racist stereotype.[360] Although Reagan didn't invent the trope, he used his international platform to raise the world's conscience of the derogatory term and made it a household idea aimed at a black woman. Ironically, actually, there are more white women enrolled in welfare than black women. Still, because of "white

---

359   Ibid.

360   "The true story behind the 'welfare queen' stereotype." *PBS News Hour*, 1 June 2019 [on-line]; accessed on 19 November 2020; accessed from https://www.pbs.org/newshour/show/the-true-story-behind-the-welfare-queen-stereotype; Internet. In his new book "The Queen," author Josh Levin tells the story of Linda Taylor, a woman who became infamous as a welfare cheat. She was a woman who went by many names, was accused of many crimes, and whose image as a Cadillac-driving welfare recipient has lived on. Her story was exaggerated for the impact of publicity and politics. As a result, Taylor became the poster child for welfare fraud. Ironically, there are far more white women on welfare or government assistance than there are black women.

privilege," they are viewed as bettering themselves and getting their entitlement, while black women are viewed as lazy freeloaders stealing money from taxpayers.

As I already stated, white slave owners would have sex with their female slaves regularly, whether they were adults or teenagers. One of the most famous cases was President Thomas Jefferson, who fathered children with his female slave Sally Hemmings. She was only 14-years-old when her sexual relationship with Jefferson began, while he was around 44-years-old.[361] Sally Hemmings had a total of about six children by Jefferson. This was normal with slavery in America because white men did as they pleased with their slaves. As already stated, black females had no rights and were essentially sex slaves. However, not only did female slaves have to deal with the abuses of the slave owners, but they were also subjected to the sexual abuses of their slave owner's sons, white plantation workers, and, yes, even black male slaves.[362]

---

361   Ibram X. Kendi, *Stamped From The Beginning*, 117. On July 15, 1787, eight-year-old Polly Jefferson, and fourteen-year-old Sally Hemings reached Jefferson's Paris doorstep. Sally Hemings had come to Monticello as an infant in 1773 as part of Martha Jefferson's inheritance from her father. John Wayles had fathered six children with his biracial captive Elizabeth Hemings. Sally was the youngest. As his peers penned the U.S. Constitution, Jefferson began a sexual relationship with Sally Hemings. Hemings was more or less forced to settle for the overtures of a sexually aggressive forty-four-year-old. Jefferson pursued Hemings as he arranged for the publication of Notes in London. He did not revise his previous stated opinion about Blacks. Jefferson was a hypocrite because he assailed interracial relationships between White women and Black or biracial men.

362   Diana L. Ramsey, "History & Archaeology: Colonial Era, 1733-1775," 10 January 2014 [on-line]; accessed on 13 November 2020; accessed from https://www.georgiaencyclopedia.org/articles/history-archaeology/slave-women; Internet. Early adolescence for female slaves was often difficult because of the threat of exploitation. For some young (black) women, puberty marked the beginning of a lifetime of physical, sexual, and emotional abuse from masters and mistresses, overseers, male slaves, and members of the planter family. For others, work in the planter's home included close interaction with their owners, which often led to intimate relationships with white men or friendships with white women. House servants spent time tending to the needs of their plantation mistresses—dressing them, combing their hair, sewing their clothes or blankets, nursing their infants, and preparing their meals. They were on call twenty-four hours a day and spent a great deal of time on their feet.

Whites Played A Role In Destroying The Black Family

In a book by Dr. Tony Evans titled, *The Kingdom Agenda: Life Under God*, he explained the family from a biblical perspective. He stated that the disintegration of the family is the single most devastating internal issue facing our nation in general and our communities in particular. Also, he talked about how families touch every area of society; their strengths and weaknesses, and to a large degree, determine the strengths and weaknesses of churches and communities.[363] The key point Evans made was that if there is weak male leadership in the home, it destroys the family. Because of the institution of slavery, the black family was destroyed long ago. Unfortunately, white America has done nowhere enough to right a terrible wrong, which is why many African Americans believe we are owed reparations.

Slavery did not recognize the sanctity of marriage. Couples and families could be broken up at any time, without warning. Commonly, except on large plantations, husbands and wives did not reside in the same place, sometimes not in the same neighborhood following sales or owners' relocation. Thus, the reality is that despite men's often incredibly heroic efforts at visiting and supporting their families, women were forced to raise their children largely on their own for as long as they could since they lived under the constant threat of being sold or their children being sold.

If Reconstruction would have been allowed to run its course, perhaps the plight of African Americans might have been far different over the years. However, with Reconstruction being left for dead,[364]

---

[363] Dr. Tony Evans, *The Kingdom Agenda: Life Under God*, (Chicago: Moody Publishers, 2013), 218.

[364] "The Compromise of 1877," *History Channel*, 27 November 2019 [online]; accessed on 13 November 2020; accessed from https://www.history.com/topics/us-presidents/compromise-of-1877; Internet. The Compromise of 1877 was an informal agreement between southern Democrats and allies of the Republican Rutherford Hayes to settle the result of the 1876 presidential election and marked the end of the Reconstruction era. Immediately after the presidential election of 1876, it became clear that the outcome of the race hinged largely on disputed returns from Florida, Louisiana and South Carolina–the only three states in the South with Reconstruction-era Republican governments still in power. As a bipartisan congressional commission debated over the outcome

Jim Crow filled the vacuum for more than 100 years and made life unbearable for black men, black women, and their children.

Before some of you reading this book get too upset, remember the title of this section is "Whites played a role in destroying the Black Family." This does not absolve African Americans of any responsibility for their current plight because it does not. However, we must at least acknowledge that African Americans didn't get in the ditch by themselves. I would argue that it has been far more difficult for American Americans to climb out of the hole that was dug for them because their starting point was different than every other race that came to America. This is why I have to give a shout-out to African American women, past and present. If it had not been for the strong, committed, courageous, God-fearing Black women, the black family, black community, and black church would have collapsed long ago. Black women lead our families, communities, and churches—all roles that were divinely appointed to men by God, primarily because our black men have been AWOL.[365] Although many of us black men got the memo from God, and are fulling our God-given roles, too many of our black brothers have not. As I have already stated, black men and black women have suffered at the hands of the white majority in America for centuries. However, black women have been far more resilient in many ways than black men. Black women have overcome many of their own challenges and are at least willing to push forward, even though they are still hurting and struggling in many ways from systemic racism, but the difference is that many black men have not.

Black, But Not Appreciated, Part 1

---

early in 1877, allies of the Republican party candidate Rutherford Hayes met in secret with moderate southern Democrats in order to negotiate acceptance of Hayes' election. The Democrats agreed not to block Hayes' victory on the condition that Republicans withdraw all federal troops from the South, thus consolidating Democratic control over the region. As a result of the so-called Compromise of 1877 (or Compromise of 1876), Florida, Louisiana and South Carolina became Democratic once again, effectively bringing an end to the Reconstruction era.

365   AWOL is a military term, and an acronym for Absent Without Leave. In other words, illegally missing in action.

Moses, Aaron, and Miriam are a unique story in Scripture about Hebrew siblings. When we first read about Moses, he is a toddler who has to be protected by his mother from an evil Pharaoh seeking to kill him and all the other Hebrew male children his age. When Moses' mother could no longer hide him, she placed him in a basket. She enlisted the help of her daughter, Miriam, in the plan to protect her beloved son from death. So, she had Miriam—a young girl—to place Moses' basket in the reeds on the Nile River. The basket did not float too far before the cries of an infant got the attention of Pharaoh's daughter, as Miriam looked on to see what would become of her brother. Pharaoh's daughter sent her maiden to retrieve the basket that contained baby Moses. When she investigated the basket, she saw that there was a Hebrew infant boy inside.

Remarkably, Pharaoh's daughter took Moses and raised him as her own. Just as amazing, Miriam approached Pharaoh's daughter and asked if she wanted her to get one of the Hebrew women to nurse the infant boy, to which Pharaoh's daughter agreed. So, Miriam went and got her mother, who was paid by Pharaoh's daughter to take care of her own son—which was nothing but the providential hand of God. Pharaoh's daughter was a black woman that had the compassion to raise a Hebrew child as a family member in Egyptian culture and heritage—giving Moses one of the best educations available of his day.

At the age of 40-years-old, Moses was forced to flee to Midian because he had killed an Egyptian. When Moses departed, Miriam, the oldest, would have been about 52-years-old at the time, and Aaron would have been about 43. Fast-forward to Numbers Chapter 12, and the relationship between Miriam, Aaron, and Moses had changed. All three siblings were more than likely over 100-years-old at this time and were all married. The major difference was, Moses had married outside their Hebrew race. He married a Cushite (Ethiopian) black woman named Zipporah, who was not appreciated by her in-laws. As you recall, Moses was raised by a black woman and spent the first 40 years of his life entrenched in African culture, so Moses did not have an issue with the black race. Also, he had interracial children with Zipporah. Perhaps, this had been an issue with his siblings long before this incident occurred, but we don't know.

However, what we do know is, Miriam and Aaron were jealous of their younger brother Moses. Each of these three siblings had important roles in God's agenda for His people. Miriam was a prophetess, Aaron was the High Priest, but Moses' role far exceeded theirs. Moses was chosen for a very special role, not only to lead the Israelites, but he represented God's law to His people.[366] As a result, God spoke to Moses differently than how He communicated with everyone else at that time. It was because of that special relationship that Miriam and Aaron were jealous of Moses.

To make matters worse, because of their jealously, they attacked the race of Moses' wife. They said, "Has the Lord indeed spoken only through Moses? Has He not spoken through us as well?" (v. 2). Ironically, Miriam was the ringleader of this rebellion against Moses.[367] The same Miriam who once risked her life to save Moses, when he was an infant. The reason why we know she was the instigator is because her name is mentioned first. Once again, we find Aaron bowing down to the pressure of someone disgruntled with Moses—like he did when built the golden calf (Exodus 32). Unfortunately, for them, their disrespect got God's attention.[368] So, God summoned Miriam and Aaron, as well as Moses, to the Tent of Meeting. The cloud pillar descended and stood erect at the entrance. From the pillar of cloud, the Lord called forth

---

366 William Sanford Laser, David Allan Hubbard, and Frederic William Bush, Old Testament Survey: The Message, Form, and Background of the Old Testament, (Grand Rapids: William B. Eerdmans Publishing), 1996, 64. Role of Moses. Moses is the key figure in the Pentateuchal narratives, from Exodus through Deuteronomy. Throughout the Old Testament, Moses is regarded as the founder of Israel's religion, promulgator of the law, organizer of the tribes in work and worship, and their charismatic leader.

367 R. D. Cole. *Numbers*, Vol. 3B. (Nashville: Broadman & Holman Publishers, 2000), 200. The section begins with the feminine singular form of the verb watĕdabber, implicating Miriam as the leader in this endeavor. As noted numerous times in the earlier chapters, the masculine singular form wayĕdabber is used regularly to refer to the process of divine instruction from Yahweh, or of Moses' response in subsequent instruction of the people.

368 W.W. Wiersbe, Wiersbe's Expository Outlines on the Old Testament: Numbers (Wheaton: Victor Books, 1993) Numbers has an important spiritual lesson for Christians today, as explained in Hebrews 3–4 and 1 Cor. 10:1–15. God honors faith and punishes unbelief. At the root of all of Israel's sins in the wilderness was unbelief: they did not trust God's Word.

the disgruntled sister and brother, for a special revelatory session. The Lord normally spoke only with Moses in this manner (v. 8), but this time He directed His words toward the prophetic challenges to Moses' authority.

The two of them stepped forward to hear what God would say to them for their rebellion.[369] In verses 6-7, in a poetic proclamation, the Lord affirmed Moses' position as the uniquely commissioned confidant of Yahweh.[370] God chastised Miriam and Aaron for not being afraid to speak to His servant Moses the way they did. By speaking to Moses in that manner, they spoke to God in that manner because Moses was God's vessel—doing God's will. The climax of the story was verse 10, "But when the cloud had withdrawn from over the tent, behold, Miriam was leprous, as white as snow. As Aaron turned toward Miriam, behold, she was leprous." This passage has often confused many Bible readers. So, why was only Miriam disciplined, but not Aaron? She was the only one that was stricken with leprosy.

Some feminists have viewed this as an affront, an example of chauvinism in the Bible. This was not what happened at all—again, context matters. The reason Aaron was spared had nothing to do with gender. It was because Aaron was the High Priest, and according to Lev. 21:10–12, was not allowed to become ceremonially unclean for any reason. The High Priest represented the people of Israel to God, and he had to always be available to minister in that capacity. So, only Miriam was stricken by leprosy, not because she was a woman or because her sin was any worse than Aaron's, but because God, in His grace, refused to deprive His people of the High Priest's ministry.[371]

What is interesting about the outcome was Aaron didn't get off scot-free. Numbers Chapter 20 records the death of Aaron. "Take Aaron and his son Eleazar and bring them up to Mount Hor, and strip Aaron of his garments and put them on his son Eleazar. So, Aaron will be gathered to his people and will die there. So, Moses did just as the Lord had commanded, and they went up to Mount Hor in the

---

369   R. D. Cole. *Numbers*, Vol. 3B, 202.

370   Ibid.

371   L. O. Richards. *The Bible Reader's Companion*, electronic ed. (Wheaton: Victor Books, 1991), 99.

sight of all the congregation. After Moses had stripped Aaron of his garments and put them on his son Eleazar, Aaron died there on the mountain top" (vs. 23-28). Once Aaron's garments were removed—which represented his covering and anointing, as well as his office of High Priest—he died. As long as Aaron occupied that office, he was only temporarily spared.

Black, But Not Appreciated, Part 2

One of the greatest honors a citizen of a democratic nation is to serve in the Armed Forces, especially as a Christian—for God and country is commendable. Having served in the U.S. Air Force for more than 30 years was one of my greatest honors, but serving as a Christian was an even greater honor. Even in the Bible, Jews, as members of the nation of Israel, were proud to serve God and the nation. In a very familiar story, in 2nd Samuel 11, David was on his rooftop because he could not sleep, and a beautiful woman bathing naked caught his eye, so he inquired about her.

This scene would seem strange to modern Bible readers. Since no Israelite house had running water at that time, bathing often may have been performed privately in the enclosed courtyard that was a part of many Israelite houses. However, David's house probably was located on the highest ground within the Old Jebusite fortress, and from there, his rooftop would have given him a commanding view of the city. Yet, there's no indication in the text that the woman deliberately positioned herself to entice David[372]

The woman's name was Bathsheba, the daughter of Eliam. David's messenger reported this to him, including she was the daughter of one of David's best fighters (cf. 23:34), the granddaughter of his most trusted counselor (cf. 16:23; 23:34), and the wife of one of his inner circle of honored soldiers, Uriah the Hittite (cf. 23:39).[373] Despite being warned about her marital status, David commanded his servant to bring the women to him to have sexual relations. Note: David already

---

372 R.D. Bergen, *1, 2 Samuel*, Vol. 7. (Nashville: Broadman & Holman Publishers, 1996), 364.

373 Ibid.

had seven wives at this time. So, why didn't Bathsheba reject David's sexual advances since she, too, was married? Why did she allow herself to be used by David?

These are age-old questions that usually come down to the man having all the power and authority. Regardless of what Bathsheba's reasons were, David could use his position as king to do as he pleased. After David slept with Bathsheba and got her pregnant, he sought to cover up his sin by having Uriah the Hittite, the husband of Bathsheba, killed. He had Joab, the commander of Israel's army, put Uriah in the hottest part of the battle and then withdraw, essentially leaving him for dead. However, not only was Uriah the Hittite killed, but because of collateral damage, some other Jewish soldiers were killed as well.

When you trace Bathsheba and Uriah's lineage, you find some fascinating revelations. Bathsheba was introduced, not by her name, but by the distinction, "the wife of a Hittite." At this point in Scripture, who she was married to, was more important than who she was. Also, when Uriah was mentioned, it was highlighted that he was "Uriah the Hittite." He was addressed by his name and race on four occasions. When he was first introduced as Bathsheba's husband, and on three other occasions after his death was it mentioned. This issue matters because the author of 2nd Samuel repeatedly emphasized the Hittite race. The Hittites were descendants of Canaan through one of his sons named Heth (Genesis 10:15). Also, Ham, the father of black African nations, was the father of Canaan. This lets us know the Uriah was a black man.

To determine Bathsheba's race, you also must trace her lineage. Bathsheba's father's name was Eliam (2nd Samuel 11:3). Her grandfather, Ahithophel, a faithful advisor to King David, until he rebelled, was a Gilonite. The Gibeonites, just like the Hittites, are believed to have descended from Canaan, which father was Ham. Therefore, David destroyed a black family whose lineage can be traced back to Ham, the father of black people. One final point about the life of David. From 2nd Samuel Chapter 11 until 1 Kings Chapter 2, when David died, his life was never the same because of his sin with Bathsheba, which included getting her pregnant, having her husband Uriah killed, and marrying her—even though he was already married. Although David repented for his sins, his family was in turmoil the rest of his earthly life, which was the cost of what he knowingly did that was a sin against God.

Therefore, there is biblical precedence of black families being destroyed by the people group in power. Again, only if white Americans would have read and followed the Bible from the beginning. Perhaps, knowing this passage in the Bible would have given them pause concerning the role they played in the destruction of the black family and their role in systemic racism.

Black, But Not Appreciated, Part 3

I applied to attend seminary in the summer of 1998. When I received my acceptance letter from the Admissions Office that fall from Southwestern Baptist Theological Seminary, I was overjoyed. I wanted to study for the ministry at one of the premier conservative Bible-centered seminaries in the country, and I thank God that I got the opportunity. I was blessed to earn a Master of Divinity and a Doctor of Ministry from such a prestigious seminary. However, my alma mater does not have a history of being kind to African Americans. Also, the seminary has not done enough to change that image. Although they have made some strides, most Blacks that have attended still walk away feeling the school is still a white male-dominated institution that is not looking to change.

I would submit that is because of four primary reasons. First, the school does not embrace its sinful past and role in systemic racism. Although from time to time, they have offered some empty apologies, actions speak louder than words. Second, the seminary's official position is that it does not recognize systemic racism as a structural problem in America. Third, the seminary is too closely linked to politics and the influence of the Republican party. Fourth, the seminary still refuses to diversify racially and allow qualified Blacks to be an influential part of the faculty and staff. For instance, why is there not an African American full-time staff person who would act as a liaison to the Fellowship of Black Seminarians and the senior leadership? Also, give this person a budget and authority to recruit Blacks on behalf of the school, and connect the school with the African American community. However, I believe what hinders the seminary from going forward is the fact that it has yet to deal with its past.

Southwestern Baptist Theological Seminary began in Waco, Texas. It received a charter on March 14, 1908, and relocated to Fort Worth in 1910, when Fort Worth Hall was erected. It housed the seminary classrooms, library offices, chapel, and dormitory. However, this seminary was only open to White students pursuing a call to ministry. Blacks who felt they were called to ministry were not welcome, which would be the case for many years. This was not surprising since the Southern Baptist Convention was founded in 1845 in Augusta, Georgia, while upholding slavery and white supremacy in America.

In an article in the *USA Today* this year, by Holly Meyer, "Southern Baptists confront the church's history of racism and slaveholding. For some members, it's not enough." [374] Meyer's article deals with the racist past and pro-slavery roots of the Southern Baptist Convention.

> *The Southern Baptist Convention, founded in 1845, formed after Baptists in the North did not want to allow slaveholders in the South to serve as missionaries, said Barry Hankins, chair of Baylor University's history department and co-author of "Baptists in America." Segregation in the church followed the Civil War, he said. Up until the last 40 years, Baptist historians downplayed slavery as the key issue for the creation of the Southern Baptist Convention, Hankins said. Now it is just acknowledged, he said. "White supremacy is still in the DNA of America. It's still in the DNA of the South. It's still in the DNA of the Southern Baptist Convention. The best leaders acknowledge that, face it head-on and work with it," Hankins said. "There are those that don't want to acknowledge it, don't believe it, and want to ignore it. So, you just have this sort of tension, even among white Southern Baptists, as to what to do about this."*[375]

---

374   Holly Meyer, "Southern Baptists confront the church's history of racism and slaveholding. For some members, it's not enough." *USA Today*, 8 August 2020 [on-line]; accessed on 15 December 2020; accessed from Southern Baptists confront the church's history of racism and slaveholding. For some members, it's not enough. (msn.com); Internet.

375   Ibid.

The article also talks about the call for more diversity among Southern Baptist leadership. There needs to be more diversity in positions of authority. A move that is desperately needed to advance racial reconciliation. Ironically, in the over 175-year history of the Southern Baptist Convention, there has only been one African American President, Dr. Fred Luter Jr., Senior Pastor of Franklin Avenue Baptist Church in New Orleans, Louisiana. He was elected in June 2012. However, Luter knew that even with his election, the SBC still had major problems with race relations.

> *"One of the things that let me know that not only a convention, a church, a denomination, but a company is also interested in leveling the playing field is when people of color or different ethnic groups are elected or appointed in positions of leadership," Luter said. "That says to me that we're serious about dealing with racial reconciliation. We have a long way to go, but we've come a long, long way."*

I had the privilege of meeting Dr, Luter on the Southwestern Baptist Theological Seminary campus when he was the guest speaker for the chapel. He is a very good preacher of the gospel and a nice man. I enjoyed my brief conversation with him at the end of chapel. However, with Luter's election to the role of President of the SBC, I couldn't help but feel the same way that I did when Michael Steele was elected as the first African American to be elected as the Chairman to lead the Republican party in 2009. At the time, I felt this was a token move as a knee-jerk reaction to the election of Barack Obama as President of the U.S. in 2008 and him taking office in January 2009.

When Michael Steele was chairman of the Republican National Committee, it did not help change the party's perception of race relations with African Americans. Likewise, when Pastor Luter was President of SBC, it did not change the race relations between White and Black Christians that fall under the Baptist umbrella. These prominent African American men's moves did not move the needle toward racial reconciliation in politics or the church. In fact, according to the article, Myers says things have gotten even worse in the age of Trump—on behalf of politics as well as the church. She states that white evangelicals align themselves with the Republican party, and thus, align themselves with Trump.

The final point that Holly Myer makes in her article is the call for the symbols of the Confederacy to come down. However, the SBC would have to deal with its house cleaning for memorializing Confederate men that fought to uphold slavery on their campuses.

> In addition to increasing diversity in leadership, some Southern Baptists also want the convention and its entities to reconsider how they honor their early slave-holding leaders. While calls for the removal of Confederate symbols intensified in communities across the U.S., Greear pushed for the convention to retire one of its own — the Broadus gavel. It was one part of Greear's efforts to bring racial equality issues back to the forefront after George Floyd's death. Greear also declared in his online presidential address in June that Black lives do matter, but he does not support the Black Lives Matter organization founded in 2013. Used by the convention president while presiding over the denomination's annual meetings, the gavel is named for John A. Broadus, the slave-holding, Confederacy-supporting second president of the convention's flagship school, Southern Baptist Theological Seminary in Louisville, Kentucky.[376]

In response to Greear's comments, Rev. Dwight McKissic, a Black senior pastor of Cornerstone Baptist Church in Arlington, Texas, wanted to go further than a simple gesture. He stated that Broadus Chapel at Southern seminary be renamed and the other honorary references to its slave-holding founders. As a side note, John Albert Broadus served as a chaplain in the Confederate Army to General Robert E. Lee.

McKissic suggested renaming the chapel for the Rev. T. Vaughn Walker, the first African American to become a full professor at the seminary. As an African American Pastor and graduate of an SBC seminary, McKissic's suggestion should be taken seriously because it would be the Christian thing to do, and it would be a step in the right direction toward racial reconciliation. McKissic didn't stop there; he went on to say, "How do you invite Black people to sit in a chapel

---

376   Ibid.

that is named after a blatant racist? The world is ahead of us. The world recognizes the hypocrisy of the fallacy here. The world wants to remove all those vestiges of racism and white supremacy construct." I say amen to Pastor McKissic!

In an opinion article by Jemar Tisby in the Religious News Service, "Report on slavery is only a start for Southern Baptists' reckoning with racism." Tisby also tackles how the Southern Seminary in New Orleans, Louisiana aligned itself with a known racist for financial gain.

> *Just over 100 years ago, Southern Baptist Theological Seminary was on the brink of financial collapse. The school's trustees were thinking about closing the doors. Then a man named Joseph E. Brown made a $50,000 donation to save the school. The seminary's leaders hailed the gift as an answer to prayer. They eventually honored Brown, who also served as governor of Georgia and a member of the seminary's Board of Trustees, with a professorship in his name. They never had a second thought about where the money came from. Joseph E. Brown, the secessionist governor of Georgia during the Civil War. Brown gained his wealth on the backs of incarcerated black men through the heinous practice of convict leasing. His business, Dade Coal Company, paid the state a fee for the work of incarcerated men and, in turn, worked these laborers under draconian conditions.*[377]

Tisby didn't stop there; he went on in this article to talk about how Evangelicals — including Southern Baptists — have continued to demonstrate complicity with racism since the civil rights era and to the present day. From slavery to Jim Crow segregation, and now in the post-civil rights era, the narrative of white racial superiority persists, particularly among white evangelicals.[378] Additionally, Tisby reports on what he terms a "quiet exodus" of people of color leaving from

---

377   Jemar Tisby, "Report on slavery is only a start for Southern Baptists' reckoning with racism: The subtitle was "A new report detailing the history of slavery and racism at Southern Baptist Theological Seminary ends more than 50 years too soon." Religious News Service, 14 December 2028. [on-line]; accessed on 15 December 2020; accessed from Report on slavery is only a start for Southern Baptists' reckoning with racism (religionnews.com); Internet.

378   Ibid.

white evangelical congregations. He says, what is driving this exodus is white evangelical support for Donald Trump. Black people and other racial and ethnic minorities express confusion and disillusionment that support a president who has trafficked in racist tropes and xenophobia. In one of Tisby's final comments, he stated that to move forward in the journey for justice, the leaders at Southern Baptist Theological Seminaries need to commit themselves to actions that affirm the dignity and humanity of black people and other racial and ethnic minorities. I would add to Tisby's comments that the trustees that hire these presidents need to take responsibility.

Not only does Southern Seminary in New Orleans have a problem with racist founders and financial benefactors of their school, so does my alma mater at Southwestern Seminary in Fort Worth. Benajah Harvey Carroll (B.H.) served for two years in the Confederate Army, assigned to the Texas State Militia from 1862-1864, from age 18-20-years-old. Forty-four years later, Carol was instrumental in founding Southwestern Baptist Theological Seminary in Waco, Texas, in 1908. He was also instrumental with the seminary breaking away from Baylor University and moving to Fort Worth, Texas, in 1910.

An academic institution should have high standards of morality, human decency, professionalism, and respect among the faculty and student body. You would not necessarily expect a non-Christian secular graduate school to embody those attributes, but you would expect a Christian college, university, or seminary to do so. Therefore, when a Christian seminary, the higher echelon of academic and theological studies, does not uphold at least the fundamentals of the Christian faith, it is the definition of hypocrisy.

After I began my studies at Southwestern Seminary, I initially wondered why there were not more Blacks among the student body, especially from the surrounding Dallas/Fort Worth metroplex. I noticed most of the Black students that did attend were not from the area. Many of them were from out of state or from Africa. I began to learn about the seminary's ties to America's racist past and how that past is viewed in the African American community. I also learned about some of the founders of the seminary serving in the Confederate Army and supporting slavery, such as B.H Carroll. I have talked to numerous black men from the metroplex that are called to preach the gospel but would never consider an education at Southwestern Seminary. Because of its past, the personal testimonies from some former black alumni that did not have a pleasant experience, and the school is seen as too "white," and not enough diversity in the faculty and leadership.

Furthermore, the feeling among African Americans is that Southwestern seminary does not care about the black church community in the city. For instance, the seminary purposely makes mission trips and even sends facility, to South Korea to recruit students, which has great returns on their investment because the second-largest group of students at the school other than Caucasian is Asian. This is astonishing because the seminary will not even travel throughout the city visiting the African American community to recruit within their own backyard.

Although numerous incidents are very troublesome about my alma mater, I will only cover a few.

In the winter of 2000, my wife and I traveled to Columbus, Georgia, with another seminary student and his wife, which we met on campus and became close friends, even to this day. My friend was scheduled to preach at his home church for the Sunday Morning service that weekend. We arrived on Saturday evening, and we all stayed in the home of a dear friend of theirs that was a longtime member of the church. That evening, I met the Baptist church pastor for the first time when he came to the home of our host. Due to the sensitive nature of the story, I purposely left out my friends, the pastor, and members of the church in Georgia. With their names, you could easily put the pieces together to locate the church as well as the pastor that kept his story secret all these years. The pastor only shared his horrific story with a select few people, and I was included in that number. Out of respect for his privacy, I tell his story without divulging his name.

Although the pastor and I had just met, he invited me to preach in his place for a joint service that Sunday evening. It was an annual special service with four pastors that were once members of the church but left to start their own ministries. Since that initial encounter, and the first time I preached for his church, the pastor and I became good friends. Our friendship came easily because we shared a similar career path. We both graduated from Southwestern Baptist Theological Seminary, were military chaplains, I was Air Force, and he was Navy, and we both had a passion for preaching the gospel correctly. Over time, I would travel back to Georgia from Texas on numerous occasions to minister to his congregation because of his kind invitations.

The reason why I bring up this story is because of our connection to Southwest Seminary. The pastor is at least 25-years-older than I am, and I consider him not only a good friend but a mentor as well. His experience as a student at the Southwestern Seminary dates back to 1970. It was around that time, the seminary first allowed African Americans to stay on campus while pursuing a degree. However, instead of putting African Americans in the regular dormitory with white students, the seminary created makeshift rooms in the cold basement, well below the standards of white students. One evening, while my friend was in his basement room studying, some white students came in behind him, threw a blanket over him, tied him up, covered his eyes, beat him, took him out to Benbrook Lake, dumped into the lake, and left him for dead.

Ironically, what saved his life was the height from which they threw him into the lake because he hit the water with such force it loosened what he was tied up with. He had never been so scared in his entire life. He thought he was good as dead. However, severely shaking and trembling with fear, he was able to free himself from being tide-up. By the grace of God, he was able to get himself out of the water and knock on the door of a nearby house of someone he never met. Benbrook, Texas has always been a predominately white city, even to this day. It was a white family that did not appreciate a black man knocking on their door and asking for help to my friend's surprise. He said they did not hide their racist feelings in his presence.

Without divulging to them the details about his ordeal, the white couple reluctantly gave him a ride back to the seminary campus. Ironically, he kept the incident a secret from his family, including his dad, who was also his pastor, who recommend he attend Southwestern Seminary. He feared he would receive more backlash if he reported the incident to any of his professors or the leadership at the seminary, so he kept it to himself. He never told his dad because he did not want to disappoint him. His dad went to his grave, never knowing what his son had endured from a school he pushed him to attend. His dad was so proud of him because he never attended seminary, and he wanted his son to be the first in the family to attend.

The white students that kidnapped him and took him to Benbrook, a suburb of Fort Worth, and tossed him in the lake to drown were his classmates. He knew their voices because they talked during the entire ordeal. It was as though they did not care if he knew who they were, so they did not attempt to disguise their voices. After the ordeal, my friend racked his brain trying to understand why human beings would treat another human being that way, especially at a Christian seminary. He realized what may have triggered the white student's racist actions against him was because he had become friends with a white female student from one of his classes. Although they never dated, they would be seen talking, walking, or sitting together on campus. The actions of the racist white students were brazen racism and attempted murder. To my friend, what they did to him was their way of saying blacks were not welcome to their predominately white school, and they were not going stand by allow him to come in as a black man and date their white women. So, they had to teach him his place because he had forgotten. My friend knew that the only reason why this happened was because he was an African American. To this day, he never told his family about what he had to endure as a young man just seeking to prepare for ministry.

The second incident of blatant racism took place while I had first started my Doctor of Ministry program at Southwestern Seminary. Our D-Min class was encouraged to attend a special celebration in chapel one day. The guest speaker was Rev. Eugene Florence. He was finally being awarded his Master of Divinity from Southwestern Baptist Theological Seminary after waiting fifty-three years. Rev. Florence was only two months shy of his one hundred and first birthday at the time. He was born during one of the worst times of American history: the Jim Crow era and segregation, on February 29, 1904.[379] Although Rev.

---

[379] The Christian Post. "Southwestern Seminary Awards Long-Overdue Degree to African-American Alumnus: Recent decision by Southwestern Baptist Theological Seminary brings ultimate redemption to dark segregationist past." 15 December 2004 [on-line]; accessed on 16 December 2020; accessed from <u>Southwestern Seminary Awards Long-Overdue Degree to African-American Alumnus - The Christian Post</u>; Internet.

Florence dreamed of becoming a scholarly ministry, there were no white seminaries at the time that allowed Blacks to attend.

However, in 1943 Rev. Florence was given an opportunity when Southwestern created the "Negro Extension Centers." Blacks were still not allowed on campus, but they could get a seminary education taught by white professors at one of these centers.[380] Florence studied for eight long years to fulfill all the recommended requirements for his master's degree, which he was so proud to do. In a tragic case of outright racial bigotry, Rev. Florence was disrespectfully denied his Master of Divinity in 1951, which he had worked so hard to rightly earn. The rationale was the seminary did not bestow such prestigious degrees on Blacks. Rev. Florence did not allow that to deter him. He used the tools he had learned in seminary and followed his dream, and preached the gospel at a high level.

He pastored four churches in his 65 years of ministry. The Baptist Press, who interviewed him after he finally received his well-deserved master's degree, asked Rev. Florence how he felt about how things were back then that caused his 50 plus year wait. He simply smiled and said, "I had not thought about it. I just thought that was the way it was operated.... I just attended regularly for eight years."[381] What humility from one of God's faithful servants. Now comes the part that bothered me the most as I stood there in chapel back in 2004. Under the leadership of Dr. Paige Patterson, the seminary president at the time, the school stuck out its chest as though it was doing something honorable. They treated the situation as the Rev. Florence had just graduated with the class of 2004 and not his original class of 1951.

On that day, I was not proud of my alma mater's actions. To make Rev. Florence wait 51 years for something he had already earned and act as though you did a great deed. I felt it would have shown that the school had understood the magnitude of their sinful past. They would have gone over and beyond their simple gesture. What would have honored this wonderful man of God would have been to acknowledge

---

380   Ibid. Although these Blacks were required to pay tuition, they still did not receive the respect and resources like their White counterparts.

381   Ibid. This was not only humility of a faithful Christian, it also showed white Christians how they should have treated him all those years earlier.

their sinful mistake, while at the same time honoring Rev. Florence's life work in ministry would have been to not only giving him his master's degree he had earned but giving him an honorary Doctor of Ministry degree. That alone would have made a remarkable statement. I brought concern among my classmates, and they stated honorary doctor's degree is not something Southwestern does. I said to them back then, this time, they should have made an exception.

The third incident of blatant racism took place in 2000. For the sake of being able to tell this African American story and protect this former student's identity, at his request, I will refer to him as Don. Don graduated from Howard University, a prestigious HBCU in Washington D.C. He had planned to attend Virginia Union University Seminary for his Master of Divinity, another historic HBCU school. However, he was strongly encouraged by the late Rev. Dr. E. K, Bailey, a pillar in Dallas, Texas, and founder of the Concord Baptist Church, to attend Southwestern Baptist Theological Seminary. When he arrived on campus from a prominent HBCU school, he says he felt unwelcomed. According to Don, HBCU schools mean absolutely nothing on the Southwestern Seminary campus. In a telephone interview, Don discussed several issues that caused him to depart Southwestern Seminary before graduating, including three.

Issue number one, Don described what it was like to live in the single male dormitory called Fort Worth Hall, which was majority white. Although the rooms were small, he had two roommates, one African American and one Caucasian. The young white man resented being placed in a room with not one but two black men from the very beginning. So, he used his white privilege to make their life miserable. During that fall/winter, it would get cold, especially overnight. So, Don and his black roommate would adjust the thermostat to keep the room warm. Repeatedly, the white roommate would complain it was too warm and would drop the temperature. They would, of course, turn it back up.

The white roommate would complain to the white building manager. However, without hearing from all sides, he only accepted the complaint of the white roommate. So, one day when Don was leaving his room to head to class, he was stopped by the white campus security, but it was not just any security that showed up; it was the chief of security. He challenged Don, not as a student but as an intruder in the door. Although he had witnessed Don walk out of his room, he demanded to see his student identification. Don asked the chief why when he knew that he lived in the dorm. Ironically, this was not the first time the chief of security stopped Don on campus and asked to see his ID. He could not believe it, but he was constantly racially profiled on campus. At that time, there were a few Blacks that lived on campus in a single housing. Apparently, to humiliate him, whites in his dormitory would call security and claim an intruder in the building. This happened routinely, so much so that his Black roommate could not take it anymore and moved off campus into his apartment. Don stuck it out until he finally left the seminary for good.

Issue number two. Don felt blessed to find employment on the seminary campus at the recreational facility known as the RAC. This facility housed an indoor swimming pool, full basketball courts, indoor track, weight room and racketball area, men and women locker rooms, a full conference area, and a lounge area. Although the RAC closed at about 9;00-10:00 PM on weekdays, it often would take hours after the facility closed to get everything clean and locked up.

After one of those late work nights, Don left the RAC at about 1:30 AM, walking to his dorm. He was first stopped by campus security, and then the Fort Worth Police arrived. He did not have his student ID on him because it was in his dorm room. However, he did have on his work shirt with the seminary and RAC logo. Someone called the security and the police and told them a suspicious black man was prowling the campus. Don ended up being humiliated and thrown to the ground. Don hadn't done anything wrong, except walking while black on campus. He was slammed to the ground and treated like a criminal on a seminary campus where he worked, attended school, and lived. Don said talking to other black students at the time, they had similar experiences of being harassed by white campus security, and the chief of security was leading the charge.

The third incident happened in the classroom. The organization of black seminarians was having a meeting. They invited the white seminary faculty to address some of their concerns, including improving race relations on campus between white and black students, adding African American faculty, and better hours and employment for blacks seminarians on campus. At that meeting was one of the well-known white tenured professors named Dr. T. B Matson, a professor of Ethnics. When the question was asked about adding African American faculty, Matson told this group of black students, "We are looking for an African American, but we are not going to lower our standards."

Don said that he and the other black men were astonished at Matson's remarks. They felt his comments were racist and demeaning. However, Matson did not act as though he said anything wrong. Don said this statement, along with how he and others like him had been treated, told him everything he needed to know about the seminary he was so excited to be accepted into. Matson probably meant well, but he was not the one to address a group of African Americans about their important concerns. When whites, especially those in leadership or a position of authority, speak to blacks, they often lack racial sensitivity or tact. Here was what Matson told Don and the other black seminarians that day, "You guys keep asking for us to add black faculty, but blacks are not smart enough to hold a candle to white professors, so why should we lower our standards, just to please you, black people." Hint to white people, when you put down a black person's intelligence, especially when you try to make yourself seem superior, that is not a "dog whistle"; it is a bullhorn shouting racism.

Since that time, I guess they still have not found any black professors that are qualified to teach whites at their prestigious school. How do I know? There have only been a handful of black professors that have ever been hired at Southwestern Seminary in its 112-year history, which remains a travesty. Speaking as a qualified African American graduate of the seminary and having talked to numerous other black qualified graduates, the issue for us is not qualifications; it is our skin color.

The sad outcome of Don's time at the Southwestern seminary ended before he was able to graduate, which he regrets. He said enough was enough and was willing to walk away and give up his dream of a seminary education due to racism. Don told me he no longer wanted to attend a seminary that did not appreciate black people's presence on campus. Don also said that during his time at Southern Seminary, he knew many other African Americans that had similar experiences to his. Although black students discussed their experiences of racism with one another in private, many of them refused to make their issues publicly known. They knew what a degree from Southwestern Seminary would have meant for their futures in ministry. So, they just wanted to keep their head down, support one another, and graduate. Unfortunately, other blacks dropped out as well.

Finally, Don did not want to reveal his real identity for our interview because he still works under the Southern Baptist umbrella. Because he is well known in those circles, he did not want to jeopardize his future in ministry where he knows God uses him to make a difference. Despite his history with the SBC, Don has a heart of forgiveness for his white Christian brothers and feels he can make a big impact in race relations as an African American in a predominately white denomination with a shady pass on racism. I told Don that I commended him for his humility and willingness to forgive—which was the right thing to do—and that he continues to work with the SBC despite how he was treated.

Application of Numbers 12:1-8

What can we learn from Aaron and Miriam about their sinful actions against Moses?

1. **Jealousy can lead to racism (v. 1)**

This verse tells us that Miriam and Aaron spoke against Moses because of the Cushite (Black) woman he had married. They allowed their jealously of Moses' relationship with God to cause them to attack the ethnicity of his wife. This is something you may expect from neighbors or strangers, but not from Christian siblings. The lesson here is the church should never interject race into matters of disagreements with leadership or church members.

2. **Racism leads to Sin (v.2)**

This verse reveals the slippery slope that Miriam and Aaron found themselves on because they wanted to continue attacking their younger brother's God-given authority. The lesson here is the church must understand that members do not appoint pastors; God does. However, if congregations pick their pastors without consulting God and waiting on an answer, they have to suffer through the division they signed off on. However, that does not mean that pastors would not be held accountable. It just means that you have to do it biblically.

3. **Sin gets God's attention (v. 2)**

This verse tells us that God didn't like the childish behavior of his leaders, so He intervened. The lesson here for the church is you never want to get God's attention because of your sin. Just remember the Scriptures tells us, "For the eyes of the LORD move to and fro throughout the earth that He may strongly support those whose heart is completely His." (2 Chron. 16:9)

4. **The wrong kind of attention with God gets you in trouble. (vs. 4-5)**

This verse tells us that God summoned Moses, Miriam, and Aaron to the Tent of Meeting. When they came forward, God called Miriam and Aaron on the carpet for their sinful behavior against Him because they disrespected Moses while he was doing God's will, not his own. This is a lesson for all Christians as well as non-Christians. Be careful how you treat a true Christian that is doing the will of God because when you attack them, you attack God, who appointed them. And when that happens, then God is going to call you on the carpet to judge your actions, as well as dispense His punishment.

How did God respond to Miriam and Aaron because of their sinful actions?

1. **He came down. (v. 5)**

Meaning God's manifest presence was made known. "And an angel of the Lord suddenly stood before them, and the glory of the Lord shone around them, and they were terribly frightened." Luke 2:9

2. He called them on the carpet. (v. 5b)

Meaning God was reminding them He was still in charge, and they had to answer to Him for their actions. "What then could I do when God arises? And when He calls me to account, what will I answer Him?" Job 31:14

3. He chastised them for their actions. (v. 6-9)

Means God chastises those He loves. "For the LORD disciplines those he loves, and he punishes each one he accepts as his child." Hebrews 12:6 (NLT)

4. He judged them. (vs. 10)

Means God will never accept the sinful actions of those that claim they are His. "For it is time for judgment to begin with the household of God; and if it begins with us first, what will be the outcome for those who do not obey the gospel of God?" 1 Peter 4:17

CHAPTER 17

PHYSICAL BONDAGE VS SPIRITUAL BONDAGE

The curse of Canaan:

Now the sons of Noah who came out of the ark were Shem and Ham and Japheth; and Ham was the father of Canaan. These three were the sons of Noah, and from these the whole earth was populated. Then Noah began farming and planted a vineyard. He drank of the wine and became drunk, and uncovered himself inside his tent. Ham, the father of Canaan, saw the nakedness of his father, and told his two brothers outside. But Shem and Japheth took a garment and laid it upon both their shoulders and walked backward and covered the nakedness of their father; and their faces were turned away, so that they did not see their father's nakedness. When Noah awoke from his wine, he knew what his youngest son had done to him. So he said, "Cursed be Canaan; A servant of servants He shall be to his brothers." He also said, "Blessed be the Lord, The God of Shem; And let Canaan be his servant. "May God enlarge Japheth, and let him dwell in the tents of Shem; And let Canaan be his servant." (Genesis 9:18-27)

One of the worst places to find yourself is in bondage. Bondage is defined as slavery, captivity, oppression, or servitude. Of course, it has been well documented that slavery in America of African people was the worse form of physical bondage—at least in American history. From the time Blacks were captured, taken across the Atlantic Ocean, on crowded slave ships (in chains), brought to American soil, hosed down like cattle, auctioned like cattle, and taken to a new home that did not put out a welcome mat. Simply based on the color of their skin, Blacks were beaten, disfigured, tortured, and constantly humiliated—often for sport.

Black women and their teenage daughters were constantly raped and abused as well. A slave mother gave birth between nine to ten children on average, definitely not by personal choice. Black families were broken up at the whim of the slave owner, and Blacks had a very high mortality rate during slavery in America—due to sickness and disease—related to poor working and living conditions. As already stated, the physical treatment of Blacks by Whites was nothing short of a human tragedy. However, I would submit to you, there was something far worse for African slaves than the physical bondage they faced, and that was the spiritual bondage they were subjected to.

To keep slaves in check and under their control, many slave owners used the Bible—although out of context. Blacks were traumatized by their ungodly treatment from many Whites. Therefore, they searched for answers about the plight they found themselves in—which is something all slaves wrestled with—so many of them were coerced into believing the answers that the slave owners provided. What was hypercritical was that slave owners called themselves teaching their slaves about a Book that they, themselves, did not understand or follow.

The Bible is God's divine Word. God gave us His Word so that we would know who He is, who we are, how we are to interact with Him and with each other. In short, the Bible is our manual for life, God's way. Therefore, the Word of God should never be used for ungodly or self-serving purposes. However, many people have learned how to manipulate the Bible for their own selfish gain—which is exactly what many slave owners did on purpose. In a sense, these slave owners remind me of many of the pastors and preachers in America today that manipulate the Bible to control their audiences for their own ends, but not for the glory of God. However, just like the slave owners will one day have to answer to God for their sinful actions—on the day of judgment—so will these fake Christian preachers.

A Theological Explanation Of Why So Many People Get The Bible Wrong

Why is there so much bad preaching and teaching in the Christian church and online, not only in America but around the world? Why do people use the Bible to hold other people in bondage, as well as hold themselves in bondage?

1. **Bad Hermeneutics of the Bible text.**

Hermeneutics refers to the proper biblical interpretation or rightly dividing the Word of God. "Study to shew thyself approved unto God, a workman that needeth not to be ashamed, rightly dividing the word of truth" (2 Timothy 2:15). The phrase "rightly dividing" is key to understanding this verse and my point about proper hermeneutics. The Greek word orthotomeo means "to cut straight" (orthos, "straight," temno, "to cut")[382] The NASB translates this word "accurately handling." 1st and 2nd Timothy are Pastoral Epistles written by the apostle Paul to encourage Timothy, a young pastor for he appointed to the church in Ephesus. Paul's message to Timothy was to properly dissect the Word so that he would be able to deliver its proper meaning to God's people. Simply put, Paul was telling Timothy not to make things up but to respect God's Word. Hence, a person who calls themselves a pastor or preacher who cannot "cut it straight" doesn't need to be preaching or teaching God's Word because they are only putting people in bondage and making them easy targets Satan to manipulate.

Therefore, Hermeneutics is the theological word for proper biblical interpretation. The ultimate goal of hermeneutics is to discover the truths and values in the Bible and what the text truly means. In reality, everyone who approaches the Bible for reading or studying it is applying hermeneutics—this does not mean they are doing it properly. They are trying to take in what it says and make sense of what it means— through their own personal hermeneutic lens. However, unless they have been taught correctly and are led by the Holy Spirit, they will not come away with what God is saying in His Word. Remember, the purpose of hermeneutics is to discover what God wants us to take away from the text so that we can properly apply it to our daily walk.

---

382 W. E. Vine, M. F. Unger, & W. White Jr., *Vine's Complete Expository Dictionary of Old and New Testament Words*, Vol. 2. (Nashville: Thomas. Nelson Publishing, 1996), 178.

2. Bad exegesis of the Bible text.

Exegesis is the exposition or explanation of a text, based on careful and objective analysis—as the Holy Spirit leads you. Exegesis means to bring out the meaning of a text as it was intended by the author—as the Holy Spirit led them. You are basically putting yourself in the position of the original hearers (when they got the right meaning) to try and understand what it meant to them at that time. Remember, the Bible can't mean something now that it didn't mean then. Only by unlocking what it meant then can we understand and apply what it means now. In its most basic Bible-relevant meaning, exegesis is to discover what the Holy Spirit originally said, through His hand-picked author, in any given Bible passage. Simply put, it means to draw out what's in the text. Always Remember, hermeneutics and exegesis work together to understand the Bible properly.

Now that we understand proper biblical hermeneutics and exegesis let's apply these principles to a difficult passage for an exercise. "If anyone comes to Me, and does not hate his own father and mother and wife and children and brothers and sisters, yes, and even his own life, he cannot be My disciple" (Luke 14:26). "If" anyone comes to Me. The word "if" is translated from the Greek word ei, which is a conditional clause. It expresses a condition that is merely hypothetical and separate from all experience in indicating a mere subjective possibility. [383]

First, no one can come to Jesus unless the Father draws them (John 6:44). Second, not everyone that God calls to Himself answers the call. For many are called, but few are chosen (Matthew 22:14). Therefore, *if anyone comes to Me*, is a hypothetical phrase, not a guarantee. However, "if" a person does respond to God's call, for them to be a disciple for Jesus, they must "hate" the people closest to them—that means everyone.

However, this is where context matters in how a word is used. A layperson with zero Bible training, or at least mature understanding, will always get these types of passages wrong because they will base their understanding on feelings, emotions, human wisdom, or someone's opinion. The Greek word *miseo*, "to hate," is used especially

---

[383] S. Zodhiates. *The Complete Word Study Dictionary: New Testament*, Electronic ed. (Chattanooga: AMG Publishers, 2000).

for malicious and unjustifiable feelings towards others, whether towards the innocent or by mutual animosity. [384] If you were to stop there, you would probably be convinced that Jesus is telling you to hate your family. Jesus uses hyperbole—a figure of speech that relies on exaggeration to make a point. He is not encouraging His followers to turn against their family members; rather, He explains that even devotion to family does not supersede the call to discipleship. Absolute loyalty to Jesus and God's kingdom agenda must come first in the life of every true believer.[385]

Therefore, hyperbole is an exaggerated statement or claim but not meant to be taken literally. The Bible is full of these types of words or phrases. However, when Jesus used hyperbole, there was always a deeper truth beneath the exaggeration. In this case, for a true Christian, your love for Christ must be so strong and to such a high level of commitment that your love for anyone is like hate because it is secondary. Therefore, Jesus' use of the word "hate" had to do with rank or order and not feelings or emotions.

When Jesus tells us to hate our family, He is telling us to rank them in the proper order—way below His status—because God is sovereign, and we are not. We are not to even hold anyone next to God, or just below him, because that would be in, and disrespectful to Him as well. This is why we should never use terms like Jesus is my "BFF," best friend forever. Yes, He is our friend that sticks closer than a brother, but when you use worldly terms that imply you and God are on the same level, which is what it means when we apply that term to our human relationships. Our relationship with God is unlike any other relationship we could ever have with anyone else. However, if we consistently keep God in His proper place in our lives (high and lifted up), with the Holy Spirit's help, then nothing or no one will ever take God's place of supremacy in our lives.

---

[384] W. E. Vine, Unger, M. F., & White, W., Jr., *Vine's Complete Expository Dictionary of Old and New Testament Words*, Vol. 2. (Nashville: Thomas. Nelson Publishing, 1996), 292.

[385] J.D. Barry, D. Mangum, D.R. Brown, M.S. Heiser, M. Custis, E. Ritzema, D. Bomar, Faithlife Study Bible: Luke 14;26. (Bellingham, WA: Lexham Press, 2016). Peter calls the people to believe that Jesus is the Messiah promised in the Old Testament.

3. **Eisegesis of the Bible text.**

The process where one leads into a study by reading a passage based on pre-conceived ideas of its meaning. When you have bad hermeneutics and bad exegesis, you end up with eisegesis, which is the opposite of what a serious Bible student should be doing. Taking your prejudices and biases to the text will always lead to the text's wrong biblical meaning. Prejudices and biases are preconceived notions; whether you take them to the Bible or use them in some other way is dangerous, especially when they are used to try to explain God's Word. Eisegesis is very common today, even among pastors, preachers, and Bible teachers. The reason why is because it is very common for people to tell the Bible what they want it to say instead of letting the Bible speak for itself.

The Myth Of The Curse Of Canaan

Myths are often the result of bad information that is accepted as reliable information or truth. If you add on top of that personal biases or prejudices based on racism, then you have the myth of the curse of Canaan. The myth of the curse of Canaan was devised to support racism in American. Ironically, most of what we know about slavery (especially American antebellum slavery) is condemned in the Bible: Human beings were not to be kidnapped and sold (Ex. 21:16); slaves were not to be abused (Ex. 21:26-27); fugitive slaves were not to be returned to their masters (Deut. 23:15-16). If someone was caught kidnapping a fellow Israelite, or treated them as a slave or sold them as a slave, the kidnapper was put to death, to purge the evil from among the people (Deut. 24:7), and if a Hebrew bought a servant, he could only serve for six years, but in the seventh year he was allowed to go free (Ex. 21:2).

After Adam and Eve and their two sons, Cain and Abel, the next prominent characters in the book of Genesis are Noah and his three sons: Shem, Ham, and Japheth. Because of the repeated wickedness and disobedience of mankind, in Genesis Chapters 7, God destroyed the world with a massive flood, whereby it rained non-stop, for forty days and forty nights, destroying everything on the face of the earth. By God's grace, Noah and his wife were allowed to survive, along with their three sons: Shem, Ham, and Japheth, and their wives—a total of only eight persons. The number eight in the Bible means new beginnings, and God used these eight people to start over with humanity. God used Shem, Ham, Japheth, and their wives, to repopulate the entire earth.

What set the stage to the climax of this passage was Noah's behavior. "Then Noah began farming and planted a vineyard. He drank of the wine and became drunk (first mention of drunkenness in the Bible), and uncovered (exposed) himself inside his tent" (vs. 20-21). The Scriptures do not explain why Ham went into his father's tent, but it does describe his actions after he saw his father naked (v. 23). It says Ham went out and told his two brothers about their father's compromised situation. Shem and Japheth responded by doing the honorable thing. They took a covering and walked backward into their father's tent and covered him, which is what Ham should have done, but without the gossip. In today's society, with its openness and exploitation of sex and nudity, this is not viewed as a big deal, but in ancient times, this was a major deal.[386]

Following the text, we arrive at the verses that have caused all the consternation. "When Noah awoke from his wine (drunken stupor), he knew what his youngest son had done to him. So, he said, "Cursed be Canaan; A servant of servants He shall be to his brothers" (vs. 24-25). Either Shem or Japheth told their father about Ham's disrespectful actions. What is interesting was Noah's response, "Cursed be Canaan." So, why didn't Noah say, "Cursed be Ham," since his disrespectful actions are debated here? The answer has to do with the context of

---

[386] J. F. Walvoord, R. B. Zuck (Eds.), A.P. Ross, *The Bible Knowledge Commentary: Genesis, An Exposition of the Scriptures*, Vol. 1. (Wheaton: Victor Books, 1985), 41. Noah, "the man of the earth" (as the rabbis translated the words a man of the soil), began to plant a vineyard. Though wine is said to cheer the heart (Jud. 9:13; Ps. 104:15) and alleviate the pain of the curse (Prov. 31:6), it is also clear that it has disturbing effects. Here Noah lay drunk and naked in his tent. Intoxication and sexual looseness are hallmarks of pagans, and both are traced back to this event in Noah's life. Man had not changed at all; with the opportunity to start a "new creation," Noah acted like a pagan (cf. Gen. 6:5; 8:21)

the statement. The telling of Noah's drunkenness and his nakedness, which resulted in the patriarch invoking blesses and curses, recalls the language of the world before the flood, especially Adam's story, but also Cain's rivalry with his brother Abel. [387] Noah is described in Scripture as a righteous man, which is why God spared his life during the flood. However, this incident reveals how even faithful Christians can fall into sin, especially if they involve themselves with the sinful entanglements of this world.

Ham's criticism was not that he saw his father naked, though his actions were certainly reprehensible (Hab. 2:15), but in his outspoken delight at his father's disgraceful condition. The penalty against Ham's son may seem too severe for mere sibling gossip, but this is because we fail to understand the gravity of the offense [388] So, when Noah said to his son, "Cursed be Canaan," what did he really mean? First, Ham had four sons, Cush, Mizraim, Put, and Canaan (Gen. 10:6), from which all black people descended. So, to claim, as many slave owners did (and some Whites still believe today), that all Blacks were cursed because of this verse, is not just wrong; it's racist. Second, Noah did not judge Ham's descendants based on Ham's actions because that was not allowed under Jewish law (Deuteronomy 24:16). Third, Noah acknowledged Ham's sinful actions would bear fruit in the immoral acts of his descendants, the Canaanites. Fourth, Noah prophesied about Ham's descendants. He began with the direct words, "Cursed be Canaan!" However, Noah did not punish Ham's son for something Ham had done. Instead, Noah's words brought out the Canaanite nation's future behavior that would come from Ham through Canaan.[389] Therefore, the curse was a prophecy about behavior, not race. Finally, it was customary, at the end of a patriarch's life, to prophecy over their children. Based on

---

[387] A. J. Tomasino, *History Repeats Itself: The Fall and Noah's Drunkenness*, Vol. 42 (1992): 128–30, and D. Steinmetz, "Vineyard, Farm, and Garden: The Drunkenness of Noah in the Context of Primeval History," *JBL* 113 (1994): 193–207.

[388] K. A. Mathews, Genesis 1-11:26 , Vol. 1A, (Nashville: Broadman & Holman Publishers, 1996), 419.

[389] J. F. Walvoord, R. B. Zuck (Eds.), A.P. Ross, *The Bible Knowledge Commentary: Genesis, An Exposition of the Scriptures*, Vol. 1. (Wheaton: Victor Books, 1985), 41.

past behavior, the patriarch would pronounce a blessing or a curse. In verses 26-27, Noah pronounced blessings on his other two sons, Shem and Japheth, because of their character, which was revealed when they covered his shameful nakedness (v. 23). However, instead of blessing Ham, Noah chose to reveal the character flaws that would continue in some, but not all, of his son's offspring—which Noah saw in his son and could not bless him because of it.

Application of Genesis 9:18-27

So, how did slave owners and those that supported slavery use the curse of Canaan out of context?

1. Their bad hermeneutics caused them to take the passage out of context without ever understanding its biblical meaning.

2. Their bad exegesis of the text caused them to fail to understand the true meaning of the passage because they neglected to study the text correctly. The passage was not about enslaving people, Black or otherwise. It was about the prophecy about Ham's son, which is Canaan, and how bad some of the people from him would become.

3. Their eisegeses the text was racist because they wholeheartedly supported slavery, while at the same time, they wholeheartedly hated black people. Therefore, they already had their preconceived prejudices and biases of black people, so they searched for Scriptures to support that bias, prejudice **as well as hatred of all black people.**

** The reason why some white people today still accept the unbiblical understanding of this text that slave owners held is for many of the same reasons they did. Unfortunately, racism is still part of the thinking of many white Americans, even after all these years later, to include: a Civil War; the Jim Crow era; the Civil Rights era; the years of multiple race riots; the mass incarceration of Blacks because of a criminal justice system slanted against them; the current racial unrest, that was triggered by the killing of multiple unarmed African Americans; and the continued division between the white church and black church.

CHAPTER 18

WHERE DO WE GO FROM HERE?

A multitude of racial and ethnic diversity:

And they *sang a new song, saying,

"Worthy are You to take the scroll and to break its seals; for You were slaughtered, and You purchased people for God with Your blood from every tribe, language, people, and nation.

You have made them into a kingdom and priests to our God, and they will reign upon the earth." (Revelations 5:9)

It is often said, "You have to know where you came from to know where you are going." From the first chapter, I have told the story of where we have come from as a nation—we were founded on white supremacy, racism, and slavery. Also, I discussed how the white Christian church was complicit in creating poor race relations between Blacks and Whites because they upheld white supremacy, racism, and slavery. However, where we started (and where we continue to be stuck) does not have to be our future—at least not the church's future regardless if America continues down its sinful path.

As I reflect on the issues that led me to write this book, I wanted to conclude by sharing some thoughts on what we can do as a racially diverse Christian community in America that can lead the way for a fallen nation and the fallen world. In Chapter 8, I talked about God's answer to racism. As I have done throughout this book, I have turned to Scripture to search for God's answers to the problems and challenges we face, including the conundrum of systemic racism that has crippled this country since 1619 when the first African slaves were brought to our shores.

As I stated before, the church was not birthed into a vacuum during the height of the Roman Empire. There was a government in-place where the state religion was based on two primary points: the emperors of Rome, who saw themselves as deities and wanted to be worshiped; and politics, which was just as influential as religion, and often treated as the same. Additionally, the Roman Empire was a very polytheistic world, whereby there was a multitude of various religions, including Judaism.

Within that background, the apostle Peter preached his famous sermon in Acts chapter 2, which caused approximately 3,000 individuals, racially and ethnically diverse, to receive Jesus Christ as their personal Savior and Lord. From this passage, we learn that the Christian church began as a multicultural, multiracial body of believers, and it was remarkable to witness God's intended design come to pass. The other important backdrop to the birth of the early church was the history of division among the Jews, Gentiles, and Samaritans. On the day of Pentecost and the birth of the Christian church, God began to unite these three people groups together into one family or fellowship of faith (in Christ) into one unified church. In Acts 2, God added the Jews into His church, referred to as the *Jerusalem Pentecost*.

In Acts 8, God added the Samaritans—half Jews-half Gentiles—into His church, referred to as the *Samaritan Pentecost*. In Acts 10, God added the Gentiles into His church, referred to as the Gentile Pentecost. These three powerful movements of the Holy Spirit were not three separate movements of the Holy Spirit, but one continuous action to fulfill God's plan of unifying broken humanity into one body of believers or the body of Christ. Only after each of the people within each of these groups surrendered their lives to Jesus Christ, as their personal Savior and Lord, did God welcome them into His church, which made them citizens of heaven. Since that time, God has been adding those that have placed their faith in Jesus Christ as Savior and

Lord into His church from all over the world, from various races and ethnicities.

Why Racial Diversity In The Church Matters?

In a book by Michael Emerson and Rodney Woo, *People of the Dream: Multiracial Congregations in the United States*, they made the profound statement that if we want to understand race relations in the United States fully, we must understand its core organizational form—the religious congregation. They define a "religious congregation" as any regular gathering of people for religious purposes: who come together to worship; have an official name; have a formal structure that conveys a purpose and identity; are open to all ages; have no restraints on how long people may stay.[390] Based on that definition, they state the majority of Americans will participate in or visit a congregation in any given year. However, sadly they mention, in a fifteen-nation study, the United States scored highest in religious membership (55 percent), and had membership rates twenty or more percentage points higher than every other nation in the study except Northern Ireland.[391]

This is important because the church is the place where Americans most often go to seek the meaning of life, worship, find direction, and receive social support. Major life events take place within the congregations; newborn babies are celebrated; marriages take place; and often is where people say goodbye to loved ones. The final important point they made concerning congregations is that how essential their role is in meeting the needs of people. Clergy and congregations are the number one place Americans turn to when they have serious problems, more than the government or human and health service professionals.[392]

Based on the significance of the church, I believe the multiracial congregation can be a greater asset as well as the vehicle to help America work toward racial reconciliation from our sinful past.

---

390   Michael O. Emerson, and Rodney M. Woo. *People of the Dream: Multiracial Congregations in the United States*. (Princeton, NJ: Princeton University Press, 2006), 6.

391   Ibid.

392   Ibid.

According to Emerson and Woo, multiracial congregations are rare. They define a multiracial congregation as one in which no single racial group is 80 percent or more of the congregation. Only 7 percent of approximately 350,000 congregations are estimated to be multiracial.[393] Although multiracial congregations are rare, they are still much needed in American society and one of the best ways to unite Blacks, Whites, Asians, Hispanics, Natives, and other races.

In a book by Curtis Paul DeYoung, Michael O. Emerson, George Yancy, and Karen Chai Kim, they state the importance of racial diversity in the Christian church in America. Although their book was published in 2003, it remains relevant in addressing our troubling times of race relations. They state, "Multiracial congregations will be called on in the years to use their experience to provide a healing salve for the wounds of racial division, cultural misunderstanding, and even the lingering pain of traumatic events." [394] Based on the skyrocketing episodes of police brutality against African Americans since DeYoung, Emerson, Yancy, and Chai published their important work, the need for more multiracial congregations is far more important today. Only God can turn around America from its sinful path of systemic racism. Since the Christian church is God's vessel, it has a vital role in being the example of unity during our turbulent times.

In my doctoral research, I came across some very interesting books about the importance of multiracial churches. One of those individuals was John Piper, a man that I admire, the former pastor of Bethlehem Baptist Church, Minneapolis, Minnesota. I return to his book *Bloodlines* that I mentioned in chapter 5. Piper shared his struggles with racism and how God delivered him. For this white pastor to admit what so many other white pastors won't was admirable—that there is a problem with systemic racism in America. Piper not only admitted there was a problem, but he was also part of the problem; he decided to be part of the solution. He decided to address the elephant in the room.

---

393   Ibid, 160.

394   Curtis Paul DeYoung, Michael O. Emerson, George Yancy, and Karen Chai Kim, *United By Faith: The Multiracial Congregation as An Answer To The Problem of Race* (New York: Oxford University Press, 2003), 75.

> Piper describes racial issues from his life story and how they helped him come to the point of racial reconciliation through Jesus Christ. In the eleventh chapter, titled, "Dying with Christ For the Sake of Christ Exalting Diversity," Piper explains how Christ's death on Calvary's cross has made it possible for racial reconciliation to take place. He says that one of the reasons he believes some Christians have a hard time relating their Christianity to issues like racial and ethnic harmony and justice is that their view of what happens in conversion to Christ is superficial. The other chapter in this book that spoke volumes was fifteen. Piper lists several practical principles that diversity brings to the kingdom of God. 1. God's pursuit of diversity glorifies his grace in the gospel. 2. Diversity is forever. 3. Diverse unity is more glorious than the unity of sameness. 4. Praise from diverse peoples points to deeper beauty. 5. A diversity of followers' points to a greater leader in Christ. 6. Diversity undercuts ethnic pride and points to grace. 7. Diversity helps bring about reverence for the cross and love for God's glory.[395]

In another book by Rodney Woo, an Asian Pastor of a white Southern Baptist Church, also adds some valuable insights on the importance of multiracial churches. Woo took a predominately white congregation and turned it into a multiracial congregation, one of the hardest things to do. An established church that is already set in its ways is much harder to change than a church that began seeking to establish a multiracial congregation.

> *In the book,* The Color of Church: A Biblical And Practical Paradigm For Multiracial Churches, *Rodney Woo provides an illuminating look at race relations in the Christian church in America. Woo states that the great divide between Jews and Gentiles in the first century closely parallels the present racial divide between Blacks and Whites in the United States. Furthermore, America is often seen as two separate nations, Black and White, surpassing all other lines of demarcation in its intensity and subordination. He argues that in the same way, the Jews and Gentiles coexisted*

---

395 Nathaniel T. Powell. *Implementing the USAF's Chaplaincy Model of Racial Diversity*, 20-21.

but did not interact with or cultivate friendships with one another. They did not share the same worship places, schools, diet, or values, and strongly discouraged intermarriage. The wall between the Jews and Gentiles pervaded every area of their existence. Likewise, he says in the United States, the Black-White racial divide also permeates every area of life.[396]

From his unique position as the pastor of a racially diverse congregation, Woo can add some important insights into race relations in America today between Whites and Blacks. Although the Christian church was predominately comprised of Jews in its beginning, it rapidly became predominately Gentile. Ironically, the Gentiles began to persecute the Jews when they became the dominant race in the church, which is one of the most grievous sins in church history, and a major stumbling block causing Jews to reject Jesus as the Messiah. A problem that still has major implications to this very day. Therefore, Christians in America today need to wake up and learn valuable lessons from the past. If not, the church in America will continue to be divided by the racial divisions from its taboo past.[397]

The final book from my research I want to add to this important discussion is by Jarvis Williams, an Associate Professor of New Testament Interpretation at New Orleans Seminary.

In *One New Man*, Jarvis Williams discusses the importance of racial reconciliation in the Christian church. In his introduction, Williams says the subject of racism is one many people will mention behind closed doors, but no one really wants to talk honestly about it in the open. He states this is how racism has produced many of the world's problems because it lies at the root of much of the violence, discrimination, hatred, murder, and a host of other atrocities in the United States. He continues his argument by stating how unfortunate it is that racism has also impacted the church. The author defines racial reconciliation as humanity's relationship with God and with fellow humans that are broken because of sin and introduced into God's good creation through the disobedience of Adam and Eve. As a result of sin,

---

396   Ibid.

397   Ibid.

every relationship needs to be restored to the original state in which God intended before the fall. All races—not just Blacks and Whites—scattered throughout the entire world need to be reconciled to God and, second, to one another because of the universal impact of sin.

Williams adds a final nugget to this conversation. He says we as Christians believe the answer to racism is found in the Bible, which is the argument that I have made throughout this book. Also, he says if the answer is found in the gospel, why have Christians so often been on the wrong side of this issue? He went on to answer his own question. "Too often we do not live by the gospel we proclaim. Cultural norms and sinful patterns crowd out the liberating message Jesus taught. Even as Christians we easily forget about the good news and live by another norm." [398] Unfortunately, the norms we live by are the acceptable norms of a sinful society, not of God's Word. So, I wholeheartedly agree with the assessment of race in America from John Piper, Rodney Woo, and Jarvis Williams. I would recommend these books, along with Tony Evans' book, Oneness Embraced, to anyone searching for the answer to systemic racism from a biblical perspective.

Application Of Christian Literature

If White and Black Christians continue their current trajectory, racial reconciliation is not possible in America. The horrible stories of police brutality against African Americans will continue to be the norm. The unequal justice system that incarcerates African Americans at a much higher rate, as far as a percentage of the population, than Caucasians Americans, will continue to be the norm. The unfair labor and housing markets that work unfairly against African Americans will continue to be the norm. Also, politics will continue to have a bigger voice than the Christian church, which has been entrusted with

---

398 Jarvis J. Williams, *One New Man: The Cross and Racial Reconciliation In Pauline Theology* (Nashville: B&H Publishing Group, 2010). These comments were by Thomas R. Schreiner, Professor of New Testament, Southwestern Baptist Theological Seminary, in a forward he wrote in this book. Schreiner also says how refreshing it was to read a book by an African American scholar where the New Testament message of reconciliation through Christ is taken seriously as the answer to our racial problems.

the gospel. If politics was the answer, we would not be in the mess we are in because of America's division and hatred. If the government was the answer, then it would be able to fix our problems. However, God did not answer, nor the spiritual power, to our politicians or our government. God, in His infinite wisdom, gave the power and ability to transform society to the Christian church, but unfortunately, we refuse to step forward and accept that mantle.

However, with more Christians speaking out and using their platforms to draw attention to the continued issues of race in America, both Black and White, it is about time for every Christian church to address the problem from their pulpit. Nevertheless, as long as they both remain in their current comfort zones, America does not have the model it needs to see its way forward. Why should the nation change if the vessel God has provided the answer to—through His divine Word—is not willing to change? If white Christians continue to hold the position that they have nothing to repent for, so what's going on with black Christians is not their problem. In contrast, black Christians continue to live in anger and resentment, then I would submit to you they are both wrongs because neither positions honor and glory of God. Furthermore, if white Christians continue to wear blinders and ignore the plight of their black Christian brothers and sisters, just like the white Christian church did in colonial America, then that position does not advance the cause of unity in Christ. And if black Christians are not willing to quit using slavery as an excuse to engage in reaching out to their white Christian brothers and sisters, nor does that position advance the cause of unity in Christ. Finally, white and black Christians need to stop hiding behind their pollical affiliation; and using politics as one of their biggest stumbling blocks to racial reconciliation. Just because a person is Democrat or Republican has nothing to with their entrance into heaven because neither is a prerequisite for entry— although many treat it as though it is. No political party corners the market on Jesus. Therefore, no political party owns Him, controls Him, or speaks for Him.

Americans need to stop wrapping their Christianity around the American flag as though that makes them more spiritual or patriotic. All that does is pollute Christianity and diminish its power. Jesus

Christ will still be on the throne no matter what the future of America holds. His deity and sovereignty are not connected to America's future or existence—just like it was not connected to the Roman Empire's survival. Rome fell, but Jesus still reigns! However, if America does not get its act together, it would follow down the same road of self-destruction.

Revelations 5:9

Now I want to turn to Revelations 5:9 and explain why it is important to what happened in Acts Chapter 2. The church began on the Day of Pentecost as a multicultural, multiracial church, thoroughly explained in Chapter 8. Revelations 5:9 tells us that the church or body of Christ will continue as a multicultural, multiracial church in heaven for all eternity. That means that Blacks, Whites, Asians, Hispanics, Natives, and many others who have accepted Christ will be together, worshiping Christ together; forever. There will no longer be racism and division. There will no longer be categories of rich and poor. There will no longer be houses of worship called "Black church," or "White Church" or "Asian Church" or "Hispanic church" or "Native church." Why? Because there will not be separate churches in heaven that are known by those designations. This division we have chosen on earth will not be allowed in heaven. So, my question is this, if the church began as a multicultural, multiracial body of believers, and will be that same way in heaven, then why does segregation continue to be the norm in the Christian church now, especially in America today? I believe there are many reasons, but I will cover a few.

How White Christians Created The Problem?

White European Christians brought Christianity to America. They began churches in the original Thirteen Colonies.[399] When God moves and invites human beings to come along to be His vessels for new work, that is an awesome responsibility. So, in a sense, these white Christians were missionaries to what would become America. They claimed they

---
399 Mark A. Noll, Nathan O. Hatch and George M. Marsden. *The Search for Christian America*, 1.

were Christians, so I will give them the benefit of the doubt, at least for now. Therefore, the example they set was extremely important for the spiritual direction of the new nation. Those early white Christians were from the following denominations: The Episcopal Church (1607) in Jamestown, Virginia; Puritans or Congregationalist Church (1620) in Plymouth, Massachusetts; Lutheran Church (1620), New York/New Jersey; Baptist Church (1639) in Rhode Island; Quakers (1660), in Philadelphia, Pennsylvania; Presbyterian Church (1705); Roman Catholics (1650), in Baltimore, Maryland.[400] Lutheran Church (1742),[401] in Pennsylvania; Methodist Church (1760),[402] in Virginia and New York; Brethren in Christ Church (1778), in Pennsylvania; and the Mennonite Church (1860), in Pennsylvania.

There were other white Christian denominations in America, but they did not begin until later, after the Civil War. Conversely, I include these churches because they were instrumental in the direction of Christianity in early America. These denominations have major as well as minor doctrinal differences but still placed themselves under the Christian umbrella. However, all these denominations had a few things in common: they were all white; they were all from Europe; they all believed in a form of white supremacy; they all upheld slavery as an acceptable institution. These white denominations in existence during and after the height of slavery did not extend the proper *right hand of fellowship*[403] to Blacks. Blacks were not treated as equal, as human, or as Christians.

---

400 Ibid.

401 Daniel G. Reid, Robert D. Linder, Bruce L. Shelley, and Harry S. Scott. Dictionary of Christianity in America, 670-671.

402 Ibid, 732-733.

403 The *right hand of fellowship* is a Christian expression based on Galatians 2:9, "And recognizing the grace that had been given to me, James and Cephas and John, who were reputed to be pillars, gave to me and Barnabas the right hand of fellowship, so that we *might go* to the Gentiles, and they to the circumcised." It is the Christian thing to do; to treat someone that was once considered outside the body of Christ, to be officially and warmly welcomed into the church, after they have accepted Jesus Christ as Savior and Lord, and granted all rights, duties, responsibilities, that go along with being a believer. However, this was denied by Whites to Blacks simply because racism and white supremacy infiltrated the church.

Whites were trying to build their survival in the New World, but it never dawned on them that the Africans they brought here, against their will, desired the same opportunities. It never dawned on them that Blacks were created in the image of God, too; even though the Bible clearly states it, they obviously didn't agree with Him. It never dawned on them that they were creating a white America and a black America—two separate Americas within the same borders. It never dawned on them that they would be responsible for their one day being a white church and a black church. And it never dawned on them that they would one day have to answer to God for their sinful actions as well as for being complicit in perpetuating racism and white supremacy in America.

In an article from *Christianity Today* titled, "Why did so many (white) Christians support slavery?" It stated that many southern Christians felt that slavery, in one baptist minister's words, "stands as an institution of God." [404] For a so-called preacher to blame God for the sinful institution of slavery reveals how far these white Christians were from biblical truth. The article went on to list the following arguments made by white Christians.

Biblical Reasons [405]

Abraham, the "father of faith," and all the patriarchs held slaves without God's disapproval (Gen. 21:9–10).
- Canaan, Ham's son, was made a slave to his brothers (Gen. 9:24–27).
- The Ten Commandments mention slavery twice, showing God's implicit acceptance of it (Ex. 20:10, 17).
- Slavery was widespread throughout the Roman world, and yet Jesus never spoke against it.
- The apostle Paul specifically commanded slaves to obey their masters (Eph. 6:5–8).

---

404   *Christianity Today: Christian History*, "Why Did So Many Christians Support Slavery?: Key reasons advanced by southern church leaders" [online]; accessed on 24 November 2020; accessed from http://Christianitytoday.com/history/issues/issues-33/why-supported-slavery.html; Internet.

405   Ibid.

- Paul returned a runaway slave, Philemon, to his master (Philem. 12).

You Can't Blame The Bible For This Mess

In chapter 17 of this book, I explained how white preachers and Bible teachers used the Bible out of context to support white supremacy, racism, and slavery. They primarily did this because of what theologians call bad hermeneutics (wrong biblical interpretation), bad exegesis (wrong biblical explanation), and eisegesis of the text (using their biases, prejudices, and false beliefs to understand the Bible), in other words, reading into the text what's not there. What these white, so-called Christians did was they believed wholeheartedly in white supremacy, racism, segregation, and slavery. So, they searched the Bible to find Scriptures to make the Bible validate their sinful unchristian views; however, because their congregations were easily persuadable, mainly because they held the same views against Blacks.

Charitable and Evangelistic Reasons [406]

- Slavery removes people from a culture that "worshipped the devil, practiced witchcraft, and sorcery" and other evils.
- Slavery brings heathens to a Christian land where they can hear the gospel. Christian masters provide religious instruction for their slaves.
- Under slavery, people are treated with kindness, as many northern visitors can attest.
- It is in slaveholders' own interest to treat their slaves well.
- Slaves are treated more benevolently than are workers in oppressive northern factories.

Note: You can't call slavery charity or evangelism and be biblically correct in your assumption.

In Chapter 5 of this book, I explained God's command for us as Christians to love our brothers and sisters in Christian, especially those

---

406 Ibid.

that do not look like us. The apostle John made this abundantly clear in 1st John 2:1-11 when he said, "The one who loves his brother abides in the Light and there is no cause for stumbling in him. But the one who hates his brother is in the darkness and walks in the darkness and does not know where he is going because the darkness has blinded his eyes." These so-called Christians could never have come to their conclusion about black people if they truly loved Jesus and wanted to obey His Word. You cannot hate your brother, which these white so-called Christians did with a passion, and at the same time claim, you are a true believer. Not only did Jesus command us to love one another, but He also gave us a clear indicator if we truly belong to Him. In John 4:20-21, John told us, "If someone says, "I love God," and yet he hates his brother or sister, he is a liar; for the one who does not love his brother and sister whom he has seen, cannot love God, whom he has not seen. And this commandment we have from Him, that the one who loves God must also love his brother and sister." Based on these verses, what white Christians believed about Blacks that caused them to hate them, enslave them, and treat them as less than human, proved that they were not true Christians because if they were, the Holy Spirit would have convicted their hearts. They would not continue to support slavery until it ended. Furthermore, they would not have supported the laws of the 100-year Jim Crow era that simply created a new form of slavery.

Social Reasons [407]

- Just as women are called to play a subordinate role (Eph. 5:22; 1 Tim. 2:11–15), so slaves are stationed by God in their place.
- Slavery is God's means of protecting and providing for an inferior race (suffering the "curse of Ham" in Gen. 9:25 or even the punishment of Cain in Gen. 4:12).
- Abolition would lead to slave uprisings, bloodshed, and anarchy. Consider the mob's "rule of terror" during the French Revolution.

---

407 Ibid.

Note: We still must care for the less fortunate among us.

In Chapter 4 of this book, I explain what it means to be my brother's keeper. Genesis 4:9 says," Then the Lord said to Cain, "Where is Abel your brother?" And he said, "I do not know. Am I my brother's keeper?" In this passage, Cain had just killed his younger brother Abel. He did so out of jealously because God accepted Abel's offering but rejected his. Although God had just warned Cain in verse 6 what would happen if he rejected His wise counsel, Cain still went out and killed his brother anyway.

This is what the Bible calls rebellion against God because when you know better, but have decided you aren't going to do any better, then you have decided that you do not care what God says. When God asked Cain where his brother was, it was not because God did know what happened; it was so Cain would come clean about what he had done. However, Cain told God that he was not his brother's keeper, which meant he did not have to love him or look for him, which was false. So, God gave Cain a fair but severely harsh judgment for his actions. God banished Cain from His presence for the rest of his. Even Cain felt his punishment was too harsh because he said, "my punishment is too great to bear!" However, God did not change His mind because Cain should have known better. This passage applies to the white Christians that believed their actions against black slaves were just because, in their mind, they were doing what was right, just like Cain thought he was right. As Christians, we are to be our brother's keeper, which they failed miserably.

Political Reasons [408]

- Christians are to obey civil authorities, and those authorities permit and protect slavery.
- The church should concentrate on spiritual matters, not political ones.

Note: Your politics should not be your religion

---

408 Ibid.

In Chapter 14 of this book, I wrote a whole chapter on God's role for government based on Romans 12:1-7. Here are some of the points taken from that chapter to show how wrong these political reasons were not Christian beliefs derived from Scripture. Christians have been called *out of this world* (John 15:18 and 17:14), but they still have responsibilities to the state or government. The best citizen ought to be a Christian citizen. However, Christians obey government laws of man-made laws if they violate God's laws.

In many cities in America today, there are not too many places you can go where there is not a church on every corner. During Colonial America, there were not too many places you go either where there was not a church in every town. The majority of Thirteen Colonies were religious in many respects. However, my problem with all of this is, what type of Christianity are these white Christians practicing? Based on the history of America, it does not appear that they were practicing the same type of Christianity found in the early church in the Book of Acts, as well as in the entire New Testament.

As I stated in Chapter 8, the early church in America should have followed the early church's example in Scripture. However, these white churches failed miserably because of how they interacted with other races that did not look like them when they came to America. I would submit that these white churches are why race relations are the way they are in 2020. Also, the white church helped America lay the foundation for systemic racism, which plagues us to this day.

In a book by Mark Noll, *Critical Issues in American Religious History*, in a section titled, *The Church (White)Responsible*, he stated the following concerning white Christians culpability in slavery.

> "The church in this country is only indifferent to the wrongs of the slave, it takes sides with the oppressors. It has made itself the bulwark of American slavery, and the shield of American slave-hunters. Many of its most eloquent Divines (preachers), who stand as the very lights of the church, have shamelessly given the sanction religion and the Bible to the whole slavery system. They have taught that man may, properly, be a slave; that the relation of master and slave is ordained of God; that to send back an escaped

bondman to his master is the duty of all the followers of the Lord Jesus Christ; this horrible blasphemy is palmed off upon the world for Christianity." [409]

Noll went on to say that the American (White) church was not only guilty for upholding slavery but also for not using their platform and numerous resources to help abolish slavery. The sin of which it is guilty is one of omission as well of commission.[410]

In Jarvis Williams's book, *One New Man*, he stated the obvious in a section titled, "Racist Churches Are Unacceptable."

Paul's theology of racial reconciliation suggests that racist churches are unacceptable. Paul calls Christians to love one another (Rom 12:10; 13:8; 1 Thess 3:12; 4:9-10), to live in harmony one another (Rom 12:16; 14:19; 15:5 1 Cor 12:25), not to judge one another (Romans 14:13), to receive once another (Roma 15:7), to greet one another with affection (Rom 16;16; 1 Cor 16:20; 2 Cor 13:12), to share the Lord's Supper with one another in the appropriate manner (1 Cor 11:33), to serve one another (Gal 5:13), and not to consume one another with insidious actions (Gal 5:15). Also, Paul calls Christians to bear the burdens of one another (Gal 6:2), to be patient with one another (Eph 4:2; Col 3:12-13), to be kind to one another (Eph 4:32), to submit to one another with reverence for Christ (Eph 5:21), to treat one another as more valuable than oneself (Phil 2:3), to live sacrificially for one another (Phil 2:5-9), not to lie to one another (Col 3:9), to encourage one another with the truths of God (1 Thess 5:15). Finally, he states that Jews and Gentiles hated one another before their faith in Christ, but God's work of regeneration in their lives converted their hatred toward one another into love (Titus 3:3-7).[411]

Williams makes three final points in this book that are very important to this discussion. First, he states that the apostle Paul did

---

409 Robert R. Mathisen. *Critical Issues in American Religious History*. (Waco: Baylor University Press, 2000), 243.

410 Ibid.

411 Jarvis Williams. One New Man, 136-137.

not say black Christians should only love or serve black Christians, or white Christians should only love or serve white Christians. Rather, the above exhortations are universal and should be universally practiced by all Christians toward all Christians. He added, genuine, sincere, Christlike love for brothers and sisters in Christ that transcends one's love for and allegiance to one's race and ethnic traditions are the essence of what it means to live our racial reconciliation.[412]

Second, he stated that so many churches are segregated because racism disgraces the gospel and Jesus' death. He stated that many pastors and parishioners attempt to appease their racist conscience and justify their segregated congregations by appealing to the various cultural differences between them. The example Williams gave is how African Americans, Caucasians, Hispanics, and Koreans all use cultural differences to excuse segregation. So, they all think the excuse justifies the presence of an entirely African American congregation across the street from an entirely Anglo congregation or an entirely Korean congregation down the block from a Hispanic congregation. He believes Paul would reject this notion, and I would agree.[413]

Also, Williams stated how many African American and Anglo pastors work to appease their racist conscience and justify their segregated conversations on Dr. Martin Luther King Jr.'s birthday during Black History Month. The event itself is a good thing; however, the hypocrisy some of these same pastors find repulsive even the thought of someone from a different race either attending or joining their church. Just to come together to save face, without ever having the intention to be true brothers and sisters in Christ misses the point of Paul's theology on reconciliation.[414]

Third, he stated that many churches are more committed to their ethnic heritage than to the gospel. This is evidenced by their misplaced commitment to a worship experience that is exclusively focused on the church's particular heritage, either intentionally or unintentionally, and thereby exclude other races, either directly or indirectly, from joining and participating in the worship experiences. Labeling worship as

---

412   Ibid, 137.

413   Ibid.

414   Ibid. 138.

"black" or "white" and calling a church "black" or "white" also erects fences around worship. Such expressions are superficial, generic, and unbiblical, Williams concluded.[415]

In a book by Susan Davies and Sister Paul Teresa Hennessee, *Ending Racism in the Church*, they stated in chapter 13, "A Call to Move Beyond the Heritage of Christian Racism," the importance of koinonia in striving for racial reconciliation in the Christian church. "Koinonia calls the churches to refuse to live any longer as racially defined and divided communities in a racially defined and divided world. Further, koinonia calls the churches to eradicate this "sin," heresy," "evil," "menace" of racism caused suffering.[416] Koinonia is the Greek generally translated as fellowship. However, the word fellowship has a much deeper meaning because it also means intimacy and participation. Also, it is an example of true reconciliation among true believers.

> *This is the message we have heard from Him and announce to you, that God is Light, and in Him, there is no darkness at all. If we say that we have fellowship with Him and yet walk in the darkness, we lie and do not practice the truth; but if we walk in the Light as He Himself is in the Light, we have fellowship with one another, and the blood of Jesus His Son cleanses us from all sin. (1 John 1:5-7)*

In this passage, the apostle John explains what true fellowship with God looks like. Therefore, if we have genuine fellowship or koinonia with God—through faith in Jesus Christ—then we would also have genuine fellowship or koinonia with our brothers and sisters in Christ, including those that do not look like us.

How Black Christians Overcame The Problem

The history of Blacks in America is well documented. Throughout this book, I talk extensively about the plight of African Americans since 1619 in America—a Caucasian-dominated nation. Although Whites did

---

415　Ibid.

416　Susan E Davies and Sister Paul Teresa Hennessee. *Ending Racism in the Church*. Cleveland: United Church Press, 1998.

eventually allow Blacks into their churches during slavery, they never treated them as equal, not even in the house of God. This was very sinful because if you cannot be treated as a child of God—in the house of God—I would submit to you that church is not a true house of worship. Jesus did not reject anyone that was seriously seeking Him, regardless of their race, background, or socioeconomic status. Jesus opened His arms and welcomed all that the heavenly Father drew to Him, even the Pharisees and Sadducees, but they rejected Him. However, America has a history of not being very welcoming or Christ-like to all people, including the church. I would add that white Christians would have to take responsibility for the domino effect their forefathers set in motion, which America has never changed course. You can only mistreat people for so long before they get tired of it and either push back or move on. As a result of their ill-treatment, Blacks moved on and left white churches in droves to begin their own churches after the Civil War. Their hasty departure was primarily for these reasons:

- Not being treated as Christians.
- Not being allowed to serve as Christians.
- Not being treated as human beings.
- Not being treated equally in the house of God.
- No longer wanting to be judged because of the color of their skin in the house of God.
- No longer wanting to hear sermons that did not resonate with them or deal with their plight in America.
- No longer wanting to have to deal with segregation and humiliation in the church.
- No longer wanting to face the acceptable sin of racism practiced inside the church.
- No longer wanting to deal with the white supremacy inside the church as well as in society at the same time.

On the other hand, what were Blacks seeking when they sought to establish their own houses of worship?

- To usher in spiritual healing and restoration.
- To experience the power of a true and loving God.

- To be allowed to pursue and utilize their spiritual gifts and be allowed to lead worship.
- To be trained in the Bible without it being done through the lenses of racism.
- To have their own style of worship that Blacks could be excited about.

They were gladly looking forward to a new start without being dominated and manipulated by whites in the church. Although Blacks knew they would still have to deal with racism in society, they sought their own sanctuary to deal with those challenges.

Ever since Blacks departed Caucasian churches, at the end of slavery in America, and started their own places of worship, division among Blacks and Whites has been the acceptable norm. However, I would place this exodus squarely on the shoulders of where it belongs, with white Christians. Nowhere in the Bible would God condone how poor Whites treated Blacks, inside as well as outside the church. Therefore, I would argue that African Americans made the necessary adjustment for them at the time—for their own spiritual survival. While I can relate to how we got here, I do not understand why we, as Christians remain segregated. The institution of slavery ended on December 6, 1865, with the passage of the Thirteenth Amendment to the Constitution, but again, the stain of slavery remains a stronghold.

> *It would take a civil war, the deaths of three-quarters of a million soldiers and civilians, the assassination of a president, Abraham Lincoln, and the passage of the Thirteenth Amendment, to bring the institution of enslavement in the United States of America to an end. For a brief window of time, the twelve years known as Reconstruction, the North sought to rebuild the South and help the 4 million people who had been newly liberated. But the federal government withdrew for political expediency in 1877 and left those in the subordinate caste in the hands of the very people who had enslaved them.*[417]

---

417 Isabel Wilkerson, *Caste: The Origins of Discontents*. 48.

Racism made its way inside the church in America because white Christians brought it in and kept it in. However, the Christian church in America has had 155 years to reverse course on this bad precedent in the eyes of God. I would argue that this is because it has not been a priority for either race. Breaking the stronghold of systemic racism, at least inside the church, is achievable because the Bible is our road map. Sadly, Blacks, Whites, Asians, Hispanics, Natives, and others insist on reaching their own and do not seem to care about reaching outside their comfort zones.

What is even more disheartening is that every other institution in America has integrated, except the church. Rev. Dr. Martin Luther King Jr. often stated, "The most segregated hour in this nation" is Sunday at 11:00 AM. Fifty-seven years ago, on December 18, 1963, Dr. King made this statement and would often repeat it because it was, and still is, a sad reality. One would argue that Dr. King was the most well-known and revered African American preacher at that time, if not, all time—and it only cost him his life fighting for equality for all Americans. On the other hand, the most well-known Caucasian American preacher at that time was Evangelist Billy Graham, and he too remains extremely popular and revered since his passing in 2018. However, by 1952 Rev. Graham was already a national figure. Up until that time, he held segregated rallies. He must have had an epiphany around that time because he stated, "There is no scriptural basis for segregation. It may be there are places where such is desirable to both races, but certainly not in the church." Graham made these comments to a crusade audience in Jackson, Mississippi, in the mid1950s. Graham's words were greeted with enthusiasm by blacks and a few whites but provoked criticism from many.[418]

However, I would disagree with Rev. Graham about his comment on segregation. With his enormous platform, he should have made a more declarative statement, not only on segregation but systemic racism as well. He could have said segregation should not be an acceptable practice, in or outside the church, but at the time, he did

---

418 "History in the Making — Billy Graham Had a Dream," [on-line]; accessed on 4 December 2020; accessed from www.http//History in the Making — Billy Graham Had a Dream | Christian History Magazine (christianhistoryinstitute.org); Internet.

not. Prominent white preachers, like Graham, could have made more of an impact on behalf of Christianity in America, but they chose not to because they did not want the blowback coming their way. During my entire Christian experience, I was always taught that you stand for Christ, even if you have to stand alone (Isaiah 6:8-10).

Also, I was taught to whom much is given, much is required (Luke 12:48). What if Rev. Graham and other prominent white pastors and preachers would have joined with Dr. King and spoken out more emphatically against systemic racism in America? Perhaps the country, as well as the church, would both be further along than where they are today. Fast forward to today, why do so many prominent white pastors, preachers, as well as seminary professors remain silent on the issue of systemic racism and segregation in the church? Because they refuse to lift their voices and use their platforms, they fail to realize their complicity continues.

Black Christians overcame one problem but inadvertently played a role in created another—and that was the current condition with the segregated church in America. In no way am I blaming African Americans for the current problems with race relations and the Christian church. They did what was necessary for them at the time, but it still affects the current climate of Christianity in America.

Many would argue that the reason why there is not more unity among the various races in the church is because of doctrinal differences. However, I would argue that is not a valid reason, even though it is a major sticking point. Case in point, when I was ordained to preach the gospel at Macedonia Missionary Baptist Church, San Antonio, Texas, under the leadership of Rev. Dr. Jerry Wm. Daily, our church was dually aligned. Although the church was organized under the National Baptist Convention of America, it was also aligned with the Southern Baptist Convention. The primary difference between these two organized national church governing bodies is race: One is predominated African American, and the other is predominately Caucasian American. As far as all major doctrines and disciplines of the Bible, they agree. So, the question is, why don't they unite into one multicultural, multiracial Baptist denomination? And if they are not willing to totally unite that way, are they at least willing to work together for the sake of the gospel? Well, I would submit to you that it is because of many of the same reasons that caused Blacks to leave white churches after slavery, to start their own remain a stumbling block. Also, I believe there are problems on both sides that continue to add to the problem.

In a book by George Yancy, *Beyond Racial Gridlock: Embracing Mutual Responsibility*, he made the following statement regarding racism in America:

> *The way we define a social problem will affect the way we conceive of its solution. If we have an incomplete definition of a problem, then we will envision a limited solution. If the real problem is larger than our restricted definition, then our solution will be insufficient.*[419]

Therefore, the problem that we have in America regarding systemic racism is a lack of agreement, depending on race. Blacks and Whites view this issue from different perspectives. While most African Americans believe there is an ongoing problem with systemic racism, most Caucasian Americans do not. As a result, not having an agreeable starting point, there can never be legitimate progress toward a workable solution.

Why The Christian Church Remains Stuck Along Racial Lines?

There are four primary reasons why I believe segregation continues to exist in the Christian church in America. First, which has already been thoroughly discussed, is systemic racism and its impact on American culture. Second, a lack of Agape love among the various racial groups within the body of Christ. If Christians in America truly loved God and loved one another, this would be an easy hurdle to overcome. However, America is not the Christian nation it claims to be, which makes unity a biblical impossibility. Also, you have stubborn Whites as well as stubborn Blacks that are stick in their

---

419   George Yancy. *Beyond Racial Gridlock: Embracing Mutual Responsibility*. (Downer Grove: InterVarsity Press, 1984), 19.

ways and do not desire to worship with others that do not look like them—at least not in large numbers. Also, some Whites and Blacks do not like attending a church where the pastor and leadership do not look like them. Third, the religion of politics and how it has become more influential than biblical views. Politics in America is a powerful force. What makes it so dangerous is when it not only controls the government but controls a vast portion of the Christian church, which is predominately white evangelicals. Fourth, underestimating Satan's influence to divide the church and keeping it divided by focusing on the wrong things. Anytime Satan can convince Christians to replace God's kingdom agenda with Americanism, then we lose. If God saw fit to allow America to be toppled, as He did with the Roman Empire, the world would still go on, at least, until God's Great White Throne Room Judgement (Rev. 20).

Application of Revelation 5:9-10

Regardless of the systemic racism that has been part of America since its founding, why current racially diverse houses of worship will fit right in—in glory?

1. **We rejoice because our unity worship now is just a dress rehearsal together in heaven.**

We will sing a new song of unity together before the presence of God.

2. **We will already have plenty of practice to do in glory what we have already been doing on earth—worshiping the Lord in unity.**

We will be united with true believers from every tongue and tribe.

3. **We will be invited to reign with Christ in our new unified roles.**

Will reign together with Christ as a kingdom of priest to God.

What disadvantages do one-race churches have that multiracial churches benefit from?

1. **How worship will be practiced together in heaven with other brothers and sisters in Christ that do not look like us.**

   The beauty of multiracial churches because they are the example God intended.

2. **The ability to appreciate God's racial diversity in humanity.**

   The beauty of the multiracial church is that it allows us to practice on earth what God requires in heaven.

3. **To learn how to see people that do not look like us through the eyes of God.**

   The beauty of the multiracial church allows us to reflect God's glory in a real visible way.

The Answer To Racism In America Is Jesus Christ

The final point I want to reiterate at the close of this book is the need for Black and White Christians to work together to spread the gospel to a dying America on its way to hell, especially if it remains on its current trajectory. Instead of continuing to allow race to stand in the way of advancing the gospel, Black, White, Asian, and Hispanic Christians all need to apply the Scriptures correctly that we claim we believe in. As our country continues to come apart at the seams, why do we remain silent? Why do we insist on using other methods to be the vehicle to do the job that God entrusted to His church, such as our sinful politics and broken government? Why do we insist on allowing our political affiliations to speak for us and not the Word of God? Why do we continue to claim that we love one another when our actions do not corroborate our words? Why do people say they love Jesus but hate the church? The answer is because we are not what God created us to be, at least not on American soil since our founding as a nation. Therefore, America will have a lot to answer for on the *day of judgment*.

Jesus is the answer to American's problem with systemic racism, and the multiracial church is God's vehicle. It was God's vehicle to unite the Jews, Gentiles, and Samaritans in the book of Acts when God birthed the Christian church. Therefore, the multiracial church can be God's vehicle now in America if the Christian church is willing to surrender to God's will and work together for His glory and not trying to build their own kingdoms. As a church planter of a multiracial church in Fort Worth, Texas, I wholeheartedly believe that the multiracial church is the answer to providing a spiritual beacon of light to this nation that desperately needs Jesus. Furthermore, not only is Jesus the answer to American's problem with race but all the other multitude of sinful problems we struggle with as well.

Acts Chapter 2 describes the benefit of having Christians work together, loving one another, and putting Jesus first. Therefore, we have the model to follow, but we must implement the biblical model. If our churches are too stubborn to diversify along racial lines, especially if we are in racially diverse communities, we should support starting new churches, where that will be the primary focus from the beginning. Multiracial churches committed to Christ will allow America to have a role model for dealing with systemic racism—because politics and government are not the answer.

An Advanced Copy of an Autopsy

Merriam-Webster dictionary defines an autopsy as an examination of a body after death to determine the cause of death or the character and extent of changes produced by disease. The Cambridge English dictionary defines an autopsy as the cutting open and examination of a dead body to discover the cause of death. According to a medical dictionary, an autopsy is a postmortem assessment or examination of a body to determine the cause of death. Consequently, an autopsy is performed by someone thoroughly trained in pathology. Pathology is the science or the study of the origin, nature, and course of diseases or any deviation from a healthy, normal, or efficient condition.

The good news is God has provided us an advanced copy of the devastating effects of sin on fallen humanity. The Bible is God's advanced copy of the autopsy of humanity. Unfortunately, many people do not bother to read God's assessment of where we stand with Him and how we can get things right with Him. The Bible not only defines the disease of sin, it tells us where it originated as well as its lasting effects. Fortunately, for us, God is the pathologist and the Christian church is his patient. Although God provided sick humanity with the antidote for its disease (sin), which is Jesus Christ our Lord, the patient remains sick because the patient refuses to follow the spiritual, medical manual (the Bible) that He provided.

Although the entire Bible provides us an advance copy of an autopsy of sinful humanity, there is perhaps no greater summary or conclusion of that autopsy than the book of Revelations. Furthermore, because the Scriptures are God's word, this autopsy is from God's divine perspective, which should matter to all people who claim they belong to Him. Within the first three chapters, we find an advance copy of seven churches' autopsy during the millennial period. Although the seven letters in Revelation are tailored to the named churches, these churches and their stated deficiencies can symbolize all churches in one respect or another. The instruction is given to Revelation's congregations, therefore, is valuable to Christian congregations today. The following is the list of the Seven Churches and their description:

- Ephesus: The church that had deserted its first love for Christ (Revelation 2:1-7).
- Smyrna: The church that faced harsh persecution (Revelation 2:10).
- Pergamum: The church that refused to repent of their sins (Revelation 2:16).
- Thyatira: The church infected by a false prophetess that was leading the congregation astray (Revelation 2:20).
- Sardis: The church that was simply going through the motions and needed to wake up (Revelation 3:2).
- Philadelphia: The church that kept the word of God and persevered (Revelation 3:10).
- Laodicea: The church with lukewarm faith (Revelation 3:16).

In many ways, a strong argument can be made that the church in American today can be compared to six of these seven churches. I would exclude the church of Philadelphia because they do not describe the church in America at all. Out of all the churches listed, Philadelphia is the lone church that gets God's approval without being rebuked or having one negative thing said about it. This would not be God's autopsy of the Christian church in America today—or in or sinful past, especially with white supremacy and systemic racism. Christ's return is imminent—it could happen at any time. Although we do not know when Christ will return, we know what He expects from His church. Chapters 2-3 represent an aspect of his plan during the church age for every properly functioning church—represented by the number seven, the number of completion.[420]

The church in America versus the church in Ephesus (Revelation 2:1-7). Since many believe the church in America was founded as a Christian church, God's rebuke to Ephesus would appropriately apply to us as well. Why? Because, we too, have lost our first love. Although we might love God, we do not love Him first. Our passion for other things far exceeds our love for Christ. Jesus said, "Those who love me will obey my teaching. My Father will love them, and my Father and I will come to them and live with them." (John 14:23) Since the Christian church in America was said to be founded on Judeo-Christian principles, we have definitely lost our first love. America is a country of perpetual sinfulness, and the church, in many ways, emulates society. Just like secular America, Christian America puts anything and everything first above our relationship with God. We are just as materialistic, judgmental, political, and worldly as a secular society; therefore, we are guilty! Therefore, the strong rebuke that God gave five of these seven churches is the same rebuke that applies to the Christian church in America.

The church in America versus the church in Smyrna (Revelation 2:8-11). Like the Smyrna church facing tribulation and poverty, the church in America is currently facing very similar problems. Our problems are primarily because of the same three main forces that are affecting the rest of the country: The Covid-19 virus; the financial downturn that has put a lot of people out of work, including many Christians; and the racial unrest triggered by the continuous shootings of unarmed black men. Furthermore, the biggest difference between

---

420 Tony Evans. *Bible Commentary*, 1397.

America and Smyrna is that our suffering is self-inflicted primarily because of disobedience, disunity, and disfunction. Smyrna was not suffering because they had sinned against God. Just like the Philadelphia Church, God did not rebuke this church for any wrongdoing. God allowed the Smyrna church to suffer because it was their time to go through adversity for three primary reasons: To grow them spiritually, to prepare them for their future, and to build their faith in Him, which are three of the primary reasons God allows obedient Christians to go through adversity today as well. "For it is better, if God should will it so, that you suffer for doing what is right rather than for doing what is wrong." (1 Peter 3:17)

The church in America versus the church in Pergamum (Revelation 2:12-17). The Pergamum church was viewed as a worldly church, which thoroughly describes the church in America. Pergamos means "married," and this church was wedded to some doctrines and practices that were wrong.[421] Likewise, the Christian church in America is married to some doctrines that make us just as worldly as a secular society. It is not for poisonous propensity doctrine; it is for political doctrine or empty unbiblical doctrine. Three were three serious problems that existed in Pergamos.

1. Satan's throne (v. 13). This passage refers to the "mystery cults" of Balaam. Balaam was a hireling prophet who led the people of Israel into sin in return for the wealth and prestige he received. He encouraged Israel to worship heathen idols and indulge in fornication. At Pergamos, the church was wedded to the world to get worldly advantages that set up their headquarters in Pergamos. It also includes the emperor worship that played a key role in this heathen city.[422]

2. The doctrine of Balaam was teaching (v. 14., see also 6.) Came from someone labeled as a false prophet. Balaam tried unsuccessfully to prostitute his prophetic gift and curse Israel for money offered him by Balak, king of Moab. So, he devised a plot to have Moabite women seduce Israelite men into

---

421 W.W. Wiersbe, Wiersbe's Expository Outlines on the New Testament, 802.

422 Ibid.

intermarriage. The result was the blasphemous union of Israel with fornication and idolatrous feasts.[423]

3. The doctrine of the Nicolaitans (v. 15, see also v. 6). What began as "deeds" in one church is now a settled doctrine in another. We now have this church divided into "priests" and "people."[424]

The church in Pergamum apparently had the opposite problem of the Ephesian church. Rather than testing and rejecting false teachers, they had uncritically accepted people that held to the teaching of Balaam. The risen Lord unleashed stinging criticism and compared it to the teachings of the Nicolaitans.[425] When a Christian church can be compared to false prophets, that says one of two things; either that church is a really bad example, or that church is not Christian. Unfortunately, many churches in America fall within these two camps because they are not churches God can use. And even though they know Christ is coming back for His church without spot, wrinkle, or blemish (Eph. 5:27), that does not seem to be enough motivation for them to change.

The church in America versus the church in Thyatira (Revelation 2:18-29). This church suffered from false prophets leading the congregation astray. The chief false teacher was a false prophetess that was compared to Ahab's wife, Jezebel. She was in a leadership position she should never have been placed on or allowed to assume (1 Tim 2:11-15). Thus, the church lacked proper ecclesiology and church discipline. The practice of church discipline that Christ instituted to maintain the holiness of the church has a twofold purpose: to call sinning believers back to righteous behavior and to purge from the church from those who stubbornly cling to their sin. In either case, the purity of the church is maintained.[426] The church in America is guilty of the same sinful offenses because of the large number of unqualified, ill-informed, unspiritual, false preachers and teachers leading many

---

423 F. J. MacArthur. *The MacArthur Study Bible.*

424 W.W. Wiersbe, *Wiersbe's Expository Outlines on the New Testament,* 803.

425 K. H. Easley, *Revelation,* Vol. 12. (Nashville, TN: Broadman & Holman Publishers, 1998), 38.

426 F. J. MacArthur., Jr. *Revelation 1–11* (Chicago: Moody Press, 1999). 94.

churches. What makes this even worse in America is for two reasons: the false preachers and teachers that have convinced themselves they are speaking God's truth, when they are not, and the people that follow them and don't seem to have a clue that their pastors and teachers don't even know the Bible, but they blindly follow anyway.

The church in America verses the church in Sardis (Revelation 3:1-6). The Sardis church was known as the dying church that needed to wake up from its slumber. The church was asleep spiritually and needed to come alive in Christ. Christ knew their deeds, and there was little about their behavior that needed to be commended. Although they had the reputation of being alive, they were dead. Subsequent verses indicate that while the entire church had not fallen into a state of complete spiritual death (vs. 4–5), the majority had so fully compromised with the pagan environment that the church was Christian in name only (i.e., "nominally" Christian). Like the prodigal son of whom the father said, "This son of mine was dead" (Luke 15:24), only by repentance and return could life be restored (cf. Eph 5:14).[427] The church at Sardis comes under the most severe denunciation of the seven. Apparently untroubled by heresy and free from outside opposition, it had so completely come to terms with its pagan environment that although it retained the outward appearance of life, it was spiritually dead. Like the fig tree of Mark 11:20, it had left but no fruit.

Furthermore, the believers at Sardis had established a name for themselves in the eyes of the community, but in God's sight (i.e., from God's point of view) their works had not measured up.[428] Like the churches at Ephesus, Pergamum, and (later) Laodicea, Sardis is told to repent (cf. 2:5, 16; 3:19).[429] As you examine the Sardis church, it reminds you of the Christian church in America. First, the church in America has been on the decline (in attendance) for years. For many, the church does not seem relevant, which has turned many away. Also, the church is very good at stating what it is against, but not always what it is for. The church is quick to condemn but not as quick to reflect God's

---

[427] R. H. Mounce. *The Book of Revelation*. (Grand Rapids: Wm. B. Eerdmans Publishing Co, 1997). 93.

[428] Ibid, 94.

[429] Ibid.

forgiveness or holiness. This does not look good in the eyes of the unsaved because there is always some church or preacher in the news for some ungodly behavior, which is why many unchurched view the church as a bunch of hypocrites. Second, the church in America has compromised its beliefs for political clout, which is a point that I make throughout this book. The church needs to get back in its lane, which is to reach the lost and disciple the saved and get out of the lane of secular affairs. Third, just like in Sardis, the church in America has established a name for itself in the community's eyes, but not in God's sight. Forth, just like the other churches in revelations were told to repent, the church in America needs to repent. For these reasons and many others, the unsaved view the church in America as irrelevant.

The church in America versus the church in Laodicea (Revelation 3:14-22). The Laodicean church was known as an apostate church. The name "Laodicea" means "the rule of the people" and suggests a democratic church that no longer followed spiritual leaders or the authority of the Word of God. The church was lukewarm, a condition that came from mixing hot and cold. It was a church with the truth that had been diluted with error. The tragedy was that this church was "rich" but didn't realize it was poor, pitiful, blind, and naked. What a picture of the apostate church of today, with its prestige, wealth, and political power, yet all the while spiritually poor.[430] The Laodicea church was a lukewarm, apostate church with a big budget and no blessing. This is the church that is materially rich and spiritually poor. And the tragedy is, the people do not know how poor and miserable they really are! Christ stands outside the church, calling for even one believer to yield to Him.[431]

In the age of the megachurch, in which many are large only because of their prosperity doctrine, this is a strong message against those types of ministries. Here Jesus rebukes a prominent lie of prosperity theology: being materially successful means God has blessed you. This is because the external appearance of prosperity was not indicative of the condition of their hearts or a close relationship with God. Although

---

[430] W.W. Wiersbe, *Wiersbe's expository outlines on the New Testament*, 805.

[431] Ibid.

they had material wealth, they were wretched, pitiful, poor, blind, and naked spiritually. Many Americans, for the most part, are generous people.[432] Therefore, they will give to a cause wholeheartedly if they believe in it, no matter how farfetched it may be. Case in point, Although President Trump lost the Presidential election in November 2020, he has been raking in hundreds of millions of dollars from his supporters based on a lie that he was cheated out of the election. It needs their money to fight to overturn the election and his right to remain in the White House. Although this is a false narrative, Trump knows his followers will stick with him no matter what. Unfortunately, many of those gullible followers that are forking up their hard earn money and savings are white evangelical Christians. Just like people can be easily manipulated in the political and secular arenas, pastors and church leaders are fleecing Christians that lack spiritual discernment in the church arena. This is yet another reason why the unsaved hate the church, because preachers are no better than crooked politicians in their eyes, and the church is not more than a scam. But woe unto the pastors, preachers, and churches that are scamming God's people. They will have to answer to God for their sinful behavior.

Note, finally, the importance of the Word of God to the churches. Seven times Christ calls the churches to hear what the Spirit is saying. When churches stop listening to the voice of the Spirit through the Word and start listening to the voices of false teachers (as many have done in the church in America), they begin to turn away from the truth. We must not deny the faith (2:23), even if it costs us our lives. We must keep His Word (3:8, 10) and not deny His name. Apart from the Word of God, there is no life or hope for the churches.[433]

Blacks Need To Forgive And Whites Need To Remove Their Blinders

When I was growing up in East St. Louis, I would often get injured from a multitude of bumps, bruises, and scrapes. I was a typical boy that was very active in sports in my neighborhood. Regularly, I would

---

432 Tony Evans, Bible Commentary, 1400.

433 Ibid, 805-806.

manage to go home bleeding with scraps on my arms, legs, elbows, or knees from playing rough because of my competitive nature. These mishaps would come from either the basketball court up the street from our house, the field down the street, or from playing in the street in front of the house. It would often take a long time for my injuries to heal because I would consistently cause the scab to come off. This was because I would somehow manage to be reinjured in the same places. All these years later, I still have the scars to prove my injuries.

My illustration explains exactly why many African Americans have a hard time forgiving Caucasian Americans. While we are still trying to heal from so many past scars and racist events, since slavery, there is something else that Whites do to us that rips the scab off, again, and again, and again! Not saying that it is right to hold grudges because it is not, but this is the reason why so many Blacks remain bitter, angry, frustrated, and lack forgiveness when it comes to Whites. It is why so many Blacks feel there are two Americas: White America and Black America. Also, this is why many Blacks do not want to have anything to do with Whites, and they try to avoid them at all costs. I recall a black lady that visited our church in the past. She was very nice and friendly when she came, and she liked our preaching, teaching, worship style, and the friendliness of our congregation (her comments). She was invited by one of our members that was a good friend of hers. One day our member came to me and said that her friend did not feel welcome in our church because I always talked about inviting white people.

To add some context to the lady's comments, from the very beginning, our church has sought to be a racially diverse congregation, so we would deliberately and purposely reach out to all races and welcomed them—a practice we still do today. We made it known from the beginning that we strived to be a multiracial church to reach our multiracial community. Additionally, we wanted everyone to feel welcome, regardless of race or ethnicity, which many people have loved about our church. However, because this lady had her issues with white people, she did not want to attend a church that was not all Black.

Surprisingly, this is where a lot of blacks, including Christians, find themselves stuck. I told our member that her friend was always welcome, but our church was probably not the place for her friend because our goal was to be part of the solution and not settle for being part of the problem. At that time, I felt that if our church were all black and not trying to be more racially diverse, this lady would have probably joined our congregation. She did not feel welcome worshiping people that did not look like her. Before any of you reading this begin to beat this lady up, you must understand her scars that had not yet healed. If I remember correctly, she suffered some bad experiences at the hands of some evil white people. She was older, so she had far more of those bad racial experiences with Whites than I ever had to deal with, even though I have had my fair share. Just like this lady, many Blacks have their own racist experiences with Whites. As a result, the sanctuary that provides them a way to escape white-dominated America, and all that it entails—at least on Sunday—is the black church. Historically, the black church has meant something totally different to Blacks than what the church has meant to Whites.

> *The Black church in the United States can be traced back to the enslavement of Black people in the 18th and 19th centuries. Enslaved African people brought to the Americas by force came with a variety of religions, including traditional spiritual practices. But the system of enslavement was built on the dehumanization and exploitation of people, and this could only be achieved by depriving those enslaved of meaningful connections to land, ancestry, and identity. The dominant white culture of the time accomplished this through a system of forced acculturation, which included forced religious conversion.*[434]

The impact of American slavery, and the trials of the Jim Crow era, are the reason why Blacks are often far more expressive in their worship than Whites. Our worship is distinctive in style, preaching,

---

434   Vanessa Taylor. "The Black Church: Religious Culture and Social Movement" 28 November 2017. [on-line]; accessed on 23 December 2020; accessed from The Black Church: Religious Culture and Social Movement (thoughtco.com); Internet. The term "Black church" is used to describe Protestant churches that have predominately Black congregations. More broadly, the Black church is both a specific religious culture and a socio-religious force that has shaped protest movements, such as the Civil Rights Movement of the 1950s and 1960s.

and congregational response during worship. Typically, we are more expressive in our emotions, so we respond to the music and the preaching with public responses. It is why we dance during worship, talk back to the preacher during the sermon, and stand with our hands toward heaven—often with tears rolling down our faces. These expressions of worship can be traced back to slavery. This is why we relate so well with the Israelites and their bondage in Egypt because we had a similar experience of bondage and deliverance after centuries of our lives being dominated by an evil oppressor.

Because of how white Christians treated Blacks during and after slavery, most Blacks prefer the black church experience when they want to worship God. For that vast majority of Blacks, we have nothing personal against Whites; we just prefer our worship style. Also, Blacks feel like they fit in better in an African American led church because we are allowed to be in leadership, we are loved and respected, and hear sermons that address our plight in life, which also can be traced back to the beginning of the Black church after slavery. Some Blacks feel that Whites have ruined so many of their experiences, so they wanted to keep the last best place they can go—that is not controlled or manipulated by Whites—the Black church. In their defense, whether you agree with how they feel, you at least should understand it and respect where they are coming from. Remember, the Blacks that arrived at this conclusion were because of the many years of ill-treatment by white America.

> *Black pastors and their congregations maintained their autonomy and identity by reading their histories into Christian texts, unlocking new routes for self-realization. For example, many Black churches identified with the Book of Exodus's story of the prophet Moses leading the Israelites to escape from enslavement in Egypt. The story of Moses and his people spoke to hope, promise, and the benevolence of a God which was otherwise absent in the systematic and oppressive structure of enslavement. White Christians worked to justify enslavement through the employment of a white savior complex, which in addition to dehumanizing Black people, infantilized them. Some went so far as to claim that Black people*

had been cursed and enslavement was the necessary, God-intended punishment.[435]

However, as an African American, I completely understand my black brothers and sisters in Christ that only want to worship among themselves. Likewise, there are many Caucasian, Asian, and Hispanic Christians that do not desire to worship with anyone outside of their race either, for various reasons. However, I choose to take a different course of action. I choose to worship with all of God's children, especially those that do not look like me, which is why we began Agape Community Fellow Church in January 2003 in Fort Worth, Texas.

In a book by Spencer Perkins and Chris Rice, *More Than Equals: Racial Healing for the Sake of the Gospel*, we find a black Christian (Spencer) and a white Christian (Chris), men from very different backgrounds, that provide a powerful message to the answer to racism in America. The book was not written by "experts" from the perspective of a sociologist, political scientists, historians, or economists—but simply by two brothers in Christ who walked a daily reality of unity.[436]

The book tells the story of a racial incident that impacted Spencer in a very profound way when he was only sixteen years old. His father, Paster John Perkins, was heavily involved in the Civil Rights Movement and was arrested because of it. Spencer recalled visiting his father in jail after the arrest. When he saw his dad, bloodied and swollen in jail, the image was seared into his heart and mind forever. The black pastor and activists were severely beaten by police. His only crime was standing up for his activist friends. This event took place in the racist city of Brenden, Mississippi, in the 1970s. Some of his friends were returning from a peaceful civil-rights protest in the streets of Brendon. On their way home, without any provocations, they were stopped by the white Brenden police. They were beaten and taken to jail for peaceful protesting. When Perkins found out about the incident, he went to jail in hopes of freeing his friends.

---

435   Ibid.

436   Perkins, Spencer and Chris Rice. *More Than Equals: Racial Healing for the Sake of the Gospel*. (Downers Grove: IVP Books, 2000), 23.

However, he was beaten and bloodied by the sheriff—a member of the local Ku Klux Klan—for simply showing up and requesting his friends be released for simply protesting peacefully. Spencer never forgot about the police brutality his father suffered at the hands of white police officers because of racism. As a result of that image, Spencer couldn't imagine living in the same community with a white person after that experience. But his plans were changed when Jesus touched his heart and gave him the ability to forgive. This was magnified when he crossed paths with Chris.

Chris Rice grew up in very different circumstances, of "Vermont Yankee stock," attending an elite Eastern college and looking forward to a career in law and government. Chris had never experienced anything remotely close to his friend Spencer and other Blacks consistently faced in America. Spencer and Chris proved that Blacks and Whites can unite and make a difference for the kingdom of God. This book illustrates how differently the issue of race has affected various ethnic groups and how similarly we can be transformed as we become part of God's story.[437]

> *We can't just snap our fingers and—presto! —suddenly be one in Christ. The task of bridging our racial divide and acting like a loving family is a journey, and three crucial steps are needed. First, admit. Christians must admit that a separation exists, that our ethnic and racial relationships are uneasy and that this represents what God intends for His people. Second, submit. We must hand ourselves over to God, fall on our faces before Him for help, and recognize we can't be healed apart from Him. And we must submit to one another by embracing across racial and ethnic barriers and begin to address the hurts and gaps between us. Finally, admit. Deep and lasting reconciliation will be realized only as we commit ourselves to a lifestyle of loving our racially different neighborhoods as ourselves.*[438]

---

437   Ibid, 23-24. At times the anger from Spencer's bitter racial experiences sends sparks out from these pages, while Chris' racial naivete is embarrassingly evident. But we all begin where we are. For the process of racial reconciliation to start, different responses are required different groups.

438   Ibid, 24. Spencer and Criss' long friendship and ministry proved that

Spencer and Chris were willing to sit in the same room and have an important conversation on race relations in America and ask the hard questions about how racial reconciliation can be achieved. Working together over the years led them to write this book. These Christian men provide us with some simple answers that would be a good first step in the right direction for healing race relations in America.

> *Four hundred years of slavery forced segregation, and discrimination has left a stubborn residue within us all. For blacks, the residue is anger, bitterness, and blame. For whites, the residue is racial blinders. Blinders were an ingenious invention designed to keep a horse single-minded, focused on one thing-moving forward in the direction the master desired. They are put around the horse's eyes, limiting its peripheral vision so that the horse can see only a partial reality. So, it forges forward in that one direction. Meanwhile, all around are dangers, difficulties, and even opportunities of which the horse is unaware. Even if the horse cannot see them, they still exist.*[439]

The illustration of a horse and blinders is an excellent example in describing how many Caucasian Americans wear blinders when it comes to systemic racism in our country. The illustration was not meant to be demeaning; it was meant to be informative and make a powerful point. The sad thing about blinders is that most people that have them are so conditioned to seeing what they want to see—based on background, socio-economic status, or race—that they are oblivious to what's going on around them. If it does not directly affect them, they have the "I don't care" or "It's not my business" attitude.

Perhaps, the biggest blinder that white America has today is President Donald Trump. For the vast majority of African Americans, Trump represents what is wrong with race relations in America because he is the epitome of systemic racism. We watched as Trump rose to political prominence by attacking one of the most successful symbols in

---

it is still possible for the embodiment of reconciliation, this new family of God, to become visible on this earth.

[439] Perkins, Spencer, and Chris Rice. More Than Equals: Racial Healing for the Sake of the Gospel. (Downers Grove: IVP Books, 2000), 71.

American history and, more importantly, in African American history; the election of Barack Obama as our nation's 44th President. Although not all African Americans agreed with all of Obama's policies while in the Oval Office, we were proud to witness a major accomplishment for our race. Many Blacks are angry because they do not feel he did enough for people of color. Nevertheless, Blacks, by far, are glad that Obama made it to such a high office. For a black man to reach the highest office in America and around the world sent a powerful message to all who were paying attention.

A house built by slaves, and now had one of its ancestors occupy it, not as a slave, a visitor, or a servant, but the one who lived there with His family to lead the nation. Simply unprecedented! Obama's accomplishment told every black child in America and around the world that they could dream the impossible and see it come to pass one day. However, Trump could not stand that a black man occupied the White House, and neither could many of his followers, so he attacked Obama's race with his "birtherism" claims. Although Trump was already nationally known in the entertainment and real-estate industries, this launched him onto the national political scene. Because so many white evangelicals still support Trump, even after all the wrong things He has done to our country and people of color, proves they are not ready to admit that they have on blinders—when it comes to helping perpetuate the Christian church's role in systemic racism.

Furthermore, historically, American Christianity has failed to challenge racial division. Sometimes we have even embraced separation—if not in theory, most definitely in practice.[440] After all these years of racial oppression of African Americans, more white Christians are not willing to work together to help alleviate the problem, instead of acting as though it does not exist.

One of the oldest strategies of warfare is to divide and conquer. Once you have isolated your enemy, you have robbed him of his strength. Then you can do just about whatever you please with him.[441]

---

440   Ibid, 30.

441   Ibid. 61. Unfortunately, Christians have used a similar strategy of divide and conquer in our attempt to deal with hard teachings of Jesus. We have separated basic principles of Scripture that God never intended to be

As I conclude this book, this statement summarizes what white America has done to black America since 1619.

Finally, I want to leave my Black and White brothers and sisters in Christ with sound biblical advice to help them with their stumbling block of racial division. This passage is from Jesus' *Sermon on the Mount*.

> *"Do not judge so that you will not be judged. For in the way you judge, you will be judged; and by your standard of measure, it will be measured to you. Why do you look at the speck that is in your brother's eye, but does not notice the log that is in your own eye? Or how can you say to your brother, 'Let me take the speck out of your eye,' and behold, the log is in your own eye? You hypocrite, first take the log out of your own eye, and then you will see clearly to take the speck out of your brother's eye. (Matthew 7:1-5)*

This sermon was preached to Jesus' disciples after the Sermon on the Mount. However, it was preached about the Pharisees that loved to judge people falsely. The word judge is the Greek word *krinos*, which means to distinguish or make a judgment and examine whether or not a thing is true. Paul used *krinos* in 1st Corinthians 5 when he addressed sexual immorality in the Corinthian church. A Christian man was sleeping with his step-mother, who was more than likely not a church member or even a Christian because she was not addressed for her part in the sinful relationship. Because of the man's actions and the fact that he refused to repent, Paul says, "For I, on my part, though absent in body but present in spirit, have already judged him who has so committed this, as though I were present. [1 Corinthians 5:3]. Paul was saying he examined the man's fruit (lifestyle) and that it did not line up with Scripture, so he made a righteous judgment or decision based on the man's actions and failure to repent.

Furthermore, after Paul's proper examination, he concluded that the man is excommunicated from the church in Corinthian. The goal was to remove the man from under the covering of Christian church fellowship. It gave Satan easier access to this Christian, so it would

---

separated, consequently robbing them of their power. An example would be the improper exegesis of the curse of Ham in Genesis chapter 4. White wrongly used this passage to validate enslaving Blacks

hopefully lead him to gladly repent and turn back to Jesus, church attendance, and the fellowship of the saints. Therefore, in Jesus' statement in the Sermon on the Mount, He was not saying we should never judge, but the emphasis should be on righteous judgment or righteous decision making—I would add that especially when it comes to dealing with others, that do not look like us. Jesus went on to say that the same measure we judge will be used to judge us and that the same measure we use will be used against us. Jesus' statements were meant to deter us from judging others improperly as the Pharisees did repeatedly.

Jesus didn't stop there because He said, "Why do you look at the speck that is in your brother's eye, but does not notice the log that is in your own eye?" The difference between a speck and a log is, one is hardly visible, while the other is very visible. This metaphor was meant to send a message to those who unrighteously judged others. The proof that this was exactly what the Pharisees were doing is why Jesus called them hypocrites. They did not care about their sins (the log in their eye) but only cared about the sins (speck) in their brother's eye. So, why do I conclude this book with this passage? Because this is what has been going on for years between Blacks and Whites—as it relates to race relations.

Since at least 1619, Whites have unrighteously judged Blacks, which allowed them to enslave us and create a whole system of systemic racism based on the false premise of white supremacy to build a foundation for America. Since this was the original false judgment, and White America does not seem to want to address this foundational sin in any meaningful way, our country will continue to spiral down the road of hatred, bitterness, and division and never achieve racial reconciliation on this side of glory. Hopefully, the Christian church, made up of all races and ethnicities, will take a stand for righteousness and racial reconciliation, regardless of what secular America does.

Sooner or later, we will have to stop pretending that the antagonistic relationship between Blacks and Whites can be headed by itself. If it could, it would have been accomplished by now, since it has only been over 400 years since slavery began in America. As Maya Angelou famously quoted, "We cannot change the past, but we can change our attitude toward it. Uproot guilt and plant forgiveness. Tear out arrogance and seed humility. Exchange love for hate - thereby, making the present comfortable and the future promising." Therefore, for the future of race relations in America to ever get better, we are going to have to do the following: First, the Christian church in America must take the lead, this includes Blacks, Whites, Asians, Hispanics, and others. Second, we must admit things are broken and that they have been broken for a long time. Third, we must be willing to admit that all races have been part in perpetuating the problem, even though one race invented the problem by agreeing with slavery, Jim crow, and white supremacy. Finally, we must submit to the Word of God for clear direction, repentance, healing, and reconciliation.

According to Spencer and Rice, although it is not easy to take on the challenge of talking honestly and working intentionally toward living like one Christian family, it is a necessary task, that's if racial reconciliation will ever be achieved.[442]

As I stated in the beginning, my goal in writing this book was to begin a serious dialogue between the many different races and ethnicities in America, not just Blacks and Whites. Furthermore, for my white Christian brothers and sisters, Spencer and Rice challenge you to put yourself in an environment where you are the minority. Why? Because it is one of the most effective ways, you can begin to understand the hurts that didn't concern you before, especially those challenges that affect the people of color in America daily.[443]

Finally, for all Christians, rather than being points of conflict, and focusing on your cultural differences, you can utilize your God-given opportunities so that we all can learn from and enrich one another.[444] This would be helpful because if we are willing to go out of our way to initiate relationships with people from other races, this can lead to some long-term payoffs for reconciliation. As Christians, the goal we should all be striving for is unity. One way this can be achieved in building racial bridges or "proving neighborhoods," which is essentially

---

442   Perkins, Spencer and Chris Rice. *More Than Equals*, 19

443   Ibid, 83.

444   Ibid.

interracial church partnerships.[445] Once again, a personal relationship with Jesus Christ and the vehicle of the multiracial church is God's answer to racism in America. The question is, are you willing to do your part to be actively involved in this new move of God that would glorify not only God but also be an example of racial reconciliation in America and the Christian church?

My experience of serving in the United States Air Force as a Christian thoroughly enriched my life in so many ways. The people I met along the way from different backgrounds and countries, as well as different races and ethnicities, was something my wife and I will cherish the rest of our lives. At each base we served, we met many wonderful people that are our dear friends for life, which many did not look like us. As a military chaplain, I was blessed to minister to a multicultural, multiracial crowd of God's people. During my last military deployment to the Middle East, as the Senior Base Chaplain for over 8,000 U.S. Armed Forces personnel, I was blessed with being able to share the gospel of Jesus Christ with Air Force, Army, Marines, and Navy personnel.

Also, I was blessed to share the gospel with troops from two of the countries from our coalition forces, Canada and Great Britain. The blessing of Christ was being able to some of them to faith in Christ, that were stationed at the same deployed base with us. The multiracial makeup of the military and our allies afforded me the opportunity to experience true racial unity in the body of Christ. And if the amazing God we serve can do that in a deployed location in the desert, he can certainly do it in the spiritual desert of the United States. However, unless all Christians in America, Black, White, Asian, Hispanic, and other races are willing to do the following: admit there is a problem with systemic racism that is keeping us divided; be willing to come out of our racial comfort zones; stop being complicit to the division and racism; be willing to obey the Bible completely and show genuine Christ-like love to one another; be willing to work together for Christ

---

445   Ibid, 220. Given our conspicuous lack of experience in bridge-building, many such partnerships begin rather clumsily. But that is a small price to pay for the benefits they can bring. Just because racial reconciliation is difficult does not mean the Christian church in America should not try, especially since we are God's created vehicle on earth to do so.

sake to reach the lost and disciple the saved; then the Christian church in America can reflect God's glory in heaven. However, if we fail to unite as a church, then America will continue to suffer and go down the same pitiful sinful path we are currently on. And if the nation continues to go down that road, the church does not have to follow. We can take a stand and be the peculiar people the Bible calls us to be (1 Peter 2:9) KJV. Furthermore, suppose the church does not make the necessary changes of unity. In that case, the unsaved will not get to see the reflection of God's glory working through all His people, our racial tensions will remain, the church will continue to be segregated, our country will lose out on the biblical example to emulate, and our country will continue down the slippery-slope of systemic racism, as well as all the other sinful issues that plague us.

APPENDIX ONE

WHITE PRIVILEGE ON STEROIDs

On 6 January 2021, as my wife and I sat in our home office working, we had the TV on the news, and what we saw was beyond heartbreaking. We watched in horror as hundreds of President Donald Trump's insurrectionist supporters breached the U.S. Capital building. They broke through police-manned barricades, charged up the steps to the entrance door, broke windows, and gained access. The uncontrollable mob chanted. "Hang Mike Pence, Hang Mike Pence."[446] This was because Vice President Pence said he would do his job and certify the 2020 Presidential election (validating Biden's win), which was simply a formality that he had no power to change.

The seditious mob even erected a hangman's gallows on the Capitol grounds, including a rope tied in a noose. So, why did this horrendous incident ever happen? It's simple; President Donald Trump wanted it to happen! He stoked his base and encouraged them to explode on his behalf in a crazy attempt to save his presidency. As a result, his millions of followers hung on his every word and believed what he told them—no matter how deranged. This strategy of the division was effective for Trump during his entire presidency. However, when people try to argue that this was simply an incident that just got out of hand, they are just as delusional as the many conspiracy theories that Trump subscribed to and retweeted daily. The attack on the Capitol building was well planned and had been brewing for months, if not

---

446   Peter Weber, "'Where is Pence?' Pro-Trump mob tried to hunt down vice president, lawmakers in Capitol siege," Yahoo News, 7 January 2020. [on-line]; accessed on 13 January 2021; accessed from https//:www.Where is Pence?' Pro-Trump mob tried to hunt down vice president, lawmakers in Capitol siege. (yahoo.com); Internet.

years. Trump had already sold his Maga-crowd on the fake news that he, their "white knight" and "savior," had been mistreated since he was elected. I said this before, but this is what "white privilege" and "white victimization" look like, but on steroids.

Trump and his zombie-followers knew that there would be a joint session of Congress on January 6, 2021, to certify the election of Joe Biden and Kamala Harris as the next President and Vice President of the United States. This was the sole purpose why so many of his angry supporters traveled to Washington D.C. Their goal was to stop Congress from certifying the election by any means necessary. Many of Trump's avid misled supporters had that date circled on their calendar, which is why they were present for the "Stop the steal" rally that morning.

In a last-ditch effort, Trump did his best to stop the certification of the election of Joe Biden from ever taking place. If Trump had succeeded and gotten enough of the Senate and House of Representatives to go along with him, America would have no longer been a democracy. The United States of America would forever be changed. Because every presidential candidate hereafter would have been able to do the same thing, especially if they were the incumbent. This would have essentially made Trump a dictator, which would have been just fine with his base, and over 150 Republican Congressmen and Senators. This is why it was not by accident that the white MAGA mob showed up at the Congress Capitol building that morning. They were simply following the orders of their deranged leader, Donald Trump.

Earlier on the morning of Wednesday, 6 January 2021, Trump held a rally not too far from the Capitol building, and as he had done many times before, he gave his mad-MAGA followers their marching orders.

> "And after this, we're going to walk down there, and I'll be there with you, we're going to walk down ... to the Capitol and we are going to cheer on our brave senators and congressmen and women," Trump told the crowd. "And we're probably not going to be cheering so much for some of them. Because you'll never take back our country with weakness. You have to show strength and you have to be strong."[447]

---

447   Antonio Fins, "What Trump said in rally speech to spark U.S. Capitol storming, "*The Palm Beach Post*, 9 January 2021. [on-line]; accessed

However, after the Capitol was under siege by his devout MAGA followers, Trump did not call off his terrorizers; he gave them his blessing. Trump tweeted the following statement:

> "These are the things and events that happen when a sacred landslide election victory is so unceremoniously & viciously stripped away from great patriots who have been badly & unfairly treated for so long. Go home with love & peace. Remember this day forever!"[448]

As things continued to deteriorate at the Capitol, Trump continued to be tone death to what was happening in real-time. He continued to tweet and incite his angry, dangerous mob.

> "We will never give up. We will never concede. It doesn't happen. You don't concede. It doesn't happen. You don't concede when there's theft involved. Our country has had enough. We're not going to take it anymore." [449]

Trump didn't stop there; he continued tweeting, making the situation worse with each passing moment.

> "I am asking for everyone at the U.S. Capitol to remain peaceful. No violence! Remember, WE are the Party of Law & Order – respect the Law and our great men and women in Blue. Thank you!" Trump tweeted. "Please support our Capitol Police and

---

on 9 January 2020; accessed from https://ww.palmbeachpost.com/story/news/politics/2021/01/06/what-trump-said-rally-speech-spark-u-s-capitol-storming/6568337002/; Internet.

448   Ibid.

449   Tony Romm, Elizabeth Dwoskin, Drew Harwell, "Twitter, Facebook lock Trump's accounts amid D.C. riots," The Washington Post, 8 January 2021. [on-line]; accessed on 9 January 2020; accessed from https://www.msn.com/en-us/news/politics/trump-e2-80-99s-election-attacks-on-twitter-spark-new-online-calls-for-violence-as-rioters-stormed-the-us-capitol/ar-BB1cxamz; Internet. Amid the onslaught of criticism, Facebook took the rare step of removing Trump's video after hours of internal debate about the president's actions, before blocking his account entirely. YouTube also removed the video, while Twitter similarly took aim at Trump throughout the day, flagging tweets that sent mixed messages about the events that had unfolded.

Law Enforcement. They are truly on the side of our Country. Stay peaceful!"

Perhaps, no one watches more TV than Donald Trump, especially no other past president. In his own words, Trump admitted his habit of binge-watching TV.

> "I watch some of the shows," Trump declared. "I watch Liz McDonald. She's fantastic. I watch Fox Business. I watched Lou Dobbs last night. Sean Hannity last night. Tucker [Carlson] last night. Laura [Ingraham]. I watched Fox & Friends in the morning. You watch these shows. You don't have to go too far into the details, they cover things that are—it's an amazing thing."[450]

Therefore, because of past behavior, Trump was thoroughly aware of how the situation was playing out in real-time. Trump spent hours watching his favorite cable news shows such as Fox News and OAN News. Also, Trump watched CNN and MSNBC—although he had repeatedly called them fake news. Trump gave himself away when he would constantly tweet in real-time, based on what irked him about their broadcast. So, Trump had to see how bad things were for him as the situation played out. Once again, each tweet was loaded with lies. The party of law and order would have never attacked the Capitol building, which represents the hallmark of our democracy, nor would they have attacked a co-equal branch of government because the majority did not agree with them.

Only after enormous pressure from his allies, which were disgusted with what they had witnessed on every news outlet in America, did Trump upload the following message on Twitter before his account was deactivated to incite violence the next day.

> I'd like to begin by addressing the heinous attack on the United States Capitol. Like all Americans, I am outraged by the violence, lawlessness, and mayhem. I immediately deployed the National

---

[450] Justine Baragona, "Trump Admits He Sits Around Watching Cable News All Night," 10 September 2020. [Internet]; ; Internet. President Donald Trump, who just last month insisted he doesn't "watch very much TV" because he works "very long hours," admitted that he basically sits around all night and morning watching cable news—specifically, of course, Fox News.

> Guard and federal law enforcement to secure the building and expel the intruders. America is and must always be a nation of law and order. My campaign vigorously pursued every legal avenue to contest the election results, my only goal was to ensure the integrity of the vote. In so doing, I was fighting to defend American democracy. Now, Congress has certified the results. A new administration will be inaugurated on January 20. My focus now turns to ensure a smooth, orderly, and seamless transition of power. This moment calls for healing and reconciliation. 2020 has been a challenging time for our people, a menacing pandemic has upended the lives of our citizens, isolated millions in their homes damaged our economy, and claimed countless lives. Defeating this pandemic and rebuilding the greatest economy on earth will require all of us to work together. It will require a renewed emphasis on the civic values of patriotism, faith, charity, community, and family. We must revitalize the sacred bonds of love and loyalty, that bind us together as one national family. To the citizens of our country, serving as your president has been the honor of my lifetime. And to all of my wonderful supporters. I know you are disappointed, but I also want you to know that our incredible journey is only just beginning. Thank you, God bless you, and God bless America.[451]

The next day, after Trump instigated the deadly riot, he finally said he agreed to a peaceful transfer of power. However, this had more to do with the bad press he was getting that tied him to the incident, not because he changed his behavior or position on the election.

> "Even though I disagree with the outcome of the election, and the facts bear me out, nevertheless there will be an orderly transition on January 20th. I have always said we would continue our fight to ensure that only legal votes were counted. While this represents the end of the greatest first term in presidential history, it's only the beginning of our fight to Make America Great Again!" [452]

---

451   Aljazeera, "Donald Trump Acknowledges Biden election win: Full transcript. Us President Donald Trump addresses the nation a day after crowds of his supports attacked the US Capitol." 8 January 2021.

452   Holly Ellyatt, "After inciting riot, Trump now promises peaceful

Throughout Trump's presidency, when he wanted people to know how he felt about anything, he tweeted it. Whenever he had stepped in it and had to do something to appease the Republicans, he would read a prepared statement. This was no different when Trump read this statement and had it posted on Twitter and YouTube. The statement was not only not Trump's own words, but it was filled with lies. First, Trump claimed he wanted a peaceful transition of power. However, his actions, leading up to the election, proved that to be a lie. Just like he did the entire time he was in office,

Trump thought he could, once again, manipulate all levels of government to remain in office. Delirious, yes, but it is how he thought and operated. Second, Trump never cared about the Covid-19 pandemic or how many American citizens were infected or died. If he had, he would not have called a hoax for months before he even admitted it was the problem.[453] Third, he did not immediately send in the Air National Guard to help quell his MAGA supporters. That point was a lie on two fronts: It was Vice President Pence that sent in the Air National Guard, and second, they were not sent in until after the mob had already done the damage, so it was not immediate.[454] Fourth, we know

---

transfer of power," 7 January 2021. [on-line]; accessed on 11 January 2021; accessed from Trump now promises an 'orderly transition' of power (cnbc.com); Internet. President Donald Trump is now promising an "orderly transition" of power, tweeting through a surrogate early Thursday minutes after Congress formally confirmed the election of Joe Biden as president following an hours long takeover of the Capitol by a mob of Trump supporters.

453   Lauren Egan, "Trump calls coronavirus Democrats' "New hoax." 28 February 2020. [on-line]; accessed on 11 January 2021; accessed from ; Internet. North Charleston, S.C. — President Donald Trump accused Democrats of "politicizing" the deadly coronavirus during a campaign rally here on Friday, claiming that the outbreak is "their new hoax" as he continued to downplay the risk in the U.S.

454   Tim O'Donnell, "Pence, not Trump, reportedly approved National Guard Deployment after Capitol breach," 6 January 2021. [on-line]; accessed on 11 January 2021; accessed from ; Internet. Per *The New York Times*, Pentagon and Trump administration officials said the green light came from the vice president, while Acting Defense Secretary Christopher Miller said he and Gen. Mark Milley, the chair of the Joint Chiefs of Staff, spoke with Pence, House Speaker Nancy Pelosi (D-Calif.), Senate Majority Leader Mitch McConnell (R-Ky.), Senate Minority Leader Chuck Schumer (D-N.Y.), and House Majority Leader Steny Hoyer (D-Md.), about what was happening at the Capitol. It

someone else wrote the statement when it said, "We must revitalize the sacred bonds of love and loyalty, that bind us together as one national family." Trump has always been a self-serving narcist, never caring about anyone but himself, and would throw anybody under the bus if it benefited him. (Ask Vice President Pence) Fifth, if serving as the President was such an honor, why was it that Trump spent his entire presidency dishonoring the office? Sixth, "Our journey is only just beginning" was said to hopefully save face with his demented MAGA base, even after he had just thrown them under the bus. This was, of course, hypocritical after Trump had excited his enraged followers to do his dirty work by attacking the Capitol.

For those of you that are reading this book and are not convinced that Donald Trump incites racism and violence and that racist white Americans are drawn to him because he speaks their language, these are the words of a wife and husband that were staunch supporters of his that attended the Capitol insurrection.

> "This is not America," a woman said to a small group, her voice shaking. She was crying, hysterical. "They're shooting at us. They're supposed to shoot BLM (Black Lives Matter followers), but they're shooting the patriots" (privileged whites).
>
> A man, possibly her husband, comforted her: "Don't worry, honey. We showed them today. We showed them what we're all about."[455]

Every time some bad racists event happens in America, at least in recent years, you hear people say, "This is not who we are."[456] However,

does not appear either Miller or Milley spoke with the president.

455 Andrew McCormick, "Madness on Capitol Hill," The Nation, 7 January 2020. [on-line]; accessed on 10 January 2021; accessed from https://www.thenation.com/article/politics/capitol-insurrection-explosions/;Internet.

456 Soraya Nadia McDonald, "The Dangerous magical thinking of 'this is not who we,'" 14 January 2021. [on-line]; accessed on 27 January 2021; accessed from The https://www.The dangerous magical thinking of 'this is not who we are' (theundefeated.com); Internet. We can't fix what's wrong with American democracy until we acknowledge the problem of white supremacy. I've long found these sorts of proclamations baffling, because if one is honest about the history of the United States, it prominently features white violence, terrorism and revanchism, particularly toward Black

I would beg to differ, because we have shone as a nation since 1619; this is exactly who we are—at least, who many white Americans are because of their treatment of black people. The statements made by this white couple are very telling. This white lady revealed her white privilege and support for systemic racism. The fact that she was in disbelief about the police response to their criminal behavior lets you know she is not used to the police shooting at them like they do with black people. Trump has called BLM a terrorist organization, which this white woman believed as well. In her eyes, when white people commit acts of sedition on behalf of Trump, it is patriotism, but when black people march peacefully for racial justice, that is un-American and criminal. Her husband thoroughly understood the motives behind their madness when he said, "Don't worry, honey. We showed them today. We showed them what we're all about." Yeh! You not only showed the country but the entire world that you are racist as well as seditionist that do not believe in the Constitution, at least not when things do not go your way.

The Capitol Police, which was supposed to stop this very thing from happening, were severely overwhelmed by Trump's Mob. This predominately white mob desecrated the Capitol building and embarrassed the United States on the world stage. However, this event was not just a spontaneous event, it had been brewing for months, because it was stoked by President Donald Trump, Republican members of Congress, conservative media outlets, such as Fox News, One American News Network OAN, and Rush Limbaugh, and a multitude of Trump followers on social media outlets.

---

people, Indigenous people and women. Such attitudes have been codified within our laws and institutions, and it has taken enormous, multigenerational work to chip away at the bigotry that metastasizes within our nation. Since the deadly attack on the U.S. Capitol on Jan. 6, there have been statements from white people across the political spectrum, including President-elect Joe Biden, that repeat variations of the same refrain: This is not who we are. Even now, we witness the defanging of the Voting Rights Act or the Violence Against Women Act, attacks on Black churches, synagogues and mosques, and the daily deployment of police officers on calls that originate with racist grievance.

In an online article posted the day after a predominately white mob broke into the Capitol building in D.C., staff writer Matt Byrne summed up the double standard in the two Americas: White and Black.

> *Watching the mob of white nationalists and Trump loyalists surge past a complacent Capitol police force on Wednesday, Nathan Allen recognized a familiar truth for Black and brown people across the nation being reinforced once again. "You and I know if it was a group of Black people who tried to storm the capitol, we wouldn't have made it to the steps. It would have been a blood bath," said Allen, 36, who spent the summer protesting police brutality and racism in southern Maine and was pepper-sprayed by police during a protest in Portland. "It's two different Americas." Allen was among millions in the country who stood toe to toe with local officers last summer to demand that police stop killing Black people, only to be met with harsher treatment than those who attempted to undo an election in broad daylight on national television, he said. To be black and to protest is to be feared, while white people seem to get a pass.* [457]

After what happened on 6 January 2021 in our nation's capital, no one in America, or around the world, should ever argue again that white privilege does not exist in America. This article, and the events that transpired by the white mob, makes it plain that we still have a systemic racism problem in America. After witnessing this horrific event portrayed on just about every news outlet, I talked to one of my dear pastor friends from seminary, Dr. Dwayne Baker. We agreed that if that had been a black group of rioting men and women, the incident would have played out with hundreds or even thousands of black bodies littering the Capitol grounds.

We do not think that Blacks would have been allowed to pass the initial Capitol Police barricade. The Capitol Police would not have been on our side, as some were on the side of the white mob. Therefore, they would not have done what the nation saw on live TV or from

---

[457] Matt Byrne, "Police Response To Capitol Insurrection Proves Double Standard, Black Mainers Say," 7 January 2021. [On-Line]: Accessed On 7 January 2021; Accessed From Https://:Www.Olice Response To Capitol Insurrection Proves Double Standard, Black Mainers Say - Portland Press Herald; Internet.

recordings by news outlets and cell phone video of rioters, such as taking selfies with us, smiling in our faces, or moving barricades and allowing us onto the Capitol steps.

Furthermore, if Blacks would have somehow gotten past the barricades, we would have been shot in the back on the steps. If Blacks had somehow managed to make it up the steps to the doors of the Capitol building, we would have been gunned down at the door. If Blacks had broken windows and broken through doors, that would have been the last stand for black people on the Capitol grounds; we would have been gunned down systemically and would have never been allowed to breach the Capitol building. Full stop![458] On the other hand, white people were treated with kid gloves, even though they proved they were violent and meant to leave their destruction mark. Not only was this white mob allowed to push their way into the building, but they were also allowed to ransack offices, steal what they wanted, damage furnishings, and march through the Capitol building proudly displaying a confederate flag.

News reports, since the seditious mob riot, stated that many of the insurrectionists were armed with weapons.[459] Why is it that when

---

458 Reuters, "How chaos at the Capitol exposed a double standard," 8 January 2020 [on-line]; accessed 8 January 2021; accessed from How chaos at the Capitol exposed a double standard (yahoo.com): Internet. At Black Lives Matter protesters in Washington in June, the National Guard was deployed along with a heavy police presence as Trump vowed to crack down on what he called lawlessness by "thugs." Police then fired smoke canisters, flashbang grenades and rubber bullets to drive peaceful protesters away from the White House, so that Trump could walk to a nearby church and be photographed holding a Bible. Nearly 300 were arrested that evening. Meanwhile 68 people were arrested in connection to Wednesday's stunning security breach, though officials say that number is expected to grow.

459 Molly Redden, "The Bloodshed Could Have Easily Been Worse': Rioters Came to Washington Heavily Armed," [on-line]; accessed on 13 January 2021; accessed from https//www. The Bloodshed Could Have Easily Been Worse': Rioters Came To Washington Heavily Armed | HuffPost; Internet. Court records show the mob at the U.S. Capitol brought assault rifles, Molotov cocktails, an ammunition cache and a plan for violence. The pro-Trump rioters brought handguns, pistols, assault rifles, and "a shit ton" of ammunition. One insurrectionist smuggled a handgun and an extra 12-round magazine onto the U.S. Capitol grounds. Another was arrested with a Smith & Wesson firearm in his pocket and had an assault rifle, a second handgun, ammunition and 11 Molotov cocktails in a truck he had parked around the corner.

black people take to the streets and peacefully protest, they cause law enforcement to come out in full force: to include, riot gear, tanks, and multiple agencies collaborating in a show of force. Just like when Black Lives Matter peacefully protested along the same street back in July 2020. Although the crowd was a fraction of the size of the white mob, and nobody from that group tried to break through a barricade, break windows, or beat Capitol Police with rods and an American flag. But yet, nearly 300 Black Lives Matter personnel were arrested on the spot in July.

In contrast, during the white mob riot, only about 60 personnel were arrested initially. Also, the Black Lives Matter personnel were not allowed to leave the scene; they were detained on the spot for a non-violent protest. For some strange reason, when law enforcement encounters white people in numbers breaking the law, they act powerless. Still, when black folk gathers together, there is always an overwhelming show of force to keep us in our place—meaning our subservient roles to whites. Furthermore, white mob rule is called patriotism, while blacks protesting for equality are labeled un-American and treasonous.[460]

As this white mob invaded the Capitol building, the congressional men and women, Senate and House of Representatives, barricaded themselves into places of shelter. As this horrific episode was unfolding, some of the most alarming photos that filled news channels saw the congressional men in women in the House chambers hiding behind furniture. At the same time, plain-clothed Capitol Police officers stood at the entrance door with their guns drawn. You could see one of the white men from Trump's mob looking through a broken window in the door that the mob had broken out. The Capitol Police officers inside the House chamber stated that if they had not barricaded the entrance door with furniture, the white mob would have certainly gained access to the House floor where congressional members and their staffs were

---

460   Ibid. Adding to the cruelty of it all, some observers have noted, is the Capitol building's history. It was built with help from enslaved Africans, whose blood and sweat later allowed the union to meet there and strategize its battle against pro-slavery Confederates. On Wednesday, images emerged showing custodial staffers of color in the Capitol sweeping up the shards of glass and trash left behind by the rioters.

located. This act of bravery more than likely saved the lives of the members of Congress and their staff, especially the Democrats, which Trump had told his followers for years, were traitors and enemies of America.

As the news continued to display the mayhem, a woman was trying to force her way into the Speaker's Lobby and was shot by Capitol Police.[461] The woman was ID's as Ashli Babbitt, a fourteen-year Air Force veteran.[462] What would cause someone to give fourteen years of her life defending the Constitution and give her life in an attempt to end the Constitution? A President likes Trump that only used his MAGA followers as pawns to advance his selfish agenda, at the cost of their freedom and lives.

As a result of following Trump's instructions, a Capitol Police office named Brian Sicknick died at the hands of the white mob. Sicknick suffered severe injuries during the violent siege of the Capitol, which was confirmed by three law enforcement sources and reported to ABC News.[463] What was normally a formality, the certifying of the electoral college votes from all 50 states by the Congress after an election, became a day of chaos, insurrection, and sedition, led by President Trump.

---

461   Nicholas Bogel-Burroughs and Mike Ives, "Woman who was killed during the attack was shote by the Capitol Police." *The New York Times*, 6 January 2021 [on-line]; accessed on 8 January 2021; accessed from; Internet. A woman who was fatally shot inside the Capitol after it was overrun by a pro-Trump mob was struck by gunfire from a Capitol Police officer, a police official said Wednesday night. Chief Robert J. Contee of the Metropolitan Police Department told reporters that the woman had been shot by a police officer on Wednesday afternoon as plainclothes police officers confronted the mob. She later died in a hospital, he said, and the shooting is being investigated. At least 14 Capitol Police officers were injured during the demonstrations on Wednesday, Chief Contee said, including two who were hospitalized.

462   Danielle Wallace, and Louis Casiano, "Capitol protests: Woman shot, killed I'd as Ashli Babbitt, Air Force veteran." [on-line]; accessed on 8 January 2021; accessed from; Internet. The woman fatally shot inside the U.S. Capitol Wednesday has been identified as Ashli Babbitt, a friend confirms to Fox News. Babbitt was a 14-year veteran who served four tours with the Air Force and resided in San Diego, according to media reports.

463   Jack Date, Mark Osborne, and Emily Shapiro, "Capitol Police officer dies form injuries suffered in riots, federal murder investigation opened," 8 January 2021 [on-line]; accessed on 8 January 2021; accessed from ; Internet.

As I stated, about six months before the MAGA mob descended on our nation's capital, there was a Black Lives Matter protest in Washington D.C. The scene was very different because there was an enormous law enforcement presence in riot gear to protect the White House and Capitol building from black people. However, with a much larger white Trump crowd, there was essentially no serious police presence. Four Trump supporters died, one from being shot by Capitol Police, as the crowd breached the Capital building, and the other three due to medical emergencies. The property was damaged, and items were stolen by Trump's angry mob, and someone in the mob crowd spread human feces on the wall inside the Capitol building.[464] As President Trump watched the horrific events play out on TV, he was pleased and motivated by his supporter's actions.[465] Following the insurrection by his supporters, the House of Representatives impeached Trump on 13 January for inciting the riot—using his own words and actions against him.

---

464   Chris Sommerfeldt, "Pro-Trump rioters smeared poop in U.S. Capitol hallways during belligerent attack," 7 January 2021. [on-line]; accessed on 13 January 2021; accessed from ; Internet. They took a dump on American democracy — literally. Some of the unhinged pro-Trump rioters who stormed the U.S. Capitol on Wednesday defecated inside the historic building and "tracked" their feces in several hallways, the Daily News has learned.

465   Andy Towle, "Trump Was 'Pleased' as Supporters Stormed U.S. Capitol with Lawmakers Inside, Called Off Rioters 'Reluctantly' — REPORT," 8 January 2021. [on-line]; accessed on 13 January 2021; accessed from ; Internet. As supporters stormed into the Capitol on Wednesday, Mr. Trump was initially pleased, officials said, and disregarded aides pleading with him to intercede. Unable to get through to him, Mark Meadows, his chief of staff, sought help from Ivanka Trump. Former Gov. Chris Christie of New Jersey, a longtime friend who has publicly criticized his efforts to invalidate the election results, tried to call Mr. Trump during the violence, but could not get through to him." In a video recorded backstage at Trump's rally ahead of the mob insurrection at the U.S. Capitol on Wednesday, Donald Trump Jr was seen gathered with his father and other members of the family praising the crowds that had arrived.

BIBLIOGRAPHY

Books

Ahmann, Matthew. *Race: Challenge to Religion*. Chicago: Henry Regnery Publishing Company, 1963.

Alexander, Michelle. *The New Jim Crow: Mass Incarceration in The Age of Colorblindness*. New York: The New Press, 2012.

Anders, Max, and Kenneth O. Gangel. *Holman New Testament Commentary on Acts*. Nashville: Broadman and Holman Publishers, 1998.

Aune, D.E. *Word Biblical Commentary: Revelation 1-5*, Vol. 52A. Dallas: Word, Incorporated, 1998.

Baker, Anni. *Life in the U.S. Armed Forces: Not Just Another Job*. Westport: Praeger Security International, 2008.

Barbour, Russell B. *Black, and White Together: Plain Talk for White Christians*. Philadelphia: United Church Press, 1967.

Battle, Michael. *The Black Church in America: African American Christian Spirituality*. Oxford: Blackwell Publishing, 2006.

Blauner, Robert. *Racial Oppression in America*. New York: Harper & Row Publishers, 1972.

Bonhoeffer, Dietrich. *Meditations on the Cross*. Louisville: Westminster John Knox Press, 1996.

_____. *Life Together: The Classic Example of Christian Community*. New York: Harper and Row Publishers, 1954.

Branch, Taylor. *Pillar of Fire: America in the King Years 1963-65*. New York: Touchtone Publishers, 1998.

Brauer, Jerald, and Martin E. Marty. *An African American Exodus: Chicago Studies in the History of American Religion*. New York: Carlson Publishing, 1991.

Bright, John. *A History of Israel*, Third Edition. Philadelphia: Westminster Press, 1972.

Bromley, David G., and Charles F. Longino, Jr. *White Racism and Black Americans*. Cambridge: Schenkman Publishing Company, Inc., 1972.

Burrell, Tom. *Brainwashed: Challenging the Myth of Black Inferiority*. New York: Smiley Books, 2010.

Campbell, Don, Wendell Johnston, John Walvoord, and John Witmer, *The Theological Workbook: The 200 Most Important Theological Terms and Their Relevance for Today*. Nashville: Word Publishing, 2000.

Campolo, Tony. *Is Jesus a Republican or a Democrat: And 14 Other Polarizing Issues?* Dallas: Word Publishing, 1995.

Carson, D.A., Douglas J. Moo, and Leon Morris, *An Introduction to The New Testament*. Grand Rapids: Zondervan Publishing House, 1992.

Chafer, Lewis Sperry and John F. Walvoord, *Major Bible Themes: 52 Vital Doctrines of The Scripture Simplified and Explained*. Grand Rapids: Zondervan Publishing, 1953.

Conde-Frazier, Elizabeth, S. Steve Kang, and Gary A. Parrett. *A Many Colored Kingdom: Multicultural Dynamic for Spiritual Formation*. Grand Rapids: Baker Academic, 2004.

Cone, James H. and Gayraud S. Wilmore. *Black Theology: A Documented History*, Volume One: 1966-1979, Maryknoll: Orbis Books, 1993.

Cone, James H., and Gayraud S. Wilmore. *Black Theology: A Documented History*, Volume Two: 1988-1992. Maryknoll, NY: Orbis Books, 1993.

Copeland, E. Luther. *The Southern Baptist Convention and the Judgment of History: The Taint of an Original Sin*. Lanham, MD: University Press of America, 1995.

Cornett, Daryl C. *Christian America?: Perspectives on Our Religious Heritage*. Nashville: B&H Publishing Group, 2011.

Culver, Dwight W. *Negro Segregation in the Methodist Church*. New Haven, CT: Yale University Press, 1953.

Davies, Alfred T. *The Pulpit Speaks on Race*. New York: Abingdon Press, 1956.

Davies, Susan E., and Sister Paul Teresa Hennessee. *Ending Racism in the Church*. Cleveland: United Church Press, 1998.

Davis, James H., and Woodie W. White. *Racial Transition in the Church*. Nashville: Abingdon, 1980.

Delgado, Richard and Jean Stefancic. *Critical Race Theory*, Third Ed. New York: New York University Press, 2017.

Demy, Timothy J., and Gary P. Steward. *Politics and Policy: A Christian Response, Crucial Considerations for Governing Life*. Grand Rapids: Kregel Publications, 2000.

Deymaz, Mark. *Building a Healthy Multi-Ethnic Church: Mandate, Commitments, and Practices of a Diverse Congregation*. San Francisco: Jossey-Bates Publishing, 2007.

DeYoung, Curtis Paul, Michael O. Emerson, George Yancey, and Karen Chai Kim. *United By Faith: The Multicultural Congregation as an Answer to the Problem of Race*. Oxford: Oxford University Press, 2003.

Dockery, David S., and Gregory Alan Thornbury, eds. *Shaping a Christian Worldview: The Foundation of Christian Higher Education*. Nashville: Broadman and Holman Publishers, 2000.

Dryden, Charles W. *A-Train: Memoirs of a Tuskegee Airman*. Tuscaloosa, AL: University of Alabama Press, 1997.

Dyson, Michael Eric. *Long Time Coming: Reckoning with Race in America*. New York: St Martin's Press, 2020.

_____. *Tears We Cannot Stop: A Sermon to White America*. New York: St. Martin's Press, 2017.

Easley, K.H. *Holman New Testament Commentary: Revelations*, Vol. 12. Nashville: Broadman & Holman Publishers, 1998.

Edgerton, Robert B. *Hidden Heroism: Black Soldiers in American Wars*. Boulder, CO: Westview Press, 2001.

Edward, Korie L. *The Elusive Dream; The Power of Race in Interracial Churches*. Oxford Press: 2008.

Edwards, Jefferson D. *Purging Racism from Christianity: Freedom and Purpose Through Identity*. Grand Rapids: Zondervan Publishing House, 1996.

Emerson, Michael O., and Christian Smith. *Divided by Faith: Evangelical Religion and the Race Problem in America*. Oxford: University Press, 2000.

Emerson, Michael O., and Rodney M. Woo. *People of the Dream: Multiracial Congregations in the United States*. Princeton, NJ: Princeton University Press, 2006.

Evans, Tony. *God's Glorious Church: The Mystery and Mission of the Body of Christ*. Chicago: Moody Publishers, 2003.

_____. *Oneness Embraced: A Fresh Look at Reconciliation, The Kingdom, and Justice*. Chicago: Moody Press, 2011.

_____. *The Kingdom Agenda: Life Under God*. Chicago: Moody Publishers, 2013.

_____. *Totally Saved: Understanding, Experiencing, and Enjoying the Greatness of Your Salvation*. Chicago: Moody Press, 2002.

_____. *What A Way to Live: Running All of Life by The Kingdom Agenda*. Nashville: Word Publishing, 2003. 1997.

_____. *What Matters Most: Four Absolute Necessities in Following Christ*. Mood Press, 1994.

Fields, W. C. Galatians. In H. F. Paschall & H. H. Hobbs (Eds.), *The Teacher's Bible Commentary*, 1972.

Floyd-Thomas, Stacey, Juan Floyd-Thomas, Carol B. Duncan, Stephen G. Ray Jr., and Nancy Lynne Westfield. *Black Church Studies: An Introduction*. Nashville: Abingdon Press, 2007.

Foster, Charles R. *Leadership in Multicultural Congregations: Embracing Diversity*. Herndon, VA: Alban Institute Publication, 1997.

George, T. Galatians (Vol. 30). Nashville: Broadman & Holman Publishers, 1994.

Gonzalez, Justo L. *The History of Christianity: The Early Church to the Dawn of the Reformation, Vol. 1*. San Francisco: Harper Publishers, 1984.

_____. *The History of Christianity: The Reformation to the Present Day, Vol. 2*. San Francisco: Harper Publishers, 1985.

Griffin, John Howard. *The Church and the Black Man*. Dayton, OH: Pflaum Press, 1969.

Groh, John E. *Facilitators of the Free Exercise of Religion: Air Force Chaplains, 1981-1990*. Vol. 5. Washington D.C.: Office of the Chief of Chaplains, USAF, 1991.

Gushee, David P., and Walter C. Jackson. *Preparing for Christian Ministry: An Evangelical Approach*. Wheaton: Victor Books, 1996.

Hacker, Andrew. *Two Nations: Black and White, Separate, Hostile, Unequal*. New York: Scribner Publishing, 1992.

Hagood, L. M. *The Colored Man in the Methodist Episcopal Church*. New York: Books for Libraries Press, 1971.

Hammett. John S. *Biblical Foundations for Baptist Churches: A Contemporary Ecclesiology*. Grand Rapids: Kregel Publications, 2005.

Hanson, K. C., and Douglas E. Oakman. *Palestine in the time of Jesus: Social Structures and Social Conflicts*. Minneapolis: Fortress Press, 1998.

Haselden, Kyle. *Mandate for White Christians*. Richmond, KY: John Knox Press,1966.

Haslam, David. *Race for the Millennium: A Challenge to Church and Society*. London: Church House Publishing, 1996.

Hatch, Nathan O. *The Democratization of American Christianity*. New Haven: Yale University Press, 1989.

Hayes, Daniel J. *From Every People and Nation: A Biblical Theology of Race*. Downers Grove, IL: InterVarsity Press, 2003.

Henderson, David W. *Cultural Shift: Communicating God's Truth to Our Changing World*. Grand Rapids: Baker Books, 1998.

Holtrop, Donald. *A Reformed Journal Monograph: Notes on Christian Racism*. Grand Rapids: William B. Eerdmans Publishing Co., 1969.

Homan, Lynn M., and Thomas Reilly. *Images of America: The Tuskegee Airman*. Chicago: Arcadia Publishing, 1998.

Hood, Robert E. *Begrimed and Black: Christian Traditions on Blacks and Blackness*. Minneapolis: Fortress Press, 1994.

Horton, Michael. *Christless Christianity: The Alternative Gospel of the American Church*. Grand Rapids: Baker Books, 2008.

Hunter, George G., III. *How to Reach Secular People*. Nashville: Abingdon Press, 1992.

Jacobs, Harriet. *Incidents in the Life of a Slave Girl*. Great Britain: Coda Books: 2012.

Jones, William R. *Is God a White Racist?: A Preamble to Black Theology*. New York: Garden City Press, 1973.

Kelsey, George D. *Racism and the Christian Understanding of Man*. New York: Charles Scribner's Sons, 1965.

Krndi, Ibram X. *Stamped From The Beginning: The Definitive History of Racist Ideas in America*. New York: Bold Type Books, 2016.

Kimball, Dan. *The Emerging Church: Vintage Christianity for New Generations*. Grand Rapids: Zondervan, 2003.

_____. *They Like Jesus but Not the Church: Insights from Emerging Generations*. Grand Rapids: Zondervan, 2007.

King, Martin Luther, Jr., *Where Do We Go From Here?: Chaos or Community?* New York: Harper and Row, 1967.

Kinnaman, David. Unchristian: What A New Generation Really Thinks About Christianity…And Why it Matters. Grand Rapids: Baker Books, 2007.

Kitagawa, Daisuke. *Race Relations and Christian Mission*. New York: Friendship Press, 1964.

Laing, John D. *In Jesus' Name: Evangelicals and Military Chaplaincy*. Eugene, OR: Resources Publications, 2010.

Lasor, William Sanford, David Allan Hubbard, Frederic William Bush. Old Testament Survey: The Message, Form, and Background of the Old Testament, 2nd Ed. Grand Rapids: William B. Eerdmans Publishing Company, 1996.

Leonard, Bill J. *Community in Diversity: A History of Walnut Street Baptist Church 1815-1990*. Louisville: Simons-Neely Publishing Co., 1990.

Lincoln, Eric C., and Lawrence H. Mamiya. *The Black Church in The African American Experience*. Durham: Duke University Press, 1990.

Lingenfelter, Sherwood G., and Marvin K. Mayers. *Ministering Cross-Culturally: An Incarnational Model for Personal Relationships*. Grand Rapids: Baker Academic, 1986.

Lloyd-Jones, Martyn D. *Revival*. Wheaton: Crossway Books.1987.

Luis, C. C. *The* Joyful Christian. New York: Macmillan Publishing Co., Inc., 1977.

Malphurs, Aubrey. *A New Kind of Church: Understanding Models of Ministry for the 21st Century.* Grand Rapids: Baker Books, 2007.

Mansfield, Stephen. *The Faith of the American Soldier.* New York: Penguin Group Publishing, 2005.

Manis, Andrew M. *Southern Civil Religions in Conflict: Black and White and Civil Rights, 1947-1957.* Athens: The University of Georgia Press, 1987.

Massey, Douglas S., and Nancy A. Denton. *American Apartheid: Segregation and the Making of the Underclass.* Cambridge: Harvard University Press, 1993.

Maston, T. B. *The Bible and Race: A Careful Examination of Biblical Teachings on Human Relations.* Nashville: Broadway Press, 1959.

Mathews, Tony. *There's More Than One Color in the Pew: Handbook for Multicultural, Multiracial Churches.* Macon: Smyth & Helwys Publishing, 2003.

Mathisen, Robert R. *Critical Issues in American Religious History.* Waco: Baylor University Press, 2000.

_____. *"Of One": A Study of Christian Principles and Race Relations.* Atlanta: Home Missions Board, Southern Baptist Convention, 1946.

McCall, Emmanuel L. *When All God's Children Get Together: A Memoir of Race and Baptists.* Macon, GA: Mercer University Press, 2007.

McNeal, Reggie. *The Present Future: Six Tough Questions for the Church.* San Francisco: Jossey-Bass Publications, 2003.

Metzger, Paul Louis. *Consuming Jesus: Beyond Race and Class Divisions in A Consumer Church.* Grand Rapids: William B, Eerdmans Publishing Company, 2007.

Mitchell, Henry H. *Black Church: The Long-Hidden Realities of the First Beginnings.* William B. Grand Rapids: Eerdmans Publishing Company, 2004.

Moskos, Charles C., John Allen Williams, and David R. Segal. *The Postmodern Military: Armed Forces After the Cold War.* New York: Oxford University Press, 2000.

Neibuhr, Richard H. *Christ & Culture.* San Francisco: Harper Collins Publishers, 1951.

Nelson, William Stuart. *The Christian Way in Race Relations.* New York: Books for Library Press, 1948.

Newman, Mark. *Getting Right with God: Southern Baptists and Desegregation, 1945-1995.* Tuscaloosa: The University of Alabama Press, 2001.

Nickelson, Ronald L. *History of the United States Air Force Chaplain Service, 1991-2000.* Vol. 6. Washington D.C.: Office of the Chief of Chaplains, USAF, 2007.

Noll, Mark A. *The History of Christianity In the United States and Canada.* Colorado Springs: William B. Eerdmans Publishing Company, 1992.

Noll, Mark A., Nathan O. Hatch, George M. Marsden. *The Search for Christian America.* Colorado Springs: Helmers & Howard Publishing, 1989.

Obama, Barack (President). *A Promised Land.* New York: Crown Publishing, 2020.

Oglesby, E. Hammond. *O Lord, Move this Mountain: Racism and Christian Ethics*. St. Louis: Chalice Press, 1998.

Oldham, J. H. *Christianity, and the Race Problem*. London: Student Christian Movement, 1925.

Osborne, William A. *The Segregated Covenant: Race Relations and American Catholics*. New York: Herder and Herder, 1967.

Patterson, Paige. *The New American Commentary: An Exegetical and Theological Exposition of Holy Scripture*, Vol. 39. Nashville: B&H Publishing Group, 2012.

Peart, Norman Anthony. *Separate No More: Understanding and Developing Racial Reconciliation in Your Church*. Grand Rapids: Baker Books, 2000.

Perkins, Spencer, and Chris Rice. *More Than Equals: Racial Healing for the Sake of the Gospel*. Downers Grove: IVP Books, 2000.

Piper, John. *Bloodlines: Race, Cross, And the Christian*. Wheaton: Crossway, 2011.

_____. Future Grace*: The Purifying Power of the Promises of God*. Colorado Springs: Multnomah Books, 2013.

Powell, Paul W. *The Church Today*. Dallas: Annuity Board of the Southern Baptist Convention: Crossway, 1997.

Reed, Gerald. *C.S. Lewis and the Bright Shadow of Holiness*. Kansas City: Beacon Hill Press of Kansas, 1999.

Reid, Daniel G., Robert D. Linder, Bruce L. Shelley, and Harry S. Scott. *Dictionary of Christianity in America: A Comprehensive Resource on the Religious Impulse that Shaped a Continent*. Downers Grove: InterVarsity Press, 1990.

Reist, Benjamin A. *Theology in Red, White, and Black*. Philadelphia: Westminster Press, 1975.

Rhodes, Stephen A. *Where the Nations Meet: The Church in a Multicultural World*. Downers Grove, IL: InterVarsity Press, 1998.

Richardson, Harry V. *Dark Salvation: The Story of Methodism as It Developed Among Blacks in America*. New York: Anchor Press, 1976.

Ridley, Charles R. *Overcoming Unintentional Racism in Counseling and Therapy*. London: Sage Publications, 1995.

Roberts, Deotis J. Bonhoeffer & King: *Speaking Truth to Power*. Louisville: Westminster John Knox Press, 2005.

Rose, Benjamin Lacy. *Racial Segregation in the Church*. Richmond, VA: Outlook Publishers, 1957.

Rothstein, Richard. The Color of Law: A Forgotten History of How Our Government Segregated America. New York: Liveright Publishing Corporation, 2017.

Salley, Columbus, and Ronald Behm. *What Color Is Your God?: Black Consciousness & the Christian Faith*. Downers Grove, IL: InterVarsity Press, 1981.

_____. *Your God Is Too White*. Downers Grove, IL: InterVarsity Press, 1970.

Sansbury, Kenneth Cyril. *Combating Racism*. Great Britain: British Council of Churches, 1975.

Schneller, Robert J. Jr. *Blue & Gold, and Black: Racial Integration of the U.S. Naval Academy*. College Station: Texas A & M University Press, 2008.

Schreiner, Thomas R. *Paul Apostle of God's Glory: A Pauline Theology*. Downers Grove, IL: InterVarsity Press, 2001.

Simms, James M. *First Colored Baptist Church in North America*. New York: Negro Universities Press, 1788.

Smith, David L. *All God's People: A Theology of the Church*. Bridge Port: Bridge Port Publisher, 1996.

Smith, R. Scott. *Truth and the New Kind of Christian: The Emerging Effects of Postmodernism in the Church*. Wheaton: Crossway Books, 2005.

Soeters, Joseph, and Jan Van Der Meulen. *Cultural Diversity in the Armed Forces*. New York: Routledge Press, 2007.

Sowell, Thomas. *Black Rednecks and White Liberals*. San Francisco: Encounter Books, 2005.

Swain, Carol M. *The New White Nationalism in America: Its Challenge to Integration*. Cambridge: University Press, 2002.

Taliaferro, Charles C. *Praying with C.S. Lewis*. Winona: Saint Mary's Press, Christian Brothers Publications, 1998.

Thompson, Oscar W. Jr., and Carol Thompson. *Concentric Circles of Concern: From Self to Others Through Life-Style Evangelism*, Nashville: Broadman Press, 1981.

Tisby, Jemar. *The Color of Compromise: The Truth About the American Church's Complicity in Racism*. Grand Rapids: Zondervan, 2011.

Toussaint, Stanley D. *Behold the King: A Study of Matthew*. Kregel Academic & Professional Publishing,1980

Trull, Joe E. *Walking in the Way: An Introduction to Christian Ethics*. Nashville: Broadman & Holman Publishers, 1997.

Unander, Dave. *Shattering the Myth of Race: Genetic Realities and Biblical Truths*. Valley Forge, PA: Judson Press, 2000.

Vogel, Joseph M., and John H. Fish III. *Understanding the Church: The Biblical Ideal for the 21st Century*. Neptune: Loizeaux Publishers, 1999.

Webb, George W. *Today's Church: A Community of Exiles & Pilgrims*. Nashville: Abingdon Press, 1979.

Webster, John. *Barth: Second Edition*. New York: Continuum Publishers, 2000.

Wiersbe, W. W. Wiersbe's Expository Outlines on the New Testament, 1992.

Wilkerson, Isabel. *Caste: The Origins of Our Discontent*. New York: Random House, 2020.

Wells, David F. *Above All Earthly Pow'rs: Christ in a Postmodern World*. Grand Rapids: William B. Eerdmans Publishing Co., 2005.

Williams, Jarvis J. *One New Man: The Cross and Racial Reconciliation in Pauline Theology*, Nashville: B & H Academic, 2010.

Williams, Mary E. *Interracial America: Opposing Viewpoints*. San Diego: Greenhaven Press, Inc., 2001.

Williams, Michael E., Sr., and Walter B. Shurden. *Turning Point in Baptist History: A Festschrift in Honor of Harry Leon McBeth*. Macon, GA: Mercer University Press, 2008.

Williams, Robin M. *Strangers Next Door: Ethnic Relations in American Communities*. Englewood Cliffs: Prentice-Hall Publisher, Inc., 1964.

Woo, Rodney M. *The Color of Church: A Biblical and Practical Paradigm for Multiracial Churches*. Nashville: B & H Academic, 2009.

Woodley, Randy. *Living in Color: Embracing God's Passion for Ethnic Diversity*.
Downers Grove, IL: InterVarsity Press, 2001.

Wright, Nathan, Jr., *Let's Face Racism: A Youth Forum Book*. New York: Thomas Nelson Inc., 1970.

Yancey, George. *Beyond Racial Gridlock: Embracing Mutual Responsibility*. Downers Grove, IL: InterVarsity Press, 2006.

_____. *One Body One Spirit: Principles of Successful Multiracial Churches*. Downers Grove, IL: InterVarsity Press, 2003.

Dissertations

Goodson, James L. "An Abbreviated History of Racial Prejudice in the Attitudes and Practices of Christians." Ph.D. diss., Southwestern Baptist Theological Seminary, 1967.

Johnston, Mark. "Behind the Wire: The Chaplain as a Catalyst for Spiritual and Social Change Within the Military Culture: A Multidimensional Model with Selected Programs for Ministry." Ph.D. diss., Regent University, 2002.

McGinnis, Timothy S. "The Controversy and Division of First Baptist Church, Birmingham, Alabama, 1968-1970." Ph.D. diss., Southwestern Baptist Theological Seminary, 1990.

Porter, Lee. "Southern Baptist and Race Relations 1948-1963." Ph.D. diss., Southern Baptist Theological Seminary, 1965.

Powell, Nathaniel T. "Implementing the USAF's Chaplaincy Model of Racial Diversity in Agape Community Fellowship Church" D-Min. diss. Southwestern Baptist Theological Seminary, 2013

Richards, Roger Charles. "Actions and Attitudes of Southern Baptists Toward Blacks." *1845-1895*. Ph.D. Diss., Florida State University, 2008.

Zemans, Daniel S. "One Baptism, One Faith; Two Races, Two Denominations: Race and the Southern Baptist and National Baptist Conventions." Ph.D. Diss., Macalester College, 1998.

Internet

ABC News. "Mother Not Charged In Hot Car Death." January 8, 2009 [online]; accessed 29 August 2020; Available From Https://Abcnews.Go.Com/Gma/Story?Id=3570651&Page=1. Internet.

Adams, Cydney. CBS News. "Rodney King beating caught on video." (3 March 2016) [online]; accessed on 5 September 2020; available from https://www.cbsnews.com/news/march-3rd-1991-rodney-king-lapd-beating-caught-on-video/. Internet

A&E Television Network. "Dred Scott Case." (27 October 2009). [online]; accessed on 5 September 2020; available from https://www.history.com/topics/black-history/dred-scott-case. Internet.

American Battlefield Trust. How so many soldiers died in the Civil War. [online]; accessed on 21 September 2020; available from https://www.battlefields.org/learn/articles/civil-war-facts#/. Internet.

Anderson, Ken. "Roman and America – Comparing to the Ancient Roman Empire" (5 May 2020) [online]; accessed on 17 September 2020; available from https://probe.org/rome-and-america/. Internet.

Andrews, William L. Harriet A. Jacob (Harriet Ann). 1813-1897. [online]; accessed on 25 September 2020; available from https://docsouth.unc.edu/fpn/jacobs/bio.html. Internet.

Balko, Radley. *"There's overwhelming evidence that the criminal justice system is racist. Here's proof."* The Washington Post. (10 June 2020) [online];. Accessed 5 September 2020; available from https://www.washingtonpost.com/graphics/2020/opinions/systemic-racism-police-evidence-criminal-justice-system/. Internet.

Beset, James D. George Mason, the Framer Who Refused to Sign the Constitution. (20 April 2011). [online]; accessed on 5 September 2020; available from http://www.whatwouldthefoundersthink.com/george-mason-the-framer-who-refused-to-sign-the-constitution. Internet.

Blair, Leonardo, "SBC wants to scrap resolution on critical race theory, Pastor Dwight McKissic says," 17 December 2020. [online]; accessed on 31 December 2020; accessed from https://www.christianpost.com.news/SBC wants to scrap CRT resolution, Dwight McKissic says - The Christian Post; Internet.

Blake, John. "Black in America 2: Why Do Americans Prefer Their Sundays Segregated?" (August 8, 2004) [online]; accessed 9 July 2009; available from http: www.cnn.com/2008/LIVING/wayoflife/08/04/segregated; Internet.

Bodenheimer, Rebecca, "What is Critical Race Theory? Definition, Principles, and Applications: A Challenge to the rhetoric of color-blindness," 6 May 2019. [online]; accessed on 30 December 2020; accessed from ;Internet.

Bradford, Thomas. "Why were African people taken as slaves and thought of as savages in early American?" (2 February 2020). [online]; accessed on 15 September 2020; available from https://www.quora.com/Why-were-African-people-taken-as-slaves-and-thought-of-as-savages-in-early-America. Internet.

Brew-Hammond, Nana Ekua. The Root. *Blacks Were Christians Before Slavery and Before White-Jesus Pieces* (29 March 2013). [online]; accessed on 5 September 2020; available from https://www.theroot.com/blacks-were-christians-before-slavery-and-before-white-1790895789. Internet.

Bright, Stephen, "Unequal Justice Under the Law," *CBS News*, (13 August 2017) [online]; accessed 5 September 2020; available from https://www.cbsnews.com/news/unequal-justice-under-the-law/; Internet.

Britannica, "Black Code," (23 October 2020) [online]; accessed on 23 October 2020; accessed from https://www.britannica.com/topic/black-code; Internet.

_____, "New Deal: United States History," (10 September 2020) [online]; accessed on 1 September 2020; available from https://www.britannica.com/event/New-Deal; Internet.

Brooks, David. The Atlantic. The Culture of Policing in Broken. (16 June 2020). [online]; accessed on 5 September 2020; available from https://www.msn.com/en-ph/news/opinion/the-culture-of-policing-is-broken/ar-BB15ADY7. Internet.

Brown, Stacey M. "The Major Role The Catholic Church played in Slavery," *Amsterdam News*, (18 September 2018) [online]; accessed on 7 October 2020; available from http://amsterdamnews.com/news/2018/sep/18/major-role-catholic-church-played-slavery/; Internet.

Brown, Tracy. Los Angeles Times. "'Cops' canceled amid nationwide protest against police brutality." (8 June 2020). [online]; accessed on 5 September 2020; available from. https://www.latimes.com/entertainment-arts/tv/story/2020-06-09/cops-canceled-paramount-protests-police-violence; Internet

Burton, Darryl. Other Missouri Exonerations with Jailhouse Informants, *The National Registry of Exonerations*, 12 June 2012 [online]; accessed 5 September 2020; available from http://www.law.umich.edu/special/exoneration/Pages/casedetail.aspx?caseid=3076; Internet.

Bureau of Justice Statistics, *Prison Population Counts*. [online]; accessed 20 August 2012; available from http://bjs.ojp.usdoj.gov/index.cfm?ty=tp&tid=131; Internet.

Burke, Minyvonne. "Breonna Taylor police shooting: What we know about the Kentucky woman's death" *NBC News* (May 15, 2020) [online]; accessed 28 August 2020; available from https://www.nbcnews.com/news/us-news/breonna-taylor-police-shooting-what-we-know-about-kentucky-woman-n1207841. Internet.

Burton, Darryl. The National Registry of Exonerations. (June 12, 2012) [online]; accessed 5 September 2020; available from http://www.law.umich.edu/special/exoneration/Pages/casedetail.aspx?caseid=3076. Internet.

Cambridge Dictionary. [online]; Accessed on 21 September 2020; available from https://dictionary.cambridge.org/dictionary/english/accountability. Internet.

Carissimo, Justine. "Woman Killed in Charlottesville, Virginia car attack identified." (13 August 2017). [online] accessed on 21 September 2020; available from https://www.cbsnews.com/news/heather-heyer-charlottesville-virginia-car-attack/. Internet.

Carrega, Christina and Delano Massey, CNN. Weeping resounded from the room where Breonna Taylor's mother learned the grand jury's decision. (24 September 2020). [online]; accessed 28 August 2020 available from https://www.cnn.com/2020/09/24/us/breonna-taylor-grand-jury-decision-reaction-tamika-palmer/index.html. Internet.

Cassidy, Captain, "The SBC's Battle Royale Over Critical Race Theory (CRT)," [online]; accessed on 31 December 2020; accessed from https//www.the SBC's Battle Royale Over Critical Race Theory (CRT) | Roll to Disbelieve: The Fight for the Emperor's Scepter (patheos.com); Internet.

Chinn, Derek Doh-lun. "The Challenges of Creating a Multiracial Church from Single Race Congregations" (2001) [online]; accessed 29 January 2010; available from http://rim.atla.com/scripts/starfinder.exe/2376/rimmarc.txt; Internet.

The Christian Post. "Southwestern Seminary Awards Long-Overdue Degree to African-American Alumnus: Recent decision by Southwestern Baptist Theological Seminary brings ultimate redemption to dark segregationist past." (15 December 2004) [online]; accessed on 16 December 2020; accessed from Southwestern Seminary Awards Long-Overdue Degree to African-American Alumnus - The Christian Post; Internet.

Christianity Today. Potter, Ronald C. "Was Slavery God's Will?" (May 2000) [online]; accessed 5 September 2020; available from https://www.christianitytoday.com/ct/2000/may22/29.80.html; Internet.

_____.Mark Galli, "So, What's an Evangelical?" (18 September 2020) [online]; accessed on 20 September 2020; available from ; Internet

Slavery and Remembrance. Transatlantic Slave Trade. [online]; accessed on 25 September 2020; available from http://slaveryandremembrance.org/articles/article/?id=A0002. Internet.

Coates, Ta-Nehisi. "Slavery Made America: The Case for Reparations," *The Atlantic* [online]; accessed 27 August 2020; available from https://www.theatlantic.com/business/archive/2014/06/slavery-made-america/373288; Internet.

Cole, Nicki Lisa, Ph.D. "Understanding and Defining White Privilege: The U.S. Hierarchy in the 21stf Century." [online]; accessed 29 August 2020 https://www.thoughtco.com/white-privilege-definition-3026087. Internet.

Connor, Ken. "Fanning the Flames of Racism" (July 19, 2008) [online]; accessed 29 November 2009; available from http://www.christianpost.com/article/20080719/; Internet.

Davis, Charles. Business Insider. Prosecutor announces homicide charges against Kyle Rittenhouse, the 17-year-old accused of shooting and killing 2 people at a Kenosha protest. [online]; accessed 28 August 2020 from https://www.yahoo.com/news/prosecutors-announce-homicide-charges-against-231210695.html. Internet.

Davis, Charles, "Prosecutor announce homicide charges against Kyle Rittenhouse, the 17-year-old accused of shooting and killing 2 people at a Kenosha protest" *Business Insider* (8 August 2020) [online]; accessed 28 August 2020 from https://www.msn.com/en-us/news/crime/prosecutors-announce-homicide-charges-against-kyle-rittenhouse-the-17-year-old-vigilante-who-shot-and-killed-2-people-at-a-kenosha-protest/ar-BB18rmSj; Internet.

Dayen, David. The American Prospect: Ideas, Politics, and Power. Trump's Impeachment and the Era of No Accountability (24 September 2020) [online]; Accessed on 21 September 2020; available from https://prospect.org/power/trump-impeachment-era-of-no-accountability/. Internet.

Dictionary.com. [online]; accessed on 21 September 2020; available from https://www.dictionary.com/browse/accountability. Internet.

Diouf, Sylviane. "Remembering the Women of Slavery," *New York Library* (27 March 2015) [online] accessed on 13 Nov 2020; accessed from https://www.nypl.org/blog/2015/03/27/remembering-women-slavery. Internet.

Easley, Timothy D. "Grand jury was never asked to mull homicide charged in Breonna Taylor case," *Politico*, 9 September 2020 [online]; accessed 5 October 2020; available from https://www.politico.com/

news/2020/09/29/kentucky-grand-jury-tapes-breonna-taylor-422864. Internet.

Ehrenreich, Barbara. Welfare: A White Secret. Time Magazine (June 24, 2001) [online]; accessed 5 September 2020; available from http://content.time.com/time/magazine/article/0,9171,156084,00.html. Internet.

Evans, Carter. CBS News. Alleged college resume of Lori Loughlin's daughters lists fake rowing achievements. (10 February 2020) [online]; accessed 19 August 2020; available from https://www.cbsnews.com/news/college-admissions-scandal-lori-loughlin-daughter-olivia-phony-rowing-achievements-resume/. Internet.

França, Valdir Xavier de. "The Challenges to the Church's Identity: A Cross-cultural Perspective from Matthew's Gospel." *Columbia Theological Seminary Journal* (2007) [online]; accessed 29 January 2010; available from http://rim.atla.com/; Internet.

Freeman, Jordan, and Justin Carissimo. "Police in Wisconsin shoot Black man in back multiple times, sparks protest." *CBS News*. (August 25, 2020) [online] accessed 27 August 2020 from https://www.cbsnews.com/news/jacob-blake-kenosha-shooting-wisconsin-police-black-man-protesters-gather; Internet.

Friedman, Zach. Forbes. *Lori Loughlin charged with Bribery, Faces 50 Years in Prison.* (October 2019). [online]; accessed 19 August 2020; available from https://www.forbes.com/sites/zackfriedman/2019/10/22/lori-loughlin-bribery-college-prison/#784ea7c8679e. Internet.

Freeman, Jordan, and Justin Carissimo. "Police in Wisconsin shoot Black man in back multiple times, sparks protest." *CBS News*. (August 25, 2020) [online] accessed 27 August 2020 from https://www.cbsnews.com/news/jacob-blake-kenosha-shooting-wisconsin-police-black-man-protesters-gather Internet.

Financial Samurai. The Wide Implications of the College Admissions Scandal. [online] accessed 19 August 2020; available from https://www.financialsamurai.com/the-wide-implications-of-the-college-admissions-bribery-scandal/. Internet.

Fox, Alex "Nearly 2,000 Black Americans Were Lynched During Reconstruction," Smithsonian Magazine. (18 June 2020) [online]; accessed on 25 November 2020; accessed from https://www.smithsonianmag,com/smart-news/nearly-2,000 Black-Americans-Were-Lynched During-Reconstruction-180975120; Internet.

Gallup Poll. "Race and Religion: Division Steeped in History" (August 10, 2004) [online]; accessed 2 July 2009; available from http:www.galloppoll.com/poll/12664; Internet.

_____. "Race and Religious Leadership" (March 9, 2004) [online]. Accessed 2 August 2009; available from http:www.galluppoll.com/poll/12718; Internet.

Gates, Henry Louis Jr. The Root. "Slavery by The Numbers. (February 10, 2014) [online]; accessed 1 September 2020. available from https://www.theroot.com/slavery-by-the-numbers-1790874492. Internet.

Gilbreath, Edward. "Race Isn't Supposed to Matter Anymore. Except When it Does" (April 22, 2009) [online]; accessed 29 November 2009; available from http://blog. sojo.net/2009/04/22/; Internet.

Glass, Andrew. Politico. "Truman ends racial segregation in armed forces." (July 26, 1948) [online]; accessed on 16 September 2020; available from https://www.politico.com/story/2018/07/26/this-day-in-politics-july-26-1948-735081. Internet.

Grimshaw, Mike. "Responding Not Believing: Political Theology and Post-Secular Society" (March 2009) [online]; accessed 29 January 2010; available from http:// firstsearch.oclc.org. Internet.

Grossie, William. "Postmodernism: What One Needs to Know" (March 1997) [online]; accessed 29 January 2010; available from http://firstsearch.oclc.org; Internet.

Haidari, Niloufar. Vice. "50 examples of white privilege to show family members who still don't get it." (June 9, 2020) [online]; accessed 29 august 2020; available from https://www.vice.com/en_uk/article/4ayw8j/white-privilege-examples. Internet.

Haag, Matthew. "*Cleveland Officer Who Killed Tamir Rice Is Hired by An Ohio Police Department.*" *New York Times*, (8 October 2018). [online]; accessed 28 August 2020; available from https://www.nytimes.com/2018/10/08/us/timothy-loehmann-tamir-rice-shooting.html. Internet.

Hill, Daniel. "Thoughts on Racial Reconciliation" (July 7, 2008) [online]; accessed 29 November 2009; available from http://www.churchsolutionsmag.com/articles/ thoughts-on-racial-reconciliation.html; Internet.

History Channel. "Black Civil War Soldiers," (7 June 2020) [online]; accessed on 31 October 2020 https://www.history.com/topics/american-civil-war/black-civil-war-soldiers. Internet.

_____. *Church of England*. [online]; accessed on 19 October 2020; available from https://www.history.com/topics/british-history/church-of-england/. Internet.

_____. Clark, Alexis. "How the History of Blackface Is Rooted in Racism. (15 February 2020). [online]; accessed on 16 September 2020; accessed from https://www.history.com/news/black-wall-street-tulsa-race-massacre. Internet.

_____. *Confederate States of America*. (21 August 2018) [online]; accessed on 16 October 2020; available from https://www.history.com/topics/american-civil-war/confederate-states-of-america. Internet.

_____. Hunter, Tera W. *"Enslaved Couples Faced Wrenching Separations, or Even Choosing Family Over Freedom."* (20 September 2019) [online]: accessed on 19 November 2020; accessed from https://www.history.com/news/african-american-slavery-marriage-family-separation; Internet.

_____. *Jim Crow Laws.* (19 August 2020) [online]; accessed on 21 September 2020; available from https://www.history.com/topics/early-20th-century-us/jim-crow-laws. Internet.

_____. "The Compromise of 1877," (27 November 2019) [online]; accessed on 13 November 2020; accessed from https://www.history.com/topics/us-presidents/compromise-of-1877; Internet.

_____. "Tulsa's Black Wall Street' Flourished as a Self-contained Hub in the early 1900s." (2 Jan 2020). [online]; accessed on 16 September 2020; accessed from https://www.history.com/news/black-wall-street-tulsa-race-massacre. Internet.

Hopfensperger, Jean, "Black pastor takes stand against Southern Baptist race statement," *Star Tribune*, (30 December 2020) [online]; accessed on 30 December 2020; accessed from ; Internet.

Jackson, David. Trump defends response to Charlottesville violence, says he put it 'perfectly' with both sides remark. CBS News (26 April 2019) [online]; accessed on 21 September 2020; available from https://www.usatoday.com/story/news/politics/2019/04/26/trump-says-both-sides-charlottesville-remark-said-perfectly/3586024002/. Internet.

Jackson, Fred, and Jody Brown. "Fewer Americans than Thought Going to Church, Says Study" (August 10, 2004) [online]; accessed 22 February 2010; available from http://www.crosswalk.com/1396537/; Internet.

Jewish Journal. "White Supremacy is Our Country's Original Sin." (16 August 2017) [online]. accessed on 5 September 2020; available from https://jewishjournal.com/commentary/opinion/223136/white-supremacy-is-our-countrys-original-sin/. Internet.

Jones, Riley. Complex. How Nike's "Just Do It" Slogan Turned the Brand into a Household Name. (17 August 2015) [online]. Accessed on 21 September 2020; available from https://www.complex.com/sneakers/2015/08/nike-just-do-it-history. Internet.

Justia, U.S. Supreme Court. 163 U.S. 537 (1896) Plessy Vs Fergusson [online]; accessed on 5 September 2020; Available From. Https://Supreme.Justia.Com/Cases/Federal/Us/163/537/. Internet.

Faith Karimi, "What critical race theory is – and isn't," (1 October 2020) [online]; accessed on 30 December 2020; accessed from https://www.cnn.com/2020/10/01/critical_race_theory_is_--_and_isn't_-_CNN; Internet.

King, Martin Luther. "The Struggle for Racial Justice" (January 27, 1965) [online]; accessed 2 March 2010; available from http//mlk-kpp01.standford.edu; Internet.

Kristian, Bonnie. Christianity Today. "Juneteenth: A Truer Independence Day." (18 June 2020). [online]; accessed on 5 September 2020; available from https://www.christianitytoday.com/ct/2020/june-web-only/juneteenth-truer-independence-day.html. Internet.

Kroll, Andy "The Plot Against America: The GOP Plan to Suppress the Vote and Sabotage the Election," *Rolling Stone*, (16 July 2020). [online]; accessed on 31 October 2020 https://www.rollingstone.com/politics/politics-features/trump-campaign-2020-voter-suppression-consent-decree-1028988/; Internet.

Lee, Alicia and Sara Sider. CNN. "99 years ago, today, America was shaken by one of its deadliest acts of racial violence." (June 1, 2020) [online]; accessed 29 August 2020; available from https://www.cnn.com/2020/06/01/us/tulsa-race-massacre-1921-99th-anniversary-trnd/index.html. Internet.

Lightman, Allan J. The Hill. "Who Rules America." (8 December 2014) [online]; accessed on 5 September 2020; available from https://thehill.com/blogs/pundits-blog/civil-rights/214857-who-rules-america. Internet.

Little, Becky. How the US Got So Many Confederate Monuments? (12 June 2020). [online]; accessed on 21 September 2020; available from https://www.history.com/news/how-the-u-s-got-so-many-confederate-monuments. Internet.

Loving v. Virginia (1967). "United States Supreme Court." [online]; accessed on 9 October 2020; available from https://caselaw.findlaw.com/us-supreme-court/388/1.html. Internet.

Lumenick, Lou. New York Post. "Why 'Birth of a Nation' is still the most racist movie ever." (7 February 2015). [online]; accessed on 23 September 2020; available from https://nypost.com/2015/02/07/why-birth-of-a-nation-is-still-the-most-controversial-movie-ever/. Internet.

Madani, Doha and David K. Li. "Lori Loughlin sentenced to 2 months, husband to 5 months, in college scam." *NBC News*, (21 August 2020) [online]; accessed 19 August 2020; available from https://www.nbcnews.com/news/us-news/lori-loughlin-s-husband-mossimo-giannulli-sentenced-5-months-college-n1237556; Internet.

Matthews, Dylan. "How today's protests compare to 1968, explained by a historian." (2 June 2020) [online]; accessed on 5 September 2020; available from https://www.vox.com/identities/2020/6/2/21277253/george-floyd-protest-1960s-civil-rights. Internet.

McKeeby, David. "End of U.S. Military Segregation Set Stage for Rights Movement: African Americans' Record of Military Service Linked to Equality Struggle" (8 February 2008) [online]; accessed 29 January 2010; available from http:// www.america.gov/st/diversity-english/2008/February/20080225120859liameruoy0. 9820215.html; Internet.

McMillon, Lynn. "Will Believers Bridge the Racial Divide?" [online]; accessed 29 November 2009; available from http://www.christianchronicle.org/article2158318; Internet.

Meyer, Holly. "Southern Baptists confront the church's history of racism and slaveholding. For some members, it's not enough." USA Today, (8 August 2020) [online]; accessed on 15 December 2020; accessed from Southern Baptists confront the church's history of racism and slaveholding. For some members, it's not enough. (msn.com); Internet.

Miller, Dave. "President Fred Luter," SBC Voices. [online]; accessed on 15 September 2012; available from http://sbcvoices.com/president-fred-luter; Internet.

Military.com. Memorial Day by the Numbers: Casualties of Every American War. [online]; accessed on 21 September 2020; available from https://www.military.com/memorial-day/how-many-us-militay-members-died-each-american-war.html. Internet.

Mills, David M. "What Would Jesus Deconstruct?: The Good News of Postmodernism for the Church." *Journal of the Evangelical Theological Society* (March 2008) [online]. Accessed 29 January 2010; available from http://firstsearch.oclc.org. Internet.

MLK at Western University Libraries. (8 June 2020) [online]; Accessed on 17 September 2020; available from https://libguides.wmich.edu/mlkatwmu/QandA.Internet.

Mohler, Albert R. "What is Truth? Truth and Contemporary Culture" (March 2005) [online]. Accessed 29 January 2010; available from http://firstsearch.oclc.org; Internet.

Murahashi, Kent. "A Church Planting Strategy for Reaching a Multi-racial Target Group in the Pacific Northwest." *Western Seminary* (2001) [online]. Accessed 29 January 2010; available from http://rim.atla.com/; Internet.

Nakao, Annie. *Her Tale Was Brutal, Sexual. No One Believed A Slave Woman Could Be So Literate. But Now Harriet Jacobs Has Reclaimed Her Name.* (23 June 2004). Accessed On 24 October 2020; Accessed From Https://Www.Sfgate.Com/Entertainment/Article/Her-Tale-Was-Brutal-Sexual-No-One-Believed-A-2747114.Php. Internet.

National Construction Center. The Reconstruction Amendments. [online]; accessed on 22 September 2020; available from https://constitutioncenter.org/learn/educational-resources/historical-documents/the-reconstruction-amendments. Internet.

National Geographic Resource Library. The Black Codes and Jim Crow Laws. [online]; Accessed On 21 September 2020; Available From https://www.Nationalgeographic.Org/Encyclopedia/Black-Codes-And-Jim-Crow-Laws/. Internet.

_____. The Founding Fathers. (24 January 2020) [online]; accessed on 9 September 2020; available from https://www.nationalgeographic.org/article/founding-fathers/. Internet.

_____. The Ku Klux Klan. [online]; accessed on 21 September 2020; available from https://www.nationalgeographic.org/article/ku-klux-klan/. Internet.

National Review. Robert Verbruggen. "Does Kyle Rittenhouse Have a Self-defense Claim?" (August 28, 2020) [online]; accessed 28

August 2020 from https://www.nationalreview.com/2020/08/does-kyle-rittenhouse-have-a-self-defense-claim. Internet.

NBC News. *Shanesha Taylor, Phoenix Mom Who Left Kids in Hot Car, Pleads Guilty to Child Abuse.* (March 16, 2015) [online]; Accessed 29 August 2020; available from https://www.nbcnews.com/news/us-news/shanesha-taylor-mom-who-left-kids-car-pleads-guilty-child-n324476. Internet.

Neary, Lynn. "*Victim Of Brock Turner Sexual Assault Reveals Her Identity,*" NPR, 4 September 2019 [online]; accessed 6 October 2020; available from https://www.npr.org/2019/09/04/757626939/victim-of-brock-turner-sexual-assault-reveals-her-identity; Internet.

New York Post. Jorge Fitz-Gibbon. "Here's everything we know about the death of George Floyd" (May 28, 2020) [online]; accessed 28 August 2020; available from https://nypost.com/2020/05/28/everything-we-know-about-the-death-of-george-floyd. Internet.

New York Times. Goldberg, Michelle. "Trump's Re-election Message is White Grievance: Republicans in D.C. Just Pretend Not To See It." (2 July 2020) [online]; accessed on 20 November 2020; accessed from https://www.opinion/trump's-re-election-message-is-white grievance - The New York Times (nytimes.com); Internet.

Nix, Elizabeth. Tuskegee Experiment: The Infamous Syphilis Study. (16 May 2017) [online]; accessed on 21 September 2020; available from https://www.history.com/news/the-infamous-40-year-tuskegee-study. Internet.

NBC News. "GOP Top Goal: Make Obama a 1-Term President" (4 November 2010) [online]; accessed on 28 November 2020; accessed from http//www.GOP leader's top goal: Make Obama 1-term president (nbcnews.com); Internet.

NPR. 8 February 2020. "100 Years Later, What's the Legacy of 'Birth of a Nation." [online]; accessed on 23 September 2020; available from https://www.npr.org/sections/codeswitch/2015/02/08/383279630/100-years-later-whats-the-legacy-of-birth-of-a-nation. Internet.

Nohstine, Ray. The Christian Post. *Trump: 'Why do I have to repent or ask for forgiveness if I am not making mistakes?'* [online]; Accessed on 15 October 2020; available from https://www.christianpost.com/news/trump-why-do-i-have-to-repent-or-ask-for-forgiveness-if-i-am-not-making-mistakes-video.html. Internet.

Norman, Christopher L. "Becoming a Church for All People: How to Become a Multicultural Church." *Trinity Evangelical Divinity School* (2007) [online]; accessed 29 January 2010; available from http://rim.atla.com/; Internet.

Nunn, Nunn, "Understanding the long-run effects of Africa's slave trades." *VoxEU* (February 2017) [online]; accessed 1 September 2020; available from https://voxeu.org/article/understanding-long-run-effects-africa-s-slave-trades; Internet.

Ortega, Ralph R. "Police apologize to black pastor who was arrested after he called cops because he was being beaten and abused by white family." (15 June 2020) [online]; Accessed on 12 October 2020; available from https://www.dailymail.co.uk/news/article-8420801/Black-pastor-called-cops-beaten-white-family-arrested-pulling-gun.html. Internet.

Ortiz, Erik. NBC News. Racial violence and a pandemic: How the Red Summer of 1919 relates to 2020. (21 June 2020) [online]; accessed on 21 September 2020; available from https://www.nbcnews.com/news/us-news/racial-violence-pandemic-how-red-summer-1919-relates-2020-n1231499. Internet.

Palmer, Brian and Seth Freed Wessler. Smithsonian Magazine. The Cost of the Confederacy. (1 December 2020) [online]; accessed on 21 September 2020; available from https://www.smithsonianmag.com/history/costs-confederacy-special-report-180970731/. Internet.

Panton, Alan. "The Church Amid Racial Tensions" (March 31, 1954) [online]; accessed 28 November 2009; available from http://www.religion-online.org/showarticle.asp? title=474; Internet.

Persaud, Winston D. "Believing in Jesus Christ in this Postmodern World" (Summer 2007) [online]; accessed 29 January 2010; available from http://firstsearch.oclc. org; Internet.

Pina, Michael. "Doc Rivers Has Been Fighting Racism All His Life." (26 August 2020). [online]; accessed on 13 October 2020; Available from Https://Www.Yahoo.Com/Lifestyle/Doc-Rivers-Fighting-Racism-Life-153313551.Html. Internet.

Polan, Emma. "'Cops' Cancelled: TV Show Has Been Accused of Racism Ever Since It First Aired 31 Years Ago, "Newsweek, 10 June 2020 [online]; accessed on 3 October 2020; available from https://www.newsweek.com/cops-cancelled-racism-criticism-paramount-1509985; Internet.

Politico. Martin, "Palin Electrifies Conservative Base." (31 August 2008) [online]; accessed on 30 November 2020; accessed from //www. Palin electrifies conservative base - POLITICOBack ButtonSearch IconFilter Icon; Internet.

Preston, Tony. "An Inquiry into the Validity of the Niche Church: An Acceptable Effort to Fulfill the Great Commission or an Ill-informed Stratagem That Threatens the Unity of the Spirit and the Witness of the Body of Christ?" *Midwestern Baptist Theological Seminary* (Fall 2001) [online]; accessed 8 February 2012; available from http://firstsearch. oclc. org; Internet.

Prentiss, Craig R. "Coloring Jesus: Racial Calculus and the Search for Identity in Twentieth-century America" (Spring 2009) [online]; accessed 28 January 2010; available from http://firstsearch.oclc.org; Internet.

"Racial Reconciliation and the Word of God" [online]; accessed 28 November 2009; available at http://www.christianidentitychurch.net/racial_reconciliation; Internet.

Ramsey, Diana L. "History & Archaeology: Colonial Era, 1733-1775," 10 January 2014 [online]; accessed on 13 November 2020; accessed from https://www.georgiaencyclopedia.org/articles/history-archaeology/slave-women; Internet.

Ray, Michael. "Tuskegee Airmen: United States Military Unit." [online]; accessed on 13 October 2020; available from https://www.britannica.com/topic/Tuskegee-Airmen. Internet.

Ray, Zola. "This is the toy that got Tamir Rice Killed 3 Years Ago." *Newsweek* (November 11, 2017) [online]; accessed 29 August 2020; from https://www.newsweek.com/tamir-rice-police-brutality-toy-gun-720120. Internet.

Roberto, Melissa. Fox News. "Lori Loughlin's request to serve prison sentence at California's Victorville signed off by judge: court docs." (18 August 2020) [online]; accessed 19 August 2020; available from https://www.foxnews.com/entertainment/lori-loughlin-prison-sentence-california-victorville-signed-judge-court-docs. Internet.

Rodney King Biography. (2 April 2014) [online]; accessed on 21 September 2020 from https://www.biography.com/crime-figure/rodney-king. Internet.

Ronald Reagan Blog. (1 May 2020). [online]; accessed on 21 September 2020; available from https://www.reagan.com/ronald-reagans-commitment-to-make-america-great-again. Internet.

Rogness, Michael. "Proclaiming the Gospel on Mars Hill" (Spring 2009) [online]; accessed 29 January 2010; available from http://firstsearch.oclc.org; Internet.

Sahadi, Jeanne. "After years of talking about diversity, the number of black leaders at US Companies is still dismal," CNN Business, (2 June 2020) [online]; accessed on 13 October 2020; available from After years of talking about diversity, the number of black leaders at US companies is still dismal - CNN; Internet.

Sam Samurai, "The Wide Implications of the College Admissions Scandal," *Financial Samurai* [online]; accessed 19 August 2020; available from https://www.financialsamurai.com/the-wide-implications-of-the-college-admissions-bribery-scandal; Internet.

Sastry, Anjuli, and Karen Grigsby Bates. "When LA Erupted in Anger: A Look Back at the Rodney King Riots." (26 April 2017). [online]; accessed on 8 October 2020; available from https://www.npr.org/2017/04/26/524744989/when-la-erupted-in-anger-a-look-back-at-the-rodney-king-riots. Internet

Sawe, Benjamin Elisha. World Atlas. Who Signed the Declaration of Independence? (16 February 2020). [online]; accessed 9 September 2020; available from Https://Www.Worldatlas.Com/Articles/Who-Signed-The-Declaration-Of-Independence.Html. Internet

"Segregated Churches Hinder Evangelism." *Baptist Standard* (February 17, 2006) [online]; accessed 22 February 2010; available from http://www.baptiststandard.com/ index; Internet.

Shah, Khushbu and Juweek Adolpe. "400 Years Since Slavery: A Timeline of American History" (Aug 16, 2019) [online]; accessed 27 August 2020; available from https://www.theguardian.com/news/2019/aug/15/400-years-since-slavery-timeline; Internet.

Shellnut, Kate, "Southern Baptists Keep Quarreling Over Critical Race Theory," (17 December 2020). [online]; accessed on 31 December 2020; accessed from ; Internet.

Smithsonian. Blackface: The Birth of An American Stereotype [online]; accessed on 21 September 2020; available from https://nmaahc.si.edu/blog-post/blackface-birth-american-stereotype. Internet.

"Statement About Race at Bob Jones University." *Criswell Theological Review* (Spring 2009): 63-64 [online]; accessed 27 January 2010; available from http://firstsearch. oclc.org; Internet.

Storey, Kate "'When They See us 'Shows The Disturbing Truth About How False Confessions Happen." *Esquire* (June 2019) [online]; accessed 6 October 2020; available from https://www.esquire.com/entertainment/a27574472/when-they-see-us-central-park-5-false-confessions/; Internet. The Netflix show depicts the Central Park Five case, one of the most important in the field of false confessions research.

Strochlic, Nina. National Geographic. "How Slavery Flourished in the United States" (August 23, 2019). [online]; accessed 1 September 2020. available online https://www.nationalgeographic.com/culture/2019/08/how-slavery-flourished-united-states-chart-maps/#close. Internet.

Sweas, Megan. "Ethnic Tensions in the Church Must be Overcome, Say African Bishops" [online]; accessed 29 November 2009; available from http://www.us catholic.org/news/2009/10. Internet.

"10 of the Worst Wrongful Imprisonment Cases," *Oddee* (November 9, 2012) [online]; accessed 5 September 2020; available from https://www.oddee.com/item_98768.aspx. Internet.

Taylor, Vanessa. "The Black Church: Religious Culture and Social Movement" 28 November 2017. [online]; accessed on (23 December 2020); accessed from The Black Church: Religious Culture and Social Movement (thoughtco.com); Internet.

The Atlantic Slavery Made America: The Case for Reparations. [online].accessed 27 August 2020; available from https://www.theatlantic.com/business/archive/2014/06/slavery-made-america/373288. Internet.

The Charlotte Observer. *Charleston shooting suspect's Burger King meal gets national attention.* (24 June 2015) [online]; accessed 28 August 2020; available from https://www.charlotteobserver.com/news/local/article25394389.html. Internet.

"The Root Causes of Racial Tensions" (September 3, 2007) [online]; accessed 29 November 2009; available from http://www.asian-nation.org/headlines/2007/09/; Internet.

Thompsell, Angela. *Timeline of the Trans-Atlantic Slave Trade.* (19 June 2019). [online]; accessed on 25 September 2020; available from https://www.thoughtco.com/trans-atlantic-slave-trade-timeline-4156303. Internet.

The **Armed Services Vocational Aptitude Battery** "ASVAB Enlistment Testing Program," https://www.officialasvab.com/: Internet.

Three-Fifths Compromise: United States History. [On Line]; accessed on 5 September 2020; available from http://www.whatwouldthefoundersthink.com/george-mason-the-framer-who-refused-to-sign-the-constitution. Internet.

Timmons, Greg. History Channel. "How Slavery Became the Economic Engine of the South." (6 March 2018). [On Line]; accessed on 15 September 2020; available from https://www.history.com/news/slavery-profitable-southern-economy. Internet.

Transatlantic Slave Trade: Slavery and Remembrance. [online]; accessed on 21 September 2020; available from http://slaveryandremembrance.org/articles/. Internet.

US Census Bureau. "An act providing for the second Census or Enumeration of the Inhabitants of the United States" [online]; accessed 27 August 2020; available from https://www.census.gov/content/census/en/library/publications/1801/dec/return.html; Internet.

_____. As of January 26, 2012, the U.S. population is 313, 232, 044 persons. White 72.4 %, Black 12.85%, Asian 4.43%, Hispanic 15.1%. [online]; accessed 26 January 2012; available from http://factfinder2.census.gov/faces; Internet.

Van Dunsen, Michael. "10 Worst Massacres of African Americans.) 23 October 2019: Accessed on 8 October 2020; available from https://listverse.com/2019/10/23/10-of-the-worst-massacres-of-african-americans-disturbing-images/. Internet.

Verbruggen, Robert. "Does Kyle Rittenhouse Have a Self-defense Claim?" *National Review*, 28 August 2020 [online]; accessed 28 August 2020 from https://www.nationalreview.com/2020/08/does-kyle-rittenhouse-have-a-self-defense-claim; Internet.

Wallenfeldt, Jeff. Britannica. "Tulsa Race Massacre of 1921." (5 February 2019). [online]; accessed on 16 September 2020; available from https://www.britannica.com/event/Tulsa-race-riot-of-1921. Internet.

Jim Wallis, "Southern Baptist seminary presidents double down on bad theology on race," 10 December 2020. [online]; accessed on 31 December 2020; accessed from Southern Baptist seminary presidents double down on bad theology on race (religionnews.com); Internet. CRT shows how white supremacy — the belief that some people are more valuable than other people because of their skin color — is not just a personal prejudice but a structural and societal practice in America.

Ward, Alex. The racist history behind the 10 US Army facilities named after Confederate leaders. (9 June 2020) [online]; accessed on 21 September 2020; available from https://www.vox.

com/2020/6/9/21285097/army-base-name-change-confederacy-marines-navy. Internet.

Wheelan, Joseph. "How the Civil War Changed America Forever" (14 April 2017). [On Line]; Accessed on 3 October 2020; available from https://www.thedailybeast.com/how-the-civil-war-changed-america-forever?ref=scroll. Internet.

Western, Dan. 50 Maya Angelou Quotes on Life and Death [online]; accessed on 21 September 2020; available from https://wealthygorilla.com/23-maya-angelou-quotes-on-life-and-death/. Internet.

Wubbenhorst, Jeffrey K. "Brothers in Heaven, Strangers on Earth: Reconciling the Black and Evangelical Churches." *Gordon-Conwell Theological Seminary* (2006) [online]; accessed 29 January 2010; available from http://rim.atla.com/; Internet.

Yeats, John L. "In Jena, Revival Overpowers Racial Tensions" (February 27, 2008) [online]; accessed 29 November 2009; available from http://www.bpnews.net/; Internet.

Commentaries

Allen, Leslie C. *Psalms 101-150*. Word Biblical Commentary. Waco, TX: Word Books, 1983.

Anders, Max and Trent C. Butler, *Holman Old Testament Commentary: Hosea, Joel, Amos, Obadiah, Jonah, Micah*. Nashville: Broadman & Holman Publishers, 2005, 177.

Barrett, C. K. *The Acts of the Apostles: A Critical and Exegetical Commentary on the Acts of the Apostles*. Edinburgh: T. & T. Clark Publishers, 1994.

Barry, J. D., Mangum, D., Brown, D. R., Heiser, M. S., Custis, M., Ritzema, E., … Bomar, D. *Faithlife Study Bible* (Ac 2:38). Bellingham, WA: Lexham Press, 2016.

Bergen, R. D. *1, 2 Samuel* (Vol. 7). Nashville: Broadman & Holman Publishers, 1996.

Boa, K. & W. Kruidenier *Romans,* (Vol. 6). Nashville, TN: Broadman & Holman Publishers, 2000.

Bock, Darrell L. *Acts*. Baker Exegetical Commentary on the New Testament. Grand Rapids: Baker Academic, 2007.

Bruce, F. F. *The Acts of the Apostles: The Greek Text with Introduction and Commentary*. London: Tyndale Press, 1951.

Carson, D. A., Douglas J. Moo, and Leon Morris, *An Introduction to The New Testament*. Grand Rapids: Zondervan Publishing House, 1992.

Chafer, Lewis Sperry. *Systematic Theology: Soteriology, Volume Three*. Grand Rapids: Kregel Publications, 1948.

Chafer, Lewis Sperry. *Systematic Theology: Soteriology, Volume Seven & Eight*. Grand Rapids: Kregel Publications, 1948.

Cole, R. D. *Numbers,* (Vol. 3). Nashville: Broadman & Holman Publishers, 2000.

Cornett, Daryl C. *Christian America?: Perspectives On Our Religious Heritage*. Nashville: B & H Academic, 2011.

Craigie, Peter C., and C. Leslie. *Psalms 1-50*. Word Biblical Commentary. Waco, TX: Word Books, 1983.

Eddleman, Leo H. *An Exegetical and Practical Commentary on Acts*. Dallas: Copy-Rite Printing Co., 1974.

Emerton, J. A., C. E. Cranfield, and G. N. Stanton. *The Acts of the Apostles*. International Critical Commentary. Edinburgh: T. & T. Clark, 1994.

Erickson, Millard J. *Christian Theology,* Second Edition. Grand Rapids: Baker Books, 1983.

Evans, Tony. *The Tony Evans Bible Commentary: Advancing God's Kingdom Agenda.* Nashville: Holman Publishing, 2019.

George, Timothy. *The New American Commentary: Galatians.* Nashville: Broadman & Holman Publishers, 2001.

Justo L. Gonzalez. The History of Christianity: The Early Church to the Dawn of the Reformation, (Vol. 1) New York: Harper Collins Publishers, 1984

_____. The History of Christianity: From the Reformation to the Present Day, (Vol. 2). New York: Harper Collins Publishers, 1985.

Kistemaker, Simon J. *Exposition of the Acts of the Apostles.* New Testament Commentary. Grand Rapids: Baker Book House, 1990.

Lasor, William Sanford, David Allan Hubbard, and Frederic William Bush, Old Testament Survey: The Message, Form, and Background of the Old Testament. Grand Rapids: William B. Eerdmans Publishing, 1996.

MacArthur, John, Jr. *Ephesians.* MacArthur New Testament Commentary. Chicago: Moody Bible Press, 1986.

_____. *The MacArthur Study Bible: New American Standard Bible.* Nashville: Thomas Nelson Publishers, 2006.

_____. *Galatians.* MacArthur New Testament Commentary. Chicago: Moody Press, 1983.

Mare, W. H. *New Testament Background Commentary: A New Dictionary of Words, Phrases, and Situations in Bible Order,* 2004.

Mathews, K.A. <u>Genesis 1-11:26</u>, Vol. 1A, Nashville: Broadman & Holman Publishers, 1996.

Miller, S. R. <u>Daniel</u>. (Vol. 18). Nashville: Broadman & Holman Publishers, 1994.

Mounce, R.H. *The Book of Revelation*. Grand Rapids: Wm. B. Eerdmans Publishing Co, 1997.

O'Brien, Peter. *The Letter to the Ephesians*. Pillar New Testament Commentary. Grand Rapids: William B. Eerdmans Publishing Co., 1999.

Ogilvie, Lloyd J. *Communicator's Commentary on Acts*. Waco, TX: Word Books, 1979.

Osborne, G.R. <u>Romans</u>. (Downers Grove: InterVarsity Press), 2004.

Polhill, John B. *Acts*. New American Commentary. Vol. 26. Nashville: Broadman Press, 1992.

Racham, Richard B. *The Acts of the Apostles*. Oxford Commentaries. London: Methuen & Co., 1901.

Radmacher, E.D., R.B. Allen, & H.W. House. <u>Nelson's New Illustrated Bible Commentary</u>: *Exodus*. Nashville: Nelson Publishers, 1999.

Richards, L. O. <u>The Bible Reader's Companion</u> (electronic ed.). Wheaton: Victor Books, 1991.

Schaff, Phillip. *The Nicene Fathers of the Christian Church*. Vol. 8. Grand Rapids: William B. Eerdmans Publishing Co., 1979.

_____. *The Nicene Fathers of the Christian Church*. Vol. 13. Grand Rapids: William B. Eerdmans Publishing Co., 1979.

Smalley, Stephen S. *1, 2, 3 John*. Word Biblical Commentary. Waco, TX: Word Books, 1994.

Talbert, Charles H. *Reading Acts: A Literary and Theological Commentary on the Acts of the Apostles*. New York: Crossroad Publishing Co., 1997.

Tate, Marvin E. *Psalms 51-100*. Word Biblical Commentary. Waco: Word Books, 1990.

Vine, W. E., Unger, M. F., & White, W., Jr. *Vine's Complete Expository Dictionary of Old and New Testament Words* (Vol. 2). Nashville, Thomas. Nelson Publishing, 1996.

White, John E. and D. S. Dockery. *Holman Concise Bible Commentary: John*. Nashville: Broadman & Holman Publishers, 1998.

Walvoord, J.F. & R. B. Zuck (Eds.), *Genesis: The Bible Knowledge Commentary: An Exposition of the Scriptures* (Vol. 1). Wheaton: Victor Books, 1985.

_____. *Jeremiah: The Bible Knowledge Commentary: An Exposition of the Scriptures*, (Vol. 1). Wheaton: Victor Books, 1985.

_____. *Romans: The Bible Knowledge Commentary: An Exposition of the Scriptures*, (Vol. 1). Wheaton: Victor Books, 1985.

Wiersbe, W. W. *The Bible Exposition Commentary* (Vol. 1). Wheaton: Victor Books, 1997.

_____. *Expository Outlines on the New Testament*. Wheaton: Victor Books, 992.

Willmington, H.L. *Willmington's Bible Handbook*. Wheaton: Tyndale House Publishers, 1997.

Witherington, Ben III. *The Acts of the Apostles*. A Socio-Rhetorical Commentary. Grand Rapids: William B. Eerdmans Publishing Co., 1998.

Grammatical, Dictionary, and Lexical Resources

Brown, John. *Brown's Dictionary of Bible Characters: A Preacher's Dictionary of Bible Character*. Christian Heritage Publishers, 2007.

Cambell, Don, Wendell Johnston, John Walvoord, and John Wetmer. *The Theological Workbook: The 200 Most Important Theological Terms and Their Relevance Today*. Nashville: Word Publishing, 2000.

Gesenius, W., and S. P. Tregelles. *Gesenius' Hebrew and Chaldee Lexicon to the Old Testament Scriptures*. Bellingham, WA: Logos Research Systems, 2003.

Gruden, Wayne. *Systematic Theology: An Introduction to Biblical Doctrine*. Grand Rapids: Zondervan, 1994.

Holman Illustrated Bible Handbook. Nashville: Holman Publishing, 2012.

Kittel, G., G. W. Bromiley, and G. Friedrich, eds. *Theological Dictionary of the New Testament*. (electronic ed.). Grand Rapids: Eerdmans, 1964.

Lexham Greek-English Interlinear New Testament. Logos Research Systems, 2008.

Lust, J., E. Eynikel, and K. Hauspie. *A Greek-English Lexicon of the Septuagint: Revised Edition*. Deutsche Bibelgesellschaft: Stuttgart, 2003.

Mounce, William D. *Mounce's Complete Expository Dictionary*: Old & New Testament Words, Grand Rapids: Zondervan, 2006.

Pfeiffer, Charles E. *The New Combined Bible Dictionary and Concordance.* Grand Rapids: Baker Book House, 1961

Reid, Daniel G., Robert D. Linder, Bruce L. Shelley, and Harry S. Scott. *Dictionary of Christianity in America: A Comprehensive Resource on the Religious Impulse that Shaped a Continent.* Downers Grove: InterVarsity Press, 1990.

Rogers, Cleon L, and Cleon Rogers III. *The New Linguistic and Exegetical Key to the Greek New Testament.* Grand Rapids: Zondervan Publishing House, 1998.

Strong, J. *A Concise Dictionary of the Words in the Greek Testament and the Hebrew Bible.* Bellingham, WA: Logos Research Systems, 2009.

_____. *The Exhaustive Concordance of the Bible.* (electronic ed.). Ontario: Woodside Bible Fellowship, 1996.

Thomas, R. L. *New American Standard Hebrew-Aramaic, and Greek Dictionaries: Updated Edition.* Anaheim: Foundation Publications, 1998.

Van Voorst, R. E. *Building Your New Testament Greek Vocabulary* (ix). Grand Rapids: Eerdmans, 1990.

Zodhiates, S. *The Complete Word Study Dictionary: New Testament* (electronic ed.). Chattanooga: AMG Publishers, 2000.

Articles

Graham, Billy. "Why Don't Our Churches Practice the Brotherhood They Preach?" *Reader's Digest* 72 (August 1960): 52-56.

Grimshaw, Mike. "Responding Not Believing: Political Theology and Post-Secular Society" *Political Theology* 10, no. 3 (March 2009): 537-57.

Grossie, William. "Postmodernism: What One Needs to Know" *Zygon* 32 no. 1 (March 1997): 83-94.

Mills, David M. "What Would Jesus Deconstruct?: The Good News of Postmodernism for the Church." *Anglican Theological Review* 91, no. 1 (March 2009): 151-54.

Mohler, Albert R. "What is Truth? Truth and Contemporary Culture" *Journal of the Evangelical Theological Society* 48, no. 1 (March 2005): 63-75.

Persaud, Winston D. "Believing in Jesus Christ in this Postmodern World," *Word & World* 27, no. 3 (July 2007): 265-73.

Prentiss, Craig R. "Coloring Jesus: Racial Calculus and the Search for Identity in Twentieth-century America" *Nova Religio* 11, no. 3 (Spring 2008): 64-82.

Rogness, Michael. "Proclaiming the Gospel on Mars Hill" *Word & World* 27, no. 3 (Spring 2009): 274-94.

"Statement About Race at Bob Jones University." *Criswell Theological Review* 6, no. 2 (Spring 2009): 63-64.

Tomasino, A.J. *History Repeats Itself: The Fall and Noah's Drunkenness*, Vol. 42, (1992): 128–30.

www.ingramcontent.com/pod-product-compliance
Lightning Source LLC
Chambersburg PA
CBHW050830230426
43667CB00012B/1939